M000308461

...ries
...ox 80611
Lansing, MI 48908
Christ Centered Pen Pals

THE REFORMATION
THEN AND NOW

THE REFORMATION
THEN AND NOW

25 Years of *Modern Reformation* Articles
Celebrating 500 Years of the Reformation

ERIC LANDRY AND MICHAEL S. HORTON, EDITORS

HENDRICKSON
PUBLISHERS

The Reformation Then and Now: 25 Years of Modern Reformation Articles Celebrating 500 Years of the Reformation

© 2017 by Hendrickson Publishers Marketing, LLC
P. O. Box 3473
Peabody, Massachusetts 01961-3473
www.hendrickson.com

ISBN 978-1-61970-890-7

Printed in the United States of America

First Printing — January 2017

Library of Congress Cataloging-in-Publication Data

A catalog record for this book is available from the Library of Congress.
Hendrickson Publishers Marketing, LLC ISBN 978-1-61970-890-7

Contents

Preface: Does the Reformation Matter?   ix
     Eric Landry

Part I: The Cause

1. The Shape of the Reformation   3
     Michael Allen

2. The State of the Church Before the Reformation   9
     Alister McGrath

3. What Drove Luther's Hammer?   20
     Rod Rosenbladt

4. "Neither Reason nor Free Will Points to Him":
Luther's Assertion That the Whole Man Is in Bondage   26
     Benjamin Sasse

5. Luther on the Freedom and Bondage of the Will   39
     R. Scott Clark

6. Luther on Galatians   43
     David R. Andersen

7. Pelagianism   51
     Michael S. Horton

Part II: The Characters

8. Reformation Pathways: Calvin and Luther   65
     Lawrence R. Rast Jr.

9. Was Martin Luther a Born-Again Christian?   68
     Rick Ritchie

10. The Lutheran Doctrine of Predestination:
A Melanchthonian Perspective   73
     Scott L. Keith

11. Neglected Sources of the Reformed Doctrine of Predestination   80
    Frank A. James III

12. "Make Your Calling and Election Sure": Predestination and
    Assurance in Reformed Theology   88
    Michael S. Horton

13. Calvin versus the Calvinists: A Bibliographic Essay   98
    R. Scott Clark

14. How the Rumors Started: A Brief History of Calvin's Bad Press   101
    Ryan Glomsrud

15. Calvin the Transformationist?   104
    David VanDrunen

16. Our Calvin, Our Council   106
    Alexandre Ganoczy

17. Calvin on the Eucharist   109
    W. Robert Godfrey

18. Calvin's Form of Administering the Lord's Supper   114
    Keith A. Mathison

19. Who Was Arminius?   117
    W. Robert Godfrey

20. Calvin and Jonathan Edwards   124
    Paul Helm

21. The Journey to Geneva: Calvin and Karl Barth   126
    Peter D. Anders

22. Going to Church with the Reformers   129
    Michael S. Horton

Part III: The Consequences

23. The Crisis of Evangelical Christianity: Reformation Essentials   137
    Michael S. Horton

24. Christ at the Center: The Legacy of the Reformed Tradition   147
    Dennis Tamburello

25. Was the Reformation Missions-Minded?   154
    Michael S. Horton

26. The Reformation and the Arts   159
    Gene E. Veith

27. Musings on the History of the Protestant Ministry 167
    Lawrence R. Rast, Jr.

28. Against the Weber Thesis 176
    Diarmaid MacCulloch

29. Christ in the Heidelberg Catechism 179
    W. Robert Godfrey

30. "Servants of Freedom": Luther on the Christian Life 184
    Rick Ritchie

31. Being and Remaining: The Apostolicity of the Church
    in Lutheran Perspective 192
    Mickey L. Mattox

32. "Comfort Ye My People": A Reformation Perspective on
    Absolution (Lutheran View) 199
    Rick Ritchie

33. "Comfort Ye My People": A Reformation Perspective on
    Absolution (Reformed View) 210
    Michael S. Horton

34. The Reformation and Spiritual Formation 218
    Michael S. Horton

35. "By These Means Necessary": Scriptural and Sacramental
    Spirituality for All Nations 227
    John Nuñes

36. A Brief History of the Westminster Assembly 234
    Michael S. Horton

37. A Defense of Reformed Liturgy 238
    Michael S. Horton

38. Calvin and Anglicanism 242
    C. FitzSimons Allison

39. Calvin and the Continuing Protestant Story 246
    Serene Jones

40. Ten Ways Modern Culture Is Different Because of John Calvin 249
    David W. Hall

41. Was Geneva a Theocracy? 270
    Michael S. Horton

42. Is Calvin Still Relevant After 500 Years? It All Depends   277
        Michael S. Horton

Conclusion: *Is* **the Reformation Over?**   285
        Michael S. Horton

Appendix:

   Who Were the Reformers?   295
   A Reformation History Lesson   298
   Key Concepts in Reformed Spirituality   300

Contributors   301

Does the Reformation Matter?

Eric Landry

In 2017, the cobblestone streets of Wittenberg, Germany, fill with pilgrims of a sort: Reformation-minded friends from around the world gathering to celebrate the five-hundredth anniversary of Martin Luther's hammer blow "heard round the world." Today, in the twenty-first century, new questions are being raised about the accuracy of that iconic picture: the brave Augustinian monk who starts a revolution by posting ninety-five theses for public disputation—chief among them, his criticism of the sale of papal indulgences used to build St. Peter's Basilica in Rome. The effect of Luther's ministry, however, is beyond doubt. Within a few short years, Brother Martin would be on the run—protected by peasant and prince alike. His sermons and lectures would be distributed by Gutenberg's new printing press, disciples from across the continent would find their way to his kitchen table, and soon, Western Christendom would be radically reshaped.

In addition to the travelogues, new biographies, and ecumenical commentary, fresh questions about the continuing effect (and relevance) of Luther and the other Reformers—such as the Frenchman John Calvin, who ministered in Switzerland—are being asked: Was the Reformation necessary? How much of the reform movement that coalesced around especially Luther and Calvin was driven by forces beyond their control? Is the five-hundred-year-old breach between the Roman Catholic Church and Protestants still necessary in an age of surging secularism and violent jihadist movements? Does the Reformation even matter anymore?

These are not questions with easy answers on which everyone agrees. Indeed, some modern Lutheran and Reformed theologians and church leaders would be among the first to criticize the Reformers as separatists who did more harm than good. Recent ecumenical movements give grudging assent—at best—to the historical necessity of the Reformation, but they quickly assert that no one on either side of the debates raging then believes today what once was worth dividing (and dying) over. So, now is the time to find common ground, to resist a common enemy, and to coalesce around a common confession of faith.

This is the tension in which the heirs of the Reformation live and worship today. The arguments that gave life to our separate churches seem old, hard to understand, and even more difficult to explain as a rationale for continued division. In light of that reality, the editors of this volume have gathered together some of the most trusted voices across the Reformation spectrum to speak to three main questions: What was the cause that led to the Reformation? Who were the characters that gave life to the incredible history of the Reformation? What are the consequences for the Reformation—both then and now?

These chapters originally appeared as articles in *Modern Reformation* magazine, which celebrates its twenty-fifth anniversary of publication in 2017. Before *Modern Reformation* was a magazine, it was a simple newsletter produced and distributed out of Southern California, designed to introduce the Reformation to disaffected American evangelicals. Today, the magazine exists at an important crossroads. It is a magazine for serious Christians: those who know the importance of being challenged, those who want to interact with more than a blog-post summary of the important theological issues of the day, and those who aren't academics but aren't afraid of academics. Even though anyone can start a conversation today via our modern technological world, *Modern Reformation* is a magazine of record in the marketplace of ideas. When the church at large wants to know what confessional Protestants think on any issue, thought-leaders often turn to the pages of *Modern Reformation* for the answer. Our strength—now twenty-five years in the making—of uniting the voices of Anglicans, Congregationalists, Baptists, Episcopalians, Lutherans, Presbyterians, and Reformed on issues of common concern has ensured that this magazine is considered, cited, defended, and disparaged by friend and foe.

With a name like *Modern Reformation*, our goal with this collection of essays cannot be missed. But we are not advocating some return to a "golden age" of church history. Instead, we firmly believe that the resources provided to the church through the Protestant Reformation (particularly through its exegetical insights and resulting ecclesiastical applications) can be faithfully applied to our contemporary situation. If the church recovers this lost treasure trove and uses it wisely, then it may be blessed to see as remarkable a transformation of its faith and practices as experienced in the Reformation. This is the focus of the final chapter in the book, newly written by Michael Horton, coeditor for this volume and editor-in-chief of *Modern Reformation*: "Is the Reformation Over?"

We are grateful to Hendrickson Publishing, especially our friend and colleague Patricia Anders, without whom this volume would have never been published. Our hope with this collection and, Lord willing, another twenty-five years of *Modern Reformation* is: to *challenge* the errors in the church that are sometimes passed over in ignorance or false piety; to *convince* our readers of the Reformation perspective on doctrine and practice; and, finally, to *communicate* this message to the broader audience seeking answers. We freely admit that our ambitious aims must be tempered with a realistic assessment of the process of sociological and ecclesiastical change. But if we can continue to be that mouthpiece of confessing Protestants—evangelicals who are eager to reclaim their heritage and their unity on the core concerns of the Reformation—then we can be assured that the work that lies ahead of us is significant enough to demand that we still take up the issues of the day and work, promoting the truths and practices of the Reformation to the contemporary church.

PART I: THE CAUSE

CHAPTER 1

The Shape of the Reformation

Michael Allen

What does it mean that the church is always being reformed? This question is integrally related to other questions about sin and grace, and authority and Scripture. To reflect on these issues that are relevant to faith and spiritual life, we must consider the Protestant Reformation and its continuing ramifications.

Understanding the Reformation

What was the Reformation? Some would argue that it was a revolt by peasants against the landed aristocracy and the tax-hungry practices of Rome. Others claim that it was an example of the politically subservient masses shirking the authority of the papacy. Still others believe that it was an ecclesiastical rebirth of the Christian church that had been awash in heresy since the days of the apostles.

None of these proposals fits, however. The Protestant Reformation was primarily a moment when God led the church deeper into the truth of the gospel and further into the teaching of their need for the Bible. The Reformation was not primarily a political, economic, or social event (though it affected all of these arenas in various ways). First and foremost, the Reformation involved deeper illumination into the revelation of Scripture and the glorious news of what Jesus had done for his people, the church.

Historians of the Reformation talk about its two principles. Its material principle, meaning the substance or stuff of the Reformation, was the debate over the gospel in which the doctrine of justification *sola fide* (by faith alone) took center stage. Along with the importance of faith, the Reformers saw that this faith was a gift of God—namely, that it was *sola gratia* (by grace alone). Scholars then go on to say that the shape of the debate about the gospel was determined or outlined by the doctrine of *sola scriptura* (scripture alone), sometimes also called the formal principle of the Reformation. We will examine each of these principles in order to explore how they are related. Along the way, we will see why a deep sense of living by grace always flows into a serious concern to live in God's word.

Faith Alone

At the time of the Reformation, God showed more pointedly than ever before the radical nature of divine grace and Christian freedom. Primarily, this illumination came through the ministry of a German monk and professor named Martin Luther. Others had known the gospel throughout the ages, but the Reformation intensified the church's grasp of the nature and articulation of the gospel. Luther had been raised to think that only faith shaped by love and consisting in rigorous adherence to a system of piety and religious activity would bring God's pardon. Though he was a most impressive monk, he still trembled before God's judgment. Eventually he gained insight into Paul's Letter to the Romans and saw that Christ was given in his place, to be received by faith alone: "For I am not ashamed of the Gospel, for it is the power of God for salvation to everyone who believes, to the Jew first and also to the Greek. For in it the righteousness of God is revealed from faith for faith, as it is written, 'The righteous shall live by faith'" (Rom. 1:16–17). His awareness of his own sinfulness and his delight in the gospel of Jesus were linked.

The gospel shows that God does not wait for us to clean ourselves up, but he pursues us while we are yet sinners (Rom. 5:6). God does not expect us to ascend to his holy hill and to heaven itself, but he descends into the agony of our world and on the cross suffers hell in our stead. God does not look for good works or meritorious pedigree, but he unites us to Christ at the moment of our first trusting him. We will obey, but this follows from the gospel and does not function as a doorway to that promise. All that we need, Jesus gives. For ungodly people like us, justification *sola fide* is the best of news.

Grace Alone

Very quickly, however, Luther and the other Reformers realized that even faith could be thought of as a work. If left to ourselves to generate such trust, we would be just as engulfed in a performance game as the Pharisees and Judaizers, as well as the late medieval Roman Catholics. We need not only a new context but a new composition as well: we need hearts of flesh and not of stone.

Luther saw that God supplies what God demands. Faith itself is a gift of God. In 1525, Luther responded to Erasmus, penning his famous volume *The Bond-*

age of the Will. He defended what is now called "biblical monergism," which literally means that salvation is "a single work" or the "work of a single person." Now, monergism can be misleading if we interpret it to mean that we don't need to believe in Christ. At its best, however, monergism speaks of the single divine motion in initiating and sustaining all our salvation—outside of us in Christ and in us by his Spirit—by his grace alone. We do believe but only because he grants us grace to do so. We do love but only because he first loved us.

Grace alone is good news for those with bound wills. Because we are children of Adam, the need for resurrection is fundamental. Charles Matthews has said that "sin is a one way street"—once you are marred by it, you are incapable of managing or fixing it, and there are no U-turns to be made here. So sinners need new life. Christ blesses us with that new life and carries us with his ongoing grace. Like a shepherd he leads, like a priest he intercedes, like a Son he is grace incarnate. He provides everything for his people—even their faith—by his life-giving Spirit. As the Heidelberg Catechism reminds us, "The Holy Spirit creates it [faith] in our hearts by the preaching of the holy gospel, and confirms it by the use of the holy Sacraments" (Q. 65).

The Bible Alone

Along with the gospel, the question of authority was also raised in this era. Historians speak of the sole and final authority of the Bible as the means by which everything we think and believe about Christianity is shaped.

In the days of the Reformation, God showed more pointedly than ever before the thoroughgoing nature of biblical authority. Again, Martin Luther served as an instrument for conveying this cherished belief. Others had professed this for centuries, but this era brought a newfound clarity and consistency to grasping and confessing this doctrine. Luther insisted that human reasoning and churchly powers could not determine his faith, famously declaring at the Diet of Worms that his conscience was captive to the word of God. He did not teach a doctrine of Scripture as if there were no other authorities. For example, he served as an authority in his capacity as professor of theology at the University of Wittenberg. But he viewed all human authorities—from the pope down to himself—as subservient to the Bible's authority in faith and practice. Therefore, when their teaching was not rooted in its claims, he had to stand with the word of God and do no other. If a seminary professor speaks contrary to the word, then the Bible trumps his opinions. When a pastor proposes a ministry method that runs against the principles of the Bible, the Bible should be heeded. The

Bible is the only norm for theology that is not itself normed by anything else—
it is the only final authority for faith and practice. This is what *sola scriptura*
means in practice.

The Golden Thread

We trust the Bible alone as our final authority, because we are sinners justified by faith alone and living by grace alone. The two claims are tied together:
erosion of one will lead to the erosion of all, just as the defense of one should
encourage a defense of all! Justification by faith alone says that we will never be
perfect in this life and yet we are accepted by God; as Luther would say, we live
a dual existence as simultaneously righteous in God's sight, and yet still sinful
and prone to sin. While in Christ we are seen as perfect by the Father and thus
justified; in and of ourselves we remain a work in progress and quite flawed.
Part of our indwelling sin is our failure to know God truly. Yes, even our minds
need renewal, for sin plagues every aspect of our being (this is what we mean
when we speak of *total* depravity). Remarkably, our minds are being renewed,
as Romans 12:1–2 says, though it is an ongoing process and not yet complete.
Part of Christian growth revolves around the smashing of our theological idols
by working in the word to form true beliefs about God. We need something and
someone reliable to lead us further into the truth day by day—and only God's
word and his Holy Spirit will do.

Grasping the gospel and our need for salvation in Christ, therefore, should
point us to the Bible. The more we see our own inability and our failure, the more
we realize we need a word from above, a word infallibly and inerrantly given by
God. Nothing else will do, for our best thoughts remain the thoughts of sinners
only gradually being changed. We err. We are misled and we mislead. We need
God to provide guidance. We need God to speak by his word and Spirit. Having
a gospel-centered understanding of ourselves leads to firm reliance on the Bible
alone to guide our practice.

We must remember that this is true both individually and corporately. The
church is a communion of sinful saints. Pastors fail. Sessions stumble. Congregations misstep. Even our best successes are not perfect. Ministry is done east of
Eden. Thus every church and denomination, if it understands that its identity is
in Christ and its hope is only in the gospel, should look to God to provide guidance. A gospel-drenched church will become more and more reliant upon the
Bible to shake it loose from its comfort zone and set it on a course of greater
faithfulness.

Trusting the God Who Reforms Us

If we cherish the gospel and trust the Bible, then we will expect to grow and to change. If we savor justification by faith alone and see our need for God's word as our final authority, then we will pursue the reformation and renewal of our theology by this very word. If we depend on grace as our spiritual oxygen, then we will turn to where it is delivered and dispensed with fervency and faith.

Most important to remember, though, is not our need to change. The most crucial news is the best: God is still in the business of reforming us, both as individuals and as communities. We not only have a need, but we have *great* hope because God has given *great promises*. The Father will continue to shed light on his word. The Son will continue to teach as our ascended prophet, priest, and king. The Spirit has been given to remind us of what Jesus taught, and he will dwell within the Christian and empower the body of Christ.[1] The Bible makes plain that God will continue to work in applying our salvation, taking us deeper into the truths of his word. All theology is by grace, a gift from our heavenly Father, so we can have tremendous hope and expectation.

Now we must remember that God's ongoing commitment to lead us further into his word does not mean that every new idea is right. We cannot afford to buy into the modern idea of progress or the contemporary cult of youth. All reforms must be guided by the word of God, and so we must discern the spirits. But it would be overreaction to oppose all change and insist that we have already arrived at perfection. Such a stance flows from fear rather than freedom in Christ. Not only is it an unbiblical stance, but it does not honestly follow the examples of those from our Christian past. When we study church history, we see the way in which leaders of the past navigated through change in their times, cognizant of the need for transformation rooted in God's word. Like many theologians of the past, we must seek ongoing faithfulness to minister the unchanging gospel and to be reformed continually by it. As Presbyterian theologian George Hunsinger writes:

> Grace, strictly speaking, does not mean continuity but radical discontinuity, not reform but revolution, not violence but nonviolence, not the perfecting of virtues but the forgiveness of sins, not improvement but resurrection from the dead. It means repentance, judgment, and death as the portal to life. It means negation and the

---

[1] Those wishing to bolster their hope that God promises to illumine his people should read John 14–17 and 1 Corinthians 1–2.

negation of the negation. The grace of God really comes to lost sinners, but in coming it disrupts them to the core. It slays to make alive and sets the captive free.[2]

So our final words must be those of praise and prayer fixed on his promises. We praise God for his work in the past, revealing truth through prophets and apostles. We celebrate his presence in the present, leading his church deeper into the gospel and further into Holy Scripture. We pray that his great work of reformation would continue within us, our churches, and to the ends of the earth, continuing to break our idols and give us better understanding of who God is for us in Christ. We are not self-assured, but we are confident in what he has promised. Because God gives his people grace, we turn to his word with expectancy. Because he is the God who reforms us, we trust that his church is always being reformed.

---

[2] George Hunsinger, *Disruptive Grace: Studies in the Theology of Karl Barth* (Grand Rapids: Eerdmans, 2001), 16–17.

CHAPTER 2

The State of the Church Before the Reformation

Alister McGrath

Why was there a Reformation? What was the church like just before the Reformation took place? Why did the Reformation have to happen? By looking at these questions we can begin to gain some understanding of our own situation today.

One of the reasons why the Reformation happened is that there was a rediscovery of the attractiveness of the gospel. A new generation arose, who by reading the New Testament firsthand began to discover for themselves that here was something exciting, something life changing, which was like new wine, which just couldn't be contained in the old wine skins of the church of the late Middle Ages. So underlying everything I'm going to say was this sense of excitement and rediscovery of the gospel. And there was a realization that there was a need to bring this into the sixteenth century, that the medieval church was lacking something. But by studying Scripture, by rediscovering the doctrine of grace, something was made available that gave new life, new meaning, new purpose to the church back in those days. You and I can rediscover today that as well.

In my hometown of Belfast, Northern Ireland, is a house owned by my grandparents. It is one of these great big old rambling houses built back in the 1890s. At the top of the house is this kind of attic, which is where my grandparents stored all the things they picked up in their youth and their early married life. Why did they do this? Their answer was, "You never know when these things come in useful." That's what the Reformation is like in many ways. It is about realizing that we can turn to our Christian past and rediscover the things that are there, that we've neglected, that we have forgotten—things that can be useful today. Studying history is not simply some kind of nostalgia, some kind of feeling that says, "Oh, they always did things better in the past." No, it's saying, "Look, we can reach into the past to enrich the present. We can reach into the past and discover things we need to hear today. It is a resource you and I can access as we try to face the tasks for today's church."

One of the big themes, then, is rediscovering the gospel. But the other side, which I'll address here, is that things had become pretty bad in the late Middle Ages. One thing you will notice is that these problems seem to be emerging again. Woody Allen once said, "History repeats itself. It has to; nobody listens the first time around." I want to impress on you the need for us to rediscover some of the ideas from the Reformation, because we are beginning to experience the same problems to which the Reformation was a solution.

Here is one of the first areas I want to look at. The late Middle Ages saw the church undergo a period of doctrinal confusion. People were not sure what they believed, nor were they sure why they believed it. This resulted in the church lacking any sense of certainty about what they believed or why they believed it. There arose a generation of Christians who didn't understand what the gospel was all about. That was enormously important for a whole range of things. One of the great themes of the doctrine of justification is that it answers the question, "What must I do to be saved?" That is an important question for a lot of people, and it is a question that needs to be answered. Yet in the late Middle Ages, people weren't certain how to answer that question at all. What must you do to be saved? Let me tell you a story to bring out the importance of this point.

In 1510 in northern Italy, there was a group of about twenty Italian noblemen who met regularly to pray and to talk. An important issue for them was this question of knowing how you could be sure you were saved. It's still an important issue for us. In the end, the group decided there was no way of answering this, so the group split into two parts. One group felt that the only way of being sure they were going to be saved was to go to the nearest monastery and spend the rest of their lives there. The others felt that somehow you had to be able to live your life as a Christian in the world and be sure that your sins had been forgiven. But they weren't sure that this was what the church taught. The point I'm trying to make is that this is a big question. It is a question we will surely be expected to answer. But these guys didn't. They weren't stupid. They weren't uneducated. Like most people in their day and age, they just did not know.

One of the themes of the Reformation is a bringing to consciousness the great truths of the Christian faith. Karl Heim, one of the renowned historians of the Reformation, once wrote a line about his Calvinist friends. He said the Calvinist knows what he believes and why. Heim made the point that the Reformation brought with it a rediscovery of the truths of the Christian faith—a rebirth of Christian understanding and Christian knowledge—something that wasn't there in the late Middle Ages. Instead, there was confusion and a lack of understanding.

Again, I sense this is beginning to happen to us today for all kinds of reasons. One of them is that people these days are often too experience oriented. What's Christianity all about? Well, they'll say, "It's about my experience of God"—and it is. Experience of God is of enormous importance. Without an experience of God, we are simply talking about an external formal shell with no fire for life. Nevertheless, that is a part of the Christian faith. There's intellectual depth there, and it has a converting power based on the strength of its ideas. If we don't know and understand this, then we sell the gospel short talking about our subjective appreciation of the gospel but not the objective truth it brings to our lives. So that is one important area where there were problems in the late Middle Ages. I think the same thing is beginning to happen today.

Let me move on and look at another major area that caused problems in the late Middle Ages: the clergy. The clergy in the late Middle Ages tended to be not well informed. They were often the target of abuse and ridicule because they knew so little. This reflected the fact that the social status of clergy wasn't very high, but deeper down there was something much more worrisome: all the clergy needed to do was tend to the pastoral needs of their flock and not worry about anything else. There was no teaching ministry grounded in the word of God. There was no sense of mission or evangelism. Bear in mind, we're talking about late fifteenth-century Europe, where the assumption was that everybody was a Christian, so there was no need to evangelize.

The result was that people didn't like the clergy, who had certain privileges. For example, they were exempt from taxation, and they were exempt from compulsory military service. Above all, they were not well informed, and they were not seen to play a decisive or important role in the life of the church. With the Reformation, this changed in a big way. It changed because enormous emphasis came to be placed upon the teaching role of the clergy. The clergy were there to enable their people to discover in its full depths the wonder and the glory of the gospel. They were there to open the word of God for their people, to help them discover what they had already discovered—namely, the depth and the attractiveness of the gospel of Jesus Christ. So the clergy began to discover a role based on their understanding of the gospel and their passionate concern to communicate this—again, taking excitement in what God had done for them through the cross of Jesus Christ, wanting their people to share in this, to know that they were benefiting from it. So we see in the late Middle Ages a church whose clergy had ceased to have any teaching function. The Reformation restored the vital elements of teaching and evangelism to the ministers of the church, which was a much needed correction. I think it's a correction we also need to rediscover today.

In the late Middle Ages, Christianity tended to be formal and external. In other words, it was simply about people doing certain things, maybe believing certain things. But often there was no sense of personal commitment or personal appropriation of the gospel. In other words, if you were a Christian, then you would behave in certain ways, as in attending church. Christianity was defined in terms of what you did. There was little sense of the dynamic, something transforming, something that could take hold of your life and turn it inside out. We see this change in a number of ways as the Reformation began to dawn.

It changed a bit through the doctrine of justification by faith, which invited its heroes to discover the wonderful truth that we can experience the touch of God's forgiving grace even though we are sinners. This was an enormously important insight for the Reformers, for here was something that made the gospel relevant to the world of ordinary people. The Reformation made this connection between the gospel and the experiential world of ordinary people. We are not talking simply about people being told to do certain things. We are talking about the gospel being able to bring new life, new hope to ordinary people, connecting the gospel to people, helping them to discover what the gospel could mean in their lives. So there was a rediscovery of the inward aspects of the gospel, taking delight in its objective truth but nonetheless insisting it also had a subjective impact on people's lives.

The relevance of the gospel, therefore, moved away from mere outward observance to a discovery of what the gospel can mean to our inward lives. Luther talked a lot about the importance of experience in the Christian life. In one of his writings, he says, "Only experience makes a theologian." That means there is no point in writing about God unless you have experienced God, unless you know what he is like. In another one of his writings, he says, "It is not reading and understanding and speculating that makes a theologian, but living and dying and being damned." He means that the gospel is about forgiveness. It is about this glorious knowledge that our sins have been forgiven through the gospel. But unless you have fully appreciated that you are a sinner, then the sweet news of forgiveness is not going to meet you in all its force. It's only by experiencing the death of sin that you can understand how wonderful this message of forgiveness is. So we see that there was a rediscovery here of the importance of the individual believer. There was a new relevance given to the ordinary layperson. That brings me to the next point.

The late Middle Ages saw the clergy living in a world different from ordinary lay Christians, who were seen to be at a lower level. The laity was simply despised. They had no place to play in the church. With the Reformation came a major change I call the rediscovery of the laity. As many of you know, one of the key ideas underlying this is the doctrine of the priesthood of all believers, the idea that every Christian believer can act as a priest, that every Christian believer has a role to play in the church. You only have to look at the late Middle Ages to see how little the laity were valued. For example, if you look at Calvin's city of Geneva, which before the Reformation had five thousand ordinary citizens and two hundred clergy, you can see how many clergy there were and how little the laity were allowed to do in the church. After the Reformation, there were still five thousand people there but only six or seven clergy whose task was primarily teaching. The laity was rediscovered and given a positive role to play in the life of the church. I think this rediscovery is a vital aspect of the Reformation heritage—a rediscovery that ordinary laypeople have been called by God, equipped by God, and given something to do by God. We to need to rediscover and value that today.

Let me tell you more about the late medieval church. The late Middle Ages are now thought to have been a period of enormous interest in Christianity. People used to think it was an era of decline, but it's now increasingly thought of as an era of growth that led to increased criticism of the church. Ordinary Christians came to have greater expectations of what the church ought to be doing. When expectations weren't met, people began to criticize the church. One of the things that developed was a cynicism on the part of ordinary Christians about the church and the clergy. They had a sense they were being exploited by those who were meant to be their pastors, their shepherds, their leaders. Often, the exploitation in question was financial. Many of you know about the indulgence controversy that was of great importance to Luther's Reformation at Wittenberg. Let me explain what this was and why it caused such a row.

In the Middle Ages, the idea developed that although God does indeed forgive sinners, it was appropriate to express your gratitude for forgiveness in various ways. One of those ways was financial. Because God forgave your sins, you could express your gratitude to God by, for example, endowing a church or giving money to charity or something like that. But by the early sixteenth century, this idea had become debased. Now people were being told, "Give money and sin will be forgiven." Often, this played on the love of people for their dead relatives. Your father or your mother has died, and you may be wondering if they made it to heaven. Well, if you buy an indulgence, then they'll make it. In fact, there was an advertising slogan for indulgences: "When the coin in the coffer rings, a soul from purgatory springs." In other words, once you've paid this sum of money, your mother, your father, or other relative will be delivered from any torment they're going through and will find their way safely through the pearly gates. Of course, it had enormous attraction for ordinary believers who were worried about what happened to their parents, their grandparents, people they loved.

At one level, this was financial exploitation. Luther reacted against this very, very negatively. For him, this was perversion of the gospel. This made forgiveness a commodity, something you could buy. Luther was outraged and felt there was a need to rediscover the idea of forgiveness, justification by faith—that you could die knowing your sins had been forgiven. Not because of anything that you had done, but because of the grace of God and what he has done for you through Jesus Christ. So there was financial corruption that made many people wonder if the church and their pastors could be trusted.

The same thing was happening in other aspects of the church. For example, in the late medieval church when someone you loved died, the priest had to say the right prayers for them. Someone had to conduct a requiem Mass to make sure they got safely to heaven—but that priest would have to be paid. Again, people began to think, "Here we are being exploited. We want to know that our loved ones are safely in the arms of God. The only way we can do this is by paying money to this priest to say certain prayers." So there was this deep unease about the quality of ministers and the integrity of the church. The Reformation tried to restore the integrity and the public image of the church.

One of the great themes of the gospel is that of forgiveness. Again, we find Luther moving this into the forefront of the Reformation struggle. You and I do not need a priest to tell us that we will die with our sins forgiven. We don't need to pay a priest to say prayers for us. We know that when we die we will be safe in the arms of God. This deep reassurance of knowing that sins have been forgiven, through what Jesus Christ has done for us, is a central theme of the Reformation. We must rediscover this theme. Often, Christians are told that they are arrogant for thinking their sins are forgiven. But they aren't arrogant; they're just trusting—trusting in the word of God that makes those promises and realizing that they are addressed to us who joyfully accept what God wants us to have.

I've talked a bit about the problem of confusion in the late medieval church. I have tried to make the point that one of the things the Reformation did was to bring home to believers the importance of knowing what they believed. That brings me to the next theme, which is that of Christian education. In the late Middle Ages, this was virtually nonexistent. The only people who were educated were the clergy. Yet, very often, they were poorly educated indeed, and they knew little about the gospel. As a result, they were simply unable to answer questions that ordinary people had. Because of this, a climate of unease built up about the trustworthiness of the gospel—not because of any problems with the gospel, but because the inadequacy of the clergy made it difficult for the people to understand what the gospel was saying.

The Reformation brought home the importance of Christian education. Not simply of having a literate and educated clergy but also a laity of ordinary Christians who understood their faith and what it meant to them. You can see this working at two different levels. At the first level, it meant being able to give a good account of what the Christian faith is. A whole range of works came into being at the time of the Reformation designed to give Christians a deeper understanding and appreciation of the intellectual resilience of the intellectual depths of the Christian faith. John Calvin's *Institutes of the Christian Religion* are an excellent example of this kind of work. They brought home to people that Christianity made sense, that it could be trusted, that by having a good understanding of the Christian faith you were well placed to deepen your own faith and also explain it to others. So, objectively, education was important.

Education was also important subjectively. It brought home to people that they could feel good about the gospel by the reassurance of its attractiveness, stability, and the fact that it did make sense. Here is something we need to rediscover. We need to rediscover that by deepening our understanding of our faith, we do two things. First, we bring about a new depth of understanding of our own faith. It's good news for us. As we begin to realize the full depths of our faith, we begin to open up and explore something we've always known was there but have never really explored in all its fullness. Second, one of the great ideas of the Reformation is to unpack the enormous riches of Scripture and to savor them as we realize just how much it means. But by appreciating for ourselves all that the gospel means, we can also be more effective evangelists as well. Having an enriched understanding and appreciation of the gospel will help us to give a far more effective witness—try to explain to others what it is about the gospel that is so attractive to us in the full knowledge that it could be attractive to them as well. This area of education was a great weakness in the late medieval church, which the Reformation was able to address and one that we too need to rediscover.

Let me make another point about the problems in the late medieval church. Often, there was a huge gap between the ordinary Christian and Scripture. In part, the reason was technological. Before the invention of printing, Scripture had to be copied out by hand, which was expensive. Not every Christian believer could read, and Christian believers were often dependent on their priest for an understanding of Scripture. But with the Reformation came this glorious rediscovery that Scripture was like bread upon which you could feed, that it was living water, which you could drink and which would quench your thirst. It was a move toward rediscovering the importance of Scripture for the church.

All kinds of developments took place to encourage this; for example, the development of exegetical sermons, biblical commentaries, and works of biblical theology such as Calvin's *Institutes*. There was a rediscovery of Scripture and a realization that you did not need to rely upon your priest to understand Scripture but that you could go to Scripture directly. One of the great themes of the Reformation is that you can go to Scripture directly, read it, and be nourished by the word of God. This relieved people of the false teachings the church was putting into circulation at the time.

Reading Scripture is not merely about rediscovering the excitement of the gospel. It's also about asking hard questions about what this religious teacher or that religious teacher is saying, asking, "Where did this come from? Is this really biblical?" As the Reformers began to open Scripture for their people, they began to rediscover that much of the teaching in the late medieval church could not be justified on the basis of Scripture at all.

The doctrine that Scripture was not easy to understand had emerged in the late medieval church: God in his providence had provided the church to interpret Scripture to the people. But by putting the church between Scripture and the people, the church took control of Scripture. To this, the Reformers said, "Go back to Scripture. Read it for yourself and ask, 'Where did these ideas come from?'" I think that is a central theme of the Reformation—that each and every believer has the right and the responsibility to ask: "Where do these ideas come from that we hear from our pulpits? Are they justified in the light of Scripture?"

I think there is a need for us to rediscover that important Reformation theme. Because even in today's church we have preachers who often say things that may be what their congregations want to hear, that may be what they want to say, but that aren't well grounded in Scripture. There is a need for us to rediscover Scripture with a view to checking our preachers' art, lest they lead us astray. To my mind, one of the greatest curses of the modern church is the personality cult that seems to descend upon some preachers. Going back to Scripture is about going back to the word of God and discovering what it is saying, rather than relying upon some preacher who may act as if he alone is the mean of communication between God and his people. So I've addressed some of the problems that were there in the late medieval church, though there were many more I could mention.

I don't want you to gain the impression that we are dealing with a whole series of problems and that the Reformation simply came along as a solution to those problems. It was a solution to those problems, but it was also something else as well. You must never think of the Reformation solely as a negative thing, as a response to weaknesses. It was also about our rediscovery of the gospel. Rediscovery of the gospel led to the correction of the weaknesses I've been talking about. But, in part, the Reformation was this glorious rediscovery of what God had already done for his people and would continue to do for them—if they were faithful to him and would rediscover his word and will through Scripture. I think this is a great theme for us, because you and I are seeking to rediscover the word and will of God for his people. The Reformation offers us a case study on how to do that.

Many of us may look at the Reformation and say something like, "Look, this is very interesting and may be academically important, but you are talking about something that happened in sixteenth-century Europe. We want to know: Does it have any relevance for us today?" I think the answer is yes. First, because we are talking about the same God who needs to restore his church, wherever that church is. By looking at the way God restored, renewed, and reformed his church back then, we can gain some ideas about what he might want to do to his church here, today, in this place. It is about looking through history to discover what God has been doing in the past; then we can say, "Maybe he wants to do that kind of thing now."

The Reformation is one of those great moments in history when a church paused and asked itself this question: "What are we here for? What is the real reason the church is here? What is different about the church? What must the church do if it is to stay the church of God?" In other words, there was a taking of stock, a posing of hard questions about the mission and purpose of the church. Every organization that has been around for a long time settles into inertia. It works on the assumption that, well, we did this today and yesterday, and it'll go on like this forever. There's no need to ask those hard questions. But the Reformers felt that the only way a church could be reformed or renewed was by asking: What does God want the church to do in the first place? By rediscovering that sense of purpose, we can bring the church back to life by allowing it to do what God wants it to do.

As many of you well know, people such as Luther and Calvin asked that question. The answer they gave is that the church is the preaching of the gospel of Jesus Christ. Wherever that takes place, there also is the true church. I think that's an important insight: the need to take stock, the need to say, "Does God want us to move in a different direction?" We are to look back at our Christian history, back at Scripture, and ask, "Where does God want us to go from here?" Luther and Calvin said that the best way of rediscovering why we are here is to go back to the New Testament, read it, and become excited at what we find in its pages.

If you read Luther, then you will discover that for him—reading the New Testament is like getting an insight into the days when faith came to life, insights to days when the church seems to have died. Luther, and many others besides us, said we have a church that is slowly but surely dying because it does not know why it's here. By going back to Scripture and rediscovering apostolic preaching, by rediscovering the dynamism of the early church, we can bring our church back to life by giving it the same mission, the same sense of encouragement we find in the early church. I think we still need to do that, to regain our sense of direction.

The Reformers say this: There is no point in going forward, forward, forward. It helps to stop and look back, and ask, why are we here, what resources do we have? Then, we need to begin to go forward again in the full knowledge of why we're here. As we seek to confront the future, this is a model we can rediscover. We're not saying that the Reformation is basically something we have to repeat like parrots. We *are* saying that, as we seek to move the church into the future, it helps to look back at those great moments in Christian history when the Lord was active and ask, "Can we learn from that time? Is there anything the Lord wants to say to us through those people of long ago as we face their task in today's age?"

One of the reasons for studying church history is for the following. I'm sure many of you have been to a Bible study or discussion group. You talk about some big issue, perhaps some moral issue, theological issue, or biblical interpretation issue. You think about this, and then somebody says something that helps you. You go away from that Bible study or discussion group feeling a lot better, because something you didn't understand is now sorted out. Studying church history—studying the Reformation—is like being at a Bible study with a great company of people who thought about those questions that are bothering you. Such as: Why is the church here? What should we do to be saved? How can we know that we are saved? It gives answers that you and I need to know because they still make sense today. You and I still ask those questions, and we want good answers. So one of the reasons we look at the Reformation is to rediscover the answers to questions that are still being asked, being able to rejoice in those answers. So there is a need to rediscover how helpful studying the past—studying the Reformation—can be. Another great reason for studying the Reformation is that you can be the person who brings these answers, which have been tried and tested in church history, to the people you minister to.

Why was there a Reformation? First, there was a Reformation because there was a gospel that had to be rediscovered in all its fullness. When it was rediscovered, all kinds of reorientation had to take place. Second, there was a Reformation because the church had run into many problems and someone had to sort them out. You and I can rediscover that gospel today. The Reformation is about that process of rediscovering and bringing to life. That is still very much our agenda. But also on our agenda, I'm afraid, is the simple fact that we are looking at a church today that often has many of the same problems we find in the late Middle Ages. There is a need for us to think through what we can do about those problems. The Reformation gives us some bearings, some landmarks, some ideas about how to address today's issues—using the resources, the methods, and above all, the inspiration that comes from the past.

CHAPTER 3

What Drove Luther's Hammer?

Rod Rosenbladt

The following is a *Reader's Digest* version of what led Martin Luther to the discovery of the gospel. It introduces Luther's upbringing, education, and life as a monk before turning to the nature of the gospel he discovered in the writings of St. Paul.

Luther's Upbringing

Luther was the second son in a family of eight children. His father and mother were sturdy German *Bauern* (peasants): coarse, credulous, and devout. Often in the beliefs of these untutored folk, elements of old German paganism blended with the Christian story: woods, winds, and water were peopled by elves, gnomes, fairies, mermen and mermaids, and sprites and witches; and witchcraft was taken for granted throughout Europe. Young Luther had ample opportunity to witness the mischief and grief of evil spirits, soon learning the marvelous power of the church to control the demons. As a result, Luther carried over many typical German peasant superstitions of his day.

Scholars tell us that there was nothing remarkable about Luther's home life. His parents were God-fearing but not unusually devout, and the children were subjected to a stern upbringing. Typical of the age, the switch and beatings were the most common way to raise a family, and young Martin received his share. But as Luther began to show academic promise, he became highly esteemed at home.

In his classic book, *Here I Stand: A Life of Martin Luther*, Yale University historian Roland Bainton summarizes these early years: "We know this much. Luther imbibed a religion in which one had to strive for future salvation, just as one had to work for material survival."[1]

---

[1] Roland Bainton, *Here I Stand: A Life of Martin Luther* (Nashville: Abingdon Press, 1987; repr. Peabody, MA: Hendrickson Publishers, 2009).

Luther's Education

School education reinforced the training of the home. Children were instructed in sacred song, singing psalms and hymns, and they attended Mass and Vespers. Bainton writes that "the entire training of home, school, and university was designed to instill fear of God and reverence for the church."

Schools of that day were not tender, but neither were they brutal. Teaching was by drill and punctuated by the rod. Luther remembered being soundly beaten for failing to conjugate a Latin verb he had not yet learned! But he knew Latin was useful: it was the language of the church, of law, of diplomacy, of international relations, of scholarship, even of travel. Luther was therefore devoted to his studies and became highly proficient in Latin and German grammar.

By age seventeen, Luther was a student at the University of Erfurt. As the university was yet untouched by the Renaissance, Luther remarked that the most popular courses were those offered in the inns and taverns (many students, including Luther, referred to the university as "a bawdy house and a beer house"). Luther's first year was nothing special. In 1505, however, he was one of seventeen students (out of an original three hundred) who graduated as a "master" of arts. During that time, he built a reputation among his fellow students as one of the finest disputants, and they dubbed him "the philosopher."

In many ways, Luther as a young man was an ordinary, although gifted, student: sociable, musical, popular, pious. He was rollicking, fond of music, proficient on the lute, and enamored of the German landscape.

Luther's *Anfectungen*

In one respect, however, Luther stood apart from his fellows: his inner bouts with the *Anfectungen* that plagued him throughout his life. The word has no English equivalent. It is stronger than "temptation" or "trial"; closer would be "assault" or "attack"—terrifying ordeals, bouts of depression, despair, perhaps what people of earlier centuries called "melancholia."

Luther often wondered if God held good intentions toward him or not—his anxieties stemming from late medieval Roman Church theology. Luther feared God and everlasting condemnation; he sensed deeply the stare of Christ the Judge standing over him, demanding of him an impossible level of inner purity. At times, he could not help fearing that these feelings were evidence that he was not one of God's elect, but rather among those destined to be damned.

After two months of attending lectures in law, Luther went home for a visit. We don't know why, but he later wrote that it was because of fear over the condition of his soul. During his return to university, a sudden storm arose, lightning flashed, and the air pressure of a bolt suddenly knocked him to the ground. In terror, he cried out, "St. Anne, save me! I will become a monk!" The thought of sudden, unexpected death terrified every medieval Christian, because it would not allow a last confession to a priest.

It was no easy vow to keep, and Luther carefully considered his obligation to it. Though his father was angry and several of his teachers thought his vow was not binding, Luther could not avoid keeping his promise. He threw a farewell party for his friends and gave away his musical instruments and Roman law books. Then, in the fall of 1505, with heaviness of heart, he arrived at the Augustinian Order's monastery in Erfurt—the most rigorous of the local monastic groups.

Like everyone else in the Middle Ages, Luther knew what to do about his plight. The wise and secure course was to "take the cowl." But why did Luther drop out of law school and join a monastery? For exactly the same reason thousands of others did—to save his soul!

Luther the Monk

Medieval monasticism reflected the deepest insight of the Roman Church concerning the relation of the holy God to man the sinner. In the last analysis, a holy, righteous, and just God could have fellowship with and could accept only a holy, just, and good man. But how could such a God of perfection accept a sinful man as his own? The real problem was to make a man sufficiently holy, so that his acceptance by God, if not certain, was at least highly probable. As Bainton explains, "[Luther] set himself to the pursuit of holiness. Monasticism constituted such a quest; Luther looked upon the cloister as the higher righteousness."

His teachers, following the Bible, taught that God demanded absolute righteousness (as in Matthew 5:48, "Be ye perfect"). People needed to love God absolutely and their neighbors as themselves; and they should have the unshakable faith of Abraham, who was willing to sacrifice his son—hence the demand that the monk fulfill all the laws and commands of God, including poverty, chastity, and obedience.

The life of a monk was terribly hard, but people of Luther's day "knew" it was pleasing to God. Its benefits were "certain." Were the monastics aware of the great gulf between God and man? Absolutely! They also knew that the fluctuation between despair and hope, between unbearable demand and partial fulfillment, would produce doubts and spiritual torment in many of the good brothers—but this served to keep them from complacency and self-righteousness. Once their sinfulness was fully exposed, there were ample ways to reassure the weak in times of trouble. At the center of this assurance was the sacrament of penance. The sinner confessed to a priest, was forgiven (absolved), and then performed penitential acts that completed the process. People were to repent in a fully contrite manner—not for the purpose of saving themselves. But Luther knew that in the midst of this most crucial act, he was at his most selfish. He confessed his sins and performed his penance out of the intensely human instinct to save his own skin. Yet because of the human tendency to sin, one could hardly confess enough. This critical issue remained vivid in Luther's mind. He later commented, "If one were to confess his sins in a timely manner, he would have to carry a confessor in his pocket!"

When Luther tried to avail himself of this comfort, it failed to produce the desired results: "Yet my conscience would never give me assurance, but I was always doubting and said 'You did not perform that correctly. You were not contrite enough. You left that out of your confession.'" How then could he stand before God?

Monasticism provided a variety of ways in which man could wash away his sin and improve his spiritual estate. The monk could fast, pray, meditate, perform Mass, beat his body, and engage in other physical/spiritual exercises. Through this, the body and pride would be defeated.

In addition to an acute sense of the holiness of God, Luther had a brutally honest picture of himself as a creature. He knew all too well that it is easy for man to see himself "in the best possible light." Man is usually willing to forgive himself and then rest assured that God has also forgiven him. "So long as one does the best that is in him," man is sure it is enough. But Luther was too sensitive to be satisfied with such "answers." What Luther saw was a self-centered sinful man holding sway under the pretense of monastic holiness. So serious were the mounting struggles that Luther began to think he may be one of those predestined for damnation.

A critical moment came when Luther's superiors ordered him to take his doctorate and become a professor of Bible at Wittenberg University. Although he initially resisted going—"It will be the death of me!"—he finally relented. As one historian famously notes, this command that Luther pursue theological study "was one of the most brilliant or stupid decisions in the history of Latin Christianity."

Although Luther's fears and anxieties drove him into the cloister, they only intensified during his time as a monk. But the command to study academic theology meant he could now also investigate his struggles intellectually. He soon acquired his mature self-identity as a professor and a doctor of Sacred Scripture.

The "Turn"

Luther's early doctrine of justification was a form of self-torture. The problem was how to love God unselfishly, to reach a state of pure love of God for God's own sake—which he learned from St. Augustine and St. Bernard of Clairvaux. Still, Luther knew that we children of Adam are "curved in on ourselves" and that we seek only ourselves. For Luther, the remedy for the evil self-love was self-hatred. This was the essential road to salvation: agree with God's verdict and the rightness of his wrath against us, even be willing to be damned. (Justification is the opposite: we agree with God's wrath against us, feeling *that* in our hearts; the just man always accuses himself.)

This thinking, however, led Luther to a deeper fear of God rather than greater love for him, thus setting up a vicious cycle of fear, resentment, and despair, which led to anger and a hatred of God. What was missing was the gospel as God's kind word of promise.

Luther felt compelled to turn to St. Paul's Letter to the Romans, particularly to wrestle with the phrase "the righteousness of God": "The Gospel is the power of God for salvation to everyone who has faith, for in it the righteousness of God is revealed from faith to faith, as it is written, 'The righteous shall live by faith'" (Rom. 1:16–17; Hab. 2:4). Luther's first understanding of the verse was that the gospel merely confirmed the dreaded juridical interpretation of "God's righteousness" as demand—a revelation of the punitive righteousness of God, God's means of further tormenting men who are already fearfully burdened with original sin and the Ten Commandments. Still, he would not let go of the passage. He struggled and raged against the demands of a God who kept demanding that which man *cannot* give and then *damns* him for not giving it!

Then the breakthrough came. God by the Holy Spirit finally cracked open the passage to Luther's understanding. In my paraphrase: "The one who gives up on his or her supposed, but really icky 'righteousness,' who shifts instead to trusting only in the Messiah's righteousness freely given or imputed to him, that sinner will live." Gratuitously (freely) that sinner is forgiven all of his sin, reconciled to God, adopted into the family of God as his child and heir, and given eternal life. "Being turned away from" obsession with our "icky" righteousness to Jesus Christ's (genuine but "alien") righteousness as the only hope we have is, what Paul calls, "faith." (Think of the old King James translation of the verse in

Jeremiah: "Turn Thou me and I shall be turned.") So we get no credit for saving faith whatsoever. Like Peter's confession as to who Jesus was, it is a gift to us from heaven: "Flesh and blood have not revealed this to you, but My Father in heaven." As a result, the sinner is made alive to God and begins to walk in his way.

The Gospel Breakthrough

In grasping the meaning of "justification," Luther saw that the heart of the gospel has to do not with what God *demands* but with what he *gives* to man in the death and resurrection of Jesus Christ. Here Luther leaned heavily on St. Paul. The "righteousness of God" that saves sinners is not an active one (something man does), but is rather entirely passive. A man is not righteous because of what he achieves, but because of what Jesus Christ did for him in his death and resurrection. Man simply trusts God at his word and hopes in the inscripturated promise of God. He trusts that God in Christ has completely accepted him while he was still a sinner, has forgiven his sin, instantly judged the sinner as completely acquitted, and given him eternal life—and all this based solely on what Christ has done outside of him and for him, not "in him."

For the first time in his life, Luther discovered what "peace" meant. It was not some self-induced tranquility of mind or even a profound resting secure in an ancient and hallowed tradition, but rather a childlike trust in God's own promises in Scripture, in texts that spoke of God's saving action in Jesus Christ. It rested not on personal vision or ecstasy, a miracle, or on the adjustment of Luther's personality to the tensions he experienced. Finally, the gospel is not about man at all (except in the sense of the God-man, Jesus Christ); it is not about merit or effort, but about *Jesus'* struggle with wrath and judgment, and with *Jesus'* victory over sin, death, and the devil. This is what drove Luther's hammer.

CHAPTER 4

"Neither Reason nor Free Will Points to Him": Luther's Assertion That the Whole Man Is in Bondage

Benjamin Sasse

In the years immediately following Martin Luther's emerging fame after posting the Ninety-Five Theses in 1517, many European observers wondered how the Renaissance and Reformation movements might relate to one another in the future. After all, both were interested in a type of reform in the church. Furthermore, each movement was led by a brilliant man who had angered the church's hierarchy, and who might therefore benefit from an alliance with another visible figure. Individually, the men might be marginalized, but together, some speculated, their reform proposals might receive more serious attention. Desiderius Erasmus (c. 1466–1536) was more than fifteen years older than Luther (1483–1546) and considerably less interested in theology proper. Yet, as J. I. Packer has written, "Many anticipated that the outspoken young Saxon and the cool clear-thinking Lowlander would join forces."[1]

Such expectations seem hardly believable to those living after the Reformation—or, more specifically, after Luther and Erasmus's heated public exchange about the human will. For Luther opened his 1525 response to Erasmus's *Freedom of the Will* by announcing that using Erasmus's brilliant eloquence to convey such a weak argument "is like using gold or silver dishes to carry garden rubbish or dung."[2] He concluded his critique by offering a sincere—but nonetheless shocking—prayer that Erasmus might one day be converted to Christianity (320). Yet, in spite of the debate's vigor, it was possible for men in earlier years

---

[1] J. I. Packer and O. R. Johnston, "Historical and Theological Introduction," in Martin Luther, *The Bondage of the Will* (Old Tappan, NJ: Revell, 1957), 25.

[2] Luther, op. cit., 63. (Unless otherwise noted, all footnotes refer to the previously cited version of Luther's *The Bondage of the Will*.)

(c. 1517–1519) to speculate about common cause. Such hopes were encouraged by the attempts of Philip Melanchthon, who was both an evangelical and a humanist, to bring the two men closer together.

Additionally, the evangelicals had been the beneficiaries of much of the humanists' work. Most obvious is Erasmus's Greek scholarship, which aided Protestant New Testament exegesis, but Erasmus had also in fact been a political asset to the evangelicals on a number of occasions: He had urged the church to be moderate in its judgment of its critics (Luther particularly), he had argued that Rome should stop burning the Reformer's books, and he allegedly declined an offer of a bishopric if he would publicly reject Luther's teaching.[3]

Ultimately, though, as the visible leader of the humanist movement too often identified with the new evangelicalism, Erasmus decided he must comment on Luther's destabilizing writings. After the death of Pope Leo X and the ascent of Adrian VI in 1521, Erasmus was on better terms with Rome. For Adrian was a friend of Erasmus. Additionally, Luther's increasingly public observations that Erasmus was able to critique the church, but was not able to offer anything better (specifically because Erasmus's theology was not Christocentric enough), surely angered the elder scholar.[4] Finally, it seems to have been Luther's dismissive statements about the human will—which Erasmus understood to degrade the entire person (and, by implication, God)—which prompted Erasmus to action.

The result was the 1524 publication of Erasmus's *Diatribe* [or *Discourse*] *Concerning Free Will*, despite a prior letter from Luther warning him that he would be better off not getting in over his head.[5] Erasmus had long made it clear that he was wary of theological dispute because it tended to be divisive. He preferred peace within the church because Christ was, after all, the agent of peace. Yet, under pressure from both friend and foe to reveal where he stood regarding Luther's teaching on Christian freedom, Erasmus concluded that engaging Luther on the will would be beneficial for at least three reasons: He could publicly distance himself from the heretical Luther, he could defend the dignity of humanity from the abuses of Luther's "extreme" view of Adam's fall, and he could offer a public sermon about the superiority of piety (which is beneficial to both the pious and their neighbors) over doctrine (which is often destructive).

Luther's response, *The Bondage of the Will* (1525), which he generally considered his best work, is surprisingly forceful. (At least Erasmus accomplished his goal of showing his distance from the zealous Luther!) The other two aims of

---

[3] Packer, op. cit., 31, 36.

[4] Packer, 26, 36.

[5] Packer, 37.

Erasmus's book (his position on the freedom of the will and his prioritization of piety over doctrine) are, Luther insists, intimately connected—for Erasmus can place his hope only in human piety because he believes that human will is free to attain piety. Protestants, on the other hand, despair of attaining righteousness by their own actions, so if man is to have any hope at all, it must be found in theology, not ethics.

But, Erasmus replies, is that to imply that theology is silent on ethical matters? Did not Jesus, God Incarnate, say that the summary of the law is love of God and love of neighbor?

Identifying the Chief Division in Theology: Law and Gospel

Clearly, our interlocutors need to reach agreement on some definitions. Most importantly, Luther complains that Erasmus "makes no distinction at all between the voices of the law and of the gospel; so blind and ignorant is [Erasmus's book] that it does not see what the law and the gospel are" (163). The problem here is that the law is not good news to a lawbreaker; it is horrifying to learn that God demands something from man that he does not have (righteousness). It is only as a consequence of this horror—that is, as a consequence of law—that the message of Christ's living and dying has any meaning. To the poor and the despairing, Luther writes,

> The gospel is preached and this is just the word that offers the Spirit and grace for the remission of sins which was procured for us by Christ crucified. It is all entirely free, given by the mercy of God the Father alone as He shows His favour towards us, who are unworthy, and who deserve condemnation rather than anything else. (180)

This is not to say that the law is unimportant. It is essential; it drives us to Christ. "By the law is the knowledge of sin" (Rom. 3:20), and an awareness of sin yields an awareness of the need for a Savior. This is what Luther calls "the work [or] the office of the law," for "it is a light to the ignorant and blind" (159, 287). The law in this most basic theological incarnation does not tell man that he is weak and exhort him to do better. Instead, it displays disease, sin, evil, death, hell, and the wrath of God. It does not help or set them free from these things; it is content merely to point them out. When a man discovers the sickness of sin, he is cast down and afflicted; nay, he despairs. The law does not help him; much less can he heal himself. Another light is needed to reveal a remedy. This is the voice of the gospel, which displays Christ as the Deliverer from all these evil things (287).

Obviously then, Luther's charge that Erasmus fails to distinguish between the voice of law and the voice of gospel is tantamount to saying that he does not understand the first point of theology. Luther argues that Erasmus seizes man's problem (the severity of the law) as if it is an answer—and thus has no real need for God's answer (the gospel). Throughout *The Bondage of the Will*, Luther reiterates both points: that Erasmus regards the unattainable standard of the law as attainable, and that he "will not take the slightest trouble to know about Christ" (164).

Helpful versus Idle Theologizing

In addition to distinguishing the parts (law and gospel) within the whole of theology, Luther also draws a distinction between theologizing that is profitable and theologizing that is pointless. This distinction is derived from the division between those things which God has revealed and those on which he has remained silent (or left hidden).

> [We] must discuss God, or the will of God, preached, revealed, offered to us, and worshipped by us, in one way, and God not preached, nor revealed, nor offered to us, nor worshipped by us, in another way. Wherever God hides Himself, and wills to be unknown to us, there we have no concern. Here that sentiment: "what is above us does not concern us," really holds good. . . .

> Now, God in His own nature and majesty is to be left alone; in this regard, we have nothing to do with Him, nor does He wish us to deal with Him. We have to do with Him as clothed and displayed in His Word, by which He presents Himself to us. (169–70)

If God has not spoken on a matter, Christian theology should not regard that matter as a topic on which it needs to speak definitively. "But if [the topic under consideration] is a matter of concern to Christians and to the Scriptures, then it ought to be clear, open and plain, just like all the other articles, which are perfectly plain" (129).

Yet to say that the word defines the theologian's business is not to say that the Christian never brings questions with him to the text. It means, instead, that the Christian will patiently trust God even if the answer in the word is neither complete nor completely satisfying. If God's answer (or lack of an answer) seems inexplicable, recall with Job who is God and who is man in this questioning. If there appears to be conflict between our sense of justice, and what God has revealed as his way of action, Luther exclaims with Paul (Rom. 3:4): "Let God be true, but every man a liar" (84). The problem in any conflict, of course, is not God but us, so Luther counsels:

> In everything else, we allow God His Divine Majesty; in the single case of His judgement, we are ready to deny it! To think that we cannot for a little while believe that He is just, when He has actually promised us that when He reveals His glory we shall all clearly see that He both was and is just! (315)

The Christian waits on God's timing, because the day of Christ's return will reveal the God "to whom alone belongs a judgement whose justice is incomprehensible, as a God whose justice is most righteous and evident—provided only that in the meanwhile we believe it" (317).

The Whole Man Is "Flesh"

But Adam's children are rebels by nature, and we are not content to wait with the word. Reason asserts herself and demands that God justify himself now. When he does not submit to our commands, we choose to engage in speculative theology. Like our parents, we believe we know better than God, and we lust after forbidden fruit.

According to this story, however a theory divides one (simply into mind and body, or into the reason, the will, and the passions), it is impossible to shield any part of a person from complicity in—and the consequences of—Adam's fall. The mind is guilty of unbelief, the will of pride, and the passions of lust. This is the foundation of Luther's entire argument in *The Bondage of the Will*: No part of the self is untainted; therefore, no part of the self either will or can seek the pure God, who neither will nor can tolerate any contamination. (The root defect of most arguments that reject predestination, then, is an insufficient grasp of the effects of the fall.) If there is to be any relation between God and humanity, then God must take the initiative. In the case of every Christian, God has been the pursuer, just as he pursued Adam and Eve as they hid from him in the garden. As descendants of a line of rebels, we have inherited fear of the just Lawgiver.

But, Erasmus asks, shouldn't some distinctions be drawn within human nature? Does not Paul distinguish between "spirit" and "flesh," implying the former is noble and the latter ignoble? Church father Jerome takes up the distinction

and lodges man's weakness first in the flesh. No, Luther bellows, Paul is not following Plato; he is not praising some higher part of man (mind) and condemning
some lower part (body). He is not talking about two parts of an individual man,
but two parts of collective humanity:

> What is the meaning of: "Ye are not in the flesh, if the Spirit is in you," but those who
> have not the Spirit are of necessity in the flesh? And he that is not Christ's, whose
> else is he but Satan's? It stands good then, that those who lack the Spirit are in the
> flesh, and under Satan.

> Now let us see what Paul thinks about endeavor and the power of "free-will" in car-
> nal men. "They that are in the flesh cannot please God." Again: "The carnal mind is
> death." Again: "The carnal mind is enmity against God." Once more: "It is not subject
> to the law of God, neither indeed can be" (vv. 5–8). Let the guardian of "free-will"
> answer the following question: How can endeavors towards good be made by that
> which is death, and displeases God, and is enmity against God, and disobeys God,
> and cannot obey him? (299–300)

Human pride wants to ensure that at least the higher or "best parts" do not
belong in the category of the corrupted. Yet, Christ "plainly proves that what is
not born of the Spirit is flesh." In other words, the man who has not become a
Christian by the converting power of the Holy Spirit is, in his reason and will
just as much as his body, entirely "flesh" or sinful (249). Paul and Luther are not
offering a Greek distinction between mind and body as higher and lower, pure
and impure. Instead, the biblical distinction is between those who have been and
those who have not been initiated into the kingdom.

Outside the kingdom are those who do not despair of their own works. Instead, they strive for (an intrinsic) righteousness by the law. (To Luther, this
lack of despair in their own merit is part of what distinguishes non-Christians
from Christians. For unlike Christians, "the rest of men resist this humiliation;
indeed, they condemn the teaching of self-despair; they want a little something
left that they can do for themselves. Secretly they continue proud, and enemies
of the grace of God" (100–101). Inside the kingdom is the other group, those
who have the righteousness of Christ, which comes by faith. This is an imputed
or "reckoned" righteousness, which "consists, not in any works, but in the gracious favor and reckoning of God. See how Paul stresses the word 'reckoned';
how he insists on it, and repeats it, and enforces it." This is significant to Luther
because it is very odd to repeat that a man is *called* or *reckoned* something that
he actually is (intrinsically). Who is surprised that the ocean, which is deep, is
called deep? The point is that man *is not* righteous (intrinsically), yet God *calls*

him righteous (on account of Christ). This is the "God who gives life to the dead and calls those things which do not exist as though they did" (Rom. 4:17).

Luther continues his exegesis of Paul:

> "To him that worketh," he says, "the reward is *reckoned*, not of grace, but of debt. But to him that worketh not, but believeth on him that justifieth the ungodly, his faith is *reckoned* for righteousness," according to the purpose of God's grace. (296)

Highlighting Paul's use of the word "reckon . . . about ten times" in Romans 4, Luther argues that "flesh" corresponds to those outside the kingdom: those who work for their salvation and trust in themselves. "Spirit" corresponds to citizens of God's kingdom: those who do not work for their salvation but instead by the power of the Spirit trust in the vicarious living and dying of Christ.

A Will, But Not a Free Will

Once the reader begins to understand that Luther is talking about the universal sinfulness (or "fleshliness") of man in his fallen state, it becomes clearer why he makes so little effort to distinguish between reason and will—and why he is even discussing (attacking) reason at all in a debate that is supposedly about the will rather than the reason. Luther's book is called *The Bondage of the Will*, but it could just as easily be titled *The Bondage of the Whole Man*. No one claims that the affections are pure. Luther's goal is to ensure that no one can claim that any other part of man is pure either. It seems self-evident that only a pure part of man would seek a pure God who destroys all impurity (e.g., Lev. 10). If God is holy, then it is only by positing that some portion of man is free from unholiness that one can argue that man (or that portion of man) yearns after such a terrifying God. Luther, as if to economize his writings, is arguing for the contamination of the reason and of the will side by side. Both of them are dead in trespasses and sin. Neither contributes anything to man's salvation.

Yet, contrary to Erasmus's reading of this argument, Luther is not saying that the will and the reason were not good creations, that they do not exist, or that they are of no earthly value. Where Erasmus, in Luther's view, is continually jumping from theology to philosophy and mixing "up everything, heaven with hell and life with death" (164), Luther is trying to have an exclusively theological discussion about whether humans contribute anything (besides the sin) to salvation.

> I cannot worship, praise, give thanks or serve Him, for I do not know how much I should attribute to myself and how much to Him. We need, therefore, to have in mind

a clear-cut distinction between God's power and ours, and God's Work and ours, if we would live a godly life. (78)

Anticipating Calvin, Luther sees this matter as intimately connected to the starting point of all existential knowledge: knowledge of God and knowledge of self (305).[6]

In an argument that could grow monotonous if it were not so wonderfully life-producing, Luther repeatedly charges Erasmus with applying Paul's condemnation of "the old man" only to the "gross affections," rather than also to "what you call the most exalted faculties, that is, reason and will" (313). Mocking Erasmus's claim that knowledge of man's complete depravity can serve no constructive purpose, Luther shouts the incapacity of humanity and the complete (and even good works-producing) work of God all the more.

Regarding the will, he writes:

> *"Who"* (you say) *"will try and reform his life?"* I reply, Nobody! Nobody can! God has no time for your practitioners of self-reformation, for they are hypocrites. The elect, who fear God, will be reformed by the Holy Spirit; the rest will perish unreformed. Note that Augustine does not say that a reward awaits nobody's works, or everybody's works, but some men's works. So there will be some who will reform their lives.

Regarding the mind, he writes:

> *"Who will believe"* (you say) *"that God loves him?"* I reply, Nobody! Nobody can! But the elect shall believe it; and the rest shall perish without believing it, raging and blaspheming, as you describe them. So there will be some who believe it. You say that *a flood-gate of iniquity is opened by our doctrines.* So be it. (99)

Contrary to many caricatures of Lutheranism (sadly, often even by her sister faith, Calvinism), Luther does not deny sanctification; he simply (and properly) will not allow it to eclipse justification. Christians do grow in intrinsic righteousness, but only as an effect of—never as a cause of—the imputed righteousness of Christ. This is his point when he criticizes Erasmus for not distinguishing between commands (law) given to Christians and those given to non-Christians. The indicative and imperative moods must be distinguished. Meaningful exhortation (what Calvinism calls the "third use" of the law) can come only after condemnation (what Calvinism calls the "first use" of the law) (189, 159, 180). This is because the will that was dead to God has been made alive by God. This is not to exalt the "free will" of the unregenerate but rather to praise the Spirit

---

[6] See also John Calvin, *Institutes of the Christian Religion,* 1.1.1–2.

who converts people and now uses them for the glory of God. So does Luther understand the productive and barren trees: "Those who are not justified are sinners; and sinners are evil trees, and can only sin and bear evil fruit" (301, 189).[7]

Erasmus, in repeatedly attacking Luther's position of "necessity," apparently thinks that Luther is embracing philosophical determinism or fatalism. What he doesn't understand, though, is that Luther isn't trying to address this philosophical problem. As noted earlier, Luther believes the theologian's task is assigned by the word, and the Christian Scriptures do not speak to the philosophical problem of the appearance of fatalism—a problem common to every articulated belief system. As he frequently reiterates, Luther is not talking about "compulsion." A will, by definition, cannot be under compulsion, or it would cease to be a will. Luther is not disputing the existence of man's will; instead, he is asserting that all of the desires of the fallen will are sinful (81, 222).

When the reader hears this, he wants to argue, offering distinctions between higher and lower objects, greater and lesser actions. Luther is not disputing these distinctions. He is arguing rather that even the noblest impulse or action of which any child of Adam can conceive is stained with sin. Luther is not saying that we shouldn't draw distinctions between civic (earthly) righteousness and unrighteousness. We should; but we shouldn't thereby conclude that God's standard (the right act proceeding from the right motive: his glory) is the same as the county courthouse standard (the right act).

When Luther says the will is bound, he is saying that it has no options that are not sinful. He is not saying that one thereby has no options at all. He frequently distinguishes these things as man's will "above" and "below" him.

> [We may] credit man with "free-will" in respect, not of what is above him, but of what is below him. That is to say, man should realize that in regard to his money and possessions he has a right to use them, to do or to leave undone, according to his own "free-will." . . . [Nonetheless,] with regard to God, and in all that bears on salvation or damnation, he has no "free-will," but is a captive, prisoner and bondslave, either to the will of God or to the will of Satan. (107)

The Christian (by the converting work of the Spirit) is willfully enslaved to the will of God; the natural person (by the receipt of Adam's nature by birth) is willfully enslaved to the will of Satan. Neither will is free (to pick its master at random), but both wills, by definition as wills, willfully serve their received master.

---

[7] See also Luther's *The Freedom of a Christian, in Three Treatises* (Philadelphia: Fortress, 1960), esp. 301–16, for further discussion of the good works of Christians.

Reason, But Not Reason As King

The same distinction between freedom below and universal bondage in things above applies to reason as much as to will. It is the universal sinfulness of reason (as it doubts or tries to go beyond the word) that Luther is attacking when he condemns reason as the "Devil's whore." He is talking again about speculation, about impatience with the Revealed God and yearning to know the secrets of the Hidden God, of believing Satan's lies about the tree, of boredom with God's incarnational revelation in Christ.

Some theologians draw a helpful distinction here between the ministerial and magisterial uses of reason. Ministerial reason is the basic way we think about things below and about those things God has chosen to reveal from above. Magisterial reason is the mind's prideful claim that it is not created, that it is the maker of reality, that it will not abide any limits God may place on it. This is the distinction at work when Luther distinguishes between the (proper) "Kingdom of Reason" (earth) and the "Spiritual Kingdom" (heaven).

Just as Luther could place no hope in a will enslaved to sin, so he could place no hope in human reason blind to this enslavement:

> Show me out of the whole race of mortal men one, albeit the most holy and righteous of them all, to whose mind it ever occurred that the way to righteousness and salvation was simply to believe on Him who is both God and man, who died for men's sins, and was raised, and is set at the right hand of the Father!

Not only will man not allow that (true heavenly) righteousness comes from another, he also will not allow that there is divine judgment for man's (earthly) righteousness: "Look at the greatest philosophers! What thoughts had they of God? What have they left in writing about the wrath to come?" The unregenerate have no ability to believe this truth apart from the "predestinating" Spirit (276, 297). For when natural man

> hears Christ teach the true way of salvation, by new birth, does he acknowledge it and confess that in time past he sought it? No; he starts back, and is confounded; and not only says that he does not understand it, but turns from it as an impossibility. . . . Who ever thought that the Son of God must be "lifted up, that whosoever believeth in Him should not perish, but have eternal life" [John 3]? Did the best and acutest philosophers ever mention it?

No, so "the whole world," and "human reason" and "free-will, are forced to confess that they had not known nor heard of Christ before the gospel entered the world" (306).

Reason is naturally self-justifying, Luther says, which is why Erasmus naturally assumes either that man can fulfill the law or that he already knows he cannot. In reality, though, the law comes to condemn, as the preparation for the gospel, telling the person what his self-justifying reason would not—that he is a sinner. For "neither reason nor 'free-will' points to [God]; how could reason point to Him, when it is itself darkness and needs the light of the law to show it its own sickness, which by its own light it fails to see, and thinks is sound health?" The person thus humbled, given the gift of faith in Christ, will then trust God even when God tells him that the penalty for sin is death—be that the death of the sinner or the death of the Substitute. "Faith and the Spirit" believe "that God is good even though he should destroy all men" (161, 287, 202).

The problem of the person who knows himself to be a sinner and naturally the enemy of God is not why God predestines only some, but why he predestines any at all! (233). This is where Luther unleashes his string of glorious paradoxes: God quickens by killing, justifies by pronouncing guilty, carries up to heaven by bringing down to hell, reveals by concealing; he is merciful though he damns, just though he creates objects for destruction (101, 176–77, 169).

When the interlocutor inquires further regarding the philosophical question of why the "will of Majesty purposely leaves and reprobates some to perish," Luther points to Romans 9 and the command that man be silent about God's "dreadful hidden will." Luther knows that man is not yet satisfied, but he thinks the theologian's task is sufficiently fulfilled when he gets Erasmus to the place where the word commands him to be silent:

> But here Reason, in her knowing and talkative way, will say: "This is a nice way out that you have invented—that, whenever we are hard pressed by force of arguments, we run back to that dreadful will of Majesty, and reduce our adversary to silence." . . . I reply: This is not my invention, but a command grounded on the Divine Scriptures. . . . Paul says: "Why then does God find fault? Who shall resist His will? O man, who art thou that contendest with God? Hath not the potter power?" and so on (Rom. 9:19, 21).[8]

---

[8] For example, "When you are to dispute with Jews, Turks, Papists, Heretics, etc., concerning the power, wisdom, and majesty of God, employ all your intelligence and industry to that end, and be as profound and as subtle a disputer as you can....Such arguments [for divine truth based on human and earthly analogy] are good when they are grounded upon the ordinance of God. But when they are taken from man's corrupt affections, they are naught." From Luther's comments on Gal. 1:3 and 3:15. He also affirms Cicero's teleological argument for God's existence.

Everyone Willfully Cooperates with God

Luther's position is neither fideist (having faith in faith) nor irrational. Instead, it is reason based on revelation. This theological task might properly be distinguished from apologetic tasks (for example, seeking to persuade the non-Christian that the Bible is in fact God's revelation).[9] But within the context of those who claim to believe in revelation (as in the case of this debate with Erasmus), it would be utterly insane for the reason of finite creatures to ignore the limits prescribed by the infinite God's revelation.

As J. I. Packer argues, Luther's picture—and indeed the biblical picture—is anything but a deistic or Epicurean god (200, 316, 206, 203–04). While Aristotle's god may be so unaware of this world that he sleeps, Luther's God is "incessantly active" in both the creative and redemptive spheres, in the initiation and sustenance of each. In this, human nature reflects God's nature, for God will not allow humans "to be idle." One does not merely exist but is always active and is always willfully desiring and acting "according to his nature" (103–4, 203–5, 268).

The only question is about that nature. Either one wills and acts according to the fallen nature received from Adam, as one "ridden" by Satan. Or one wills and acts as the new creation of God, trusting in Christ and directed by the Spirit. Both the non-Christian and the Christian, though, are animated by God—that is, both receive their existence and energy from him, for there is no such thing as an act independent of God. And both individuals in a sense fulfill the will of God: the first his hidden will (of glorification in justice); the second his revealed will (of glorification in mercy).

> Yet God does not work in us without us; for he created and preserves us for this very purpose, that He might work in us and we might cooperate with Him, whether that occurs outside His kingdom, by His general omnipotence, or within His kingdom, by the special power of His Spirit. (312)

Luther is not saying that the "dead" person cooperates with God as God makes him alive; this is God's action alone. Nonetheless, after God's justification and regeneration, one does indeed cooperate with God in the glorification of his Creator and Redeemer. The redeemed person does this willfully—but because God gave him the will, not because his will was free to change itself.

> Though the great theologians who guard "free-will" may not know, or pretend not to know, that Scripture proclaims Christ categorically and antithetically, all Christians

---

[9] Packer, op. cit., 51. See also Luther, 262.

know it, and commonly confess it. They know that there are in the world two king-doms at war with each other. In the one, Satan reigns (which is why Christ calls him "the prince of this world" [John 12:31], and Paul "the god of this world" [2 Cor. 4:4]). . . . In the other kingdom, Christ reigns. His kingdom continually resists and wars against that of Satan; and we are translated into His kingdom, not by our own power, but by the grace of God, which delivers us from this present evil world and tears us away from the power of darkness. The knowledge and confession of these two kingdoms, ever warring against each other with all their might and power, would suffice by itself to confute the doctrine of "free-will," seeing that we are compelled to serve in Satan's kingdom if we are not plucked from it by Divine power. The common man, I repeat, knows this, and confesses it plainly enough by his proverbs, prayers, efforts and entire life. (314)

In yet another paradox, while the Christian begins with despair, he receives complete assurance:

I have the comfortable certainty that I please God, not by reason of the merit of my works, but by reason of His merciful favour promised to me; so that, if I work too little, or badly, He does not impute it to me, but with fatherly compassion pardons me and makes me better. This is the glorying of all the saints in their God.

CHAPTER 5

Luther on the Freedom and Bondage of the Will

R. Scott Clark

As Luther climbed the *Santa Scala* in 1510 on his knees in Rome, the principal thing on his mind was the possibility of salvation. The farthest thing from his mind was the certainty of salvation, and this was because, to that point, the only theology of salvation Luther knew taught him to count on two factors: the freedom of the human will, and the necessity of human cooperation with grace toward attaining salvation. Fifteen years later, in 1525, Luther's understanding of salvation had changed completely, and he published a book that transformed the landscape of Western Christianity: *The Bondage of the Will*.

Setting

Luther was not the first to discover the free, sovereign grace of God. In fifth-century North Africa, Augustine wrestled with the teaching of Pelagius and came to see that sin brings death and human inability and that grace is free and sovereign. In the intervening centuries, there were voices that kept this message alive, but they were a minority.

As a student, Luther learned a theology that downplayed the effects of sin in ways that would cause Pelagius to smile. His teachers held the view that God has promised to impute perfection to those who do their best, and that humans, even after the fall, have it within themselves to do what God's law requires.

In the following century, there was a significant and vehement reaction to what was perceived as a resurgence of Pelagianism. Indeed, in his monastery the young Luther regularly heard a proponent of Augustine's doctrines of sin and grace, but it was not until he found those doctrines in Scripture for himself that they penetrated his heart. Thus it was a low view of sin and grace that Luther imbibed in university, and it was this view he took with him as he began his own teaching career.

In 1513 to 1514, his first course of lectures as a professor took him through the Psalms and Augustine's homilies on the Psalms. He found that Scripture disagreed with the theology he had been taught in university, and he began to see that sin brought death and an inability to cooperate with grace. On Psalm 51 he wrote, "It is indeed true. For we are still unrighteous and unworthy before God, so that whatever we do is nothing before him."[1] Luther was moving in a Pauline-Augustinian direction. Years later he commented, "I did not learn my theology all at once, but had to search deeper for it, where my temptations took me" (*LW* 54.50).

After his lectures on the Psalms, Romans, and Galatians, Luther announced his recovery of the Pauline and Augustinian doctrines of sin, grace, and divine freedom. In the *Heidelberg Disputation* (1518), Luther expressed one of the central arguments of his later work *The Bondage of the Will*: "'Free will' after the fall, exists in name only, and as long as it is 'doing what is within it' it is committing mortal sin" (revised from *LW* 31.40). When, however, Erasmus read Luther's Protestant views, he did not like the aftertaste they left in his humanist mouth. In the treatise *The Freedom of the Will* (1524), Erasmus restated the dominant medieval view that downplayed the effects of the fall, insisting on the ability and necessity of human cooperation with grace unto (final) justification.[2]

In 1525, Luther responded, moving the Reformation to a new level of clarity about its most essential convictions: salvation by grace alone (*sola gratia*), through faith alone (*sola fide*), in Christ alone (*solo Christo*), and Scripture alone (*sola scriptura*) as the unique normative authority for faith and the Christian life.

God's Freedom and Our Bondage

The God that Luther announced in *Bondage of the Will* is sovereign, free, and had determined from all eternity those to whom he would freely give new life through the preached gospel and those whom he would leave in sin and death. For Luther, the existence of God's eternal determinations about humanity was revealed in Scripture but the particulars were not; many of God's ways and decisions are hidden to us. The God with whom we have to do is the God who reveals his word to us in Scripture, his law and his gospel, which reveals to us everything we need to know about God and salvation (*LW* 33.138–147).

---

[1] *Luther's Works*, American ed. (St. Louis: Concordia Publishing House, 1958), 10.236; hereafter *LW*.

[2] Roland H. Bainton, *Erasmus of Christendom* (New York: Scribner's Sons, 1969; repr. Peabody, MA: Hendrickson Publishers, 2016), 158.

The work is in two parts. The first two-thirds of *Bondage of the Will* responded point by point to Erasmus. Along the way, he articulated the most essential biblical and Reformation truths. Erasmus had reasoned that if Scripture tells us to do something, it must be the case that we can do it or else God is unjust. Such reasoning demonstrated that Erasmus did not know how to distinguish between the principles of law and gospel in Scripture.

> Now I ask you, what good will anyone do in a matter of theology or Holy Writ, who has not yet got as far as knowing what the law and the gospel is, or if he knows, disdains to observe the distinction between them? Such a person is bound to confound everything—heaven and hell, life and death—and he will take no pains to know anything at all about Christ. (*LW* 33.132)

According to Luther's criticism, Erasmus had managed to turn the good news into bad news! Erasmus was guilty of a sort of rationalism, of sitting in judgment over Scripture, because he had not utterly abandoned himself to the teaching of Scripture, even when the Scripture presented hard truths. For example, on Exodus 4:21 concerning the hardening of Pharaoh's heart, Luther wrote: "The Divine Author says, 'I will harden Pharaoh's heart,' and the meaning of the verb 'to harden' is plain and well known. . . . By what authority, for what reason, with what necessity is the natural meaning of the word twisted for me?" (*LW* 33.165). Luther repeatedly asserted and defended the essential clarity of God's word on those points necessary for faith and life.

Luther found the same clarity of Scripture in Romans 9. It is not possible to "resist" God's will. People may feel and desire things to be otherwise, but Luther knew Scripture to be "transparently clear" on these points. God hardens whom he wills. He has mercy upon whom he wills (*LW* 33.187). God's eternal foreknowledge and omnipotence are "diametrically opposed to our free choice," and so much so that they "completely abolish the dogma of free choice" (*LW* 33.189).

It was not that Luther denied that humans exercise any sort of freedom; he only recognized a distinction between necessity and compulsion (*LW* 33.192–212). Whatever God wills happens necessarily, but humans are not forced to action or inaction. Fallen humans will freely according to their natures, without compulsion, and within the limits of God's wise and governing decree.

Conclusion

Luther was a pastor and recognized how difficult then (as now) these words are to hear. It was not as if he himself had not struggled with it: "I myself have more than once been offended [by this doctrine] almost to the very depth and abyss of despair, so that I wished I had never been created a man, until I realized how salutary was this despair and how near to grace" (*LW* 18.719).

He insisted on God's freedom and our natural, fallen inability to do anything except sin because he came to see how intertwined God's free, eternal choice is with grace. It is of the essence of grace (divine favor) that God be free. If it is true that God *must* save a certain person, then grace is no longer grace. If grace depends on our cooperation, then grace is no longer grace (*LW* 33.241–44).

He also insisted on this teaching because to say, as the medieval church had said, that a fallen sinner still has power to cooperate with divine grace, is to deny the necessity of Christ's work. For Luther, it was utterly perverse to say that the doctrine of unconditional election leads to doubt. Rather, it is the basis of our assurance. This is because there are two spiritual kingdoms in the world, that of Christ and the other of Satan. By nature we are citizens of the kingdom of Satan. We can become a member of Christ's kingdom only by the sovereign, free, gracious choice and work of God (*LW* 33.288). If we believe, it is only because of God's free, gracious choice, not our own. If it were my choice, "I should be unable to stand firm and keep hold of it amid so many adversities and perils and so many assaults of demons" (*LW* 33.288). Without this doctrine of divine free will, believers could never be assured of God's favor because we might always lose it; but if we do come to faith, we can have firm confidence that it is because God has chosen us, made us alive, given us faith, and united us to Christ. He cannot lose us, and this is something of which we should have no doubt.

CHAPTER 6

Luther on Galatians

David R. Andersen

It is a marvelous thing and unknown to the world to teach Christians to ignore the Law and to live before God as though there were no Law whatever. For if you do not ignore the Law and thus direct your thoughts to grace as though there were no Law ... you cannot be saved. (6)[1]

Thus the German Reformer Martin Luther provocatively sets the tone for his 1535 lectures on Galatians. His argument is based on the fact that in Galatians the Apostle Paul draws, in effect, a crucial distinction between two kinds of righteousness: active and passive. Active righteousness involves our relying on our own fulfillment of the law for our ultimate justification before God (see Gal. 3:3, 12; 5:2–4). Passive righteousness consists in our permitting someone else—namely, God—to bring about our salvation. Active righteousness consists in our actively working to appease God's wrath. Passive righteousness involves our passively accepting by faith a gift we in no way deserve because God has acted in Christ to justify us (see Gal. 1:3–4; 2:15–16, 20–21; 3:2–14).

This distinction is easy to understand, but it is incredibly difficult to practice. Why? Because, Luther argues, a natural connection exists between sinful human reason and the law. We know the law by nature (see Rom. 1:18–2:16), so in the terrors of conscience and danger of death we naturally look to our own works of the law for eternal hope. Because the connection is so natural, Satan's primary goal in effecting human destruction lies in aggravating our hopeless devotion to the law and thus ensuring that our minds remain turned in upon themselves (see 2 Cor. 11:1–12:10; esp. 11:12–15). But the trouble with such an inward turn is that there is nothing within us except sin and death, so we cannot find solace by looking there.

---

[1] All of the quotations identified only by a page number are from Martin Luther, *Luther's Works*, vol. 26, trans. Jaroslav Pelikan (Saint Louis, MO: Concordia Publishing House, 1963).

This continuous battle between the law and Christ's work to redeem us from the law's curse forms the framework for many of Luther's Galatian lectures. For him, the battle must be waged by all of us, because if we stray away from passive righteousness we necessarily relapse into active righteousness. There is no middle ground. We either look to ourselves or we look to Christ for our justification before a holy God. Religion, whether medieval or modern, always succeeds in focusing attention on our worthiness and the law. It always triumphs in focusing attention on individual sins and thus ignoring completely the depth of our sinful predicament. Luther stresses that, according to Scripture, we are radically corrupt from the *inside out*. Focusing on individual sins only draws us down into despair, in the same way that Peter sank as he began to focus on the individual waves instead of on Christ. Sin erupts from the human heart with infinitely more force than water from behind a ruptured dam, so preoccupation with this or that sin is not only useless, it ultimately drags the sinner down to the deadly rocks below.

The solution must be as radical as the problem—and Luther finds it in the wounds of the crucified God. At that haunting scene of suffering and death, there is no room for human self-sufficiency, no room for trivializing sin and death. Recognizing human weakness in a way unique in Christian history, Luther turns our attention with piercing clarity to the flesh of Christ. To that end, he highlights in his Galatian lectures two temptations that both believer and unbeliever battle daily. The first involves our tendency to speculate about God's naked being; and the second involves our hopeless devotion to our own self-sufficiency. We prize both of these. To human reason, with its preconceptions about holiness and its preoccupation with itself, Christ could hardly be more offensive. So what does reason do to remove the offense? It remakes Christ according to its own notions. Thus we are led away from God by turning our gaze away from Christ, and Satan is successful in keeping us in sin and death.

Speculation and Its Devastating Consequences

From Luther's perspective, Adam's fall had two devastating consequences: (1) we lost knowledge of God; and (2) our wills became perverted and hopelessly turned in upon themselves. Before the fall, Adam had by nature a proper understanding of God, but now without that correct understanding we tend to run amuck in our imaginations as to who God is and what he desires. In other words, our tendency is to speculate about God's naked being rather than focus on God as he reveals himself in Christ and Scripture. We are incapable of knowing God apart from what he reveals about himself; and, of course, we must first come to know what something is like before we can offer theories about it. Yet we are much happier offering theories about God before we take the time to understand what God reveals about himself. We are passionately committed to our own wisdom. Human reason wants to flatter itself about what it knows in any and every situation; and so it becomes its own worst sycophant.

But such egocentricity produces idolatry rather than true worship. Sinful human beings naturally put the cart before the horse and refuse to stay on the road that God himself has paved. We always want to have and to do something unusual. Luther sees this as an enormous problem, for we cannot grasp our salvation if we fail to understand what our salvation actually involves. He explains:

> True Christian theology, as I often warn you, does not present God to us in His majesty, as Moses and other teachings do, but Christ born of the Virgin as our Mediator and High Priest. Therefore when we are embattled against the Law, sin, and death in the presence of God, nothing is more dangerous than to stray into heaven with our idle speculations, there to investigate God in His incomprehensible power, wisdom, and majesty, to ask how He created the world and how He governs it. If you attempt to comprehend God this way and want to make atonement to Him apart from Christ the Mediator, making your works, fasts, cowl, and tonsure the mediation between Him and yourself, you will inevitably fall, as Lucifer did (Is. 14:12), and in horrible despair lose God and everything. For as in His own nature God is immense, incomprehensible, and infinite, so to man's nature He is intolerable. Therefore if you want to be safe and out of danger to your conscience and your salvation, put a check on this speculative spirit. Take hold of God as Scripture instructs you. . . . Therefore begin where Christ began—in the Virgin's womb, in the manger, and at His mother's breasts. For this purpose He came down, was born, lived among men, suffered, was crucified, and died, so that in every possible way He might present Himself to our sight. He wanted us to fix the gaze of our hearts upon Himself and thus to prevent us from clambering into heaven and speculating about the Divine Majesty. . . . Therefore whenever you consider the doctrine of justification and wonder how or where or in what condition to find a God who justifies or accepts sinners, then you must know that there is no other God than this Man Jesus Christ. Take hold of Him; cling to Him with all your heart, and spurn all speculation about the Divine Majesty; for whoever investigates the majesty of God will be consumed by His glory. I know from experience what I am talking about. But these fanatics, who deal with God apart from this Man, will not believe me. . . . Take note, therefore, in the doctrine of justification or grace that when we all must struggle with the Law, sin, death, and the devil, we must look at no other God than this incarnate and human God. (28–29)

For Luther, this point cannot be expressed too often: There is no other God than the One who presents himself in the dereliction of the cross. Why does he make such an absolute statement? Because, as he read in Genesis, the fall wiped out a saving knowledge of God; and this disaster is compounded only by the fact that we are incurably religious by nature. So in the absence of a clear, simple word from God as to his nature and will, we naturally create a god to our own liking—i.e., one that conforms to our own twisted views of holiness and salvation. In other words, we create our own religions with their strict moral rules and guidelines for earning salvation. The law, already written on our hearts (see Rom. 2:15), becomes our hope for eternal bliss. Our perverted inwardness causes us to believe the false claim that if the law exists, then it must be capable of being fulfilled. So fulfilling the law becomes the key to pleasing God and inheriting the kingdom of heaven.

In opposition to this, Luther argues that our only hope is found in the Christian message—a message rooted in history and not in some supersensible, metaphysical reality. Christianity has a fleshly point of departure:

> It does not begin at the top, as all other religions do; it begins at the bottom. . . . Therefore whenever you are concerned to think and act about your salvation, you must put away all speculations about the Majesty, all thoughts of works, traditions, and philosophy—indeed, of the Law of God itself. And you must run directly to the manger and the mother's womb, embrace this Infant and Virgin's Child in your arms, and look at Him—born, being nursed, growing up, going about in human society, teaching, dying, rising again, ascending above all the heavens, and having authority over all things. In this way you can shake off all terrors and errors, as the sun dispels the clouds. (30)

For Luther, the historic Christ is the key who unlocks our preoccupation with ourselves and frees us from bondage to sin, death, and the devil. Our only hope is in that which is *outside* us, in Christ; to fasten our gaze on the One who was crucified for the world's sins is the only hope for *unbeliever* and *believer* alike. As Paul Althaus has put it: Jesus does not point us to God; he presents the eternal God himself in his very person. So to gaze upon that scene of total desolation where God in Christ bears in his own body the sins of the world is to gaze directly into God's fatherly heart. Here the human mind must subdue all of its own ideas about who God is and what he wills for humankind.[2]

But what if we fail to fix our attention on that bronze serpent (see Num. 21:8–9 with John 3:14)? From Luther's perspective, this failure can produce nothing other than despair and eternal death. This is why the bulk of the devil's

---

[2] Paul Althaus, *Theology of Martin Luther*, trans. Robert C. Schultz (Philadelphia: Fortress Press, 1966), 182.

efforts are focused on drawing us toward the contemplative life and away from knowing "Christ and him crucified." But Jesus in the flesh is the only profitable object of contemplation. Those who forsake it and speculate about the naked God by self-invented "spiritual" means are swallowed by the Divine Majesty. The incarnate Son is the covering in which the Divine Majesty presents himself to us with the gift of salvation.

Our Sense of Self-Sufficiency versus Christ's Sufficiency

For Luther, we can hardly submerge Jesus in the human situation too much. The union of the divine and human natures in one person is what assures us that Christ's work stands secure. This union is so wondrous that the angels descend as though there were no God in heaven to come to Bethlehem to adore and worship him as he lies in the manger at his mother's breast. The incarnation makes Jesus' humanity subject to death and hell, yet in that very humiliation it devours them both in itself.

As incredible as this is, the Christian church in every generation manages to place humanity at the center of the religious relationship. As Luther saw it, our self-love produces a Jesus in our own image, one who conforms to our inward sense of self-sufficiency. It does so by making Jesus our great example. He becomes, in effect, our role model. It is claimed that, by daily patterning our lives after his, we can produce the godly lives that God wants us to live. In this way we achieve the synthesis we want between our love for ourselves and our reading of certain New Testament passages, and our lives give off an appearance of piety.

But this synthesis has a horrible price. It segregates Christ from sins and sinners. Christ, as a mere example to be imitated, becomes useless to us. He also becomes a judge and tyrant who is angry at our sins and who damns us on their account. Such a perverted view of Jesus can be achieved only by disregarding God's self-revelation at the cross. At the cross, Luther argues, we must conclude that, just as Christ is wrapped up in our flesh and blood, so he is also wrapped up in our sins, our curse, and our death. Whatever sins we have committed or will commit must be seen as Christ's own, as if he himself had committed them. In other words, our sin must become Christ's own or we shall perish eternally. And so Luther comments:

> And this is our highest comfort, to clothe and wrap Christ this way in my sins, your sins, and the sins of the entire world, and in this way to behold Him bearing all our sins. When He is beheld this way, He easily removes all the fanatical opinions of our opponents about justification by works. (279)

When we make Jesus our example, we direct the human race toward the very thing that holds it captive—namely, the law. For fallen humankind, the law is a judge and tyrant that justly pronounces a curse on everything we are and do. We may misunderstand the law's true intent—thinking it has been given to us for us to fulfill—but it nevertheless rightfully condemns the human heart. And, from Luther's point of view, the solution to our plight must be as radical as the curse.

He finds the heart of the solution to our predicament in the apostle's words, "Christ redeemed us from the curse of the law *by becoming a curse for us*" (Gal. 3:13). We must, Luther insists, distinguish carefully Christ from the law. For all who do not keep the law are under a curse, and since no one keeps the law, it follows that all human beings are under a curse (see Gal. 3:10 with Deut. 27:26 and Rom. 3:9–20). Therefore, the law and works of the law do not redeem us from the curse. "On the contrary," Luther concludes, "they drag us down and subject us to the curse." Christ is entirely different from the law and its works; and so redemption in him is different than merit based on works of the law. Only Christ himself could redeem us from the law's curse, bearing in his own body our sins, our curse, and our death. "By this fortunate exchange with us He took upon Himself our sinful person and granted us His innocent and victorious Person" (284). So, in his characteristic language, Luther explains:

> When the merciful Father saw that we were being oppressed through the Law, that we were being held under a curse, and that we could not be liberated from it by anything, He sent His Son into the world, heaped all the sins of all men upon Him, and said to Him: "Be Peter the denier; Paul the persecutor, blasphemer, and assaulter; David the adulterer; the sinner who ate the apple in Paradise; the thief on the cross. In short, be the person of all men, the one who has committed the sins of all men. And see to it that You pay and make satisfaction for them." Now the Law comes and says: "I find Him a sinner, who takes upon Himself the sins of all men. I do not see any other sins than those in Him. Therefore let Him die on the cross!" And so it attacks Him and kills Him. By this deed the whole world is purged and expiated from all sins, and thus it is set free from death and from every evil. But when sin and death have been abolished by this one man, God does not want to see anything else in the whole world, especially if it were to believe, except sheer cleansing and righteousness. (280)

Wise men indeed find the highest God lying in a lowly manger. But he descends to that manger, to the level of our suffering and pain, for only one purpose: that by bearing our curse and death in himself we might find a gracious God, a God *for us*. Thus Luther rightly concludes:

With gratitude and with a sure confidence, therefore, let us accept this doctrine, so sweet and so filled with comfort, which teaches that Christ became a curse for us, that is, a sinner worthy of the wrath of God; that He clothed Himself in our person, laid our sins upon His own shoulders, and said: "I have committed the sins that all men have committed." Therefore He truly became accursed according to the Law, not for Himself but, as Paul says, *for us*. (284)

Why We Must Heed Luther's Words

Does Luther highlight a battle for faith that is culturally bound to the medieval church, with its devotion to shrines and saints, or do his words have applicability in our contemporary situation? For him, human nature remains constant this side of heaven, and consequently the tendencies toward trying to know God outside Christ and to love ourselves dominate all human history. Modern movements such as Pietism and some manifestations of American and European evangelicalism serve to confirm our abiding inward focus. While they differ in particulars, the result is always the same: Jesus becomes our example, and salvation—despite the constant language of grace—ultimately rests with us. Luther constantly warned against remaking Jesus to our own liking. In fact, he could hardly stress it too often, because we all without exception cling to the law and resist Jesus' insistence that we are the broken reeds and smoldering wicks of Isaiah's text—the very reeds and wicks he promises not to break off and snuff out (see Matt. 12:17–21).

So Luther's fervent call to behold Christ's flesh is as necessary today as it was in his day. Our only consolation is to be found in an ignominious death two thousand years ago and in our appropriation of that death in word and sacrament, by which the forgiveness of sins is distributed to beggars who have nothing to offer but sin and death. And so Luther urges us to fight our natural inclination to make Jesus an angry lawgiver. We must learn to regard him as Paul portrays him: He is the God who pays the penalty of our sin with his own blood. It is only with this objective view of God in mind that we can begin to comprehend the unqualified freedom that the Father provides in the bloody death and resurrection of the Son. It is only by clinging to this picture that we can finally, in our struggles against the law and the accusations of our conscience and the devil and in the face of our own mortality, declare with steady confidence:

Law, you have no jurisdiction over me; therefore you are accusing and condemning me in vain. For I believe in Jesus Christ, the Son of God, whom the Father sent into the world to redeem us miserable sinners who are oppressed by the tyranny of the Law. He poured out His life and spent it lavishly for me. When I feel your terrors and threats, O Law, I immerse my conscience in the wounds, the blood, the death, the resurrection, and the victory of Christ. Beyond Him I do not want to see or hear anything at all. (369)

CHAPTER 7

Pelagianism

Michael S. Horton

Cicero observed of his own civilization that people thank the gods for their material prosperity but never for their virtue, for this is their own doing. Princeton theologian B. B. Warfield considered Pelagianism "the rehabilitation of that heathen view of the world" and concluded with characteristic clarity, "There are fundamentally only two doctrines of salvation: that salvation is from God, and that salvation is from ourselves. The former is the doctrine of common Christianity; the latter is the doctrine of universal heathenism."[1]

But Warfield's sharp criticisms are consistent with the witness of the church ever since Pelagius and his disciples championed the heresy. St. Jerome, the fourth-century Latin father, called it "the heresy of Pythagoras and Zeno," as in general paganism rested on the fundamental conviction that human beings have it within their power to save themselves. What, then, was Pelagianism and how did it get started?

This heresy originated with the first human couple, as we shall see soon. It was actually defined and labeled in the fifth century when a British monk, Pelagius, arrived in Rome. Immediately, he was deeply impressed with the immorality of this center of Christendom, and he set out to reform the morals of clergy and laity alike. This moral campaign required a great deal of energy, and Pelagius found many supporters and admirers for his cause. The only thing that seemed to stand in his way was the emphasis that emanated particularly from the influential African bishop, Augustine. Augustine taught that human beings, because they are born in original sin, are incapable of saving themselves. Apart from God's grace, it is impossible for a person to obey or even to seek God. Representing the entire race, Adam sinned against God. This resulted in the total corruption of every human being since, so that our very wills are in bondage to our sinful condition. Only God's grace, which he bestows freely as he pleases upon his elect, is credited with the salvation of human beings.

---

[1] B. B. Warfield, *The Plan of Salvation* (Grand Rapids: Eerdmans, 1980), 33.

In sharp contrast, Pelagius was driven by moral concerns and his theology was calculated to provide the most fuel for moral and social improvement. Augustine's emphasis on human helplessness and divine grace would surely paralyze the pursuit of moral improvement, since people could sin with impunity, fatalistically concluding, "I couldn't help it; I'm a sinner." So Pelagius countered by rejecting original sin. According to Pelagius, Adam was merely a bad example, not the father of our sinful condition—we are sinners because we sin—rather than vice versa. Consequently, of course, the second Adam, Jesus Christ, was a good example. Salvation is a matter chiefly of following Christ instead of Adam, rather than being transferred from the condemnation and corruption of Adam's race and placed "in Christ," clothed in his righteousness and made alive by his gracious gift. What humanity needs is moral direction, not a new birth; therefore, Pelagius saw salvation in purely naturalistic terms—the progress of human nature from sinful behavior to holy behavior, by following the example of Christ.

In his commentary on Romans, Pelagius thought of grace as God's revelation in the Old and New Testaments, which enlightens us and serves to promote our holiness by providing explicit instruction in godliness and many worthy examples to imitate. So human nature is not conceived in sin. After all, the will is not bound by the sinful condition and its affections; choices determine whether one will obey God and thus be saved.

In 411, Paulinus of Milan came up with a list of six heretical points in the Pelagian message: (1) Adam was created mortal and would have died whether he had sinned or not; (2) the sin of Adam injured himself alone, not the whole human race; (3) newborn children are in the same state in which Adam was before his fall; (4) neither by the death and sin of Adam does the whole human race die, nor will it rise because of the resurrection of Christ; (5) the law as well as the gospel offers entrance to the kingdom of heaven; and (6) even before the coming of Christ, there were men wholly without sin.[2] Further, Pelagius and his followers denied unconditional predestination.

It is worth noting that Pelagianism was condemned by more church councils than any other heresy in history. In 412, Pelagius's disciple Coelestius was excommunicated at the Synod of Carthage; the Councils of Carthage and Milevis condemned Pelagius's *De libero arbitrio—On the Freedom of the Will*; Pope Innocent I excommunicated both Pelagius and Coelestius, as did Pope Zosimus. In AD 430, Eastern emperor Theodosius II banished the Pelagians from the East. The heresy was condemned by the Council of Ephesus in 431 and the Second

---

[2]Taken from the entry on Pelagianism in the *Westminster Dictionary of Church History*.

Council of Orange in 529. In fact, the Council of Orange condemned even semi-Pelagianism, which maintains that grace is necessary but that the will is free by nature to choose whether to cooperate with the grace offered. The Council of Orange even condemned those who thought that salvation could be conferred by the saying of a prayer, affirming instead (with abundant biblical references) that God must awaken the sinner and grant the gift of faith before a person can even seek God.

Anything that falls short of acknowledging original sin, the bondage of the will, and the need for grace to even accept the gift of eternal life, much less to pursue righteousness, is considered by the whole church to be heresy. The heresy described here is called "Pelagianism."

Pelagianism in the Bible

Cain murdered Abel because Cain sought to offer God his own sacrifice. The writer to the Hebrews tells us that Abel offered his sacrifice in anticipation of the final sacrifice, the Lamb of God, and did so by faith rather than by works (Heb. 11). However, Cain sought to be justified by his own works. When God accepted Abel instead, Cain became jealous. His hatred for Abel was probably due in part to his own hatred of God for refusing to accept his righteousness. This pattern had already emerged with the fig leaves Adam and Eve sewed to cover their nakedness. Running from God's judgment and covering up the shame that results from sin—these are the characteristics of human nature ever since the fall. "There is no one who is righteous, not even one; there is no one who understands, no one who seeks after God. All have turned away, they have together become worthless; there is no one who does good, not even one" (Rom. 3:10–12). The nearer God comes to us, the greater sense we have of our own unworthiness, so we hide from him and try to cover up our shame with our own clever masks.

At the Tower of Babel, the attitude expressed is clearly Pelagian: "Come, let us build ourselves a city, with a tower that reaches to the heavens, so that we may make a name for ourselves." In fact, they were certain that such a united human project could ensure that nothing would be impossible for them (Gen 11:4–6). But God came down, just as they were building upward toward the heavens. "So the LORD scattered them from there over all the earth, and they stopped building the city" (v. 8). This is the pattern: God provides the sacrifice and judges those who offer their own sacrifices to appease God. God comes down to dwell with us; we do not climb up to him. God finds us; we do not find him.

The people of Israel regularly found themselves reverting to the pagan way of thinking. God had to remind them, "Cursed is the one who trusts in man, who depends on flesh for his strength and whose heart turns away from the Lord. But blessed is the man who trusts in the Lord, whose confidence is in him." Jeremiah responds, "The heart is deceitful above all things and beyond cure. Who can understand it? . . . Heal me, O Lord, and I will be healed; save me and I will be saved, for you are the one I praise" (Jer. 17:5, 7, 9, 15). Jonah learned the hard way that God saves whomever he wants to save. Just as soon as he declared, "Salvation comes from the Lord," we read: "And the Lord commanded the fish, and it vomited Jonah onto dry land" (Jon. 2:9–10). The Babylonian king Nebuchadnezzar faced a similar confrontation when God turned his self-confidence into humiliation. Nebuchadnezzar then raised his eyes toward heaven and confessed, "All the peoples of the earth are regarded as nothing. He does as he pleases with the powers of heaven and the peoples of the earth. No one can hold back his hand or say to him: 'What have you done'" (Dan. 4:35). The message is clear: God saves freely, by his own choice and action, to his own praise and glory.

We find Pelagianism among the Pharisees in the New Testament. Remember, the foundation of Pelagianism is the belief that we do not inherit Adam's sinful condition. We are born morally neutral, capable of choosing which way we will turn. Sin is something that affects us from the outside, so that if a good person sins, it must be due to some external influence. This is why it is so important, according to this way of thinking, to avoid bad company and evil influences for this will corrupt an otherwise good person. This Pelagian mentality pervaded the thinking of the Pharisees, as when they asked Jesus why they he did not follow the Jewish rituals. "Jesus called the crowd to him and said, 'Listen and understand. What goes into a man's mouth does not make him 'unclean,' but what comes out of his mouth, that is what makes him 'unclean.'" This theological orientation was so unfamiliar to the disciples that Jesus had to restate the point: "For out of the heart come evil thoughts, murder, adultery, sexual immorality, theft, false testimony, slander. These are what make a man 'unclean'" (Matt. 15:10–20). Later, Jesus scolded the Pharisees with these harsh words:

> Woe to you, teachers of the law and Pharisees, you hypocrites! You clean the outside of the cup and dish, but inside they are full of greed and self-indulgence. Blind Pharisee! First clean the inside of the cup and dish, and then the outside also will be clean. Woe to you, teachers of the law and Pharisees, you hypocrites! You are like whitewashed tombs, which look beautiful on the outside but on the inside are full of dead men's bones and everything unclean. In the same way, on the outside you appear to people as righteous, but on the inside you are full of hypocrisy and wickedness. (Matt. 23:25–28)

Therefore, Jesus told them that they must be "born from above" (John 3:5). The Pharisees believed that God had given them his grace by giving them the law; if they merely followed the law and the traditions of the elders, then they would remain in God's favor. But Jesus said that they were unbelievers who needed to be regenerated, not good people who needed to be guided. "No man can even come to me unless my Father who sent me draws him" (John 6:44), for we must be born again, "not of the will of the flesh or of the will of man, but of God" (John 1:13). "Apart from me you can do nothing. You did not choose me, but I chose you and appointed you to go and bear fruit—fruit that will last" (John 15:5, 16).

This message was at the center of the apostolic message, as Paul defended the grace of God against the Judaizing heresy that sought to turn Jesus into another Moses. Centering on the person and work of Christ, Paul and the other apostles denied any place for self-confidence before God. Instead, they knew that we don't possess the ability, free will, power, or righteousness to repair ourselves and escape the wrath of God. It must all be God's work, Christ's work, or there is no salvation at all. Surely the Judaizing heresy that troubled the apostles was larger than the issue of Pelagianism, but self-righteousness and self-salvation lay at the bottom of it. As such, the Council of Jerusalem, as recorded in Acts 15, was the first church council to actually condemn this heresy in the New Testament era.

Pelagianism in Church History

Every dark age in church history is due to the creeping influence of the human-centered gospel of "pulling oneself up by the bootstraps." Whenever God is seen as the sole author and finisher of salvation, there is health and vitality. To the degree that human beings are seen as agents of their own salvation, the church loses its power, since the gospel is "the power of God unto salvation for everyone who believes" (Rom 1:16).

Throughout the period popularly known as the Dark Ages, Pelagianism was never officially endorsed, but it was certainly common and perhaps even the most popular and widespread tendency among the masses. That should come as no surprise, since thinking good of our nature and of possibilities for its improvement is the tendency of our sinful condition. We are all Pelagians by nature. There were debates, for instance, in the eighth century, but these did not end well for those who defended a strict Augustinian point of view. Since Pelagianism had been condemned by councils, no one dared defend a view as "Pelagian," but semi-Pelagianism was acceptable since the canons of the Council of Orange, which condemned semi-Pelagianism, had been lost and were not recovered until after the closing of the Council of Trent in the sixteenth century.

On the eve of the Reformation, there were fresh debates over free will and grace. Reformers benefited from something of a renaissance of Augustinianism. In the fourteenth century, two Oxford lecturers, Robert Holcot and Archbishop of Canterbury Thomas Bradwardine, became leading antagonists in this battle. Two centuries before the Reformation, Bradwardine wrote *The Case of God against the New Pelagians*, but "Holcot and a host of later interpreters found Bradwardine's defense of the 'case of God' was at the expense of the dignity of man."[3] If that sounds familiar, it should, since the truth and its corresponding objections never change. The archbishop's own story gives us some insight to the place of this debate:

> Idle and a fool in God's wisdom, I was misled by an unorthodox error at the time when I was pursuing philosophical studies. Sometimes I went to listen to the theologians discussing this matter [of grace and free will], and the school of Pelagius seemed to me nearest the truth. In the philosophical faculty I seldom heard a reference to grace, except for some ambiguous remarks. What I heard day in and day out was that we are masters of our own free acts, that ours is the choice to act well or badly, to have virtues or sins and much more along this line.

Therefore,

> Every time I listened to the Epistle reading in church and heard how Paul magnified grace and belittled free will—as is the case in Romans 9, 'It is obviously not a question of human will and effort, but of divine mercy,' and its many parallels—grace displeased me, ungrateful as I was.

But later, things changed:

> However, even before I transferred to the faculty of theology, the text mentioned came to me as a beam of grace and, captured by a vision of the truth, it seemed I saw from afar how the grace of God precedes all good works with a temporal priority, God as Savior through predestination, and natural precedence. That is why I express my gratitude to Him who has given me this grace as a free gift.

Bradwardine begins his treatise, "The Pelagians now oppose our whole presentation of predestination and reprobation, attempting either to eliminate them completely or, at least, to show that they are dependent on personal merits."[4]

---

[3] Heiko Oberman, *Forerunners of the Reformation* (Philadelphia: Fortress, 1966), 134.
[4] Oberman, 151–62.

These are important references, since many think of the emphasis of Luther in *The Bondage of the Will* and of Calvin in his many writings on the subject as extreme, when in actual fact they were in the mainstream of Augustinian revival. In fact, Luther's mentor, Johann von Staupitz, was himself a defender of Augustinian orthodoxy against the new tide of Pelagianism and contributed his own treatise, *On Man's Eternal Predestination.*

> God has covenanted to save the elect. Not only is Christ sent as a substitute for the believer's sins, he also makes certain that this redemption is applied. This happens at the moment when the sinner's eyes are opened again by the grace of God, so that he is able to know the true God by faith. Then his heart is set afire so that God becomes pleasing to him. Both of these are nothing but grace, and flow from the merits of Christ Our works do not, nor can they, bring us to this state, since man's nature is not capable of knowing or wanting or doing good. For this barren man God is sheer fear.

But for the believer, "the Christian is just through the righteousness of Christ." Staupitz even goes so far to say that this suffering of Christ "is sufficient for all, though it was not for all, but for many that his blood was poured out."[5] This was not an extreme statement, as it is often considered today, but was the most common way of talking about the atonement's effect: sufficient for everyone, efficient for the elect alone.

To be sure, these precursors of the Reformation were not yet articulating a clear doctrine of justification by the imputation of Christ's righteousness, but the official position of the Roman Catholic Church even before the Reformation was that grace is necessary for even the will to believe and live the Christian life. This is not far enough for evangelicals, but to fall short of this affirmation is to lose touch with even the "catholic" witness shared at least on paper by Protestants and Roman Catholics.

What About Today?

Ever since the Enlightenment, Protestant churches have been influenced by successive waves of rationalism and moralism that have made the Pelagian heresy attractive. It is fascinating, if frustrating, to read the great architects of modern liberalism as they triumphantly announce their project. They sound as if it were a new theological enterprise to say that human nature is basically good, history is marked by progress, that social and moral improvement will

---

[5] Oberman, 175–200.

create happiness, peace, and justice. Really, it is merely a revival of that age-old religion of human nature. The rationalistic phase of liberalism saw religion not as a plan of salvation but as a method of morality. The older views concerning human sinfulness and dependence on divine mercy were thought by modern theologians to stand in the way of the Enlightenment project of building a new world, a tower reaching to heaven, just as Pelagius viewed Augustinian teaching as impeding his project of moral reform.

Instead of defining Christianity in terms of an announcement of God's saving work in Jesus Christ, Schleiermacher and the liberal theologians redefined it as a "feeling." Ironically, the Arminian revivals shared with the Enlightenment a confidence in human ability. This Pelagian spirit pervaded the frontier revivals as much as the New England academy. Although poets such as William Henley might put it in more sophisticated language ("I am the master of my fate, the captain of my soul"), evangelicals out on the frontier began adapting this triumph of Pelagianism to the wider culture.

Heavily influenced by the New Haven theology and the Second Great Awakening, Charles Finney was nearly the nineteenth-century reincarnation of Pelagius. Finney denied original sin: "Moral depravity is sin itself, and not the cause of sin."[6] In his criticism of the Westminster Confession, he explicitly rejected original sin,[7] referring to the notion of a sinful nature as "anti-scriptural and nonsensical dogma."[8] According to Finney, we are all born morally neutral, capable either of choosing good or evil. Finney argues throughout by employing the same arguments as the German rationalists, and yet because he was such a successful revivalist and "soul-winner," evangelicals call him their own. Finney held that our choices make us either good or sinful. Here Finney stands closer to the Pharisees than to Christ, who declared that the tree produced the fruit rather than vice versa. Finney's denial of the substitutionary atonement follows this denial of original sin. After all, according to Pelagius, if Adam can be said to be our agent of condemnation for no other reason than that we follow his poor example, then Christ is said to be our agent of redemption because we follow his good example. This is precisely what Finney argues: "Example is the highest moral influence that can be exerted. If the benevolence manifested in the atonement does not subdue the selfishness of sinners, their case is hopeless."[9] But how can there be a "benevolence manifested in the atonement" if the atonement

---

[6] Charles Finney, *Finney's Systematic Theology* (Minneapolis: Bethany, 1976), 172.
[7] Finney, 177.
[8] Finney, 179.
[9] Finney, 209.

does not atone? For those of us who need an atonement that not only subdues our selfishness but covers the penalty for our selfishness, Finney's "gospel," like Pelagius's, is hardly good news.

According to Finney, Christ could not have fulfilled the obedience we owe to God, since it would not be rational that one man could atone for the sins of anyone besides himself. Furthermore, "If he obeyed the law as our substitute, then why should our own return to personal obedience be insisted upon as the sine qua non of our salvation?"[10] One wonders if Finney was actually borrowing directly from Pelagius's writings. Many assume "that the atonement was a literal payment of a debt, which we have seen does not consist with the nature of the atonement. It is objected that, if the atonement was not the payment of the debt of sinners, but general in its nature, as we have maintained, it secures the salvation of no one. It is true, that the atonement, of itself, does not secure the salvation of any one."[11]

Furthermore, Finney denies that regeneration depends on the supernatural gift of God. It is not a change produced from the outside. "If it were, sinners could not be required to effect it. No such change is needed, as the sinner has all the faculties and natural attributes requisite to render perfect obedience to God."[12] Therefore, "regeneration consists in the sinner changing his ultimate choice, intention, preference." Those who insist that sinners depend on the mercy of God proclaim "the most abominable and ruinous of all falsehoods. It is to mock [the sinner's] intelligence!"[13]

Of the doctrine of justification, Finney declared it to be "another gospel," since

for sinners to be forensically pronounced just, is impossible and absurd. As has already been said, there can be no justification in a legal or forensic sense, but upon the ground of universal, perfect, and uninterrupted obedience to law. . . . The doctrine of an imputed righteousness, or that Christ's obedience to the law was accounted as our obedience, is founded on a most false and nonsensical assumption [and] representing the atonement as the ground of the sinner's justification has been a sad occasion of stumbling to many.[14]

From Finney and the Arminian revivalists, evangelicalism inherited as great a debt to Pelagianism as modern liberalism received from the Enlightenment

---

[10] Finney, 206.
[11] Finney, 213.
[12] Finney, 221.
[13] Finney, 226.
[14] Finney, 319–23.

version directly. When evangelists appeal to the unbeliever as though it was his choice that determines his destiny, they not only operate on Arminian assumptions but also on Pelagian assumptions that are rejected even by the official position of the Roman Catholic Church as a denial of grace. Whenever it is maintained that an unbeliever is capable by nature of choosing God, or that men and women are capable of not sinning or of reaching a state of moral perfection, that's Pelagianism. Finney even preached a sermon titled, "Sinners Bound to Change Their Own Hearts." When preachers attack those who insist that the human problem is sinfulness and the wickedness of the human heart—that's Pelagianism. When one hears the argument—whether from the Enlightenment (Kant's "ought implies can"), Wesley, Finney, or modern teachers—that "God would never have commanded the impossible,"[15] they echo the very words of Pelagius. Those who deny that faith is the gift of God are not merely Arminians or semi-Pelagians but Pelagians. Even the Council of Trent (condemning the Reformers) anathematized such a denial as Pelagianism.

When evangelicals and fundamentalists assume that infants are pure until they reach an "age of accountability," or that sin is something outside—in the world or in the sinful environment or in sinful company that corrupts the individual—they are practicing Pelagians. That which in contemporary evangelicalism is often considered "Calvinism" is really "Augustinianism," which embraces orthodox Roman Catholics and Lutherans as well. And that which in our circles today is often considered "Arminianism" is really Pelagianism.

The fact that recent polls indicate that 77 percent of the evangelicals today believe that human beings are basically good and 84 percent of these conservative Protestants believe that in salvation "God helps those who help themselves" demonstrates incontrovertibly that contemporary Christianity is in a serious crisis. No longer can conservative, "Bible-believing" evangelicals smugly hurl insults at mainline Protestants and Roman Catholics for doctrinal treason. It is evangelicals today, every bit as much as anyone else, who have embraced the assumptions of the Pelagian heresy. It is this heresy that lies at the bottom of much of popular psychology (human nature, basically good, is warped by its environment), political crusades (we are going to bring about salvation and revival through this campaign), and evangelism and church growth (seeing conversion as a natural process, just like changing from one brand of soap to another, and seeing the evangelist or entrepreneurial pastor as the one who actually adds to the church those to be saved).

---

[15] B. R. Rees, ed., *The Letters of Pelagius and His Followers* (Woodbridge, UK: The Boydell Press, 1991), 169.

At its root, the Reformation was an attack on Pelagianism and its rising influence, as it choked out the life of Christ in the world. It asserted that "salvation is of the LORD" (Jonah 2:9) and that "it therefore does not depend on the decision or effort of man, but on the mercy of God" (Rom. 9:16). If that message is recovered, and Pelagianism is once more confronted with the word of God, then the glory of God will again fill the earth.

PART II: THE CHARACTERS

CHAPTER 8

Reformation Pathways: Calvin and Luther

Lawrence R. Rast Jr.

Why do Calvinists claim Luther (at least to a point), and why do some Lutherans ignore (or even condemn) Calvin? To put it more narrowly, why does Calvinism seem more inclined to recognize the work of Luther than Lutheranism to recognize the work of Calvin? The answer is simple, at least historically speaking: Calvin "needed" Luther, but Luther didn't "need" Calvin.

Now, please, don't get too worked up over this statement! Please note my qualifier, "historically." Luther was a first-generation Reformer; Calvin helped transition the Reformation into a second generation. Simple chronology distinguished the work and defined the relationship between the two men.

There is, of course, more to it than that. Politically, the Peace of Augsburg (1555) formalized the principle of *cuius regio eius religo*—"whose the realm, his the religion"—within the Holy Roman Empire. This effectively forced the Reformed in Germany to claim the Lutheran tradition and its Augsburg Confession, at least in edited form. By the 1560s, with the publication of the Heidelberg Catechism, the Lutherans were increasingly suspicious of Reformed departures from the unaltered Augsburg Confession. By 1580 and the publication of the Book of Concord, the Lutherans had staked out their theological ground. And, as the Formula of Concord (1577) makes clear, the Lutherans viewed the Reformed tradition (including those outside of Germany by this time) with at least as much suspicion as Roman Catholicism.[1]

And so how do we address the breach? Lutheranism and the Reformed tradition clearly share a common background over against Roman Catholicism. But are they simply different branches of the same path, or are we talking about entirely different roads?

---

[1] Friedrich Bente, *Historical Introductions to the Book of Concord* (St. Louis: Concordia Publishing House, 1965), 174.

Luther and Calvin never met, and there is no meaningful correspondence extant between the two. Still, the two men were aware of and spoke favorably about each other's work. Luther reported that he had read Calvin "with singular enjoyment." For his part, Calvin believed that Luther was "a remarkable apostle of Christ" through whom "the purity of the gospel has been restored in our time."

There was much that the two held in common. A deep commitment to the Bible as the sole authority for teaching in the church resulted in a rich corpus of biblical commentaries. Both emphasized the reality of original sin and its effects on human efforts to win salvation. They agreed that human beings contribute nothing to their salvation. God works monergistically—that is, salvation is a divine act of grace received through faith because of Christ. Many in the Reformed tradition also note Luther's strong commitment, as expressed in his *Bondage of the Will*, to the Augustinian tradition. Further, Calvin's first edition of the *Institutes of the Christian Religion* (1536) shows unmistakable evidence of Luther's catechisms.

And yet pronounced differences existed between the two. Interpreters of Luther are divided over his understanding of the place of the law in the life of the Christian. For Calvin there is no question. The third use is clearly defined and defended as the "best instrument for them to learn more thoroughly each the nature of the Lord's will to which they aspire, and to confirm them in the understanding of it" (*Inst.* 2.7.12).

While both Luther and Calvin affirmed the efficacy of the word *and* the sacraments, their understandings differed markedly. On the sacrament of the altar, both men affirmed that Christ is present in the sacrament. However, where Luther affirmed a sacramental presence of Christ, sometimes described as "in, with, and under" the bread and the wine, Calvin affirmed Christ's spiritual presence. Calvin rejected Luther's position, convinced that it "exaggerated" the claims of the Scripture. Calvin believed that Christ "is always among his own people," feeding them "with his own body, the communion of which he bestows upon them by the power of his Spirit" (*Inst.* 4.17.18).

On baptism, Karen Spierling's book *Infant Baptism in Reformation Geneva* is a helpful treatment of Calvin's views.[2] As noted, Calvin upheld original sin, but for him baptism neither specifically addressed the root problem of original sin nor did it grant forgiveness of sins. Calvin baptized infants because the word of God commanded it as a way of incorporating them into the community of the

---

[2] Karen Spierling, *Infant Baptism in Reformation Geneva: The Shaping of a Community, 1536–1564* (Louisville, KY: Westminster John Knox, 2009).

church. The church then provided the setting in which knowledge of the faith might be nurtured and the individual's calling and election might become sure.

For Luther, baptism is God's act whereby he gives the gift of faith, which then receives the benefits of Christ's death and resurrection. Put another way, baptism is essentially christological for Luther—the place where the saving righteousness of Christ is applied to sinners. It is God's act through water and the word of God that works "forgiveness of sins, delivers from death and the devil, and grants eternal salvation to all who believe" (Small Catechism). For Luther, baptism is the enacted gospel. "Ah, dear Christians, let us not value and administer this unspeakable gift so indolently and indifferently; for baptism is our only comfort and admits to every blessing of God and to the communion of the saints" (*Luther Works*, 53:103).

The differences between Luther and Calvin are there. Are they, however, simply a matter of emphasis? Are they located in a different hermeneutic? Though he had a deep and abiding respect for Luther—perhaps even saw himself as a "conscious debtor"—Calvin pushed the Reformation beyond Luther, even while he sought to remain authentic to Luther's purpose. For Calvin, however, authenticity did not demand unequivocal agreement with Luther's exegetical or doctrinal conclusions. Rather, one must follow along the path of reformation that Luther had rediscovered. As Brian Gerrish puts it, "Luther, for Calvin, was not an oracle, but a pathfinder—a pioneer, in whose footsteps we follow and whose trail has to be pushed on further. We hurry on, still today, in the path he opened up."[3] They worked in the same context and even shared the road at times, though the paths they pursued sometimes led them in different directions.

---

[3] Brian Gerrish, "John Calvin on Luther," in *Interpreters of Luther: Essays in Honor of Wilhelm Pauck*, ed. Jaroslav Pelikan (Philadelphia: Fortress, 1968), 80.

CHAPTER 9

Was Martin Luther a Born-Again Christian?

Rick Ritchie

Martin Luther was a Protestant. He was the father of Protestantism. Martin Luther was an evangelical. He defended the authority of Scripture and restored the gospel to its central position in the church. Martin Luther was a Protestant and an evangelical, but was he a born-again Christian?

Absolutely yes! Jesus told Nicodemus that he had to be born again to enter the kingdom of heaven (John 3:3). Clearly, in order to be a Christian, one must be born again in the way Jesus intended. If Martin Luther was a Christian—and he certainly was—then he must have been a born-again Christian.

Absolutely no! In contemporary America, there are many zealous Christians whose experience of the faith bears little resemblance to that of Luther. We may think that if we just strip away the cultural accretions that have attached themselves to today's born-again Christianity, then we might discover the type of faith that Luther advocated, but this is mistaken. When all the cultural layers are peeled back, what is revealed is, at best, the faith that Luther left behind in the monastery when he discovered the gospel. If Martin Luther was a born-again Christian in the biblical sense, then he was not a born-again Christian in the modern sense.

Born-Againism versus the Gospel

The thought of pitting born-again Christianity against the gospel is bound to strike some as bizarre. If it is not the born-again Christians who know the gospel, who does? How many times have we heard of staunch churchgoers who were converted at a Billy Graham Crusade after years of spiritual deadness in their mainline churches? Are we to discount all of these stories? If not, what does it mean to say that born-again Christianity is in conflict with the gospel?

It is not its emphasis on evangelistic outreach for which the born-again movement is to be faulted. Its evangelistic crusades and campus ministries are probably responsible for more unchurched Americans hearing the gospel than all other means combined. The born-again movement is to be commended for preaching the cross to those who have not heard, wherever it has done this faithfully. The real problem is that this movement preaches not only two births but two gospels and is not even aware of it. One gospel tells us of our estrangement from God and how, while we were dead in sin and hostile to God, God reconciled us to himself on the cross. The other gospel tells us how we can be saved by making a decision for Christ and asking him into our hearts. Most of us were taught to think that these teachings were two parts of the same message. When we study the life of Martin Luther, we find that the Reformation occurred when Luther abandoned the second message for the first.

Martin Luther the Monk

Just like their spiritual brethren today, Christians in the Middle Ages tried to pattern their lives after the great saints in the Bible. It has been said that the entire monastic movement was a commentary on the text, "We have left all to follow you." Like St. Paul before him, Martin Luther had a powerful conversion experience while journeying on a road. Caught in a violent thunderstorm, Luther was filled with dread at the majesty of God. He knew he had to get right with his divine Judge.

Luther did this by vowing poverty, chastity, and obedience, dedicating himself to a lifestyle of learning about God and subduing the flesh. Praying and fasting, his consecration and effort was to no avail. The harder Luther strove to please God, the more distant God seemed. The harder Luther struggled, the greater his sense of sin became. To make matters worse, God could read Luther's heart and know that he was motivated by fear and not love. How could Luther escape?

Mortifying the flesh would not help. One cannot get to heaven by works. But what about love? Luther was advised by the mystics to come to God by loving him. This mystical piety was the sixteenth-century version of "Christianity is not a religion but a personal relationship." Instead of being a solution to Luther's spiritual anxiety, however, it only made things worse. He wanted to love God so that God would grant him salvation, but how could he produce this love within himself? How could he be sure that his love for God was genuine when it sprang not from a desire for God but a desire to escape wrath? No, this would not work.

If law-keeping was an impossibility, then producing a pure love for God in one-self was doubly impossible.

Luther the Evangelical

If the new life that Luther found after his conversion experience was a living death, then Luther found true life when he repented of his youthful repentance. While teaching on the book of Romans as a university professor, Luther's anxiety was only intensified by those passages that spoke of the righteousness of God. At first Luther thought that this righteousness meant solely his justice—that God must punish the wicked. Then he came to see that if the righteous were to live by faith, and if there were to be *any* righteous, then God's righteousness must find its foremost expression in his demonstration of mercy, when he declared the wicked to be righteous by punishing Christ in their place. It was in abandoning the manufacture of a new life within himself (even with the help of the Holy Spirit—with which medieval Christians were quite familiar!) that Luther discovered the gospel.

Luther the Enemy of Free Will

Luther discovered that trying to find peace with God apart from the work of Christ was a dead-end, even if pursued by a devoted person desiring a personal relationship with God. This may be an indictment against the excesses of born-again Christianity, but Luther's criticisms of medieval Catholicism do not seem to militate against its essence. What about those churches in which people are warned that the only way to God is through Christ? Surely Luther would not have had harsh words for any of them—or would he?

Many of those who were raised in churches that advocate born-again Christianity are taught that they are the true heirs of Luther's reformation. The evidence used to support this claim is the fact that we could compare born-again Christianity to medieval Catholicism and, of the two, born-again Christianity has produced a more biblically literate laity less attached to superstitious ceremony. Was not this the result that Martin Luther envisioned for his work?

The problem with this reasoning is not that there is no difference between today's born-again Christians and their medieval Catholic cousins, but that this contrast does not run deep enough. This becomes more apparent to us when we discover how hospitably today's born-again Christianity would have been received by one of Luther's opponents. While Pope Leo would have been irate over the success of our present born-again Christianity, one of his fellow churchmen, Desiderius Erasmus, would have been quite pleased.

Erasmus was a brilliant contemporary of Luther who agreed with him concerning the need for church reform, but who disagreed with Luther's understanding of the gospel. For Luther, the gospel was an offense to our reasoning, harsh in its condemnation of sinners, and generous in forgiving them. It was a message of guilt and grace. For Erasmus, the Bible was God's guide to a better lifestyle: an owner's manual. During the early years of the Reformation, Erasmus and Luther appeared to be heading in the same direction. Erasmus's scholarship had provided Luther with the Greek New Testament from which Luther produced the first widely circulated German translation of the Bible. Both men hoped that increased Bible knowledge among the laity would bring about a changed society. It was later that the divergence between the two men's understandings of reformation was made evident.

In 1524, seven years into the Reformation, Erasmus wrote *The Freedom of the Will* in which he argued that individuals were saved by a combination of God's mercy and their efforts. While he tried to give proper credit to the operation of God's grace in salvation, Erasmus's focus was on the need for human effort. In his response to Erasmus, *The Bondage of the Will*, Luther thanked Erasmus for uncovering the true difference between Erasmus's Romanism and Luther's Protestantism. It was not in the presence or absence of ceremony, or in the formality or informality of one's approach to God, but in how they were to be made right with God in the first place.

Scripture is clear that in salvation God must act first. Had our debt not been paid on the cross, there would have been no way back to God for us no matter what we did. The question then arises as to what part we play now that the debt has been paid. Did God merely set up a system whereby we could use our free will to save ourselves? That is what synergism (the teaching that we work together with God to save us) always boils down to, and this is what Luther saw in Erasmus's teaching.

Erasmus taught that our salvation resulted from the working of new powers imparted to fallen humans by God's grace. At first this sounds like a grace-centered theology. God makes the first move; we cannot save ourselves without his help. Who is supposed to use these new powers, though? Fallen man? The Bible teaches that man is dead in trespasses and sins and hostile to God (Eph. 2:1; Rom. 8:5–8). Will a dead man follow his doctor's orders? Will a hostile man help his enemy to conquer him? We have wills that can choose to follow one course or another, but these wills always will sinfully even when they will what is outwardly good. As Luther used to say, we have all the free will in the world to choose which path to follow to hell. Getting into heaven will require something other than our sinful wills, even contrary to them. Perhaps it might be asked, "Might credit not be shared with the new wills that God gives us?" At best, this is how Erasmus's position can be understood.

While Luther insisted that God does change our wills in salvation, he would flatly deny that our new nature was the cause of salvation. If God chose to save us when we were hostile, would it make sense to say that we were saved because we were not hostile? Even when credit was given not to fallen man but to the new nature, Luther saw lurking behind this the desire of the old sinful nature to steal God's glory. What Erasmus really wanted to do was to give the old nature credit. If the new nature was responsible for salvation, then how come it did not turn out the same for all? All are equally sinful, and one would suppose that God gave equally good new natures to people, yet in the end some were not saved. Erasmus was trying to locate the explanation for this in man. Whether we are rewarded for cooperating with the new nature or for resisting it less, Erasmus taught that some people were more deserving of salvation than others. Luther would have none of it. The only credit man could receive was for his own damnation. All glory, honor, and credit for the salvation of the saved belonged to God who could save us in spite of our wills.

Is it not strange that many who call themselves Protestant teach that a person is saved by doing what Luther, the father of Protestantism, declared that a lost person could not do? Is it not even stranger that the type of conversion experience that evangelicals take to be the litmus test of genuine Christianity is based on the doctrine of free will, a doctrine that Erasmus had to defend against Luther, against Protestantism, and against the gospel that had just been rediscovered?

CHAPTER 10

The Lutheran Doctrine of Predestination: A Melanchthonian Perspective

Scott L. Keith

In the earliest editions of his *Loci Communes Theologici* ("Common Topics of Theology"), Luther's friend and colleague Philipp Melanchthon did not address in great detail the doctrine of predestination. In the *Loci* of 1521, for instance, he discussed it only briefly in the section dealing with the freedom of the human will. Following the teaching of Luther he stated: "If you relate human will to predestination, there is freedom in neither external nor internal acts, but all things take place according to determination."[1] Other than this statement, he avoided the discussion of predestination, stating that man should be cautious about delving into the mysteries of God, but rather look to Christ and his redemption.

Later in his career (c. 1535), however, while never claiming to drift from the doctrine as taught by Luther, he began to focus not on the sovereignty of God and his power to elect, but rather on God's gift of election as a comfort to the Christian believer. "First, he has demonstrated with manifest miracles that there certainly is a definite gathering of people which he loves, cares for, and will adorn with blessings. . . . And in order that we may continue to possess this comfort, it is useful to say something about the doctrine of predestination."[2] Thus believers are to cling to the words of Christ in John 10:27, "My sheep hear my voice, and I know them and they follow me, and I give them life eternal, and they shall never perish, and no one will snatch them out of my hands." Therefore, says Melanchthon, a church of the elect will always remain.

---

[1] Philipp Melanchthon, *Loci Communes Theologici* (1521), trans. Lowell J. Satre, ed. Wilhelm Pauk (Philadelphia: Westminster Press, 1969), 30.

[2] Philipp Melanchthon, *Loci Communes* (1543), trans. J. A. O. Preus (St. Louis: Concordia, 1992), 172.

Concerning the causes of election, Melanchthon gives three. "First is that we might judge regarding our election not on the basis of Law but on the basis of Gospel. Second is that the entire number of those who are to be saved is chosen (*electus*) for the sake of Christ (*propter Christum*). The third is that we may seek no other cause."[3] Election is predicated upon the redemption we have in Christ that we apprehend by faith. "Thus Peter is elect because he is a member of Christ, just as he is righteous, that is, pleasing to God, because by faith he has been made a member of Christ."[4]

Melanchthon affirms that God wills all to be saved because the immutable will of God is that we hear his Son, as he has said, "Hear him" (Matt. 17:5). "And just as the preaching of repentance is universal and accuses all, as it is clearly stated in Romans 3, so also the promise of grace is universal, as many passages testify."[5] "Romans 11:31, 'God has imprisoned them all under disobedience, that he might have mercy upon them all,' that is, he accuses the disobedience of all, he calls all to repentance, and again he offers mercy to all."[6]

As to the cause of reprobation, according to Melanchthon, there is only one—that is, the sin of men who do not hear the voice of the gospel or who reject the faith. "In those people it is certain that the cause of their reprobation is sin and human will. For it is a completely true statement that God is not the cause of sin and does not will sin."[7]

On the other hand, Melanchthon teaches it is correct to say that the cause of election is the merciful will of God, who on account of his Son gathers and preserves the church. There is no doubt that the elect are those who in faith take hold of God's mercy in Christ and never give up that confidence. "Assuredly all are elected for eternal life who, through faith in the Lord Christ, in the conversion of this life receive comfort and do not fall away before their death; for thus says the text, 'Blessed are the dead who die in the Lord'" (Rev 14:13).[8] God calls the elect to himself on account of his Son through faith (*propter Christum per fidem*). "God begins and draws us by his holy Word and the Holy Spirit, but it is necessary for us to hear and learn, that is, to take hold of the promise and assent to it, not to fight against it or be hesitant and filled with doubt."[9]

---

[3] Preus, *Loci Communes*, 172.

[4] Preus, *Loci Communes*, 172.

[5] He cites as examples Matt. 11:28; John 3:16; Rom. 3:22; 10:12; 11:32.

[6] Preus, *Loci Communes*, 173.

[7] Preus, *Loci Communes*, 173.

[8] Philipp Melanchthon, *Melanchthon on Christian Doctrine Loci Communes* (1555), ed. and trans. Clyde L. Manschreck (Grand Rapids: Baker, 1982), 188.

[9] Later "followers" of Melanchthon known as the "Philippists" would partially develop this teaching into a form of synergism.

"In Ephesians 1:4 he says, 'He has chosen us in Christ,' in order that he may teach us that the cause of our election is not our own worthiness, but Christ, so that we do not consider our election apart from Christ and the Gospel, but always seek the cause of our election in the promise of Christ."[10] According to Melanchthon, this truth brings the believer a threefold comfort. First, they who are called are those who hear, learn, and confess the gospel. "So, it is very comforting and true that only those who are called are numbered among the predestined, that is, among those who listen to and learn God's Word, for 'Those whom he has chosen, he also calls.'"[11] Second, God has chosen us because he has decreed to call us to the knowledge of the Son, and because of this his blessings will be upon us. Third, the testimony of God is present with the visible company he has called and is efficacious in this called company, the church. "Therefore we should not turn our eyes away from the universal promise, but include ourselves in it and know for certain that in it the will of God is expressed."[12]

This is the doctrine that Melanchthon taught until his death in 1560. For Melanchthon, the cause of election is the mercy of God on account of Christ and is to be seen in light of the gospel promise. For those who confess Christ as their Savior it brings great assurance. God's offer of grace is to be seen as universal and the cause of reprobation is to be assigned only to the sin of men who do not hear the voice of the gospel or the unbelief of those who reject the faith. "Therefore let us strengthen our faith and pray that the Son of God will preserve his sheep, because at the same time he also says, 'They hear me and follow me.'"[13]

Did Melanchthon and Luther Agree?

In his formulation of the doctrine of election, Melanchthon continually placed great stress on God's electing people on account of Christ through faith. Furthermore, election is never to be viewed apart from this gospel message. In many ways, the same could be said of Luther. In fact, on this point the two men were not as different as some have thought. Says Luther: "If men believe the Gospel, they shall be saved. Indeed all the saints have had confidence and comfort with their election and with eternal life, not because of a special revelation of their predestination, but rather by faith in Christ."[14] When asked where to look for assurance

---

[10] Manschreck, *Melanchthon on Christian Doctrine*, 174.

[11] Manschreck, *Melanchthon on Christian Doctrine*, 190; cf. Num. 16:5; Rom. 8:30; 2 Thess. 2:13–14; 1 Pet. 1:2.

[12] Manschreck, *Melanchthon on Christian Doctrine*, 174.

[13] Manschreck, *Melanchthon on Christian Doctrine*, 175.

[14] *WA*, 21:514.

of election, Luther responds, "Rather, hold to the promise of the Gospel. This will teach that Christ, God's only Son, came into the world in order to bless all nations on the earth, that is, to redeem them from sin and death, to justify and to save them."[15] Here one sees the many similarities between Luther and Melanchthon.

Yet Luther places more importance on the fact that election is all part of God's immutable sovereignty. In Melanchthon, we can see Luther's affirmation of the sovereign will of God being replaced by the universal saving will of God effectuated through the universal call of the gospel. Always affirming that it is the power of the Holy Spirit that allows us to believe, Melanchthon explains that we must, therefore, assent to the promise of the gospel. Luther teaches that we are unable to ascend to God and reiterates the absolute necessity for God to descend to us. "They are elect, Peter says. How? Not of themselves but according to God's purpose; for we are not able to raise ourselves to heaven or create faith within ourselves. God will not admit all men into heaven. He will very carefully count those who belong to him."[16] The difference is thus subtle but real. For both men, the faith that results from the election of God on account of Christ is a gift of God through the word. Yet, for Melanchthon, it is necessary to act on this gift, while Luther allows this gift of God to stand alone through grace. In other words, Luther's doctrine of election is summed up by the Reformation hallmarks *sola gratia* and *soli Deo gloria* (by grace alone and to God alone goes all the glory). On the other hand, for Melanchthon, election can be explicated by the phrase *propter Christum per fidem* (on account of Christ through faith).

As is often the case, these small differences did not lead the two men to disagree with one another significantly concerning this doctrine. But the followers of these men did seem to side with either one or the other. In other words, later Lutheranism faced some turmoil concerning which is the proper emphasis in election: God's sovereignty or God's universal saving will through the call of the word.

The Impact of Melanchthon's View of Predestination on Lutheran Theology

The Formula of Concord, which is the Lutheran Confession written seventeen years after Melanchthon's death, in many ways reads as though it had been written by him. It affirms all the hallmarks of a Melanchthonian view of election:

---

[15] *SL*, 9:1115.
[16] *WA*, 12:262.

1. Election as *Propter Christum*: "We should accordingly consider God's eternal election in Christ, and not outside of it."[17]

2. The universal call to repentance and belief: "If we want to consider our election to salvation profitably, we must by all means cling rigidly and firmly to the fact that as the proclamation of repentance extends over all men (Luke 24:47), so also does the promise of the Gospel."[18]

3. The elect are brought into salvation *per fidem:* "God has ordained in his counsel that the Holy Spirit would call, enlighten, and convert the elect through the Word and that he would justify and save all who accept Christ through faith."[19]

4. Finally, that the only cause of reprobation is man's stubborn will in rejecting the call through the Word: "The reason for such contempt of the Word is not God's foreknowledge but man's perverse will."[20]

The Formula of Concord, though, goes further in delineating the difference between God's eternal foreknowledge and God's eternal decree of election. The formula states that God's eternal foreknowledge extends to all, while his eternal election extends only to the children of God.[21] In doing so, the formula clarifies an area that Melanchthon (with his stress on faith) leaves unclear. It affirms a sort of "middle road" between Luther and Melanchthon. God's decree of election remains sovereign and his call universal. "Our election to eternal life does not rest on our piety or virtue but solely on the merit of Christ and the gracious will of the Father, who cannot deny himself because he is changeless in his will and essence."[22]

Later Lutheranism, as represented by the seventeenth-century dogmaticians, did not always follow this careful formulation. Some of the dogmaticians lost this paradoxical image of God as having a will that is partly hidden and partly revealed, sovereign and merciful, the freedom of his divine will and the bondage of ours, the careful distinction between God's law and his life-giving

---

[17] *The Lutheran Book of Concord*, trans. and ed. Theodore G. Tappert, et al. (Philadelphia: Fortress, 1959), "The Formula of Concord," *Art. XI*. 65, 627.

[18] *The Lutheran Book of Concord*, Art. XI, 28, 620.

[19] *The Lutheran Book of Concord*, Art. XI, 40, 623.

[20] *The Lutheran Book of Concord*, XI, 41, 623.

[21] *The Lutheran Book of Concord*, XI, 4–5, 616–17.

[22] *The Lutheran Book of Concord*, XI, 75, 628.

gospel. In many of the dogmaticians, these concepts were philosophically formalized, thus losing their life and vitality. The careful molding of Luther's concept of God's sovereign will with Melanchthon's teaching of God's saving will was lost. Rather, many of the great dogmaticians followed Melanchthon's emphasis on God's universal saving will alone. This led many (for example, the great Johann Gerhard) to teach the synergistic doctrine of *intuitu fidei* (God elects in view of foreseen faith). The efficacy of God's eternal decree became dependent on the faith of each individual. God wills all to be saved, but God's will does not come to pass unless we make the decision to believe. Says Gerhard, "And because God from eternity foresaw which humans might finally believe, and so that he decides to save these, that the eternal decree about the eternal salvation being shared to the finally believing, in view of the merits of Christ and the foreseen faith in Christ, done and precisely seen it is called especially by the name of predestination or election."[23] This led many to look to themselves for assurance rather than to Christ. Faith became a human work that had the ability to manipulate the decree of God. The result is a theology that focuses on man rather than God, a theology of glory rather than the theology of the cross.

Conclusion

Much can be learned from Melanchthon's teaching concerning election. It is certainly profitable and biblical to view election not on the basis of law but on the basis of gospel. Surely, it is proper to teach that the entire number of those who are to be saved is chosen (*electus*) for the sake of Christ (*propter Christum*), and we should seek no other cause. Great benefit is also found in affirming the scriptural teaching that the gospel must be believed. That we must trust in Christ alone as our only hope for salvation is the whole of the good news of Christ. This Melanchthon not only affirmed but taught until his death.

Yet, to take this doctrine and lose sight of God's sovereignty to save those whom he elects is to go against the Scriptures themselves. This Melanchthon did not do. Nevertheless, it must be admitted that Melanchthon's followers took his emphasis on faith and the universality of the call beyond his own position and thereby fell into great error. Our faith must be not seen as the cause of our election. Rather, faith is the product of election through the word, by which we

---

[23] *John William Baier, Compendium of Positive Theology*, ed. C. F. W. Walther (St. Louis: Concordia, 1877), trans. Theodore Mayes (1996). *Loci* 12, "Predestination," 19.

are brought into the benefits of Christ. As Melanchthon himself has said: "God's mercy is the cause of election, but it is necessary that this be revealed in the Word and that the Word be accepted. Thus he definitely offers this universally, and this is repeated in other chapters: 'All who believe in the Son shall not be confounded (Romans 9:33; 10:11).'"[24]

---

[24] *Loci praecipui theologici* (1559), CR 21, 919.

CHAPTER 11

Neglected Sources of the Reformed Doctrine of Predestination

Frank A. James III

Although its reception has been varied, the doctrine of predestination—and particularly double predestination—has nevertheless had a significant impact throughout church history. Augustine, Fulgentius of Ruspe, Isodore of Seville, Gottschalk of Orbais, Thomas Aquinas, the sixteenth-century Reformers, and, more recently, Karl Barth all devoted careful attention to this question, even if the church did not always appreciate their efforts. But of all the religious movements in history, few have been more closely associated with the doctrine than the early Reformed theologians.[1]

At this point, a caveat ought to be issued against overgeneralizations. Not all of the major Protestant Reformers agreed with Calvin's doctrine of double predestination. Some Protestants (both Lutheran and Reformed)—such as Bullinger, Bibliander, and later Melanchthon—found double predestination objectionable.[2] Furthermore, not every Roman Catholic rejected this doctrine out of hand. Although the vast majority of Roman Catholic theologians strongly refuted a rigorous doctrine of double predestination, nevertheless a few early sixteenth-century Roman Catholics, such as Konrad Treger, considered it a legitimate part of their Augustinian heritage.[3]

---

[1] Paul K. Jewett, *Election and Predestination* (Grand Rapids: Eerdmans, 1985), 10.

[2] For Heinrich Bullinger's views, see J. Wayne Baker, *Heinrich Bullinger and the Covenant: The Other Reformed Tradition* (Athens: Ohio University Press, 1980), 27–54. For Theodore Bibliander's view, see J. Staedke, "Der Zuricher Predestinationstreit von 1560," *Zwingliana* 9 (1953): 536–46. For Melanchthon's views, see Clyde L. Manschreck, ed., *Melanchthon on Christian Doctrine: Loci Communes 1555* (Grand Rapids: Baker, 1982), xii–xiv, xl–xlii, 187–91.

[3] Adolar Zumkeller, "The Augustinian Theologian Konrad Treger (ca. 1480–1542) and his Disputation Thesis of May 5, 1521," in Via Augustini: *Augustine in the Later Middle Ages, Renaissance and Reformation*, ed. H. A. Oberman and F. A. James III (Leiden: Brill Academic, 1991), 130–42.

Despite the common historical misconception, John Calvin was not the exclusive source of the Reformed branch of Protestantism. From a distance, he may appear to tower over other Reformed theologians, but the intervening centuries have distorted the historical reality. In recent years, it has been increasingly recognized that the origins of Reformed theology do not derive exclusively from Calvin, but rather from a coterie of theologians who were associated with Swiss reform, including Ulrich Zwingli, Heinrich Bullinger, Peter Martyr Vermigli, and Wolfgang Musculus.[4]

This study concentrates on two of the leading lights from this constellation of theologians who gave formative shape to early Reformed theology: Ulrich Zwingli (1484–1531) and Peter Martyr Vermigli (1499–1562). These men represent two important but different strains within the Reformed tradition. Zwingli was a first-generation magisterial reformer and inaugurator of Swiss reform. He did not give much attention to the topic of predestination until his meeting with Luther at the Colloquy of Marburg in 1529. While there, Zwingli preached a sermon on providence and predestination to an audience that included Luther himself. This sermon was later expanded and published as *De providentia* (On Providence).

Peter Martyr Vermigli belonged to the second-generation of Reformed theologians who, along with Calvin, gave definitive shape to the Reformed branch of Protestantism. Vermigli is somewhat unusual in that he had been a prominent Roman Catholic theologian before embracing Protestantism. During his first forty-three years in Italy, he was an active reformer within the Roman Catholic Church, but in 1542 he fled the Roman inquisition and sought refuge among the Protestants. Almost immediately after his flight from Italy, he rose to prominence as a Protestant theologian. In this new Protestant capacity, his sphere of influence extended to the major centers of the Reformation movement—Bucer's Strasbourg, Archbishop Cranmer's Oxford, and Bullinger's Zurich. His prominence in the Reformed community was such that one contemporary could say that "the two most excellent theologians of our times are John Calvin and Peter Martyr."[5]

Vermigli does not make predestination the signature doctrine of his theological system. But like Calvin, his name became associated with it because he was repeatedly called on to defend it, and thus he became one of the principal

---

[4] Richard Muller, *Christ and the Decree: Christology and Predestination in Reformed Theology from Calvin to Perkins* (Grand Rapids: Baker, 1988), 39.

[5] Gordon Huelin, "Peter Martyr and the English Reformation" (PhD diss., University of London, 1954), 178.

apologists for a Reformed doctrine of predestination.[6] He championed it against Johann Marbach in Strasbourg and Theodore Bibliander in Zurich.[7]

Like most of the early Protestants, both Zwingli and Vermigli held strong views on predestination. Although there was diversity, this doctrine came to be inextricably linked to Reformed theology. But how did the Reformed doctrine of predestination develop?

Sources for the Reformed Doctrine of Predestination

Historically, as noted above, predestination was not a doctrine that distinguished Protestants from Roman Catholics. The Reformed doctrine of predestination was essentially a recovery of Augustine's view, yet it was not just theological mimicry, for the Reformers sought above all to return to the teaching of the Apostle Paul. Paul was, however, interpreted through an Augustinian theological grid.

It is well known that the apostle employed the term "predestination," as well as its near equivalent "election," on a number of occasions in his Epistles.[8] Furthermore, Paul derived the essence of his conception of predestination from the Old Testament—broadly from the idea of Israel as God's chosen people, and narrowly from the divine choice of Jacob and the divine rejection of Esau.[9] The language and idea of God choosing some to the exclusion of others is an important substratum throughout the biblical writings.

Like every predestinarian before the sixteenth century, Reformed theologians drew particular inspiration from Paul. Romans 9 served as the biblical epicenter of their doctrine of predestination. This passage contains the powerful language of the divine hardening of Pharaoh's heart, God's election of Jacob and rejection of Esau before their birth, as well as the imagery of vessels of wrath pre-

---

[6] Charles Schmidt, *Leben und ausgewahlte Schriften nach handschriftlichen und gleichzeitigen Quellen* (Elberfeld: R. L. Friderichs, 1858), 106.

[7] Frank A. James III, *Peter Martyr Vermigli and Predestination: The Augustinian Heritage of an Italian Theologian* (Oxford: Clarendon Press, 1998), 31–36.

[8] Paul employs the term repeatedly (Rom. 8:33, 29; Eph. 1:5). Jesus also made comments concerning the elect (Luke 18:7; Matt. 24:22; Mark 13:27). For a more complete summary of the biblical data, see Paul K. Jewett, *Election and Predestination* (Grand Rapids: Eerdmans, 1985), 24–29.

[9] Paul's discussion of predestination in Romans 9:10–24 is self-consciously derived from the Old Testament. Much of Romans 9 is a recitation of Old Testament passages, including Mal. 1:2–3; Exod. 9:16 and 33:19.

pared for destruction and vessels of mercy prepared for glory. Whatever criticism may be leveled against Reformed theologians, they were determined to forge their theology from Scripture, and Paul especially served as the chief source of their doctrine of predestination.

History also reveals that, beginning with Augustine, a distinctive hermeneutical tradition emerged that drew from Paul's words an unequivocal doctrine of predestination. Reformed theologians knew the writings of all of the major fathers, both Greek and Latin, but it was Augustine who occupied first place in the pantheon of fathers. Although not infallible, he was viewed as the preeminently judicious and wise mentor on most theological questions, not the least of which was the doctrine of predestination.[10]

Just as these Reformed theologians interpreted Paul under the guidance of Augustine, they also encountered Augustine under the shaping influence of late medieval theology. As such, one cannot understand the development of the Reformed doctrine of predestination without some acquaintance with the late medieval theological influences that shaped their thought.

Stoicism and Ulrich Zwingli

Gottfried Locher judges that of all the major Protestant Reformers, Zwingli articulated the most extreme doctrine of predestination.[11] Calvin himself expressed concern about the "immoderate" and "paradoxical" formulation of Zwingli's view of providence and predestination. It was not until the publication of his work *De providentia* that Zwingli expressed his mature understanding of predestination. He was deeply indebted to Erasmian humanism and its penchant for seeing the classical pagan authors as rhetorical mentors. The important catchphrase of the humanists was *ad fontes* (back to the fount or original sources). Humanists such as Zwingli took this to mean a return not only to classical authors but also to the church fathers and the Bible in its original languages. It was Zwingli's humanism that made him highly amenable to appropriating insights from pagan philosophers for his theology.

Zwingli's *De providentia* reveals his strongly philosophical cast of mind. Indeed, because of the philosophical strains in this treatise, many scholars have concluded that Zwingli is more philosopher than theologian.[12] Most obviously,

---

[10] James, *Peter Martyr Vermigli*, 94–95.

[11] G. Locher, *Zwingli's Thought: New Perspectives* (Leiden: E. J. Brill, 1981), 54.

[12] W. P. Stephens, *The Theology of Huldrych Zwingli* (Oxford: Clarendon Press, 1986), 81.

his philosophical orientation is signaled by the constant parade of ancient philosophers across the pages of this work. While Calvin and Vermigli also alluded
to classical authors, there is a fundamental difference between Zwingli's use of
ancient philosophers and that of Vermigli and Calvin. These two looked to the
classical philosophers as illustrations of Christian truth, whereas Zwingli saw
them as guides to it.

Of all the ancients, Zwingli's highest praise was reserved for the last great
representative of Roman Stoicism, Lucius Annaeus Seneca, "that unparalleled
cultivator of the soul among pagans." For Zwingli, Seneca was a "theologian"
and his writings were "divine oracles."[13] So prevalent is the spirit of Seneca
throughout the *De providentia* that Francois Wendel concludes that it "reads
almost like a commentary on chosen passages from Seneca."[14] The most significant impact from Seneca is found in Zwingli's all-encompassing doctrine
of providence, of which predestination is a subcategory. Following Seneca, he
insists there is no secondary causality: "It is established therefore that secondary
causes are not properly called causes." He adds, "Nothing is done or achieved
which is not done and achieved by the immediate care and power of the Deity."
Providence in fact looms so large that there appears to be no room for human
will or human responsibility. Thus Zwingli's understanding of predestination as
indistinguishable from providence logically inclines him to the conclusion that
God is the cause of human sin. If, as Zwingli affirms, absolutely everything is
under divine providence, then is not human sin also under the direct control of
divine providence? To be sure, God is absolved of any personal culpability, yet
Zwingli can assert that God is the "author, mover and instigator" of human sin.[15]

When this all-pervasive divine providence is applied to the matter of reprobation and to eternal condemnation, it necessarily follows that God is the direct
and exclusive cause, since God is the cause of everything. Eternal condemnation
is explicitly traced back to the pretemporal rejection by the will of God. Temporal sins may be the occasion for eternal condemnation, but they are not the
ultimate and direct cause. For him, reprobation, as well as election, is conceived
teleologically.[16] The divine will does not simply reject; it rejects with a specific
purpose in view. To Zwingli's mind, reprobation includes eternal consequences.
Just as election is unto eternal life, so reprobation is unto eternal punishment.

---

[13] *Huldreich Zwinglis Werke*, ed. M. Schuler and J. Schulthess (Zurich, 1828–1842),
IV, 95.

[14] F. Wendel, *Calvin: The Origins and Development of His Religious Thought* (London: Collins, 1963), 29.

[15] Werke, IV, 96, 134, 112.

[16] Werke, IV, 126, 139.

At the core of Zwingli's predestinarian thought about election and reprobation is the notion that both issue directly from the divine will. Zwingli attributes
both to the divine will in the same way, constructing an absolutely *symmetrical*
doctrine of double predestination. The cause and means of both election and
reprobation are precisely the same. For Zwingli, God is the exclusive and immediate cause of all things.

Late Medieval Augustinianism and Peter Martyr Vermigli

As a Roman Catholic theologian, Vermigli actually read Zwingli but did not
embrace a Stoical-flavored view of predestination. Although Vermigli's primary
inspiration came from Augustine, he went beyond his mentor in his interpretation of Paul's predestinarianism.[17] The explanation for this intensified Augustinianism is found at the University of Padua, where as a student Vermigli
first read and appreciated the robust Augustinian theology of Gregory of Rimini.
What is significant for our purposes is that Gregory was "the first Augustinian of
Augustine."[18] Reading Gregory at the formative stage of his theological training,
Vermigli had encountered one of the most vigorous double predestinarians of
the late medieval period. The modern editor of Gregory's works offers this caveat
to unwary readers: "Leafing through Gregory's pages one may be shocked by
the predestinarianism, and ask oneself whether Gregory's God was the Mexican
War God."[19] Gregory was probably unfamiliar with Mexican deities, but there
was indeed a militancy in his defense of Augustine's doctrine of predestination.

Gregory is credited with having given birth to a late medieval "academic
Augustinianism" committed to the pursuit of—and obedience to—the genuine
theology of Augustine. This intensive form of late medieval Augustinianism
began a concerted effort in the fourteenth century to recover the whole corpus of Augustine's works and to develop a systematic acquaintance with his
entire thought. Gregory of Rimini not only knew the writings and followed the
doctrines of Augustine more closely than any other late medieval theologian,
but he also restored long neglected works to circulation and evidenced a highly
developed critical sense to distinguish genuine from apocryphal works.[20] In the

---

[17] James, *Peter Martyr Vermigli*, 104–5.

[18] Damasus Trapp, "Augustinian Theology in the Fourteenth Century: Notes on Edi-
tionis, Marginalia, Opinions and Book Lore," *Augustiniana* 6 (1956): 181.

[19] Damasus Trapp, "Notes on the Tubingen Edition of Gregory of Rimini," *Augustiniana* 29 (1979): 238.

[20] Trapp, "Augustinian Theology," 181–213.

fourteenth century one can speak of an "Augustinian renaissance," which some have designated the *schola Augustiniana moderna*.[21] This new intensified Augustinianism developed a ferociously anti-Pelagian theology of grace, including a vigorous doctrine of double predestination.

Although more than a century separates these two theologians, there are remarkable parallels between the predestinarianism of Gregory and that of Vermigli. Time and time again, the same issues are isolated and resolved with the same theological conclusions, often employing the same terms, and always based upon the same twin sources, Scripture and Augustine. Vermigli's most mature exposition of this doctrine occurs in an extended locus from his commentary on Romans, where he, much like Gregory, develops the doctrine of predestination within a causal nexus.[22] On the matter of election (which he technically equated with predestination), God's will in eternity was the exclusive cause. Vermigli follows Augustine's line, thinking of all humanity as a *massa perditionis* (mass of perdition), doomed to eternal condemnation unless God intervenes. Divine election is construed as the rescue of doomed sinners, who can do nothing to aid in their own rescue. After being elected from the mass of fallen sinners in eternity past and granted the gift of faith, the elect exercise that gift of faith in time and thus will inherit eternal life.[23] In sum, Vermigli, like Gregory before him, taught an unconditional election.

Vermigli did not shy away from the difficult matter of reprobation. There are two important features in his understanding of reprobation that underscore this. First, he understood reprobation as a passive expression of the sovereign will of God. Although the will of God is absolutely free and sovereign, God wields it passively in reprobation. By passive willing, Vermigli meant something more than mere permission but less than an active willing. For Vermigli, God is not to be pictured as sitting back and simply permitting matters to take their course. Rather, God engineers and orchestrates men and events without coercion in order to produce his predetermined salvation result. To reprobate is characteristically described as "not to have mercy" or "passing over."[24] Yet, it does not conjure up visions of a dispassionate deity arbitrarily hurling helpless victims into a lake of fire. Vermigli's vision of election and reprobation is more compli-

---

[21] Heiko A. Oberman, *Masters of the Reformation: The Emergence of a New Intellectual Climate in Europe* (Cambridge, MA: Harvard University Press, 1981), 70–71.

[22] James, *Peter Martyr Vermigli*, 133.

[23] Peter Martyr Vermigli, in *Epistolam S. Pauli ad Romanos commentarii doctissimi* (Basel, 1558), 410, 413–14.

[24] Romanos, 37, 381, 480, 430.

cated; it portrays God as actively rescuing some sinners, but deliberately and mysteriously bypassing others.

A second major feature of Vermigli's view of reprobation is the adoption of the distinction between reprobation and condemnation. Reprobation has reference to the decision not to have mercy in eternity past, and its cause lies in the inscrutable sovereign will of God. Condemnation, on the other hand, has a temporal orientation, where causality lies within the matrix of original and actual sins. For Vermigli, "sins are the cause of damnation but not the cause of reprobation."[25] God's role in condemnation is confined to the institution and execution of the general principle that sins are to be punished. Condemnation is the expression of divine justice. So then, the true cause of condemnation is sinful man, but the true cause of reprobation is the unfathomable purpose of God (*propositum Dei*). Vermigli's version of double predestination differs from that of Zwingli in that the latter has a symmetrical double predestination, while the former has an asymmetrical version of double predestination. For Vermigli, God does not deal with the elect in precisely the same way as he does with the nonelect. For the elect, God not only is the ultimate eternal cause, but by granting the gift of faith, he is also the temporal cause of the elect attaining eternal life. That parallel is not sustained when it comes to reprobation. Although the ultimate eternal cause of election and rejection is precisely the same, the cause for condemnation does not correspond to the cause for eternal blessing. For the condemned, it is their sins that cause their eternal destruction.

Conclusion

The development of the Reformed doctrine of predestination reminds us first and foremost that the primary source for Reformed theology is and must continue to be the Scriptures. Second, a good knowledge of church history can be a useful guide to the interpretation of Scripture, and on most issues there is no better guide than Augustine. Third, we must exercise caution about the subtle cultural and intellectual influences that infiltrate our theological system. Doctrine is never formed in a theological vacuum, and so we must examine and refine our presuppositions to conform to historic Christianity. Finally, predestination—although alien to most modern minds—is a vital, indeed necessary, truth that stops us in our tracks, destroys our pride, and relieves us of the arrogance of thinking that we did it our way.

---

[25] Romanos, 414.

CHAPTER 12

"Make Your Calling and Election Sure": Predestination and Assurance in Reformed Theology

Michael S. Horton

According to the lengthiest of the Church of England's Thirty-Nine Articles of Religion:

> The godly consideration of Predestination and our Election in Christ is full of sweet, pleasant, and unspeakable comfort to godly persons, and such as feel in themselves the working of the Spirit of Christ, mortifying the works of the flesh in their earthly members, and drawing up their mind to high and heavenly things, as well because it doth establish and confirm their faith of eternal Salvation to be enjoyed through Christ, as because it doth fervently kindle their love towards God. And yet, the study of the subject has most dangerous effects on the "carnal professor."[1]

Speaking of the doctrine of election as "a comforting article when it is correctly treated," the Formula of Concord (Lutheran) offers a similar caution:

> Accordingly we believe and maintain that if anybody teaches the doctrine of the gracious election of God to eternal life in such a way that disconsolate Christians can find no comfort in this doctrine but are driven to doubt and despair, or in such a way that the impenitent are strengthened in their self-will, he is not teaching the doctrine according to the Word and will of God.[2]

During the magisterial Reformation, the doctrine of election was regarded as a corollary to justification, the nail in the coffin of synergism (justification and

---

[1] W. H. Griffith Thomas, ed., *The Principles of Theology: An Introduction to the Thirty-Nine Articles, with the Text of the Articles* (Grand Rapids: Baker, 1979), 236.

[2] *The Book of Concord*, tran. and ed. Theodore G. Tappert (Philadelphia: Fortress, 1959), 497.

regeneration by human cooperation with grace). Pastorally, election was used to drive away despair and anxiety over one's salvation. John Bradford, an Edwardian divine who was martyred under "bloody Mary," wrote that this doctrine was a "most principal" tenet, since it places our salvation entirely in God's hands. "This, I say, let us do, and not be too busybodies in searching the majesty and glory of God, or in nourishing doubting of salvation: whereto we all are ready enough."[3] As we will see, all of this is carefully expounded by Calvin as well.

Did Calvin Invent Predestination?

More than anything else, Calvin and Calvinism are known for this doctrine. In one sense, that is quite surprising. First, the doctrine held by Calvin—namely, predestination to both salvation (election) and damnation (reprobation)—was insisted upon by many of the church fathers. Augustine took it for granted as the catholic teaching, in opposition especially to Pelagius. Aquinas wrote,

> From all eternity some are preordained and directed to heaven; they are called the predestined ones: "Having predestinated us unto the adoption of children according to the good pleasure of his will" [Eph. 1:5]. From all eternity, too, it has been settled that others will not be given grace, and these are called the reprobate or rejected ones: "I loved Jacob, and I hated Esau" [Mal. 1:2–3]. Divine choice is the reason for the distinction: " . . . according as he has chosen us in him before the foundation of the world." . . . God predestines because he loves. . . . The choice is not dictated by any goodness to be discovered in those who are chosen; there is no antecedent prompting of God's love [Rom. 9:11–13].[4]

Lodging the cause of election in the foreknowledge of human decision and action, says Aquinas, is the fountainhead of Pelagianism.[5] Thomas Bradwardine, the fourteenth-century archbishop of Canterbury, recalled his discovery of this great truth:

> Idle and a fool in God's wisdom, I was misled by an unorthodox error at a time when I was still pursuing philosophical studies. Sometimes I went to listen to the theologians discussing this matter [of grace and free will], and the school of Pelagius seemed to

---

[3] John Bradford, *The Writings of John Bradford*, vol. 2 (Cambridge: Cambridge University Press, 1858), 316.

[4] Thomas Aquinas, III *Contra Gentiles* 164; Disputations, VI *de Veritate*, I, in *St. Thomas Aquinas: Theological Texts*, trans. Thomas Gilby (Durham, NC: Labyrinth, 1982).

[5] Thomas Aquinas, *Summa Theo.*, Ia. xxiii.5, op. cit.

me nearest the truth. . . . In this philosophical faculty I seldom heard a reference to grace, except for some ambiguous remarks. What I heard day in and day out was that we are masters of our own free acts, that ours is the choice to act well or badly, to have virtues or sins, and much more along this line. . . . But every time I listened to the Epistle reading in church and heard how Paul magnified grace and belittled free will—as in the case in Romans 9, "It is obviously not a question of human will and effort, but of divine mercy," and its many parallels—grace displeased me, ungrateful as I was. . . . However, even before I transferred to the faculty of theology, the text mentioned came to me as a beam of grace and, captured by a vision of the truth, it seemed I saw from afar how the grace of God precedes all good works. . . . That is why I express my gratitude to Him who has given me this grace as a gift.[6]

This personal revolution was so deeply practical that Bradwardine turned his energies toward the recovery of the doctrine of grace and, with it, a strong emphasis on God's unconditional election. *The Case of God against the Pelagians* was his declaration of war on "the new Pelagians who oppose our whole presentation of predestination and reprobation, attempting either to eliminate them completely or, at least, to show that they are dependent on our merits."[7]

"I received it all from Staupitz," Luther said of his mentor, Johann von Staupitz, the Augustinian abbot whose most famous work was titled *Eternal Predestination and its Execution in Time.*[8] "And thus the claim for man, namely, that he is master over his works from beginning to end, is destroyed," Staupitz wrote. "So, therefore, the origin of the works of Christian life is predestination, its means is justification, and its aim is glorification or thanksgiving—all these are the achievements not of nature but of grace."[9] Luther's defense of a rigorous version of predestination in *The Bondage of the Will* is well known and is also defended in both earlier and later editions of his Romans commentary.

Countless other examples from church history could be offered. It is not all of one piece, of course, especially in the Middle Ages when confidence in human ability was a practically if not always officially held dogma. *Facienti quod in se est Deus non denigat gratium* was the medieval slogan: "God will not deny his grace to those who do what lies within them."

Nonetheless, predestination was well established before the Reformation and then defended again by the first-generation Reformers. As such, there was

---

[6] Cited by Heiko Oberman, in *Forerunners of the Reformation: The Shape of Late Medieval Thought Illustrated by Key Documents* (Philadelphia: Fortress, 1981), 135.

[7] Oberman, 151.

[8] Oberman, 175ff.

[9] Oberman, 186.

little peculiar about a young Frenchman defending this doctrine in his commentaries, tracts, and in his famous *Institutes of the Christian Religion*. The predestination that Calvin taught was catholic and evangelical, as it was faithful to the biblical text despite the scandal to human wisdom, speculation, and pride.

How Central Was Predestination to Calvin's Thought?

Many of Calvin's critics would concede that he was not the first to promote such a doctrine. What made Calvin's system distinct, however, was that it was the first to make predestination central. Or, at least, that is how the story is often told. But there are some serious flaws in this popular assumption.

First, as historical theologian Richard Muller has indefatigably pointed out, the notion of a "central dogma" is itself imported from the Hegelian tradition of historical theologians. "According to Schweizer's reading of the older dogmatics," says Muller, "the orthodox Reformed theologians attempted to build a synthetic, deductive, and therefore irrefutable system of theology upon the primary proposition of an absolute divine decree of predestination."[10] Later, the Reformed writer Heinrich Heppe just assumed this central dogma idea, and it became a way of reading (or misreading) the literature. Even before Muller's thorough critique, François Wendel complained,

> After Alexander Schweizer in 1844 and Ferdinand Christian Bauer in 1847 had claimed that predestination was the central doctrine of Calvin's theology and that all the originality of his teaching proceeded from it, historians and dogmaticians went on for three-quarters of a century repeating that affirmation like an article of faith which did not even need to be verified.[11]

The problem with this approach is, well, Calvin. One simply cannot read the most representative of his works and conclude that he is obsessed with predestination. When the subject comes up, as in his exposition of key biblical passages, or when he is engaged in specific polemical battles with opponents of the doctrine, he faces it squarely and rigorously. He does not, however, spin a systematic web around a predestinarian core. Calvin's emphasis on this doctrine grows over time in the crucible of pastoral questions and debates. One does not find the doctrine spelled out in his early catechetical and confessional work.

---

[10] Richard Muller, *Christ and the Decree* (Grand Rapids: Baker, 1988), 1.

[11] François Wendel, "Justification and Predestination in Calvin," in *Readings in Calvin's Theology*, ed. Donald K. McKim (Grand Rapids: Baker, 1984), 160.

Even in the final edition of the *Institutes* (1559), Calvin declares concerning the doctrine of justification that we must "consider it in such a way as to keep well in mind that this is the principal article of the Christian religion" (*Inst.* 3.11.1).[12] If one is searching for a central dogma, then such references (viz., justification is "the main hinge upon which true religion turns," and so on) would seem to support justification, rather than predestination, as the most likely candidate.

While this point can be overstated, it is interesting that even in his final edition of the *Institutes*, Calvin placed the discussion of election after the treatment of prayer. Surely it does not occupy systematic centrality in the *Institutes*. But then, nothing does. Calvin's classic work was a defense of the Reformed faith in the teeth of practical life (namely, persecution) organized around the articles of the Apostles' Creed and Paul's Letter to the Romans. The discussion of election begins (*Inst.* 3.21.1) with the pastoral concern for assurance: "We shall never be clearly convinced as we ought to be, that our salvation flows from the fountain of God's free mercy, till we are acquainted with his eternal election." But speculation on this topic is deadly. He writes:

> The discussion of predestination—a subject of itself rather intricate—is made very perplexed, and therefore dangerous, by human curiosity, which no barriers can restrain from wandering into forbidden labyrinths, and soaring beyond its sphere, as if determined to leave none of the Divine secrets un-scrutinized or unexplored. . . . [The curious] will obtain no satisfaction to his curiosity, but will enter a labyrinth from which he will find no way to depart. For it is unreasonable that man should scrutinize with impunity those things which the Lord has determined to be hidden in himself. (*Inst.* 3.21.1)

It follows, says Calvin, that if we want to know anything about predestination in general, or our own election in particular, we are to look no further than Christ and the gospel. If some want to boldly transgress the word, then others want to extinguish even the knowledge of this great truth that the Scriptures plainly and repeatedly afford. The only approach to the subject, then, is for the Christian to be addressed by God, making sure that "as soon as the Lord closes his sacred mouth, he shall also desist from further inquiry" (*Inst.* 3.21.5). We cannot obtain certainty of our election by attempting "to penetrate to the eternal decree of God," for "we shall be ingulfed [*sic*] in the profound abyss." We must not seek to "soar above the clouds" but must be "satisfied with the testimony of God in his external word."

---

[12] All citations from the *Institutes of the Christian Religion* in this article are from John Allen, trans. (Philadelphia: Presbyterian Board of Christian Education).

For as those who, in order to gain assurance of their election, examine into the eternal counsel of God without the word, plunge themselves into a fatal abyss, so they who investigate it in a regular and orderly manner, as it is contained in the word, derive from such inquiry the benefit of peculiar consolation (*Inst.* 3.24.3–4).

When timid souls seek to discover their election beyond this external word ("Come unto Christ all ye sinners"), they will doubtless question their salvation, occupied with the questions: "Whence can you obtain salvation but from the election of God? And what revelation have you received of election?" These questions can only torment the conscience, Calvin says. "No error can affect the mind, more pestilent than such as disturbs the conscience, and destroy its peace and tranquillity [*sic*] towards God" than such speculations. The discussion of predestination is a dangerous ocean unless the believer is safely standing on Christ the rock (*Inst.* 3.24.4).

So how does one obtain assurance of election from the external word?

In the first place, if we seek the fatherly liberality and propitious heart of God, our eyes must be directed to Christ, in whom alone the Father is well pleased. . . .

Consider and investigate it as much as you please, you will not find its ultimate scope extend beyond this. . . . If we are chosen in Christ, we shall find no assurance of election in ourselves; nor even in God the Father, considered alone, abstractly from the Son. Christ, therefore, is the mirror, in which it behooves us to contemplate our election; and here we may do it with safety. (*Inst.* 3.24.5)

This "external word," therefore, is nothing other than the universal offer of the gospel. Embracing Christ alone, one is assured of "every spiritual blessing in heavenly places in Christ," including election (Eph. 1:4). It is to be sought neither in God's eternal hiddenness nor in ourselves, but in Christ alone as he is offered to us in the external call. If we were to find assurance of our election in ourselves, who would be confident enough to say with certainty, "I am chosen in Christ"? Further, says Calvin, to be "in Christ" is an ecclesiological matter: it is to be in the church, which is Christ's body. Thus the external word is joined to baptism, catechesis, the Eucharist, and the discipline and fellowship of the Savior's commonwealth. Although the reprobate are scattered among the elect in this community, there is no way of separating the sheep from the goats until the last judgment. Assurance of election, therefore, is linked to the proper use of the means of grace and incorporation into the visible church (*Inst.* 3.24.5–6). Thus certainty of election is obtained neither within oneself nor by oneself, but in Christ and with his chosen people.

Is Predestination Central for Calvinists?

There is a popular thesis, promoted largely by neo-orthodox scholars, that drives a wedge between Calvin and the Calvinists. In other words, everything we have said thus far is granted by these thinkers: Calvin was utterly Christocentric and avoided speculation like the plague. But, say the proponents of the "Calvin versus the Calvinists" debate, Calvin was followed by those who were eager to return to the scholastic method of doing theology. Led by Theodore Beza, Calvin's successor in Geneva, these Aristotelian theologians placed the discussion of predestination under the doctrine of God instead of under the discussion of salvation.

In reality, however, Beza's own writings reflect diversity in the placement of predestination. Sometimes it is under the doctrine of God, but it is also positioned there in Melanchthon's *Loci communes*, and Melanchthon was hardly a Calvinist. Furthermore, the Westminster divines—often targeted as the epitome of scholastic Calvinism—placed the discussion under "The Covenant of Grace and Its Mediator."

The bottom line is this: Predestination is not the central dogma in Calvin, his colleagues, or his successors. There are differences in pastoral strategy. For instance, while the Puritans directed consciences to Christ, they also emphasized Peter's admonition to "make your calling and election sure." This could be done, they said, not by searching out God's hidden decree but by leaning on Christ. Yet how do I know that I'm truly leaning on Christ and not on my own merits? How do I know that my faith is strong enough, that my repentance is sincere enough? This, the Puritans (at least most of them) insisted, was to make faith and repentance new works that could earn justification. So they separated faith from assurance, arguing that one was justified simply by looking to Christ alone—even if one did not have assurance.

While both Calvin and the English Puritans were driven by pastoral concerns to preserve the clarity of God's free grace in justification, the Puritan view of assurance (as not necessarily an element of saving faith) marks an important difference with Calvin and the magisterial Reformation. After all, the magisterial Reformation insisted that faith simply was assurance. This difference is easily discerned by comparing the continental Reformed view (Belgic Confession and Heidelberg Catechism) with the Westminster Confession (see especially Article 18) and catechisms. The continental Reformed view regards assurance as belonging to faith itself. The Westminster Confession, however, sees assurance as a reflexive effect of discerning even the slightest traces of God's work in one's life. Although faith did not come and go depending on one's obedience, assurance could. Like the Reformers' teaching, the Puritan view was calculated to console disquieted consciences, but it could also be used to disturb consciences with the fear of not discerning one's election through introspective measures. In fact, the practical and casuistic literature of the English Puritans often reflects a preoccupation with attaining assurance. As we have seen, this was the very course Calvin warned against in his treatment of election. Many later Puritans complained of this tendency and sought to redress imbalances.

In 1619, the Synod of Dort issued its famous canons, from which the popular expression, "Five Points of Calvinism" or "T.U.L.I.P" (Total depravity, Unconditional election, Limited atonement, Irresistible Grace, Perseverance of the Saints) emerged. An international synod, the meeting included delegates from the established churches of England, Scotland, and Ireland, as well as the continental churches of Switzerland, France, Germany, Hungary, Bohemia, and the Netherlands. At least publicly, King James I was as eager to extinguish Arminianism from his kingdom as the delegates he sent to Dort. (Interestingly, the patriarch of Constantinople drew up his own version of the Canons of Dort for the Orthodox Churches, but this was rescinded and repudiated after his death.) In this definitive confession, the Reformed churches condemned Arminianism and asserted the Calvinistic distinctives. No other document in Reformed history has been so useful in offering a careful but concise treatment of the differences between Calvinism and Arminianism.

But Dort has to be seen in its context. It was a response to a crisis in the Dutch church, which sister Reformed churches were battling as well, even as they continue to do to this day. Unlike the confessions and catechism of the Reformation period, Dort was a polemical statement targeting a particular error. It was never intended as a stand-alone statement of the Reformed faith. Those, like myself, who subscribe to the Reformed confession, embrace Dort along with the Belgic Confession and the Heidelberg Catechism, where predestination is not only not central but is mentioned only in passing. Together, they are the "Form of Subscription." The Westminster Confession and catechisms, drafted three decades later by order of the English Parliament, also had Arminianism in view but sought to offer a full explanation of Calvinism beyond the dispute over the "Five Points."

The reason for mentioning these historical facts is to point out that it is highly problematic to reduce Calvinism or Reformed theology to the "Five Points." Genuine Calvinism is certainly more than this. It involves a distinct covenantal hermeneutic, including the covenant of works ("in Adam") and the covenant of grace ("in Christ"), and this entails certain views of the sacraments and the church. Even the isolated defense of "T.U.L.I.P." can present election or the sovereignty of God in a way that is markedly different from the Reformed understanding. Ironically, the mistake of critics who reduce Reformed theology to predestination is too often repeated by friends of Calvinism. They have discovered the richness of the doctrines of grace and yet fail to see that it is a doctrinal system that comprehends the essential teaching of Scripture.

By abstracting the "Five Points" from that system, many contemporary "Calvinists" have failed to see the sovereignty of God in his electing and redeeming grace in the covenantal unfolding of God's plan in redemptive history. Thus their treatment of predestination sometimes appears to be bold speculation into God's eternal hiddenness, apart from the external call offered to everyone and sealed by the Holy Spirit through the external means of grace. Furthermore, it seems to be a central motif in their thinking, either relegating the more central themes under which election is properly ordered to the outer edges or rejecting them altogether. No wonder, then, that such distorted versions of "Calvinism" often result in morbid introspection, severe piety, and a lack of assurance that gives no rest to the conscience. As we have seen, Calvin and the Reformed confessions (including Westminster) regard Christ and union with him as central. Even the sovereignty and glory of God are not to be considered in themselves, for apart from Christ our knowledge of God will result only in terror and judgment.

If our critics should be expected to deal more responsibly with the actual development of Reformed theology, then our friends should also be encouraged not to pull up the "tulips" from their native soil in God's redemptive scheme.

The Consolation of Election

There are various reasons why people reject the biblical doctrine of election. Some do so, as Luther surmised, because of "the wisdom of the flesh," seeking glory for self. Others, of a more philosophical bent, curiously probe beyond Scripture, demanding an accounting of God for why some, but not all, are chosen. It is just at that point where the biblical witness forbids further speculation ("Who are you, O mortal, to question God?"), and where human wisdom often prefers to reject God's revealed utterance. Further questions ensue about the problem of evil, which is, we should add, not just a problem for Calvinists. In fact, it's a problem for everyone but God. And God knew that we would throw up just such objections: "You will then say to me, how can God still blame us? . . . Is God unjust?" (Rom. 9).

As Luther said, the doctrine of election is as plainly revealed in Scripture as the notion of a supreme being. Thus Luther answered Erasmus's weak refrain of ignorance of this doctrine with the reply, "The Holy Spirit is not a sceptic!" God revealed election, not for our curiosity or to confirm us in our laziness, but to raise our eyes to him in gratitude, acknowledging that he alone is worthy to receive praise. This doctrine is the occasion for worship and not for speculation or debate. It is just such thoughts of God's goodness that lead us to exclaim, "Who shall lay anything to the charge of God's elect?" As we have been reminded, knowledge of this truth is of sweet comfort to those who have been crushed by the law and raised to life by the gospel, but it is deadly for those who have not.

Since God has entrusted his word to his church, it is only a measure of our pride and self-will that we should attempt to silence God's voice on a matter of such importance. It is difficult to find a doctrine that is so clearly and prominently proclaimed in Scripture and yet so obscured and ignored in the church. And yet, every great recovery of the apostolic gospel throughout church history has involved a rediscovery of this great truth.

If I may be permitted to conclude on an autobiographical note, I remember well the day I finally "got" Romans 9. Already disoriented and reoriented by the first eight chapters, despite my meager understanding, I was at first outraged by the sheer freedom of God. Throwing my Bible across the room, I determined not to pick it up again, but my resolve was short-lived. After reading the chapter several times, I found my hard heart softening under the warm rays of God's unmerited favor. Grace really is grace, I began to say to myself. God is greater, I am smaller, and salvation is sweeter. Whenever I get into a discussion of grace, I find that sooner or later (usually sooner), the conversation turns to election. And no wonder. While it may not be the center of Christianity, it is certainly the test of just how central the central things really are.

CHAPTER 13

Calvin versus the Calvinists: A Bibliographic Essay

R. Scott Clark

Was John Calvin a warm, biblical, humanist, evangelical, Christ-centered Reformer, and were the Reformed theologians (e.g., Theodore Beza), churches, and confessions (e.g., the Canons of Dort or the Westminster Confession) that succeeded him unfaithful to his theology, piety, and practice? Did they corrupt his biblical theology and heartfelt piety by replacing them with human reason? This was the argument of Charles Augustus Briggs (1841–1913), who claimed "the successors of the Reformers in the seventeenth century" replaced Calvin's emphasis on the word and Spirit with "Aristotelian philosophy." In the early 1950s, Perry Miller repeated a version of this argument. Indeed, for most of the twentieth century it was held widely in the Protestant mainline that the only way to understand John Calvin was by distinguishing him sharply from "the Calvinists" who had corrupted his thought and work. Two of the most influential books arguing this case were Brian G. Armstrong, *Calvin and the Amyraut Heresy* (1969), and R. T. Kendall, *Calvin and English Calvinism to 1649* (1979).

About the same time that Armstrong and Kendall were restating the majority view, scholars such as W. Robert Godfrey, Jill Raitt, and Richard Muller began to raise questions about the "Calvin vs. the Calvinists" approach to the history of Reformed theology. Their questions arose from their careful research not only into the writings of John Calvin but also those of his successors, something that has been frequently missing in the older approach. They found that the caricature of Calvinists such as Theodore Beza—which portrayed their theology as cold, dry, and rationalist—was simply untrue. In 1982 Paul Helm replied to Kendall in *Calvin and the Calvinists*, and in 1986 Richard Muller published *Christ and the Decree*. Muller has summed up much of his research in the four-volume work, *Post-Reformation Reformed Dogmatics* (2003).

This reinterpretation of Reformed orthodoxy is also reflected in the following books: Carl R. Trueman and R. Scott Clark, eds. *Protestant Scholasticism* (1999);

Mark Dever and Richard Sibbes, *Puritanism and Calvinism in Late Elizabethan and Early Stuart England* (2000); Willem J. Van Asselt, *The Federal Theology of Johannes Cocceius (1603–1669)* (2001); Richard A. Muller, *After Calvin* (2003); and Carl R. Trueman, *John Owen* (2007).

In my seminary course on Reformed orthodoxy, I begin by describing the Calvin versus the Calvinists approach and then have students read a primary source from the period, Theodore Beza. Grove City College professor Paul Schaefer observes that for many advocates of this approach, Beza is the "bad boy" of Reformed theology. Every year, the Calvin versus the Calvinist rhetoric ringing in their ears, the students find a great discontinuity between their experience of Beza as a pastoral, passionate, Christ-centered writer and their expectations. So edifying is Beza's book *The Christian Faith* that it sometimes seems to them that their professor must be misrepresenting the earlier approaches. He isn't.

What our students and many other readers find is that the Calvinists—some of whom were Calvin's colleagues (e.g., Beza), and students and who heard him preach and lecture and who spent time with him—understood his theology, piety, and practice. They understood how he read the Scriptures (i.e., his hermeneutic), and they understood the principles on which he operated (e.g., his approach to worship). After his death, they took what they learned and applied it to new circumstances and questions. Thus, when Jacob Arminius (1560–1609) rejected basic Reformation theology, the Reformed Churches of Europe and England applied the hermeneutic and principles they inherited from Calvin and replied with Canons of the Synod of Dort. In the middle of the seventeenth century in England, the Westminster Assembly did the same.

More than thirty years after the revolution in Calvin studies began, the old Calvin versus the Calvinists approach has been entirely discredited. Today, thanks to the pioneering work of earlier writers, there is a growing appreciation of primary texts from the period of Reformed orthodoxy. For example, Reformation Heritage Books recently published a three-volume series titled Classic Reformed Theology. Also, a growing movement to recapture and apply the insights of earlier Reformed theology to contemporary questions is evident in the *Confessional Presbyterian* journal and in the work of D. G. Hart. Where most scholars analyze American Christianity as either "conservative" or "liberal," in *The Lost Soul of American Protestantism* (2002), Hart suggests a third category, "confessional," to account for writers and movements such as J. Gresham Machen (1881–1936) and the confessional Presbyterians who followed him.

Thoughtful readers of Calvin know him to have been a Protestant, evangelical, biblical theologian who knew the difference between law and gospel and who saw Christ at the center of the history of redemption. Careful readers of the

Calvinist tradition are finding that the same adjectives to be true of his followers and of most of the rest of the Reformed tradition beyond Calvin. What he taught and practiced, however, was nothing less than the Reformed faith and piety, and it was this faith that the Reformed churches, pastors, and theologians practiced in their own time and in their own circumstances.

CHAPTER 14

How the Rumors Started: A Brief History of Calvin's Bad Press

Ryan Glomsrud

Myths about Calvin survive in high school history textbooks, collegiate lectures on "Intro to Western Civilization," and, even worse, untold areas of divinity school curricula. Even with careful, reproving scholarship rolling off the presses, Marilynne Robinson has sarcastically written,

> Many of us know that Calvinism was a very important tradition among us. Yet all we know about John Calvin was that he was an eighteenth-century Scotsman, a prude and obscurantist with a buckle on his hat, possibly a burner of witches, certainly the very spirit of capitalism. . . . We want to return to the past, and we have made our past a demonology and not a human narrative.[1]

Such is the case even five hundred years after Calvin's birth. It is never fun to ruin a punch line, but for those not in on the joke: Calvin was a sixteenth-century Frenchman living in exile in Geneva, the eighteenth-century Puritans wore the buckles, the prudes were the Victorians, and the rest belong to other unseemly episodes several degrees removed from Calvin himself.

John Calvin's place in Western intellectual and cultural history is important, certainly important enough to demand a fair accounting of these legends and others, the various wildly inaccurate tidbits of supposed common knowledge, oral tradition, and received lecture-hall wisdom.

It is sometimes thought that Calvin was the hired gun of the Reformed branch of Protestantism, the executioner of Counter-Reformation Catholics and religious progressives, or even a social and sexual deviant with a loose tongue

---

[1]The quotations from this column are taken from Irena Backus, "Roman Catholic Lives of Calvin from Bolsec to Richelieu, Why the Interest?" in Randall C. Zachman, ed., *John Calvin and Roman Catholicism: Critiques and Engagements, Then and Now* (Grand Rapids: Baker, 2008).

and even looser morals. More frequently, it is claimed that Calvin was a heretic of epic proportions, usually on the alleged grounds that he dismissed the Trinitarian creeds and developed a unique and "strict" or "harsh" doctrine of election and reprobation. Along these lines, it is difficult to imagine a more despised theological doctrine in the modern world than predestination, and the subscribers and witnesses to this biblical teaching, past and present, are surely doomed in our day to scathing—even if unfair—criticism. But perhaps this has always been the case.

Recent scholarship has shown that *most* of the libelous stories and myths about Calvin can be traced back to one original source, even one particular individual. The man's name was Jerome Bolsec. He was a refugee and layman who returned to the Catholic Church after a spell as Calvin's theological nemesis in Geneva and Bern, who later failed to be ordained in the Reformed Church in Paris. In 1577, Bolsec became Calvin's first Catholic biographer, and the stories he narrated have a *long* tail in European history.

Bolsec's own life was a curious one, and he provides an excellent example of how the biographical genre was used for outrageous polemical purposes in sixteenth-century Europe, coming in every form from pamphlets to woodcarvings to the first early modern encyclopedias. According to one scholar, Bolsec "wanted to destroy the image of Geneva [and Calvin] as quickly and effectively as possible." Coming up for mention in his biography, then, was the following: (1) Calvin's "calamitous influence" on France and his personal role in the destruction of Christian peace in Europe; (2) Calvin as the "reincarnation of all heresies" previously known in the church; (3) Calvin as the convicted sodomite who should have been burned at the stake by church officials in Noyon, only to have his sentence commuted at the last minute instead to receive a branding of a fleur-de-lis on his shoulder blade; (4) Calvin as the promiscuous tyrant who had "intercourse with most of Geneva's married women under the cover of pastoral guidance"; and more infamously, (5) Calvin as the sole person responsible for the execution of Michael Servetus ("a myth that turned out to have an astonishingly long life"). Bolsec, however, was not the only party guilty of spreading tales of immorality in order to undermine Calvin's authority.

As Protestant Christians, we sometimes relish our own opportunities to spread a little dirt about Roman Catholicism. The Renaissance Papacy (1447–1521) comes to mind, for example, and we must admit there is great irony that popes named Pius II and Innocent VIII fathered illegitimate children, were previously married (at least in the case of the latter), and appointed many of their children as cardinals while they were still infants, all the while claiming them as "nephews." This is to say nothing of Pope Alexander VI, whom Luther called "the Mystery of Iniquity," or Julius II, who according to legend once served the Eucharist in full battle armor while brandishing a sword in his other hand. Leaving confirmation of the veracity or falsity of these legends to readers, suffice it to say both Catholics and Protestants at the time of the Reformation engaged in a unique form of embellished biographical polemic. To tarnish moral character was to strike at the heart of the message, or so it seemed at the time.

But it does seem that some of the utterly ridiculous stories about Calvin have persisted in the general populace far longer than Lutheran or Reformed tales of Catholic corruption, and this despite the fact that later Catholic interpreters advanced by leaps and bounds in the intervening decades, in fact pioneering "objective and historical methodologies" that radically called Bolsec's *Life of Calvin* into question. After investigating each individual claim about Calvin's life, these later Catholic writers discarded most if not all of these myths on the grounds that Bolsec had fabricated sources (surely a mortal sin in the historical-biographical genre) and was inappropriately clouded by his personal animosity toward Calvin, which was significant.

In the case of Calvin, sometimes explaining the origins of the vast majority of myths and legends is a more effective apologetic strategy than debunking each slanderous claim. The same holds true for the doctrine of predestination and its place and function in Reformed theology. For now, with each regurgitated lecture about Calvin's life and thought, that buckle-hatted tyrant of Geneva, one may be tempted to call for a moratorium on popular opinions.

CHAPTER 15

Calvin the Transformationist?

David VanDrunen

The question that I have been asked to address—was Calvin a transformationist?—can be a tricky one. Generally speaking, a transformationist is someone who believes that Christians should be actively involved in cultural life and
should seek to bring all areas of life into conformity with God's will through the
power of Christ's redemptive grace. But this can mean different things to different people. I suggest that in a certain sense Calvin was a transformationist, but
that in other important respects he was not. In this yes-and-no response that I
impute to Calvin, I perceive a helpful guide and challenge for us today.

Calvin was a transformationist in the sense that he encouraged Christians
to perform their various earthly vocations faithfully and sought to promote the
welfare of his own adopted city, Geneva. Like other reformers, Calvin rejected
the common medieval notion that monasticism represented the highest ideal of
godly living. He praised the ordinary labor of ordinary people and argued that
all sorts of vocations are noble and God-honoring when pursued honestly and
industriously. Calvin also had a high view of the civil magistrate. Over against
certain factions in his day that deprecated civil authority, Calvin praised magistrates as established by God and necessary for preserving social order. Yet even
while he instructed Christians to submit to their civil rulers (even wicked ones),
he exhorted magistrates to seek justice and to be mindful of their accountability
before God. Calvin was a lawyer by training, and he was involved in efforts to
revise both the government of the church and the civil laws in Geneva. Civil
and ecclesiastical discipline in Geneva sought to shape the commercial, moral,
familial, and religious life of all the residents in the city. Viewed from this perspective, Calvin sounds like an enthusiastic transformationist. But Calvin was
certainly not a transformationist as many would understand that term today, in
at least three respects.

First, Calvin was not a transformationist in the way that H. Richard Niebuhr
used the term. Calvin is often labeled a transformationist because Niebuhr famously identified him as such in his influential book *Christ and Culture* (1951).

For Niebuhr, however, a genuine transformationist vision affirms that God redeems the whole of fallen creation and hence that all individuals will be saved in the end—that is, universalism. Calvin was certainly no universalist, and Niebuhr himself had to admit that Calvin did not quite fit into the category after all.

Second, Calvin's understanding of the kingdom of Christ distinguishes him from many contemporary transformationists. Many people today understand transformation as the task of redeeming all spheres of cultural life and hence of bringing the kingdom of Christ to expression in all of them. Calvin looked at things differently. He did not seek to bring all spheres of earthly life under the orbit of the one heavenly kingdom that Christ purchased by his own blood. Instead, Calvin believed that God governs this world by means of *two kingdoms*. He looked to the *church* as the earthly community in which believers have present fellowship with the kingdom of heaven. The church is where the redemptive message of the gospel is preached, and in the church Christians enjoy the liberty of conscience bestowed by the gospel in a unique way. But God also governs the civil kingdom, which includes the state and other earthly institutions and activities. Christians have honorable vocations within this kingdom, but God rules it not as its redeemer but as its creator and sustainer. Calvin adamantly asserted that civil government, for instance, was not to be identified with the spiritual kingdom of Christ. Calvin therefore would have rejected the notion of transformation insofar as it implies bringing all spheres of life into conformity with the life of Christ's redemptive kingdom.

Finally, Calvin was not a transformationist if that implies, as it sometimes does, a triumphalistic view of the Christian's life in this world. While Calvin believed that much good can be accomplished here and now, he also had a vivid sense that the Christian life is a life of suffering. He described our present existence as one of a pilgrimage under the cross, and he often exhorted his readers to lift their eyes to heaven and to be sustained by the great hope held out for them there.

Calvin lived in cultural circumstances very different from our own, and this makes it difficult to know how to apply contemporary terms such as "transformationist" to him. Even this brief study, however, draws attention to several points at which we can be challenged by Calvin. Perhaps most pointedly, Calvin's theology points us in a direction that avoids two dangerous extremes: on the one hand, he encourages us not to denigrate ordinary earthly activities or to doubt that they honor God and benefit our neighbor; on the other hand, he warns us against identifying our earthly labors and political involvement with the kingdom of Christ and against forgetting that the present age is one of suffering rather than conquest.

CHAPTER 16

Our Calvin, Our Council

Alexandre Ganoczy

It seems appropriate for a Catholic theologian, who for many years has studied the history and work of John Calvin, to participate in the concert of voices that honor him for the 500th anniversary of his birth. Such a participation seems to me all the more justified as I perceive considerable convergences between his conception of the church and the ecclesiology of the Second Vatican Council, to which I remain—unlike certain traditionalists who have been rehabilitated by Pope Benedict XVI—strongly attached.

In my view, a first point of convergence is established by the role attributed to the Holy Spirit in the walk of God's people in history. Although the church needs sociologically identifiable and effective institutional structures in order to act in our world, the power that allows her to fulfill this task has a divine origin. Calvin follows the Apostle Paul in recognizing that the Spirit is the one who "distributes his gifts as he sees fit" (cf. 1 Cor. 12:11). It is also the Spirit who secures the cohesion and cooperation between the diverse members of the ecclesial body (cf. v. 13). The Reformer follows both the apostle and the tradition of the Greek Fathers when he affirms that Christ makes himself present at the Lord's Supper by the work of the Spirit (cf. *Inst.* 4.17.12). Finally, the comprehension of the true sense of a given biblical text is only possible through "the internal witness of the Spirit" (cf. *Inst.* 1.7.4 and 12). Calvin, however, is not a spiritualist given to ecstatic experiences, or in favor of the "Invisible Church" whose members are known to God alone. His knowledge of Latin theologians of the early church (especially Cyprian and Augustine, who integrated components of Roman law to their ecclesiology, as well as his legal training) influenced him toward an ecclesiology that is both spiritual and institutional. Vatican II seems to have achieved a similar synthesis by placing a simultaneous emphasis on the charismatic and hierarchical structure of the church. This is reflected in both the apostolate of the laity and the apostolate given to the priests and bishops. The theme of "common priesthood" to all those who are baptized also signals a movement in the same direction.

For the Reformer, there existed a neo-testamental model that could be adapted to the requirements of his time. It consisted of the four ministries of "the reformed Church according to the Word of God": pastors, deacons, doctors, and elders. The first two exercise their functions on the basis of an ordination that is almost sacramental. Pastors secure the ministry of the word connected to the sacraments, while deacons fulfill the ministry of service and hospitality. Doctors assume the ministry of catechetical teaching, which includes both theological and so-called profane instruction, and elders are responsible for temporal (in effect lay) governance of the community.

However, it is especially in the four ministries' "collegial" method of work that a new analogy between the Calvinian and conciliar models is revealed. These are groups or "teams" for which leadership, or moderating, is provided by a "first among equals" who is elected by all the other members. Their meetings provide an exchange of information and debates, which prepare the way for decisions based on solidarity. Thus the "college" is able to avoid the danger of authoritarian and arbitrary deviation in the governing of the community. This "balance of power" sometimes gave concerns to Calvin himself, but it was especially motivated by a refusal of papal authority.

Regarding the papacy, the many "antipapal" declarations by Luther and Calvin reflect only one side of the coin. Those who know the *Institutes* are aware that Calvin's refusal of a functional primacy of the bishop of Rome was far from absolute. He occasionally reflected positively on the matter. Speaking of the church of the first six centuries up to the time of Gregory the Great (540–604), Calvin still recognized the "petrinian" ideal of primacy as both an effective symbol of ecclesial unity and a place of appeal in case of controversies between local churches (cf. *Inst.* 4.7.12). At that time, the authority exercised by Peter's successor was moral and non-monarchical. Is it then unrealistic for Calvin to think that ten centuries later (i.e., in the sixteenth century) the reestablishment of this view of apostolic succession should be realized? "Had it pleased God," wrote Calvin, "that this succession, for which they boast falsely, would have lasted up to now! We would have gladly given it the honor it deserves" (*Opera* 7, 611). Following John XXIII, the pope of Vatican II, many Catholics have been able to join their Reformed brethren to say again, "Had it pleased God." In reality, this collegial principle seems to have gradually lost its primordial role in the post-conciliar years. However, should not fidelity to both its Calvinian and conciliar heritage make a departure from Vatican II undesirable? Instead, should we not pursue and complete the work of Vatican II through perhaps a Vatican III?

Confident in the activity of the Spirit, but also in constant ecumenical and conciliar collaborative work (as was meant by Lukas Fischer), we today have the duty not to reserve the title of church to only one Christian confession. Or, at least, we should recognize among our so-called separated brethren, the "vestige" of the church, which Calvin noted the presence in non-Reformed communities. These were possible anchor points toward reestablishing Communion. For Calvin, the most important "vestige" was the sacrament of baptism (cf. *Inst.* 1539; *Opera* 1, 560; 1559, 4.2.12).

For Calvin, this Communion was not uniform but catholic. Evidently, the term is not to be taken in its confessional sense where the adjective "Roman" is necessarily added, but in its fundamental meaning of universality. "The Church," wrote the Reformer, "is called catholic or universal because we could not speak of two or three without tearing Jesus Christ" (*Inst.* 4.1.2). Beginning with a similar Christology, Vatican II also advocates, "The catholic unity of the people of God," a unity in perpetual growth and reform, the one "that prefigures and promises universal peace," and to which "men are called . . . both the catholic faithful [in the confessional sense] and the others who believe in Christ, and finally . . . all men . . . called to salvation" (*Lumen Gentium* 13/3).

More than ever today, where powers of disunity are working in so many areas, the churches that form the universal church are called to overcome what deeply separates them. And this not only by reforming themselves in dispersed order, but also in thinking and acting "conciliarly." This should be accomplished with the courage inherent to a missionary catholicity that, far from retreating into a secure traditionalist ghetto, accepts the risks of modernity.

In spite of some erring by its protagonists, this courage also fueled Luther and Calvin's reform. Likewise, it characterized the reforms of Vatican II. Current fundamentalist tendencies, with their push to conserve gains preceding the council or to revoke its fundamental reforms, must be countered. This is especially true if we, as Reformed and Catholics, want to commemorate Calvin by allowing ourselves to say from both sides, "our Calvin" and "our council."

English translation from the French by Thomas D. Petter, associate professor of Old Testament at Gordon-Conwell Theological Seminary in South Hamilton, Massachusetts.

CHAPTER 17

Calvin on the Eucharist

W. Robert Godfrey

Both Luther and Zwingli had crucial points to make in the debate over the Lord's Supper, but in my judgment, it was John Calvin who best resolved the question. Calvin began by agreeing with both sides on certain matters. He agreed with Zwingli that Christ is ascended and that his body is in heaven. He agreed with Zwingli that faith must be central in any adequate doctrine of the Lord's Supper; it is only by faith that we can receive a blessing. But Calvin's heart was really much closer to Luther because Calvin believed deeply and passionately that the Lord's Supper is God's gift to us. It is primarily God who acts in the Lord's Supper. God is the giver; we receive that gift. With great passion Calvin agreed with Luther that we must seek our redemption in the body and blood of Christ and in his sacrificial death. We are united to Christ in his body and blood by the Holy Spirit. But that union is so intense, so real, that we can rightly say we are "bone of his bone and flesh of his flesh" (*Inst.* 3.1.3; cf. Gen. 2:23). Calvin said that we are *embodied* in Christ, as Ephesians 5:30 declares: "We are members of his body." That is where our redemption comes from, Calvin insisted. Salvation is that union with Christ.

Calvin's view, however, was not just that of a compromiser, taking bits and pieces from different people and fitting them together. He had his own distinct, important, and, I think, clear statement of what the sacrament was about.

First, he insisted that the word is crucial. The preached word makes the sacrament intelligible, he said. It is only in union with the word that we know the Lord's blessing. It is only by the Spirit working through the word that the blessing is ministered to us and sealed upon us. Yet—and this is the second point—the blessing is represented and presented to us in the bread and the wine. What are bread and wine? They are food, nourishment. So, says Calvin, that is what they represent spiritually: spiritual food. As by the mouth we receive bread and wine to the nourishment of our bodies, so by faith (which is the mouth of the soul) we receive the body and blood of Christ unto everlasting life.

That food is Jesus Christ himself. We will find life in Christ only when we seek the substance of Christ in his flesh. For as soon as we depart from the sacrifice of his death, we encounter nothing but death. In Christ's flesh was accomplished man's redemption. In it a sacrifice was offered to atone for sin in an obedience yielded to God to reconcile him to us. That flesh of Christ is our food, Calvin insists.

We are to feed upon the word, to be sure. But Calvin would say we must feed upon Christ too—on Jesus himself, who offers himself and all his benefits to us in the Supper—because it is only by being in and with Jesus that we can find redemption. That is why the Supper is so important to us, so central in our life. It draws us back to the center and heart of the gospel. It is, you see, a visible word; and the visible word declares to us that there is salvation only in the body and blood of Christ. That body and blood are not just once and for all offered on the cross as a past and finished thing, but that body and blood, that real Christ, continue to be the life-giving spirit among us. It is our present union with Christ that builds us up and strengthens us. It is only as we seek union with the true Christ that we can be built up in that way.

Moreover, as Calvin says, that promise of communion with Christ is offered in the sacrament to everyone. He says, "Truly he offers and shows the reality there signified to all who sit at that spiritual banquet, although it is received with benefit by believers alone, who accept such great generosity with true gratefulness of heart" (*Inst.* 4.17.10). He says that the sacrament is like rain from heaven. It comes down as the offer and promise of God of new life in Christ. But, like rain, it falls on different kinds of ground. When it hits ground prepared by faith it comes as blessing, nourishment, and a source of growth. When it hits the hard rock of unbelief, it is still the same offer and promise, but it flows away with no profit to the soul (see *Inst.* 4.17.33).

Faith remains crucial to Calvin's doctrine. It is only the faithful who know Christ. But when the faithful come to the table, they meet Christ himself. What Christ represents in the bread and wine he presents to faith as life-giving nourishment.

Frequency of Observance

On this basis, Calvin reflected on how often we ought to receive the sacrament. Zwingli was in favor of administering the sacrament once a year; and, of course, if you are having a memorial service, once a year is probably adequate. It is like Christmas. Christmas is delightful once a year, but it would be a bit much once a week. It is good once a year to spend some special time thinking about the birth of our Lord. But to do that every week would be impossible.

Calvin, on the other hand, said that the sacrament is much more than just a memorial. It is not just a time when we sit and think good thoughts. It is a time in which we are fed, nourished. We meet the risen Christ. Therefore, it should be frequent. How often should you pray? Once a year? No, we should pray and feed upon the word frequently. So, said Calvin, we should feed upon Christ himself frequently. In the *Institutes* he says twice, "The Lord's Supper should be administered at least once a week" (*Inst.* 4.17.44, 46).

Many Reformed Christians today administer communion only four times a year. We do that for a "good" reason. Geneva's city council refused to let Calvin administer the sacrament once a week and let him offer it only four times a year. So we follow the spiritual wisdom of those wise men, the city councilmen of Geneva, and ignore Calvin himself.

For those of you who are more influenced by things British, it is interesting to note that in the 1644 Directory of Public Worship drawn up by the Westminster Assembly of Divines, it is said that the administration of communion should be frequent. Still, most Presbyterians have also followed something close to the wisdom of the Geneva councilmen.

The frequency of administration may say something about what we expect to find at that table (or, maybe I should say, whom we expect to find at that table) and what the blessing of meeting Jesus Christ there really is. Calvin himself was the first to admit that the ins and outs of that blessing were a mystery. In fact, Calvin, who so often is represented as sort of a grim logician, reveals quite a mystical streak at this point. He says,

> It is a mystery of Christ's secret union with the devout which is by nature incomprehensible. If anybody should ask me how this communion takes place, I am not ashamed to confess that that is a secret too lofty for either my mind to comprehend or my words to declare. And to speak more plainly, I rather experience than understand it. (*Inst.* 4.17.32)

There is a shock! Good Presbyterians do not experience anything. We are God's frozen people. But Calvin found such a meeting with Christ in the Lord's Supper and such great blessings attached to it that his heart was filled by the Spirit. He found Christ and all his benefits. He found joy. He was gladdened by meeting his Lord, gladdened that he could come to the table and have his faith strengthened by that sure promise of God represented there. Indeed, Calvin becomes so mystical that he speaks of the believer, as he receives the bread and wine, actually being lifted up to heaven. Christ does not descend into the bread, but by the Holy Spirit the believer ascends into heaven, there to commune with the glorified Christ and all the blessings of his crucifixion, resurrection, and ascension (*Inst.* 4.17.32; cf. Eph. 2:5–6).

Here again we can see Calvin's use of the idea of God ministering to our weakness in the sacrament. We come to the table with nothing to offer God, but we come to be blessed by the Lord.

> [We come] to offer our vileness and our unworthiness to him so that his mercy may make us worthy of him: we come to despair in ourselves so that we may be comforted in him; to abase ourselves so that we may be lifted up by him; to accuse ourselves so that we may be justified by him; moreover, we come to aspire to that unity which he commends to us in his Supper; and as he makes all of us one in himself to desire one soul, one heart, one tongue for us all. (*Inst.* 4.17.42)

Calvin felt the pull of unity in the sacrament, and he labored all his life to see that this unity was expressed. It grieved him deeply to see Protestant warring with Protestant over the Supper.

God's Help and Media

Sacraments, as Calvin put it, are "God's help and media." When I ran across that quotation it set my mind to whirring. *Media* is just an untranslated word from the Latin; it should be "means." The sacraments are God's means. But I thought that in our day of emphasis upon media, it is rather nice perhaps to leave it in the Latin. God gave his church media, visible statements of his promise. And those visible statements are a way in which we can receive the blessing of the Lord.

Luther, in reflecting on this, once said, "For 'we must have something new.' [Luther always sounds so contemporary, does he not?] Christ's death and resurrection, faith and love, are old and just ordinary things; that is why they must count for nothing, and so we weigh ourselves down with big piles of new teaching."[1]

That is just what has happened and will continue to happen. How easy it is for us to develop twitching ears that love to hear new things on the periphery of our faith or perhaps beyond the periphery of our faith—fascinating things that pique the interest. How we have a tendency to say, "Jesus' death and resurrection, faith and love. That's all sort of 'ho hum.' We've heard all that before. We

---

[1] "On Councils and the Church," *Luther's Works*, vol. 41, 127–28.

know all about that stuff. We've got to get on to bigger and better things." The Reformers call us back to the center and say that there is nothing bigger and better. There is nothing more important. There is nothing more central. There is nothing more necessary at every point in our Christian life than to go back to this: our redemption is in the body and blood of Christ.

I sometimes wonder how it might affect preachers if every sermon had to end in the Lord's Supper. Would it give a healthy new dimension to the way our sermons develop and conclude? Would it force us back to the central things of the gospel? Is it possible that to some extent the development of the altar call in evangelicalism is a response to the felt inadequacy of our services when they do not end in the heart of the gospel? Is it perhaps an unspoken desire to have that central message made in the sacrament that God has instituted? Might not our church life be strengthened by frequent communion? To be sure, there can be nothing magical here. There are churches that have the Lord's Supper every week and have no blessing from it. But when we come to the Lord's Table properly, we will experience that communion with Christ by faith. Calvin commented most eloquently on this when he said:

> Let us carefully observe then, when we wish to use the sacraments as God has or-
> dained, that they should be like ladders, for raising us on high. For we are heavy and
> cumbersome, held down by earthly things. Thus, because we are unable to fly high
> enough to draw near to God, he has ordained sacraments for us like ladders. If a man
> wishes to leap on high, he will break his neck in the attempt; but if he has steps, he
> is able to proceed with confidence. So also if we are to reach our God. Let's use the
> means which he has instituted for us, since he knows what is suitable for us.[2]

Christian growth is a gradual process. The sacraments are one key element in that process when rightly used. They are like ladders we may go up one rung at a time, coming ever to deeper fellowship with our Lord, to deeper knowledge of his redemption, to deeper gladness and strength in what he has promised. We never outgrow the sacraments. On the contrary, as we climb, we come more and more to appreciate the ladder just as firemen do as they go up and up. We come more and more to be glad that the ladder on which we stand is stable, sure, and firm.

I hope as time goes on and you participate in the sacraments—observe (and recall your) baptism and receive the Lord's Supper—that you will think on these things and realize what a great blessing the Lord has given to us in them. The sacraments, like the word, present and offer Christ and when received in faith give us Christ and all his blessings.

---

[2] Cited in Marcel, 179–80.

CHAPTER 18

Calvin's Form of Administering the Lord's Supper

Keith A. Mathison

Among the many doctrines debated at the time of the Protestant Reformation, none was the source of more discussion and debate than the Lord's Supper. John Calvin wrote and spoke extensively on the subject in his sermons, tracts, and theological treatises, and numerous studies have examined what Calvin taught in these. However, we can also gain insight into his understanding of this sacrament by examining the liturgy he prepared for use at the church in Geneva.[1]

It is clear from even a cursory glance at the liturgy that Calvin wanted the communicants to understand the meaning of the Supper. The liturgy of the church of Geneva included much more than the recitation of the words of institution. At times, the minister was to make the Supper the topic of the entire sermon in order to explain its meaning to the people. But even when this did not occur, the observance of the Supper was to be a time for instruction. According to Calvin's liturgy, when the Supper is celebrated, the minister must first turn the attention of the church to the sacrament. After doing so, the minister recites the words of institution found in 1 Corinthians 11:23–29.

The words of institution are then followed by a warning to the unworthy. Here the seriousness with which Calvin took the Supper is evident. The minister declares that unbelievers are not to be admitted and then verbally excommunicates "all idolaters, blasphemers, despisers of God, heretics" and a number of others, "declaring to them that they must abstain from this holy table, for fear of polluting and contaminating the sacred viands [items of food] which our Lord Jesus Christ gives only to his household and believers."

---

[1] In this essay, the author has used the Henry Beveridge translation of the *Form of Administering the Sacraments Composed for the Use of the Church of Geneva*. This translation is found in the second volume of the *Tracts and Letters of John Calvin* (Edinburgh: Banner of Truth, 2009), 113–28.

After warning unbelievers and unrepentant sinners to abstain, Calvin's liturgy warmly encourages the repentant believers who have carefully examined themselves to come to the table. In spite of all the sins we know remain within us, "let us all be assured that the vices and imperfections which are in us will not prevent his receiving us, and making us worthy of taking part at this spiritual table; for we do not come to declare that we are perfect or righteous in ourselves; but, on the contrary, by seeking our life in Christ, we confess that we are in death." Communicants are to understand that the Supper "is a medicine for the poor spiritual sick."

Following this invitation, the minister offers an explanation of the promises that are sealed in the sacrament of the Supper. First, communicants are to believe that Christ "is indeed willing to make us partakers of his own body and blood, in order that we may possess him entirely in such a manner that he may live in us, and we in him." Therefore, "although we see only bread and wine, yet let us not doubt that he accomplishes spiritually in our souls all that he shows us externally by these visible signs; in other words, that he is heavenly bread, to feed and nourish us unto life eternal." Christians are also to be grateful for the "infinite goodness of our Saviour, who displays all his riches and blessings at this table, in order to dispense them to us." Calvin encourages believers further to "receive this sacrament as a pledge that the virtue of his death and passion is imputed to us for righteousness, just as if we had suffered it in our own persons."

At this point in the liturgy, the minister is to encourage believers to "raise our hearts and minds on high, where Jesus Christ is, in the glory of his Father, and from whence we look for him at our redemption." Believers are reminded not to look for Christ in the elements as if he were enclosed in the bread and wine. "Let us be contented, then, to have the bread and wine as signs and evidences, spiritually seeking the reality where the word of God promises that we shall find it." At this point, the bread and wine are distributed while psalms are sung or some passage of Scripture relevant to the Supper is read.

Calvin's liturgy is instructive for us today in a number of ways. In many churches, the observance of the Lord's Supper is accompanied by little more than the words of institution. Is this sufficient today? Calvin found it important to include not only explicit warnings to unbelievers but also good news (the gospel) and warm encouragement for believers fighting the world, the flesh, and the devil. It is also instructive that Calvin included a basic explanation of the meaning and significance of the Lord's Supper in the liturgy to be recited every time the Supper was observed. Most of the people of his day had been brought up with the Roman Catholic Mass and were ignorant of the true meaning of the sacrament. While most Christians today may not have been brought up in the Roman Catholic Church, there is still widespread ignorance of the meaning of the Supper that could be rectified by following Calvin's example during our own celebration of the Lord's Supper.

CHAPTER 19

Who Was Arminius?

W. Robert Godfrey

James Arminius (Jacob Harmenszoon) is undoubtedly the most famous theologian ever produced by the Dutch Reformed Church. His fame is a great irony since the Dutch Reformed Church historically was a bastion of strict Calvinism, and Arminius has given his name to a movement very much in opposition to historic Calvinism. Who was this Arminius? What did he teach? Are the differences between Calvinism and Arminianism important today?

Who Was Arminius?

Arminius was born in 1559 in Oudewater, a small city in the province of Holland. Holland was one of seventeen prosperous provinces then known as the Netherlands or the Low Countries, which today are divided into the Netherlands, Belgium, and part of northern France.

In 1559, Philip II was the Catholic king of Spain and sovereign of the Netherlands. Despite Philip's ardent Roman Catholicism and persecuting zeal, Reformation movements had been strong in the Low Countries for decades. In the late 1540s, Calvinism emerged as an attractive, popular religion in the Netherlands, especially in the southern provinces. In 1559, Guido de Bres wrote the first edition of the Belgic Confession, which clearly summarized the Calvinistic faith and set it off from Roman Catholicism and Anabaptism. The Belgic Confession became one of the basic doctrinal standards of Dutch Calvinism.

The decade of the 1560s saw dramatic developments in the Netherlands. The Belgic Confession was published. A storm of iconoclasm broke out, destroying many images in Roman Catholic churches throughout the provinces. Guido de Bres was martyred for the faith. Philip II increasingly alienated the nobility and the people with his fiscal and religious policies. Revolts broke out against royal authority.

By the early 1570s, civil war had begun in earnest against Spain. History knows this revolt as the Eighty Years War, which was not settled until 1648. Growing up in the midst of civil war in state and church, Arminius knew the bitterness of war. In 1575, his mother and other members of his family died at the hands of Spanish troops in a massacre at Oudewater.

In October 1575, Arminius entered the newly founded University of Leiden. He was the twelfth student to enroll in the school that honored the heroic resistance of Leiden to Spanish siege in 1574. He was a talented student and like many students of his day continued his education at other schools, studying from1581 to 1586 in Geneva and Basle.

While in Geneva, Arminius seemed to have some trouble with Theodore Beza, Calvin's staunch successor. The evidence suggests not theological but philosophical differences. Indeed, there is little evidence as to exactly what Arminius's theology was in his student years. What is clear is that when Arminius was ordered to return to the Netherlands in 1586 to take up pastoral responsibilities in Amsterdam, he was given a good letter of recommendation from Beza to the Dutch Reformed Church. Before returning to Amsterdam, Arminius took a trip into Italy to see the sights. This trip was later used by some Calvinists to accuse Arminius of having Roman Catholic sympathies, but such charges were clearly untrue and unfair.

In Amsterdam, he became one of several pastors there, and in 1590 he married Lijsbet Reael, a daughter of one of Holland's most influential men. Arminius became allied to a regent family, and his convictions on the relation of church and state were the same as that of most regents. Indeed, in 1591 he was appointed to a commission to draw up a church order in which the church was given a position clearly subordinate to and dependent on the state. This position (usually called Erastianism) was not held by most clergy in the Dutch Reformed Church. Most followed Calvin's conviction that the church must have a measure of independence from the state, especially in matters of church discipline.

The issue of discipline was a controversial one in the Netherlands. The Belgic Confession had stated that discipline was one of the marks of the true church, and Calvinists strongly believed that the church ought to have the right especially to regulate the teaching of its ministers. But in the Netherlands, the government had at times protected ministers who were targets of church discipline. Arminius's Erastianism distinguished him from most of his ministerial colleagues.

Most of the years of Arminius' pastorate (1587–1603) in Amsterdam were peaceful, although there were some controversies. Arminius preached through the book of Romans, and some of his sermons evoked opposition. In 1591, he preached on Romans 7:14 and following. The standard Calvinist interpretation argued that Paul in these verses is speaking as a regenerate Christian. Romans 7 then presents the Christian's continuing struggle resisting sin in his life. By contrast, Arminius taught that Paul is remembering his previous, unregenerate state. For Arminius, the struggle against sin in Romans 7 is a struggle before conversion. The Calvinists objected sharply to this interpretation, asking how the unregenerate can delight in the law in the inner man (Rom. 7:22). In 1593, Arminius preached on Romans 9, and his sermons on predestination seemed inadequate to many Dutch Calvinists.

Still these controversies passed. When in 1603 two vacancies in the theological faculty at the University of Leiden had to be filled, people of influence in the government thought Arminius ought to be appointed, but strict Calvinists objected, unsettled by too many questions about his orthodoxy. The disagreement was resolved when both sides agreed to allow the one remaining member of the faculty, Franciscus Gomarus, to interview and evaluate Arminius for this position. Gomarus was a strict Calvinist of undoubted orthodoxy. After the interview, Gomarus declared himself satisfied with Arminius, who was then installed as a professor at Leiden.

The reason Gomarus was satisfied with Arminius is unclear. It is as unclear as the reason why Beza recommended him or that his orthodox colleagues in Amsterdam got along with him as well as they did. Perhaps Gomarus failed to ask the right questions or Arminius was not candid with his answers. Another possibility is that Arminius's theology changed significantly after the interview, but it is difficult to speculate.

Within a few years, however, suspicions began to arise about Arminius. People criticized the books he assigned students. Others worried about his private sessions with students. Gomarus became convinced that Arminius was not orthodox on the doctrine of predestination. These suspicions led Arminius's classes to try to examine his doctrine, but the trustees of the university would not permit that. Some said the issues surrounding Arminius's teaching could be resolved only at a national synod. But the government was unwilling to allow a national synod to meet.

Tensions within the church finally led to a government investigation in 1608. In the course of that investigation, Arminius wrote his "Declaration of Sentiments," probably the best summary of his beliefs. Arminius had been insisting that he was only trying to protect the church from the extremes of Calvinism, especially supralapsarianism. Gomarus replied that the issue was not peripheral matters such as supralapsarianism, but rather the Reformation doctrine of justification by faith. With no satisfactory resolution to the matter, Arminius became ill and died in 1609, a minister in good standing in the Dutch Reformed Church.

What Did Arminius Teach?

Arminius is best known theologically for his rejection of the Calvinist doctrine of predestination. In this definition Arminius states his belief that faith is the cause of election: "It is an eternal and gracious decree of God in Christ, by which He determines to justify and adopt believers, and to endow them with eternal life, but to condemn unbelievers, and impenitent persons." But such a position reverses the biblical pattern (e.g., Rom. 8:30; Acts 13:48) in which election is clearly the cause of belief. For orthodox Calvinists, faith is a gift of God. If election—God's purpose to give faith according to his sovereign will—does not precede faith, then faith is not truly a gift.

Arminius expanded his basic definition of predestination in four theses. First, God decreed absolutely that Christ is the Savior who will "destroy sin," "obtain salvation," and "communicate it by his own virtue." Second, God decreed absolutely to save "those who repent and believe, and, in Christ, and for His sake and through Him to effect salvation of such penitents and believers as persevered to the end." Third, God decreed "to administer *in a sufficient and efficacious manner* the means which were necessary for repentance and faith," according to divine wisdom and justice. Fourth, God decreed "to save and damn particular persons based on the foreknowledge of God, by which He knew from all eternity those individuals who would, through his preventing [i.e., prevenient] grace, believe, and through his subsequent grace *would persevere.*"

In his exposition of predestination, Arminius sought to have a theology of grace and avoid all Pelagianism. He stated that "that teacher obtains my highest approbation who ascribes as much as possible to divine grace, provided he so pleads the cause of grace, as not to inflict an injury on the justice of God, and not to take away *the free will of that which is evil.*" Arminius wanted a theology of grace that made God seem fair in all his dealings, and he also wanted to leave room for people to reject grace. Like many others, Arminius thought this kind of theology would make it easier to preach the gospel and emphasize human responsibility. But Arminius ultimately failed to have a true theology of grace. For Arminius, grace is essential and grace is necessary, but God's grace is not absolutely efficacious. Man's response to grace remains the final, decisive factor in salvation. Jesus is no longer the actual Savior of his people. He becomes the one who makes salvation possible. Man's contribution, however sincerely Arminius tried to limit it, became central for salvation.

Arminius also gave faith a different place in his system to the role faith had occupied in earlier Reformed theology. Arminius taught that faith itself was imputed to the sinner for righteousness, whereas the earlier teaching stressed that it was the object of faith—namely, Christ and his righteousness—that was imputed to the sinner. This shift is important because again it shifts the primary focus of salvation from God's work in Christ to man's faith. Arminius can even speak of faith being the one work required of man in the new covenant. This kind of teaching led to Gomarus's charge that Arminius undermined the Protestant doctrine of justification by faith. Arminius's teaching turns faith from an instrument that rests on the work of Christ to a work of man, and tends to change faith from that which receives the righteousness of Christ to that which is righteousness itself.

After the death of Arminius, controversy continued in the Netherlands about the teachings of Arminianism. In 1610, forty-two ministers signed a petition or Remonstrance to the government asking for protection for their Arminian views. The heart of this Remonstrance summarized their theology in five points: conditional election, universal atonement, total depravity, sufficient but resistible grace, and uncertainty about the perseverance of the saints. In 1611, the Calvinists answered with a Contra-Remonstrance. It is surely ironic that through the centuries there has been so much talk of the "Five Points" of Calvinism, when in fact Calvinists did not originate a discussion of five points. Indeed, Calvinism has never been summarized in five points. Calvinism has only offered five responses to the five errors of Arminianism.

Controversy raged in the Netherlands over Arminianism, even threatening civil war. Finally, in 1618, after a change of leadership in the government, a national synod was held at Dordrecht—the Synod of Dort—to judge the Arminian theology. By the time the Synod of Dort met, the issues raised by the Arminians were being widely discussed in the Reformed community throughout Europe. Reformed Christians from Great Britain, France, Switzerland, and Germany expressed great concern for the dangers posed by the Arminian theology.

William Ames, one of the great English Puritans, wrote that Arminianism "is not properly a heresy but a dangerous error in the faith tending to heresy . . . a Pelagian heresy, because it denies the effectual operation of internal grace to be necessary for the effecting of conversion and faith." In this evaluation, Ames rightly saw the conflict between Calvinists and Arminians as related to the conflict between Augustine, the champion of grace, and Pelagius, who insisted that man's will was so free it was possible for him to be saved solely through his own natural abilities.

The Synod of Dort had delegates not only from the Netherlands but also from throughout Europe, the only truly international Reformed synod. The synod rejected the teaching of the Arminians, and in clear and helpful terms presented the orthodox Calvinist position in the Canons of Dort. Unanimously approved by the synod, they were hailed throughout the Reformed churches of Europe as an excellent defense of the faith

The Canons of Dort responded to the five errors of Arminianism and expressed the Calvinist alternative to those errors: (1) God freely and sovereignly determined to save some lost sinners through the righteousness of Christ and to give to his elect the gift of faith; (2) God sent his Son to die as the substitute for his elect, and Christ's death will certainly result in the salvation of his own; (3) man is so utterly lost in sin that without the regenerating grace of God, man cannot desire salvation, repent, believe, or do anything truly pleasing to God; (4) God's grace saves the elect sinner irresistibly since only irresistible grace can overcome man's rebellion; and (5) God in mercy preserves the gift of faith in his elect to ensure that the good work he began in them will certainly come to completion in their salvation.

Do the Differences Between Arminians and Calvinists Matter Today?

Many argue that the differences between Calvinists and Arminians no longer matter. After all, some argue, Arminius lived four hundred years ago. Are his views still important and influential? The answer to that question must be a resounding yes, as Arminianism is still influential in evangelical and Pentecostal circles. Indeed, Arminianism today usually goes much further in emphasizing free will than Arminius did or would ever have approved of doing.

Some downplay the differences between Arminians and Calvinists out of an activism that is rather indifferent to theology. Such activists often argue that, with so much to do for Christ in the world and with so much opposition to Christianity in general, theological differences must be minimized. It is certainly true that the theological differences between Calvinists and Arminians should not be overemphasized. Most Arminians have been and are evangelical Christians. But the differences between Calvinists and Arminians are important precisely for the work that all want to do for Christ. What is the work that needs to be done and how will it be done? The answers to those questions depend very much on whether man has a free will or not. Does one seek to entertain and move the emotions and will of men whose salvation is ultimately in their own hands? Or does one present the claims of God as clearly as possible, while recognizing that fruit ultimately comes only from the Holy Spirit? Those kinds of concerns will affect the ways in which Christians worship, witness, serve, and live.

Some argue that the differences between Calvinism and Arminianism are unimportant because the theological terms of the controversy were wrong or are now outmoded. They argue that just as progress has been made in so many fields, so theological progress has transcended the old controversies. This claim may be an attractive one until it is closely examined, and then such a claim proves to be false: either salvation is entirely the work of God, or it is partially the work of man. There is no way to "transcend" this reality. On close examination, those efforts to transcend Calvinism are at best other forms of Arminianism.

Some try to split the difference between Arminianism and Calvinism. They say something like, "I want to be 75 percent Calvinist and 25 percent Arminian." If they mean that literally, then they are 100 percent Arminian since giving any determinative place to human will is Arminian. Usually they mean that they want to stress the grace of God and human responsibility. If that is what they mean, then they can be 100 percent Calvinist for Calvinism does teach that God's grace is entirely the cause of salvation and that man is responsible before God to hear and heed the call to repentance and faith.

Today, some Calvinists are hesitant to stress their distinctives because they feel that they are such a small minority within the church. They must remember that in the providence of God, Calvinism has gone through varying periods of flourishing and declining. God does not call his people to be successful; he calls them to be faithful.

Calvinists should still confidently teach the sovereign grace of God as it was summarized in the Canons of Dort. They should do so because, according to this author and the witness of Reformed Christians in church history, Calvinism is both biblical and helpful. It is helpful because in a world that is often foolishly optimistic and man centered, Calvinism teaches the seriousness of sin and the glories of the redemptive work of Christ for sinners. In the face of so much religious shallowness, the profundity of Calvinism is needed. Shallow religion produces shallow Christian living. The depths of God's grace should lead Christians to live gratefully, humbly, joyfully, and carefully before God. Today, the church of Jesus Christ does not need less Calvinism. Rather it needs to recover a forceful and faithful commitment to the God-centered biblical message.

CHAPTER 20

Calvin and Jonathan Edwards

Paul Helm

In his *Freedom of the Will* Jonathan Edwards wrote, "I should not take it at all amiss, to be called a Calvinist, for distinction's sake: though I utterly disclaim a dependence on Calvin, or believing the doctrines which I hold, because he believed and taught them; and cannot justly be charged with believing everything just as he taught."

Edwards lived in an age different from Calvin, and he had different projects. Not to further an "orderly" reformation of the church by the word of God, but to confront the rationalism of his day with its own weapons—with the help of the philosophy of his hero John Locke (theologically, an Arminian), as well as that of Sir Isaac Newton (a deist), and with a robust and self-confident appeal (when necessary) to "reason" and a remorseless use of logic. His project was to turn the intellectual weapons of "enlightened" thinkers against themselves, and to find in these very weapons support for the Reformed orthodoxy and Puritanism of New England. So he largely replaced the scholasticism of another of his heroes, Peter van Mastrict, with this more "modern" outlook. So why, with all these changes, did Edwards not take it amiss to be called a Calvinist?

To try to answer that question, we must note two or three factors. To begin with, though Calvin had been widely translated into English and the translations were best-sellers in Elizabethan England, by Edwards's time his personal influence among Anglophone readers had faded. It is almost impossible to find a direct quotation from Calvin in Edwards's voluminous writings, hence the appropriateness of Edwards's statement that he did not treat Calvin as a personal authority. But, he says, was nevertheless a Calvinist "for distinction's sake." What did he mean?

The term "Calvinist" had been coined by Lutherans who objected to John Calvin's distinctive view of the "real presence" of Christ at the Supper. But then, after Calvin's death and with the onset of the Arminian movement on the continent of Europe and through Laudian influence in England, "Calvinism" became colored and identified by the agenda of the Arminian conflict. Calvinism came to refer to a set of tenets defined in terms of the struggle with the Arminians. That was the "distinction"—between Arminian and Calvinist—for the sake of which Edwards was prepared to be known as a Calvinist. Calvinism came to have an exclusively soteriological connotation; Calvin's view of church and state, together with his ecclesiology—the whole of the matter of Book 4 of the *Institutes*—was largely lost from view. This was the era of "doctrinal Calvinists," when—along with Presbyterians and Episcopalians—Baptists and Congregationalists could equally be "Calvinists."

Edwards was a Calvinist in this sense: restricted in one way, broadened in another. What did this mean in practice? One thing it meant was Edwards's adherence to the Puritan theology of his forbears, such as Shepherd and Norton and Owen and Flavel and their contemporaries in Holland. So the parameters of Edwards's great works—*Religious Affections*, *Freedom of the Will*, and *Great Christian Doctrine of Original Sin*—were set by this "Calvinist" theology.

Whereas Calvin was at home in the philosophy and the culture of the ancient world—the world of Plato, Cicero, and Augustine, for example—Edwards had a modern outlook. His fear was Arminianism; but beyond that, deism. And one recurring theme in his writings is an attempt to make God immediate to his readers. Anyone who thought he could keep God at a distance by the exercise of his free will, or by participating in the half-way covenant (the invention of his grandfather Solomon Stoddard), or who thought that God was bound by the iron laws of the newly discovered physics, was in for a shock. The title of his best-known, notorious sermon "Sinners in the Hands of an Angry God" contains the key. We are all "in the hands of" God, whether we like it or not. Our efforts to shake free of his fingers will fail. But the Savior beckons. This was Calvin's and the Reformers' emphasis on the sovereignty of God's grace, but with a new twist.

Edwards conveyed this same message, whether it was through the pulpits of Northampton and Stockbridge in Massachusetts, or through his writings reaching the studies and libraries of the East Coast and of Europe. Whether, as he came to articulate this message, his project was a success, continues to be debated. Did he so stress divine immediacy as to undermine the reality and efficacy of created causes? Perhaps he did. Did he so stress the divine sovereignty as to articulate a form of panentheism? Perhaps he did. What cannot be doubted is that he attempted to rearticulate the tenets of "Calvinism" in a trenchant and confident way that has not been matched since.

CHAPTER 21

The Journey to Geneva:
Calvin and Karl Barth

Peter D. Anders

In 1909, Karl Barth became assistant pastor to the German congregation in Geneva. Preaching in the very auditorium and from the same pulpit as Calvin himself, and in the city then commemorating the 400th anniversary of Calvin's birth, Barth couldn't help but take a closer look at the theology of this celebrated Reformer. "It may have been the spirit of the place," he recalls, "which caused me to deepen the experience I had gained from reading Schleiermacher again and again by making considerable inroads into Calvin's *Institutes*."[1] Barth did not experience any sudden conversion to Calvinism. He initially engaged Calvin from the perspective of his liberal theological education, seeking to "combine idealist and romantic theology with the theology of the Reformation."[2] His early preaching focused on the Christian ethical task of manifesting the kingdom of God through the reformation of society, preaching he would later admit was also at odds with the Reformer's teaching: "I'm afraid that Calvin would hardly have been very pleased at the sermons which I preached in his pulpit then."[3]

Although there are important criticisms concerning Barth's theological discontinuities with Calvin—and concerning Barth's perception of later Reformed theology's discontinuities with Calvin—it should not be overlooked that Barth's early theological development was greatly influenced by Calvin's theology. This *theological* journey to Geneva began in earnest only after Barth left Geneva. Through the difficult pastorate in Safenwil, the disillusionment of the First World War, and the frantic professorate at Göttingen, his determined journey toward Calvinism is representative of many who have traveled a similar road

---

[1] Eberhard Busch, *Karl Barth: His Life from Letters and Autobiographical Texts*, trans. John Bowden (Grand Rapids: Eerdmans, 1994), 57.

[2] Busch, 57.

[3] Busch, 52–54.

since the Reformation. With honesty and insight, Barth brings into focus the face of Calvin's theology that compels such a journey.

Barth was confronted with the disturbing strangeness of Calvin's theology. As he famously expressed in a 1922 letter to his lifelong friend, Eduard Thurneysen:

> Calvin is a cataract, a primeval forest, a demonic power, something directly down from the Himalayas, absolutely Chinese, strange, mythological; I lack completely the means, the suction cups, even to assimilate this phenomenon, not to speak of presenting it adequately. . . . I could gladly and profitably set myself down and spend all the rest of my life just with Calvin.[4]

Yet, while he sought to deal with this strangeness of Calvin, Barth also recognized that it is precisely in the challenge of its unfamiliarity that this theological orientation is so valuable: "The little bit of 'Reformed theology' that I teach is really nothing in comparison to the trumpet blast which needs to be blown in our sick time."[5]

In Barth's view, what is so strange about Calvinism is essentially what is so strange about the theology of the Reformation itself.

> [It] did not fall victim to the illusion that gripped the whole of the middle ages and that has gained force again in the modern age, the illusion that there is a continuous path that leads step by step from an earthly city of God to the kingdom of heaven. For him [Calvin] the divine was always divine and the human always human.[6]

Calvin affirms both theology and ethics, yet always together in the serious and consistent application of the critical principle of God's absolute and glorious sovereignty. Here Barth recognized that in Calvin's theology it is "the glory of God itself that brought disaster to the theology of glory."[7] He saw in Calvin the heart of the Reformation's discovery that theology has to do with *God*.

> The secret was simply this, that it took this theme seriously in all its distinctiveness, that it names God God, that it lets God be God, the one object that by no bold human grasping or inquiry or approach can be simply one object among many others. God *is*. *He* lives. *He* judges and blesses. *He* slays and makes alive [cf. 1 Sam. 2:6]. *He* is the Creator and Redeemer and Lord.[8]

---

[4] *Revolutionary Theology in the Making: Barth-Thurneysen Correspondence 1914–25*, trans. James D. Smart (London: Epworth Press, 1964), 101.

[5] *Revolutionary Theology*, 101.

[6] Karl Barth, *The Theology of John Calvin*, trans. Geoffrey W. Bromily (Grand Rapids: Eerdmans, 1995), 201.

[7] Barth, 39.

[8] Barth, 39.

For Barth, Calvinism is not a theology of symmetrical completeness, rational subtleties, or pietistic introspection, but a theology that continuously makes problems for us, asks questions, and establishes tensions that lead us from law to gospel, from what is impossible for humans to what is alone possible with God.

What Barth found so compelling in Calvin's theology is what others also have found traveling the same road. Calvin's theology is a passionate and creative drive toward synthesis, yet with no other agenda save the glory of God.[9] It is grounded in the truths of Holy Scripture, yet truths that are only apprehended through the Spirit and not merely through the careful employment of scientific methods of exegesis.[10] It possesses an apologetic power, yet "not an apologetics that seeks to justify Christianity before courts outside itself, for example, philosophy or science," but one that "proceeds with the silent summons: Those who have ears to hear, let them hear! [Mark 4:9]."[11]

How far a Reformed and evangelical theologian can walk with Barth, and how far Barth actually walks with Calvin, are important contemporary issues. While this debate continues, so will Barth's theological journey to Geneva continue to represent a road many others have traveled, as it brings into focus a face of Calvin's theology that will compel many more to follow.

---

[9] Barth, 159–60.

[10] Karl Barth, *The Epistle to the Romans*, 6th ed., trans. Edwin C. Hoskyns (Oxford: Oxford University Press, 1968), 18.

[11] Barth, *The Theology of John Calvin*, 159.

CHAPTER 22

Going to Church with the Reformers

Michael S. Horton

Many of us were raised to believe that we had all the answers (whatever they were) and that Roman Catholicism believes in Mary and the pope rather than in Jesus and the Bible, and in salvation by works rather than grace. And yet, as the surveys demonstrate, we don't really know what we believe or why we believe it—at least beyond a few slogans. If someone asked the question in the correct form, we could possibly give the right answer to some of the big ones. However, a rising generation now is indistinguishable in its beliefs from Mormons, Unitarians, or those who check the "spiritual but not religious" box. We're told that "Moralistic Therapeutic Deism" is the working theology of most Americans, including evangelicals. So when it comes to authority and salvation—the two issues at the heart of the Reformation's concern—Protestantism today (mainline and evangelical) seems increasingly remote from anything that the Reformers would have recognized as catholic and evangelical faith and practice.

In my "cage phase" (when emerging Reformed zealots should be quarantined for a while), I read from a sixteenth-century confession the section on grace and justification. The audience was a rather large group of fellow students at a Christian college. "Do you think we could sign this statement today?" I asked. Several replied, "No, it's too Calvinistic." That was interesting, because I was quoting the Sixth Session of the Council of Trent, which anathematized the Reformation's teaching that justification was by Christ's merits alone, imputed to sinners through faith alone. I didn't quote the whole section, but only the part that affirmed that we are saved by grace and that our cooperation in the process of salvation—even our will to believe—requires God's grace.

You have to dig beneath the sweeping slogans and generalizations; it's precisely in the details—where many eyes glaze over—that the massive differences between Rome and the Reformation appear.

Coming to Terms with the Church's Past

Pelagianism—the view that we are saved by our own choice and effort apart from grace—was condemned by several ancient church councils and bishops of Rome. Even semi-Pelagianism—the view that we make the first move by free will and then grace assists us—was also condemned. For example, the Second Council of Orange in 529 even anathematized those who say that we're born again by saying a prayer, when it is only God's grace that gives us the will to pray for Christ's mercy.

Yet the Latin Church always struggled with the Pelagian virus in varying degrees. Medieval leaders such as Archbishop Thomas Bradwardine wrote treatises titled "Against the New Pelagians." Thomas Aquinas emphasized the priority of God's grace in predestination and regeneration. Luther's own mentor and head of the Augustinian Order in Germany, Johann von Staupitz, wrote "A Treatise on God's Eternal Election" in which he expressed concern that free will and works-righteousness had begun to undermine faith in God's grace in Christ.

By the time of the Reformation, popular piety was corrupted by countless innovations and superstitions. Luther was first aroused to arms by the arrival of a preacher with papal authority to dispense indulgences (time off in purgatory) for money that would help build St. Peter's Basilica in Rome. The Reformation couldn't be dismissed, precisely because it resonated with so many who knew that Rome had drifted far from its ancient moorings into myriad corruptions. Awakened by the new biblical scholarship, many of Europe's leading Renaissance humanists became convinced that the Reformers were correct in their interpretation and application of Scripture to the church's condition.

The Council of Trent, which anathematized the Reformation's convictions, affirmed the importance of grace going before all of our willing and running. Nevertheless, it condemned the view that, once regenerated by grace alone in baptism (our first justification), we cannot merit an increase of justification and final justification by our works. Trent said in no uncertain terms that Christ's merits are not sufficient for salvation.

Everything turned on different understandings of grace:

Rome: Grace is God's medicine infused to help us cooperate
Reformers: Grace is God's favor toward us in Christ

This in turn resulted in two different doctrines of justification:

Rome: Justification is a process of inner renewal
Reformers: Justification is a declaration based on the imputation of Christ's righteousness alone

Pelagian Revivalism in America

As Presbyterian theologians Charles Hodge and B. B. Warfield pointed out, the explicit convictions of the famous evangelist of the Second Great Awakening, Charles G. Finney, were much further down the Pelagian road than Rome. Finney denied justification through faith alone in Christ's merits alone. He based this on a rejection of original sin, the substitutionary atonement, and the supernatural character of the new birth. Consequently, his "new measures"—i.e., methods whose only criterion was whether they were "fit to convert sinners with"—replaced the divinely ordained means of grace, and his "protracted meetings" (revivals) radically altered the shape of most Protestant services and ministries in America. As Arminian theologian Roger Olson has pointed out, much of evangelical preaching today isn't really Arminian but is closer to Pelagianism.

The result is a distinctly Protestant kind of hazy moralism (works-righteousness) and an equally hazy notion that somehow Rome believes we're saved by works rather than grace. It can be a fatal combination, especially when people realize that Rome does in fact believe in original sin and the necessity of grace—more, in fact, than many who call themselves evangelicals.

Too Catholic? Welcome to the Reformation

Now we see many evangelicals being attracted to the Reformation's emphases, discovering a tradition that is both catholic and evangelical without many of the trappings of evangelicalism. As their encounter with the Reformation widens beyond election and justification, they bump into views that sound at first "too Catholic." *Sola scriptura* (by Scripture alone) doesn't mean that creeds and confessions and the decisions of church councils and assemblies don't have any authority. Although Scripture alone has *magisterial* authority, these faithful summaries of Scripture nevertheless have a *ministerial* authority. *Sola gratia* (by grace alone) is not set over against the regular ministry of preaching and the sacraments; rather, these are the means of grace through which the Spirit delivers Christ with all of his benefits. It's not Roman Catholic, to be sure, but to many evangelical brothers and sisters it sounds "too Catholic." Reformed and Lutheran churches include the children of believers in baptism, and liturgy, orders and offices, discipline, and the accountability of local churches to one another in wider assemblies. These characteristics of Reformed ecclesiology also strike many evangelicals, again, as "too Catholic."

That makes some sense. After all, despite its critique of the magisterial authority assigned to the pope officially at the Council of Trent, the Reformation differs at least as much from the freelance ministry of "anointed" preachers who act like popes, only without any accountability to the magisterium.

Churches of the Reformation not only challenged the hierarchical government of the Roman Church, but also the sects that followed their own self-appointed prophets. Yes, said the Reformers, individual members and ministers are accountable to the church in its local and broader assemblies. God doesn't speak directly to individuals (including preachers) today, but through his word as it is interpreted by the wider body of pastors and elders in solemn assemblies. Tragically, evangelical hierarchies today are more prone to authoritarian abuses and personal idiosyncrasies than one finds in Rome.

Reformation Churches and Rome

Dislodged from confidence in Pastor Bob and the givens of the evangelical subculture, Christians need to realize that the Reformation was, well, a *reformation* and not a revolution or a "do over." Luther was not the founder of a new church but an evangelical-catholic reformer. As expressed in the title of one of the great works of Elizabethan Puritanism—William Perkins's *The Reformed Catholic*—there is a deep continuity within the undivided church.

On the Roman Catholic TV network (EWTN) recently, Fr. Pacwa interviewed a professor who had graduated from Wheaton and Trinity Evangelical Divinity School. Becoming more interested in the Reformation, the professor pursued a PhD at the University of Iowa focusing on the theology of Calvin. The title of this segment was "How Calvin Made Me a Catholic." The Reformers were eager to show their connection to the pre-Reformation church. They did not believe that the church had basically gone underground—much less extinct—between Paul and Luther. Rather, they argued that a gradual decay had been accelerated by recent emphases and innovations that needed to be corrected. Calvin is recognized by Roman Catholics and Protestants alike as a scholar of the early fathers, and his *Institutes* and commentaries are replete with citations from writers of the East and the West. The great theologians of Reformed and Lutheran orthodoxy engaged the ancient and medieval theologians as their own, yet these were always subject to critique as well as approval on the basis of their interpretation of Scripture according to a shared confession.

So I can understand why some evangelicals find the Reformation "too Catholic" or, weary of Protestantism in any form, look back to their "Reformation episode" as a gateway drug to the mysteries of Rome. For a long time now, American Protestants have defined their faith and practice in reaction against Rome. Now a growing number are defining their faith and practice in reaction against evangelicalism. "If the Reformers were alive today, they'd be Roman Catholic before they would join an evangelical sect." I've heard that sentiment on more than one occasion.

Which Church Would the Reformers Join?

However, the men and women who risked their lives in the sixteenth century to defend the sufficiency of Scripture and the sufficiency of Christ would refuse the false choice between a chaotic Protestantism and a Roman Catholicism that still maintains the theology of Trent. It would be perverse to imagine that Luther or Calvin would find Rome more acceptable today than it was in their day. Even in the much-publicized "Joint Declaration on Justification," it was the mainline Lutherans who surrendered their confessional convictions; Rome did not change any of its official positions. And in any case, the Vatican has made it clear that this consultation in no way has any magisterial weight.

Is the growing interest in Reformation theology among younger evangelicals going to mean that, for some, Geneva, Wittenberg, and Canterbury will be a rest stop before moving on to Rome or Antioch? I suspect there will be this kind of trend of some sort in the future. We dare not treat those struggling with these issues among us as "necessary casualties," a minimal loss compared to net gains. Pastoral love, wisdom, and patience will be more valuable than gold. There are real questions here—existential, exegetical, theological, and practical—with real lives being affected. It's not a time for us to grandstand or to shoot from the hip with speculations about peoples' motives or character. Rather, we should strive to make a persuasive case, leaving the results to the Spirit of truth.

PART III: THE CONSEQUENCES

The Crisis of Evangelical Christianity: Reformation Essentials

Michael S. Horton

In May 1989, a conference jointly sponsored by the National Association of Evangelicals and Trinity Evangelical Divinity School was held at the Trinity campus in Illinois. Dubbed a consultation on Evangelical Affirmations, the meeting revealed more than it settled. In the published addresses (Zondervan, 1990), Carl F. H. Henry, the dean of American evangelicalism, set the tone for book with his opening line: "The term 'evangelical' has taken on conflicting nuances in the twentieth century. Wittingly or unwittingly, evangelical constituencies no less than their critics have contributed to this confusion and misunderstanding." He warned that "evangelical" was being understood, not according to scriptural teaching and "the theological 'ought,'" but according to the sociological and empirical "is." In other words, Henry was disturbed that evangelicalism is increasingly being defined by its most recent trends rather than by its normative theological identity. Author after author (presumably, speaker after speaker) echoed the same fears that before long "evangelical" will be useless as any meaningful identification.

The term itself derives from the Greek word *euangelion*, translated "gospel," and it became a noun when the Protestant Reformers began their work of bringing the "one holy, catholic and apostolic church" back to that message by which and for which it was created. People still used other labels, such as "Lutheran" and "Reformed," and later, "Puritans," "Pietists," and "Wesleyans." Nevertheless, the belief was that the same gospel that had united the "evangelicals" against Rome's errors could also unite them against the creeping naturalism and secularism of the Enlightenment in the eighteenth century. The so-called "Evangelical Awakening" in Britain coincided with America's own "Great Awakening," as Wesley, Whitefield, Edwards, Tennant, and so many others centered their preaching on the atonement. Later, of course, Wesley's zeal for Arminian emphases divided the work in Britain, but the Reformation emphases were clearly and unambiguously articulated in the Great Awakening.

Out of this heritage, those today who call themselves "evangelicals" (or who are in these churches but might not know that they are in this tradition) are heirs also to the Second Great Awakening. Radically altering the "evangel" from a concern with the object of faith, the Second Great Awakening and the revivalism that emerged from it focused on the act and experience of faith, in dependence on the proper "excitements," as Finney and others expressed it, to trigger the right response. In our estimation, this Second Great Awakening was the most important seismic shift in American religious history. Although the Reformation emphases of sin and grace continued to exercise some influence, they were being constantly revised to make the "gospel" more acceptable to those who thought they could pull themselves up by their own bootstraps.

Only in the last decade of the twentieth century did many of the movement's mainstream leaders consider the loss of an evangelical substance. No longer is the evangel the focus of the movement's identity, but it is now known more by a subculture—a collection of political, moral, and social causes, and an acute interest in rather exotic notions about the end-times. At a loss for words, one friend answered a man's question "Who are the evangelicals?" with the reply "They're people who like Billy Graham."

It is at this point that those of us who are heirs to the Reformation—which bequeathed to evangelicalism a distinct theological identity that has been since lost—call attention once more to the *solas* (*only* or *alone*) that framed the entire sixteenth-century debate: "*Only* Scripture," "*Only* Christ," "*Only* grace," "*Only* faith," and "To God *alone* be glory."

Sola Scriptura: Our Only Foundation

Many critics of the Reformation have attempted to portray it as the invitation to individualism, as people discover for themselves from the Bible what they will and will not believe. "Never mind the church. Away with creeds and the church's teaching office! We have the Bible and that's enough." But this was not the Reformers' doctrine of *sola scriptura*—only Scripture. Luther said of individualistic approaches to the Bible, "That would mean that each man would go to hell in his own way."

On one side, the Reformers faced the Roman Church, which believed its teaching authority to be final and absolute. The Roman Catholics said that tradition can be a form of infallible revelation even in the contemporary church;

one needs an infallible Bible and an infallible interpreter of that sacred book. On the other side were the Anabaptist radicals, who believed that not only did they not need the teaching office of the church, but they really didn't seem to need the Bible either, since the Holy Spirit spoke to them—or at least to their leaders—directly. Instead of one pope, Anabaptism produced numerous "infallible" messengers who heard the voice of God. Against both positions, the Reformation insisted that the Bible was the sole final authority in determining doctrine and life. In interpreting it, the whole church must be included, including the laity, and they must be guided by the teachers in the church. Those teachers, though not infallible, should have considerable interpretive authority. The creeds were binding and the newly Reformed Protestant communions quickly drafted confessions of faith that received the assent of the whole church, not merely the teachers.

Today, we are faced with similar challenges even within evangelicalism. On one hand, there is the tendency to say, as Luther characterized the problem, "I go to church, hear what my priest says, and him I believe." Calvin complained to Cardinal Sadoleto that the sermons before the Reformation were part trivial pursuit, part storytelling. Today, this same process of "dumbing down" has meant that we are, in George Gallup's words, "a nation of biblical illiterates." Perhaps we have a high view of the Bible's inspiration: 80 percent of adult Americans believe that the Bible is the literal or inspired word of God, but 30 percent of the teenagers who attend church regularly do not even know why Easter is celebrated. "The decline in Bible reading," says Gallup, "is due in part to the widely held conviction that the Bible is inaccessible, and to less emphasis on religious training in the churches." Just as Rome's infallibility rested on the belief that the Bible itself was difficult, obscure, and confusing, so today people want the "net breakdown" from the professionals: what does it mean for me, and how will it help me and make me happy? But those who read the Bible for more than devotional meditations know how clear it is—at least on the main points it addresses—and how it ends up making religion less confusing and obscure. Today, the Bible—especially in mainline Protestant churches—is a mysterious book that can be understood only by a small cadre of biblical scholars who are "in the know."

But we have the other side too. There is a popular trend in many "evangelical" churches to emphasize direct communication with the Holy Spirit apart from the word. In these circles, tradition and the teaching ministry of the church through the ages are treated not only as fallible (as the Reformers believed) but as objects of mockery. The sentiments of Thomas Muntzer, who complained that Luther was "one of our scribes who wants to send the Holy Ghost off to college," would find a primetime spot on the nation's leading evangelical radio and television broadcasts. Calvin said of these folks, "When the fanatics boast extravagantly of the Spirit, the tendency is always to bury the Word of God so they may make room for their own falsehoods."

Christianity is not a spirituality but a religion. Wade Clark Roof and other sociologists have pointed out that evangelicals today are indistinguishable from the general cultural trends, especially when it comes to preferring to think of their relationship to God more in terms of an experience than in terms of a relationship that is mediated through words. Ours is a visual or image-based society, much like the Middle Ages. Yet Christianity can flourish only through words, ideas, beliefs, announcements, and arguments. There can be no communication with God apart from the written and living word. Everything in the Christian faith depends on the spoken and written word delivered by God to us through the prophets and apostles.

Further, *sola scriptura* meant that the word of God was sufficient. Although Rome believed it was infallible, the official theology was shaped more by the insights of Plato and Aristotle than by Scripture. Similarly today, psychology threatens to reshape the understanding of the self, as even in the evangelical pulpit sin becomes "addiction"; the fall as an event is replaced with one's "victim" status; salvation is increasingly communicated as mental health, peace of mind, and self-esteem, and my personal happiness and self-fulfillment are center stage rather than God's holiness and mercy, justice and love, and glory and compassion. Does the Bible define the human problem and its solution? Or when we really want facts, do we turn somewhere else, to a modern secular authority who will really carry weight in my sermon? Of course, the Bible will be cited to bolster the argument. Political ideology, sociology, marketing, and other secular "authorities" must never be allowed priority in answering questions the Bible addresses. That is, in part, what this affirmation means, and evangelicals today seem as confused on this point as was the medieval church.

Solus Christus: Our Only Mediator

In the Middle Ages, the minister was seen as having a special relationship with God, as he mediated God's grace and forgiveness through the sacraments. But there were other challenges. We often think of our own age as unique, with its pluralism and the advent of so many religions. But not too long before the Reformation, the Renaissance thinker Petrarch was calling for an Age of the Spirit in which all religions would be united. Many Renaissance minds were convinced that there was a saving revelation of God in nature and that, therefore, Christ was not the only way. The fascination with pagan philosophy encouraged the idea that natural religion offered a great deal—indeed, even salvation—to those who did not know Christ.

The Reformation was, more than anything else, an assault on faith in humanity and a defense of the idea that God alone reveals himself and saves us. We do not find him; he finds us. That emphasis was the cause of the cry, "Christ alone!" Jesus was the only way of knowing what God is really like, the only way of entering into a relationship with him as Father instead of judge, and the only way of being saved from his wrath.

Today, once more, this affirmation is in trouble. According to University of Virginia sociologist James Hunter, 35 percent of evangelical seminarians deny that faith in Christ is absolutely necessary. According to George Barna, that is the same figure for conservative, evangelical Protestants in America: "God will save all good people when they die, regardless of whether they've trusted in Christ," they agreed.

Eighty-five percent of American adults believe that they will stand before God to be judged. They believe in hell, but only 11 percent think they might go there. R.C. Sproul observed that to the degree people think they are good enough to pass divine inspection, and are oblivious to the holiness of God, to that extent they will not see Christ as necessary. That is why over one-fourth of the "born-again" evangelicals surveyed agreed with a statement one would think might raise red flags, even for those who might agree with the same thing more subtly put: "If a person is good, or does enough good things for others during life, they will earn a place in heaven." Furthermore, when asked whether they agreed with the following statement: "Christians, Jews, Muslims, Buddhists, and others all pray to the same God, even though they use different names for that God," two-thirds of the evangelicals didn't find that objectionable. Barna observes "how little difference there is between the responses of those who regularly attend church services and those who are unchurched." One respondent, an Independent Fundamentalist, said, "What is important in their case is that they have conformed to the law of God as they know it in their hearts."

But this cultural influence toward relativism is not only apparent in the masses; it is self-consciously asserted by some of evangelicalism's own teachers. Clark Pinnock states, "The Bible does not teach that one must confess the name of Jesus Christ to be saved. The issue God cares about is the direction of the heart, not the content of their theology." For those of us who have some inkling of the direction of their heart (see Jer. 17:9), that might not be as comforting as Pinnock assumes.

To say *solus Christus* does not mean that we do not believe in the Father or the Spirit, but it does insist that Christ is the only incarnate self-revelation of God and redeemer of humanity. The Holy Spirit does not draw attention to himself but leads us to Christ, in whom we find our peace with God.

Sola Gratia: Our Only Method

The reason we must stay with the Scriptures is because it is the only place where we are told that we are saved by the unprovoked and undeserved acceptance of God. In *The Sound of Music*, Maria, bewildered by the captain's sudden attraction to her, rhapsodizes, "Nothing comes from nothing, nothing ever could. So somewhere in my youth or childhood, I must have done something good." Deep down, human nature is convinced that there is a way for us to save ourselves. We may indeed require divine assistance. Perhaps God will have to show us the way, or even send a messenger to lead us back, but we can actually follow the plan and pull it off.

The law is in us by nature. We were born with a conscience that tells us we are condemned by that law, but our reason concludes immediately that the answer to that self-condemnation is to do better next time. But the gospel is not in nature. It is not lodged somewhere in our hearts, our minds, our wills, or our emotions. It is an announcement that comes to us as foolishness and our first response, like that of Sarah, is to laugh. The story is told of a man who fell off a cliff, but on his way down managed to grab a branch. He broke his fall and saved his life, but before long he realized he could not pull himself back up onto the ledge. Finally, he called out, "Is there anyone up there who can help me?" To his surprise, a voice boomed back, "I am here and I can help you, but first you're going to have to let go of that branch." Thinking for a moment about his options, the man looked back up and shot back, "Is there anyone else up there who can help me?" We are looking for someone to save us by helping us save ourselves. But the law tells us that even our best works are like filthy rags; the gospel tells us that it is something in God and his character (kindness, goodness, mercy, compassion) and not something in us (a good will, a decision, an act, an open heart, and so on) that saves us.

Many in the medieval church believed that God saved by grace, but they also believed that their own free will and cooperation with grace was "their part" in salvation. The popular medieval phrase was, "God will not deny his grace to those who do what they can." Today's version, of course, is, "God helps those who help themselves." Over half the evangelicals surveyed thought this was a direct biblical quotation and 84 percent thought that it was a biblical idea, that percentage rising with church attendance at evangelical churches.

On the eve of the Reformation a number of church leaders, including bishops and archbishops, had been complaining of creeping Pelagianism (a heresy that denies original sin and the absolute need for grace). Nevertheless, that heresy was never tolerated in its full expression. However, today it is tolerated and even promoted in liberal Protestantism generally, and even in many evangelical circles.

In Pelagianism, Adam's sin is not imputed to us, nor is Christ's righteousness. Adam is a bad example, not the representative in whom we stand guilty. Similarly, Christ is a good example, not the representative in whom we stand righteous. How much of our preaching centers on following Christ—as important as that is—rather than on his person and work? How often do we hear about his work *in* us compared to his work *for* us?

Charles Finney, the nineteenth-century revivalist, is a patron saint for most evangelicals. And yet he denied original sin, substitutionary atonement, justification, and the need for regeneration by the Holy Spirit. In short, Finney was a Pelagian. This belief in human nature, so prominent in the Enlightenment, wrecked the evangelical doctrine of grace among the older evangelical Protestant denominations (now called "mainline"), and we see where that has taken them. Conservative evangelicals are heading down the same path and have had this human-centered, works-centered emphasis for some time.

The statistics bear us out here, unfortunately, and again the leaders help substantiate the error. Norman Geisler writes, "God would save all men if he could. He will save the greatest number actually achievable without violating their free will."

Sola Fide: Our Only Means

The Reformers said that it is not enough to say we are saved by grace alone, for even many medieval scholars held that view, including Luther's own mentor. Rome viewed grace more as a substance than as an attitude of favor on God's part. In other words, grace was like water poured into the soul. It assisted the believer in his growth toward salvation. The purpose of grace was to transform a sinner into a saint, a bad person into a good person, a rebel into an obedient son or daughter.

The Reformers searched the Scriptures and found a missing ingredient in the medieval notion of grace. To be sure, there were many passages that spoke of grace transforming us and conforming us to the image of Christ. But there were other passages, too, that used a Greek word meaning "to *declare* righteous," not "to *make* righteous." The problem was that the Latin Bible everyone was using mistranslated the former and combined the two Greek words into one. Erasmus and other Renaissance humanists "laid the egg that Luther hatched" by cleaning up the translation mistakes.

According to Scripture, God *declares* a person righteous before that person actually begins to become righteous. Therefore, the declaration is not in response to any spiritual or moral advances within the individual, but is an imputation of the perfect righteousness that God immediately requires of everyone who is united to Christ by faith alone. When a person trusts Christ, that very moment he or she is clothed in his perfect holiness, so that even though the believer is still sinful, he or she is judged by God as blameless.

This apostolic doctrine, proclaimed to Abraham and his offspring, has fallen on hard times again in church history. Not only do most Christians today not hear about the doctrine of justification by grace alone through faith alone, many cannot even define it. Although justification is the doctrine by which, according to the evangelical Reformers, "the church stands or falls," it has been challenged. Finney openly declared,

> The doctrine of an imputed righteousness is another gospel. For sinners to be forensically pronounced just is impossible and absurd. The doctrine of an imputed righteousness is founded on a most false and nonsensical assumption, representing the atonement, rather than the sinner's own obedience, as the ground of his justification, which has been a sad occasion of stumbling to many.

In our own time, Clark Pinnock wonders why we cannot embrace the notion of purgatory:

> I cannot deny that most believers end their earthly lives imperfectly sanctified and far from complete. [Most? How about all!] I cannot deny the wisdom in possibly giving them an opportunity to close the gap and grow to maturity after death. Obviously, evangelicals have not thought this question out. [We have: It is called the Reformation.] It seems to me that we already have the possibility of a doctrine of purgatory. Our Wesleyan and Arminian thinking may need to be extended in this direction. Is a doctrine of purgatory not required by our doctrine of holiness?[1]

Russell Spittler, a Pentecostal theologian at Fuller Seminary, reflects on Luther's phrase concerning justification: *simul iustus et peccator* (simultaneously just and sinner):

---

[1] Clark H. Pinnock, "The Conditional View," in *Four Views on Hell, Counterpoints: Bible and Theology*, ed. William Crockett (Grand Rapids: Zondervan, 1996).

But can it really be true—saint and sinner simultaneously? I wish it were so. Is this correct: "I don't need to work at becoming. I'm already declared to be holy." No sweat needed? It looks wrong to me. I hear moral demands in Scripture. *Simul iustus et peccator*? I hope it's true! I simply fear it's not.

The Wesleyan emphasis has always been a challenge to the evangelical faith on this point, although in his best moments Wesley insisted on this heart of the gospel. To the extent that the consensus builders and institutional abbots of the evangelical monasteries have attempted to incorporate Arminianism under the label "evangelical," it seems to me that it ceases to be evangelical indeed.

Soli Deo Gloria: Our Only Ambition

The world is full of ambitious people. But Paul said, "It has always been my ambition to preach the Gospel where Christ was not known" (Rom. 15:20). Since God has spoken so clearly and saved so finally, the believer is free to worship, serve, and glorify God and to enjoy him forever, beginning now. What is the ambition of the evangelical movement? Is it to please God or to please men?

Is our happiness and joy found in God or in someone or something else? Is our worship entertainment or worship? Is God's glory or our self-fulfillment the goal of our lives? Do we see God's grace as the only basis for our salvation, or are we still seeking some of the credit for ourselves? These questions reveal a glaring human-centeredness in the evangelical churches and the general witness of our day.

Robert Schuller actually says that the Reformation "erred because it was God-centered rather than man-centered," and Yale's George Lindbeck observes how quickly evangelical theology accepted this new gospel: "In the fifties, it took liberals to accept Norman Vincent Peale, but as the case of Robert Schuller indicates, today professed conservatives eat it up."

Many historians look back to the Reformation and wonder at its far-reaching influences in transforming culture: the work ethic, public education, civic and economic betterment, a revival of music, the arts, and a sense of all life being related somehow to God and his glory. These effects cause historians to observe with a sense of irony how a theology of sin and grace, the sovereignty of God over the helplessness of human beings, and an emphasis on salvation by grace apart from works could be the catalyst for such energetic moral transformation. The Reformers did not set out to launch a political or moral campaign, but they proved that when we put the gospel first and give voice to the word, the effects inevitably follow.

How can we expect the world to take God and his glory seriously if the church does not? The Reformation slogan *soli Deo gloria* was carved into the organ at Bach's church in Leipzig, and the composer signed his works with its initials. It's inscribed over taverns and music halls in old sections of Heidelberg and Amsterdam, a lasting tribute to a time when the fragrance of God's goodness seemed to fill the air. It was not a golden age, but it was an amazing recovery of God-centered faith and practice. Columbia University professor Eugene Rice offers a fitting conclusion:

> All the more, the Reformation's views of God and humanity measure the gulf between the secular imagination of the twentieth century and the sixteenth century's intoxication with the majesty of God. We can exercise only historical sympathy to try to understand how it was that the most brilliant intelligences of an entire epoch found a total, a supreme liberty in abandoning human weakness to the omnipotence of God.

Soli Deo gloria!

CHAPTER 24

Christ at the Center: The Legacy of the Reformed Tradition

Dennis E. Tamburello

When I was preparing for ministry as a Catholic priest in the late 1970s, one of the professors in our theology program announced that he would be teaching a course in "Calvin's Sacramental Theology." At the time I remember thinking, "What could Calvin possibly have to say to Catholics about the Sacraments?" Needless to say, I didn't take the course. Years later, as luck would have it, I became a serious student of Calvin's thought. The more I learned about Calvin, the more I grew in appreciation of him, and the more embarrassed I was by the ignorance and arrogance of my earlier judgment. I came to realize that if I had been smart, I would have taken that course.

In this essay, I will reflect on the significance of the Reformed tradition for the Christian church, focusing mainly on the contributions of John Calvin.[1] I speak as an outsider to the tradition, but also as an admirer. In our own day, thank God, we have been able to build bridges of understanding where there were once only walls of hatred and division. This is not to say that the walls have all come tumbling down. As recently as a few years ago, the Roman Catholic Church released a statement, *Dominus Iesus*, that in my view represented a major step backwards in ecumenical and interfaith relations.[2] This makes it only more important for a Catholic to engage in this kind of reflection.

I once had the opportunity to speak to a class at the London Bible College about what I liked and disliked about Calvin. It was interesting to discover that everything I had to say about Calvin corresponded to parallel things that I liked

---

[1] This abridged essay is reprinted here by kind permission of Fr. Tamburello and the Institute for Reformed Theology. It was first published in *The Bulletin of the Institute for Reformed Theology* 4, no. 1 (Winter 2004).

[2] See Dennis E. Tamburello, "*Dominus Iesus*: A Stumbling Block to Reformed-Catholic Dialogue?" in *Concord Makes Strength: Essays in Reformed Ecumenism*, ed. John W. Coakley (Grand Rapids: William B. Eerdmans, 2002), 77–87.

or disliked in Roman Catholicism. For example, I liked Calvin's emphasis on piety, which he defined as "that reverence joined with love of God which the knowledge of [God's] benefits induces."[3] This is the goal of knowledge of God—not to know God theoretically or intellectually, but to give glory and praise to God, whom Calvin described as the "fountainhead and source of every good" (*Inst.* 1.2.2). I saw Calvin's focus on piety as a point of contact with my own tradition's approach to spirituality. Indeed, in recent times, scholars have begun to speak without embarrassment of a spirituality in Calvin.[4]

On the negative side, I critiqued Calvin for being too sure of himself on a lot of issues—precisely a criticism I would also lay at the door of the Catholic Church at that time. In the sixteenth century, arrogance and pig-headedness were in ample supply, and Calvin's conviction about the absolute rightness of his own views was no more (or less!) obnoxious than that of his Roman opponents.

The exercise of compiling a list of likes and dislikes about Calvin was a helpful reminder of how much our traditions have in common even in their differences. With this in mind, I offer the following reflections on the contributions of the Reformed tradition to theology and to the life of the church.

The Grace of Christ

Perhaps the most common thread I see running through the teachings of the Reformed tradition, from Calvin's time to today, is the centrality of Christ. We see this in Calvin's own description of faith as engrafting us into Christ: "Christ, when he illumines us into faith by the power of his Spirit, at the same time so engrafts us into his body that we become partakers of every good" (*Inst.* 3.2.25). One of the foundations for this christological accent in Reformed theology is surely Calvin's teaching on the twofold grace of Christ. This teaching is laid out with particular clarity in the *Institutes* 3.16.1, where Calvin argues that we have both justification and sanctification in Christ.

This articulation of the work of grace in human beings is one of the most significant contributions of Reformed theology to the church. It is debatable whether the Scriptures themselves posit such a clear distinction between the graces of jus-

---

[3] *Institutes* 1.2.1. Translations are taken from *Institutes of the Christian Religion*, ed. John T. McNeill, trans. Ford Lewis Battles, Library of Christian Classics, vols. 20 and 21 (Philadelphia: Westminster Press, 1960).

[4] For example, a Calvin volume was recently added to Paulist Press's *Classics of Western Spirituality* series: Elsie Anne McKee, ed., *John Calvin: Writings on Pastoral Piety* (New York: Paulist, 2002).

tification and sanctification. Thus Roman Catholic theology traditionally considered justification to *include* sanctification, i.e., the transformation of the believer. Calvin's formulation preserved the Roman emphasis on the importance of works, but placed them completely under the rubric of sanctification, thus avoiding any danger of slipping into the language of works-righteousness. The Council of Trent was not receptive to such a formulation. Today it is easier to see that Calvin's conception of the twofold grace was a healthy corrective to a theology (and, more important, a piety) that had sometimes veered into Pelagianism.

Anna Case-Winters suggests yet another point that could be a "distinctive contribution" of the Reformed tradition:

> For Calvin . . . sanctification is not primarily about good works, but about "union with Christ." We do not attain or even approach sinless perfection, but "with a wonderful communion, day by day, he (Christ) grows more and more into one body with us, until he becomes completely one with us" (*Inst.* 3.2.24).[5]

I would go further than this and point out that justification too is about union with Christ. Calvin explicitly makes this connection in his commentary on Galatians 2:20:

> Christ lives in us in two ways. The one consists in His governing us by his Spirit and directing all our actions. The other is what He grants us by participation in His righteousness, that, since we can do nothing of ourselves, we are accepted in Him by God. The first relates to regeneration [sanctification], the second to the free acceptance of righteousness [justification].[6]

Sacramental Theology

Another major contribution of Reformed theology has been Calvin's teaching on the sacraments, especially the Eucharist. Contrary to what many Catholics have supposed, it is not true that Protestants in general deny the "real presence." In fact, in the Reformed-Roman Catholic joint statement on "The Presence of

---

[5] Anna Case-Winters, "Joint Declaration on Justification: Reformed Comments," in *Concord Makes Strength: Essays in Reformed Ecumenism, Historical Series of the Reformed Church in America* (Grand Rapids: Eerdmans, 2002), 91–92.

[6] David and Thomas Torrance, eds., *Galatians, Ephesians, Philippians, and Colossians*, vol. 11, Calvin's New Testament Commentaries, trans. T. H. L. Parker (Grand Rapids: Eerdmans, 1965), 43. For a more complete treatment of this topic, see my *Union with Christ: John Calvin and the Mysticism of St. Bernard*, Columbia Series in Reformed Theology (Louisville: Westminster John Knox Press, 1994), 86–87, 100–101.

Christ in Church and World," the dialogue commission stated: "We gratefully acknowledge that both traditions, Reformed and Roman Catholic, hold to the belief in the Real Presence of Christ in the Eucharist."[7]

Of course, there are some significant differences here. Calvin rejected the doctrine of transubstantiation, believing that it was a wrongheaded way of understanding the Eucharist. In his mind, it made no sense to speak of Christ becoming attached to the elements of bread and wine. Rather, he believed that in receiving the Eucharist, the believer was drawn up into the life of Christ through the power of the Holy Spirit. Calvin insisted that this communion was both spiritual and real.[8]

Although I struggle with the teaching on transubstantiation, tied as it is to the archaic Aristotelian categories of substance and accident, as a Catholic I believe that in a real sense the bread and the wine do become "different" than they were before the consecration. But Calvin was absolutely right in stressing that what was most important in the theology of the Eucharist was not what happens to the bread and wine, but what happens to *us* who receive the Eucharist in faith.

All too often in Catholicism, Eucharistic piety has centered on adoration of the sacred species. This focus misses the crucial point that Calvin grasped: that we are the most important "tabernacles" where Christ dwells. The union with Christ that we experience in the Eucharist should have a transformative effect in our lives. This was hardly a new idea in the sixteenth century. Several centuries before Calvin, John Chrysostom described Christians who came to receive at the Lord's Table, yet would not give food or show mercy to their brothers and sisters who were poor, as missing the point of the Eucharist.[9] Calvin himself followed Augustine in referring to the Eucharist as "the bond of love" that inspires compassion and care for one another (*Inst.* 4.17.38). Thus Calvin can be seen as an important resource in current discussions of the Eucharist and social justice.

It seems to me that Calvin's rich theology of the Eucharist should have led historically to the Lord's Supper having a more prominent and more frequent place in Reformed worship. Calvin himself says in the *Institutes*:

> [The Sacrament of the Lord's Supper] was not ordained to be received only once a year. ... Rather, it was ordained to be frequently used among all Christians in order that they

---

[7]"The Presence of Christ in Church and World," in *Growth in Agreement: Reports and Agreed Statements of Ecumenical Conversations on a World Level*, ed. Harding Meyer and Lukas Vischer (New York: Paulist Press, 1984), 456.

[8]See especially *Institutes* 4.17.16 and 4.17.33.

[9]See the *Catechism of the Catholic Church* (United States Catholic Conference, Inc.-Libreria Editrice Vaticana, 1994), par. 1397.

might frequently return in memory to Christ's Passion, by such remembrance to sustain and strengthen their faith, and urge themselves to sing thanksgiving to God and to proclaim his goodness; finally, by it to nourish mutual love, and among themselves give witness to this love, and discern its bond in the unity of Christ's body. (*Inst.* 4.17.44)

Calvin's argument here is directed against the teaching of the Fourth Lateran Council (1215), which required that Catholics receive Communion at least once a year. Note that Calvin is misrepresenting the council when he says that it decreed that Communion be received *only* once a year. This was the minimum, not the maximum requirement.

Be that as it may, Calvin's words can be turned against his own tradition, inasmuch as many Reformed churches celebrate the Lord's Supper somewhat infrequently. Calvin goes on to say in the *Institutes* that "the Lord's Table should have been spread *at least once a week* for the assembly of Christians, and the promises declared in it should feed us spiritually" (*Inst.* 4.17.46; emphasis added).

This is one area where I frankly think Catholicism has been more on target with its practice, at least until recently. The tradition of celebrating the Eucharist on a weekly basis is an ancient one that the Catholic Church has consistently upheld as important. On this point, Calvin seems to be in agreement. Why, then, did the Lord's Supper come to be neglected in Reformed practice? Is it possible that the sacrament was celebrated less frequently partly as an overreaction against the perceived shortcomings of the Catholic Mass? The good news is that there does seem to be some positive movement on this question in recent Reformed thinking. A good example would be the book by Keith A. Mathison, *Given for You: Reclaiming Calvin's Doctrine of the Lord's Supper* (P & R Press, 2002), which raises many of the issues touched on above.

Unfortunately, the Catholic Church is currently in no position to gloat over the priority it gives to the Eucharist. While proclaiming the Eucharist as the source and summit of the Christian life, our institutional leadership has allowed an intolerable situation to develop, whereby many Catholics are deprived of a weekly Eucharist because of narrow and outdated requirements for priestly ordination. Thus, in our own day, some Catholics end up having access to the Lord's Supper even less frequently than their Reformed sisters and brothers. Clearly, we Catholics have as much work to do in this area as the Reformed.

The Holy Spirit

Whenever Calvin talked about Christ, mention of the Holy Spirit was not far behind. This brings us to another contribution of Reformed theology: its pneumatology. Calvin's awareness of the role of the Holy Spirit pervaded every aspect of his thought. He defined faith, for example, as "a firm and certain knowledge of God's benevolence toward us, founded upon the truth of the freely given promise in Christ, both revealed to our minds and sealed upon our hearts through the Holy Spirit" (*Inst.* 3.2.7). Similarly, he spoke of the Holy Spirit bringing us through faith to union with Christ (*Inst.* 3.1.3), and of the Holy Spirit as effecting the bond we experience with Christ in the Lord's Supper (*Inst.* 4.17.33). Following Calvin's lead, Schleiermacher theorized that "every regenerate person partakes of the Holy Spirit, so that there is no living fellowship with Christ without an indwelling of the Holy Spirit, and vice versa."[10]

This focus on the Spirit continues to pervade Reformed thought today. For example, in "The Presence of Christ in Church and World," Reformed and Catholic theologians proclaim:

> It is through the Spirit that Christ is at work in creation and redemption. As the presence in the world of the risen Lord, the Spirit affirms and manifests the resurrection and effects the new creation. Christ who is Lord of all and active in creation points to God the Father who, in the Spirit, leads and guides history where there is no unplanned development.[11]

In our own day, much attention has been given to the Spirit's role in salvation and in the church. But historically, pneumatology has often taken a back seat to Christology. The Reformed tradition's emphasis on the Spirit has been a good corrective to this tendency. How much this emphasis has filtered into the everyday life of Reformed Christians is a question I am not qualified to answer.

Religion As Thankfulness

I would not want to leave the impression that the Reformed tradition has contributed only to our understanding of God. It has also enriched the church's understanding of the Christian life in myriad ways. In closing, I would like to focus on a key element of piety that is rooted in the thought of John Calvin: the notion of thankfulness.

We have mentioned that Calvin defines God as the fountainhead of all goodness. For Calvin, the only proper response to God's gifts of creation and re-

---

[10] Friedrich Schleiermacher, *The Christian Faith*, eds. H. R. Mackintosh and J. S. Steward (Philadelphia: Fortress Press, 1976), 574.

[11] "The Presence of Christ in Church and World," 445.

demption is a life filled with gratitude, giving thanks and praise to God. Calvin expresses this point with particular poignancy in his famous "Reply to Sadoleto," where he argues that preoccupation with one's own salvation is theologically unsound:

> It is not very sound theology to confine a man's thoughts so much to himself, and not to set before him as the prime motive of his existence zeal to show forth the glory of God. . . . I therefore believe that there is no man imbued with true piety, who will not regard as in poor taste that long and detailed exhortation to a zeal for heavenly life, which occupies a man entirely concerned with himself, and does not, even by one expression, arouse him to sanctify the name of God.[12]

This point is echoed in the *Institutes'* definition of piety as "that reverence joined with love of God which the knowledge of [God's] benefits induces" (*Inst.* 1.2.1).

It is not hard to see how religion can degenerate into self-interest or fear. Even the most ardent believer in justification by grace through faith can fall into the trap of becoming preoccupied with his or her salvation. Calvin was accused of presumption for daring to assert that believers could have certitude of salvation; but he thought it obvious that if salvation is in fact God's gift, then we should not worry about earning it. Rather, we should simply trust in God's promises and live our lives in thankful praise and love of God, expressing that gratitude in our love of neighbor.[13] This is perhaps the most practical contribution of the Reformed tradition to the everyday life of Christian believers.

---

[12] J. K. S. Reid, ed., *Calvin: Theological Treatises*, vol. 22, Library of Christian Classics (Philadelphia: Westminster Press, 1954), 228.

[13] Calvin makes this point with particular clarity in his commentary on Galatians 5:14, where he describes love of neighbor as proof of our love of God. *Calvin's New Testament Commentaries*, vol. 11, 100–101. See also B. A. Gerrish's excellent study, *Grace and Gratitude: The Eucharistic Theology of John Calvin* (Minneapolis: Fortress Press, 1993).

CHAPTER 25

Was the Reformation Missions-Minded?

Michael S. Horton

> Martin Luther was so certain of the imminent return of Christ that he overlooked the necessity of foreign missions. . . . Calvinists generally used the same line of reasoning, adding the doctrine of election that made missions appear extraneous if God had already chosen those he would save.

Thus writes Ruth Tucker, professor at Trinity Evangelical Divinity School, in *From Jerusalem to Irian Jaya: A Biographical History of Christian Missions.*[1] Well-meaning, but ill-informed, accounts such as this have been repeated so frequently they have become clichés in discussions of missions. Tucker repeats the caricature: The Reformers were not terribly interested in evangelism and missions, but the Anabaptists and Pietists gave birth to the modern missionary movement.[2] While I am not a missiologist, I do have an interest in this subject, and if the Reformation had negative effects on the advance of the Great Commission, then we ought to be the first to point it out. The facts, however, indicate quite a different direction.

First, there is the nature of the Reformation itself. Throughout the late Middle Ages, there was something of a lull in Roman Catholic missions. That is not to say they did not exist, but it was nothing like the evangelization of the Roman Empire or of the pagan European tribes that preceded it, nor like the missions of the Jesuits and other Counter-Reformation groups that followed it. It was, in fact, the Reformation itself, combined with other factors (such as exploration and the rise of colonialism), that not only gave birth to Protestant missions but revitalized Roman Catholic missions by reaction.

---

[1] Ruth Tucker, *From Jerusalem to Irian Jaya: A Biographical History of Christian Missions* (Grand Rapids: Zondervan, 1983), 67.

[2] Tucker, 24.

But what was the Reformation? One's answer to this question will determine one's appraisal of its missiological significance. If the Reformation was simply a period of internecine squabbling that interrupted the more important activity of the church, then it was indeed an appalling distraction. But if one maintains that it was the greatest recovery of the biblical faith since the first century, then the Reformation constitutes the most remarkable missionary movement in post-apostolic church history. For those of us who agree with the Reformers that the doctrine of justification by grace alone through faith alone because of Christ alone is "the article by which the church stands or falls," and the gospel—"the power of God unto salvation"—one can only interpret the Reformation as the re-evangelization of Europe. Is this not the point of the Great Commission? The Jews to whom the gospel first came were certainly aware of the prophecies concerning the Messiah, but they did not properly understand them as referring to Christ. The Reformers believed that those who confused the law and the gospel, merit and grace, judgment and justification, were in precisely the same category as the unconverted, even if they were part of "Christendom."

This is why—as we read Luther, Calvin, and the other Reformers—we cannot help but come away with a deep sense of admiration for the pastoral, missionary, and evangelistic heart of this movement. Designating themselves the "evangelicals" because they were recovering the gospel ("evangel"), these Protestants so indefatigably preached the gospel through print, pulpit, and in everyday conversations that the good news spread quickly throughout the Empire. Had the same movement occurred on another continent, with the same extensive effects, the Reformation would be considered the most significant missionary enterprise since the apostles. Therefore, the starting point is essential. Those who cannot see the Reformation as anything more than an in-house dispute over less than ultimate issues will not regard this as the re-evangelization of Christendom.

Second, there is the matter of categorization. For instance, in Ruth Tucker's book, distinguished Calvinistic missionaries—such as John Eliot, David Brainerd, Eleazer Wheelock, Isaac McCoy, William Carey, the Judsons and the Boardmans, David Livingstone, and many others—are treated as products of Pietism, when in actual fact these men and women had their roots in the Reformation-Puritan tradition. In fact, the most prominent names of the modern missionary movement were Calvinists! So much for the caricature that the "doctrine of election . . . made missions appear extraneous if God had already chosen those he would save." This is merely an inference of Tucker rather than an effect of this doctrine on the minds and hearts of those great missionary heroes who embraced it. They saw their theology as the engine behind their efforts, not as an embarrassing obstacle.

Besides Carey, Eliot, Brainerd, and Livingstone, there were evangelists such as Whitefield, Edwards, the Tennents, Spurgeon, and on we could go. All of these disciples of the Great Commission credited their theological convictions with their energy and motivation, knowing it was God alone who saves sinners whenever and wherever he will. While we carry the good news to the poor, only God can grant repentance and faith, and this relieved missionaries and evangelists of either despair on the one hand, or proud triumphalism on the other.

At last, however, we return to the Reformers themselves. While their followers may have been great evangelists and missionaries, were men such as Luther, Calvin, Bucer, Knox, and Melanchthon interested in such things? Interestingly, Tucker herself makes an observation that appears to contradict her previously cited remark that appears even in the same paragraph:

> Calvin himself, however, was at least outwardly the most missionary-minded of all the Reformers. He not only sent dozens of evangelists back into his homeland of France, but also commissioned four missionaries, along with a number of French Huguenots, to establish a colony and evangelize the Indians of Brazil.[3]

These missionaries were killed by Jesuits, but another group was sent from Geneva. Not only were the New England Puritans busy building Harvard; they were simultaneously evangelizing Native Americans. (The first book published in the New World was the Bible in Algonquin, by John Eliot.) In fact, the Reformed missionary enterprise integrated the proclamation of the gospel with the interests of justice and cultural betterment long before it became popular. One thinks of David Livingstone (1813–73), the Scottish missionary who was also an explorer and who, in the words of one historian, "exercised a greater influence on the history of central Africa than any other person, Christian or non-Christian, in the nineteenth century." But history records Livingstone as more than a missionary and explorer; he was an indefatigable opponent of the slave trade. Livingstone knew that the same God who cared for the salvation of the lost also abhorred the bondage of injustice, and sin had not only personal but institutional aspects. He sought to interrupt the slave trade by building East African commercial trade; he pursued some extraordinarily brilliant ideas, but the British government ended his expedition in 1863. And yet, Brian Stanley concludes, "The Protestant churches of sub-Saharan Africa, many of them born in the aftermath of Livingstone's explorations, are today among the strongest in the world."

American Presbyterian missionary and educator Samuel M. Zwemer (1867–1952) is another example of this integration of preaching grace and doing justice.

---

[3] Tucker, 67.

As a missionary in the Middle East, he earned the title of "the modern apostle to the Moslem world," and he opened up doors to missions throughout the region, especially by building hospitals and schools—a traditional approach to pre-evangelism taken by Reformed and Lutheran missionaries alike. Because these institutions are still among the most important to the locals, these missionaries and their spiritual descendants are among the only trusted Westerners. Zwemer himself argued that Calvinism could conquer the Muslim world because it was a system and the Muslims thought very systematically; they would not be won by mere pietistic sentimentality. Various cultural institutions bear his name in Cairo and in other cities in the Middle East.

Far East missions were no less led by Reformed Christians. One thinks of the Scot Robert Morrison, who was the first Protestant missionary to go to China. Confident in God's sovereignty, he prayed for God to place him in a part of the world "where the difficulties are the greatest, and to all human appearance the most insurmountable." Like Zwemer, who saw few converts in the entire tenure of his missionary enterprise, Morrison saw fewer than a dozen converts and, as Tucker informs us, "at the time of his death there were only three known native Christians in the entire Chinese empire." Nevertheless, both missionaries translated the Scriptures for the first time into the native languages and left these few converts to plant the seeds that would eventually produce a harvest of new believers. They did not despair in spite of few "results," because all results are God's results, and he will see to the success of his own mission. The story of Korean missions is full of amazing twists and turns; figuring prominently throughout it all is the Orthodox Presbyterian Church. By American standards, a small but faithful church, the O.P.C. had an inordinately large hand in the evangelization of the region before and after the division of North and South Korea.

The greatest tragedy in modern missions, from this writer's point of view at least, is the sad reality that although Reformation Christians launched modern missions, the "Pentecostalization" of the missionary movement has devastated almost overnight the regions where missionaries labored carefully for decades. Huge crusades with spectacular sideshows have replaced the careful exposition of Scripture in large parts of the world. The two-thirds world, where the earliest missions produced deep conversions and strong churches, is now dominated by successive waves of Pentecostal phenomena. The results are evident everywhere on the mission field (even more so than in America): hysteria and numerical growth, leading almost as quickly to despair and disillusionment, until the cycle repeats itself.

Just as British missions reflected worldwide missionary activity in the nineteenth century, American leadership in the twentieth is obvious. "Evangelicalism" around the world is equivalent to American evangelicalism, and the influence of such institutions as the Fuller School of World Missions, along with the leading trends evident in *Christianity Today*, leading evangelical seminaries and popular movements rather quickly overpower indigenous distinctives, many of the latter derived from the period of earlier missionary activity. Like so many other trappings of American popular commercial culture, when something gets started on the American evangelical scene, it eventually makes its way into the remotest regions.

Speaking for my own tradition, while many Reformed Christians are interested in restoring a sense of vocation and calling, including the vision of transforming culture as "salt" and "light," there does not seem to be a parallel interest in spreading the gospel, either in terms of local evangelism or missions. This is not to say that Reformed Churches, whether local or at the denominational level, are not interested in missions: many of them have proportionately large missions budgets. But it is to say that at least this writer is unaware of much thoughtful discussion of what a second Reformation might look like in, say, Thailand or Tanzania. If we truly believe that many of the crowds turning out for a healing crusade in Uganda or Tulsa are filled with people who have an erroneous understanding of the gospel, then we are in precisely the same position as the first Reformers, where "missions" and "evangelism" means first recovering the biblical gospel. It is not enough for Reformed and Lutheran evangelicals to work side by side with mainstream evangelicals and attempt to influence them. The evangelicals are not simply "off a little" on this or that emphasis; there is quite often these days a fundamentally different message, leading to methods and a general agenda at cross-purposes with biblical, historic Christianity. There must be a distinctive Reformational agenda—one that neither attempts to recreate the sixteenth-century European movement in Bombay nor capitulates to American evangelical tendencies.

May God set our hearts and minds to this urgent task, and then may he prepare our feet to bring good news to the captives, whether down the street or around the world.

CHAPTER 26

The Reformation and the Arts

Gene E. Veith

A major controversy during the time of the Reformation involved the proper use of the arts. Despite the artistic glories of the medieval church, the Reformers believed that art was being misused, that it was obscuring the gospel behind a haze of aesthetic experience. In some ways, the medieval approach to the arts, as condemned by the Reformers, is coming back among contemporary evangelicals.

The Reformation, however, did not stifle the arts. Rather, in distinguishing art from religion, the Reformation liberated the arts, sparking an explosion of creativity and artistic excellence. Both the contemporary church and the contemporary art world have a lot to learn from the artistic heritage of the Reformation.[1]

The New Graven Images

The popular religion of the late Middle Ages was centered around works of art. Unable or not allowed to read the Bible, ordinary folk learned what they knew of Scripture from stained-glass windows and street dramas. While the priests would perform Mass in barely audible Latin behind the rood screen, ordinary worshippers would contemplate the statues and icons that filled the church. In the popular mind, special images of the Virgin Mary had special power, and multitudes would embark on pilgrimages to pay devotion to a miraculous shrine. Instead of viewing art for its aesthetic value, many medieval Christians viewed it for its religious value. In doing so, the message of the gospel was often obscured.

Today's popular religion also centers on works of art. While most evangelicals—unlike medieval Christians—are uninterested in the "high culture" of serious paintings, sophisticated music, and quality craftsmanship, many eagerly embrace the "popular culture" of the media and the entertainment industry. The

---

[1] Some of the material in this article is adapted from Michael Horton, *State of the Arts: From Bezalel to Mapplethorpe* (Wheaton, IL: Crossway Books, 1991).

kinds of art forms associated with today's popular culture—contemporary music, television shows, consumer-oriented communication—define the so-called evangelical style.[2]

Today's Christian bookstores typically have more "art" than books: shelves of religious knickknacks, plaques, posters, and sentimental figurines; tapes and CDs of Christian rock, rap, and heavy metal; Christian thriller films, how-to's, and exercise routines; Christian T-shirts, toys, greeting cards, and gifts. If there is still room for books, most of them will follow the popular genres of the secular best-seller lists: Christian pop psychology, diet, and self-help; Christian romances, science fiction, mysteries, and horror. Such art forms play an important role in contemporary Christianity. Many people find their religious experience not in congregational worship but in "inspirational" videos and contemporary Christian concerts complete with mosh pits and body passing.

During the Reformation, the controversies over art centered on the question of whether religious art violated the biblical injunction against the use of graven images in worship (Exod. 20:4). To their credit, the medieval Christians, though led astray, were led astray by high-quality art. Even works of great merit, however, can become idolatrous when human expressions become substitutes for God's revelation and when aesthetic pleasure is confused with spiritual truth.

The taste of contemporary Christians for the artifacts of the pop culture has a similar danger: The glossy creations of human authors, musicians, and media specialists often take the place of the word of God. Aesthetic criteria—such as how much we like something or how much we enjoy it—replace standards of theological truth. We say, "I really like that church," instead of "I believe in what that church teaches." We tell the pastor how much we "enjoyed" the sermon rather than how it convicted us of sin and of salvation. We even discuss theology in aesthetic terms rather than the language of truth: we say, "I don't like the idea of hell," instead of asking whether there is such a place.

Even when today's religious junk is not idolatrous, it carries another danger. Much of today's "inspirational" art and music might not teach false doctrine—though it often does—but it does trivialize and vulgarize the Holy One of Israel. Such carelessness about what is holy is, literally, profanity and is sternly warned against in Scripture. If our popular religious art does not violate the commandment against graven images, then it risks violating the commandment against taking the name of the Lord in vain (Exod. 29:7).

---

[2] See Kenneth Myers, *All God's Children and Blue Suede Shoes: Christians and Popular Culture* (Wheaton, IL: Crossway Books, 1989).

The Sacred and the Secular

If you walk through an art museum, you will notice that the medieval wing is packed with religious paintings—Madonnas, saints, and icons of Christ. When you get to the Reformation section—that is, art from northern Europe of the 1500s and 1600s—there is a dramatic change. Instead of Mary and the Christ child on a throne, you will see paintings of families, pictures of people at their workplace, and portraits of ordinary men and women. You may find a few biblical scenes in the Reformation gallery, but the biblical characters look like doughty German farmers or down-to-earth Dutch matrons instead of idealized saints. The background is not beaten gold as in the medieval paintings, but realistic villages and forests. The Reformation art seems secular. Does this mean that the Reformation had no religious impact on the arts? Not at all. The Reformation's rediscovery of Scripture and of the gospel inspired a new flowering of the arts. The Reformers saw little problem with secular art. Ironically, their main complaint was against religious art.

The secular quality of Reformation art, however, had a religious motivation. Paintings of families reflected the new awareness that marriage and child raising—as opposed to the medieval exaltation of celibacy—were high spiritual callings. The paintings of butcher stalls, farmers in their fields, and women at their spinning wheels reflected the Reformation insight that all vocations, not just the clerical ones, were ways of serving God and one's fellow human beings. The portraits grew out of the Reformation emphasis on the individual. The realistic biblical scenes came from the realization that the Bible is not only true, in a down-to-earth way, but it is for and about ordinary people.

If the Reformation helped to secularize art, then it did so not by eliminating the sacred but by seeing even the secular sphere in the light of God's grace. Reformation art made the secular sacred. Today's religious art, on the other hand, often does the reverse, making the sacred secular. Christianity is presented as the key to having a happy family, finding success on the job, and feeling good about yourself. The overt subject may be religious, but the prime emphasis is on this world. In Reformation art, the subject may be secular, but—as in a painting by Rembrandt—it will be transfigured by spiritual light.

The Reformers As Art Critics

In seeking to restore the gospel and to place the Bible at the center of the Christian life, the Reformers attacked what they saw as the idolatry of the medieval church. In reaction to the devotion to images and the use of art to promote false doctrines, many Reformers became iconoclasts, smashing stained-glass windows and burning crucifixes, reliquaries, and triptychs. Nevertheless, Reformation iconoclasm was not intrinsically anti-art.

Calvin and Zwingli objected to the religious use of art, but not to art as such. "I am not gripped by the superstition of thinking absolutely no images permissible," writes Calvin, "but because sculpture and paintings are gifts of God, I seek a pure and legitimate use of each."[3] Zwingli, an extreme iconoclast, even permitted paintings of Christ as long as they were not in churches nor offered reverence. According to Zwingli, "where anyone has a portrait of His humanity, that is just as fitting to have as to have other portraits."[4]

Leo Jud, a colleague of Zwingli and a fellow iconoclast, distinguished between artificial images of God made by human beings and the true image of God made by God himself. In other words, those interested in seeing the image of God need only look at a human being, whom God himself made in his own image. Portraits, therefore—paintings of ordinary men and women—became a means of contemplating the divine image. According to Jud, portraits depict "living images made by God and not by the hands of men."[5]

As a result of this profound insight, portraiture flourished throughout the Reformed countries. The concept of the *imago Dei* underlies the work of those painters known as the Dutch Masters, including perhaps the greatest Protestant painter, Rembrandt. In the faces of his subjects—children, merchants, ordinary families—the depths of their personalities are suggested, and one can discern their dignity and value as having been created in the image of God.

Not all of the Reformers were iconoclasts. After his condemnation by the emperor, Luther came out of hiding at the risk of his life precisely to put down the riots of image burning and stained-glass window smashing that had broken out in Wittenberg. Luther's rule for church art was to reject only art that interfered with the message of Christ. Images of Mary and the legendary saints were removed, with all of the attendant devotions and "works" associated with them. Crucifixes, depicting the all-sufficient atonement for sin, and other biblical paintings and church decorations were retained.

---

[3] John Calvin, *Institutes of the Christian Religion*, trans. Ford Lewis Battles, ed. John T. McNeill (Philadelphia: Westminster Press, 1960), 1.11.12.

[4] Quoted in Charles Garside, *Zwingli and the Arts* (New Haven: Yale University Press, 1966), 171.

[5] Quoted in Garside, 182.

Luther, in a sermon on the subject, articulated an important principle of Christian freedom: "Although it is true and no one can deny that the images are evil because they are abused, nevertheless we must not on that account reject them, nor condemn anything because it is abused. This would result in utter confusion." Some people worship the sun and the stars, says Luther, but this does not mean we should try to pull them from the skies. Some are led astray by women and wine, but this does not mean we should kill all the women and pour out all the wine. Images, Luther maintains, "ought to be abolished when they are worshipped; otherwise not." "That yonder crucifix," he continues, "is not my God, for my God is in heaven, but . . . this is simply a sign." To be sure, many consider putting up an image to be a good work, a way to earn God's favor. For them, images are harmful, but "there are still some people who hold no such wrong opinion of them, but to whom they may be useful. . . . We cannot and ought not to condemn a thing which may be any way useful to a person."[6]

Luther appreciated the arts and, in turn, his theology was appreciated by artists. One of Luther's good friends—they stood as godfathers to each other's children—was the artist Lucas Cranach. His religious paintings, in marked contrast to the transcendent mysticism of the Middle Ages, are down to earth, locating biblical and spiritual events squarely in the ordinary, natural world. Albrecht Dürer, one of the greatest innovators of realistic art, was a follower of Luther.

The great nonrepresentational art form of the Reformation was music. The Reformers from Luther to Zwingli reveled in music. "My love for music," said Luther, "which often has quickened me and liberated me from great vexations, is abundant and overflowing." Luther ranked music as second in importance only to theology.[7] Music, praised throughout Scripture, involves no graven images whatsoever, yet it is art of the highest craftsmanship and aesthetic impact. The Reformation created an outpouring of music not only in the form of hymns (music with the content of the word) but also in instrumental music.

The Reformation's legacy to music finds its culmination in the piety and artistry of perhaps the greatest of composers, Johann Sebastian Bach. A devout Lutheran, Bach would begin many of his scores with the Latin abbreviation for "Jesus Help." He would end them with the Reformation slogan *sola Deo gloria*: "To God alone be the glory." These inscriptions can be found not only in his church music but also in his secular music. Bach's fugues and minuets written for the court may have been secular, but they were born in prayer and praise.

---

[6] *Luther's Works*, ed. Helmut T. Lehmann (Philadelphia: Muhlenberg Press, 1959), 51:84–85.

[7] *Luther's Works*, 49:428.

Reforming the Arts

Not many Christian bookstores today sell Bach CDs, Rembrandt prints, or for that matter the writings of Luther or Calvin. For some reason, contemporary Christians uncritically embrace the art of Hollywood and Madison Avenue, while being averse to the art that actually emerged out of a biblical worldview. Spenser, Herbert, and Milton are still lauded even in secular universities, but despite their fervent Reformation spirituality they are not read much by today's Protestants. These works of these poets, as well as those of the Reformation painters and the great classical composers, demand effort, attention, and reflection on the part of their audiences. A number of Christian artists are continuing in their tradition, creating works of honesty, complexity, and quality, but they are often spurned by the contemporary church.

Cultivating taste may be an important survival skill for Christians. That contemporary Christians are addicted to pop music and pop art (music and art that recognizes no higher values than entertainment, commercialism, self-gratification, and shallow emotionalism) means that they are opening themselves up to a pop spiritual life. It is little wonder that many contemporary Christians insist on entertaining worship services, commercialistic evangelism, feel-good sermons, and subjective spirituality. Pop art leads to pop theology. Responding to quality is a valuable self-discipline. Becoming knowledgeable about the arts, practicing discernment—both theological and aesthetic—and patronizing excellence are ways that Christians can actively resist mediocrity and corruption.

To be sure, aesthetics is no substitute for faith. The sophisticated patrons of the symphony and the galleries often use art for their religion, looking to aesthetic experience for their values, meaning, and inspiration. This kind of aestheticism may be sophisticated, but it is no less idolatrous than the most primitive superstition, insofar as human creations—however beautiful—are allowed to take the place of the transcendent God of Scripture. Ironically, when art becomes a substitute for God, the result tends to be not only bad religion but also bad art. The emptiness, immorality, and absurdity of so much of contemporary art are evidence of the spiritual condition of today's art world, which stands in sore need of the Reformation gospel.

Christians who do not look to the arts for their religion, however, are freed to appreciate them as they were intended to be appreciated. In his discussion of Greek culture, classical historian Werner Jaeger points out that "it was the Christians who finally taught men to appraise poetry by a purely aesthetic standard—a standard which enabled them to reject most of the moral and religious teaching of the classical poets as false and ungodly, while accepting the formal elements in their work as instructive and aesthetically delightful."[8] What the early church did for Greek culture, the Reformation reiterated.

This means that Christians can enjoy the whole range of the arts, but their standards should be high. Christians—recognizing that art testifies to the human condition rather than necessarily to divine truth—can approach even the most secular art from a theological point of view, while also enjoying it from "a purely aesthetic" perspective. As for explicitly religious art, Christians can agree with a work theologically while criticizing its craftsmanship. Christians can also disagree with its theology while admiring its form. Work that is both theologically profound and aesthetically powerful—the poetry of George Herbert, the music of Handel, a landscape by Thomas Cole—should be treasured. Because our faith comes not from art, but from the Bible, we can approach the arts in a spirit of Christian freedom.

Because I have written extensively on Christianity and the arts, I often hear from Christian artists who tell me about their struggles in finding acceptance within today's church. A young woman wrote me about how hard she worked to suppress her artistic gifts. Her church led her to believe that if she really wanted to serve the Lord, she needed to give up her artistic career to become an evangelist. She joined a parachurch organization and threw herself into witnessing programs. The problem was that she was unsuccessful. She had not the temperament, the talent, nor the people skills to be a home missionary. She came to realize, though, that what she was good at—namely, art—was an ability given to her by God. She realized she could serve God as an artist. In other words, she came to the Reformation understanding that being an artist is her vocation.

I know another artist and musician whose devotion to Christ led him into a career in contemporary Christian music. As he started studying Reformation theology, he became increasingly repelled by the shallow religiosity, false doctrines, bad quality, and sappy commercialism of so much of the contemporary Christian music industry. He finally decided to switch to the secular music scene. Today he writes love songs, blues, and ballads and sings them in coffeehouses and concert halls. His songs grow out of a deeply biblical worldview, expressed with honesty and artistic integrity. His songs and his drawings speak freely of a faith that informs the whole spectrum of his life. He is a true Reformation artist.

I have found that there are many Christians who have discovered their vocation in the arts, whether in the church or in the secular arena. Many of them are frustrated with the opposition or indifference they have encountered from their

---

[8] Werner Jaeger, *Paideia: The Ideals of Greek Culture*, trans. Gilbert Highet (New York: Oxford University Press, 1965), xxvii–xxviii.

fellow evangelicals, many of whom prefer tackiness and mediocrity to aesthetic excellence. These artists, who are bringing a biblical vision into contemporary culture, deserve the understanding and support of the church. Ordinary Christians, in turn, would find their lives enriched by cultivating their tastes.

The Apostle Paul's admonition to "approve the things that are excellent" (Phil. 1:10) and to meditate on "whatever things are lovely [and] praiseworthy" (Phil. 4:8) must also apply to the arts. The Reformation teaches us how to avoid idolatry—whether that of the fetish worshipper, the aesthete, or the entertainment industry—while freeing us to enjoy the fullness of beauty that God structured into his creation and into the human soul.

CHAPTER 27

Musings on the History of the Protestant Ministry

Lawrence R. Rast, Jr.

Fifteen years ago the sign in the front of the Oneida Baptist Church caught my attention. It read: "Pastor, Fred Russell; Ministers, The Entire Congregation."[1] "Aren't pastors ministers?" I mused. "Wait—if everyone is a minister, then, in effect, no one is a minister," I concluded. My thoughts haven't changed. In the years since that experience I've seen the gimmicky slogans of a local congregation evolve into a full-fledged theology. Let me make myself clear: I'm not singling out the Baptists here. I've seen identical signs in front of the church buildings and in the bulletins in my own denomination, The Lutheran Church-Missouri Synod. However, I firmly believe that those who advance such a saying have staked out a theological position of which, perhaps, they do not entirely understand the ramifications. To adopt the idea that "everyone is a minister" compromises the Reformation understanding of the doctrine of the ministry.[2]

When one mentions "the ministry" among evangelicals, one is speaking of those persons in the church who undertake some form of official activity on behalf of and for the church. The key is the little word *the*, which points to the Office of the Holy Ministry, established by Christ himself for the good of his church. Ministry without the definite article, on the other hand, has come to mean just about any kind of church activity loosely related to the proclamation of the gospel. Unfortunately, these kinds of so-called ministry often take some ridiculous forms (such as a "clown ministry"). "Ministry" has become so confused a word as to become almost meaningless.

But what about "The Ministry"? In our time we cannot simply assume that most who hear this phrase will automatically think of the pastoral ministry. I

---

[1] The name of the pastor is fictitious.

[2] That is not to attack the motives of those who do so; as I implied, they likely do so out of a well-meaning ignorance.

submit that this situation is unacceptable for the heirs of the Reformation. Further, I believe it is time for the churches of the evangelical tradition to reclaim this word and not allow its misuse to relegate it to obscurity. The means by which we will achieve this are two. First of all, rigorous theological instruction—something no Protestant should find distasteful. Second, and here lies the burden of this article, we need to be historically aware of the idea of the ministry, and why and how it is that we have arrived at the point of linking the office that preaches Christ crucified and risen again for the sins of the world with such silliness as a clown ministry. We can only move into the future faithfully if we are fully informed both doctrinally and historically. To that end, let us look at the basic history of the Protestant conception of the ministry.

Priests and Pastors According to Martin Luther

The use of the word *minister* to indicate a person who functions in a particular role as proclaimer of the gospel and administrator of the sacraments of baptism and the Lord's Supper can be traced primarily back to the Reformation period. Roman Catholicism preferred the use of the term "priest" for its clergy, underscoring that tradition's doctrine of the ministry. A "priest" is one who sacrifices on behalf of another. The Reformers favored "minister" because it means "one who serves."

To understand Martin Luther correctly, one must be familiar with his disagreement with Rome over the nature of the Christian priesthood. Luther rejected what he believed was Rome's mistaken understanding of the relationship of the believer to God. Rome, said Luther, had placed the pope and his bishops and priests in the place of Christ. They had become the mediators of divine grace in place of the Lord. As successors of Peter, they were the ones who reenacted the sacrifice of Christ for the church. In contrast, Luther argued that Christ had been sacrificed only once and for all—Christ alone was *the* priest and *the* sacrifice. By virtue of their baptism all believers are "priests," and as such had the privilege of administering the sacraments and preaching. However, for the sake of good order, Christ himself had established the Office of the Ministry. The community of the faithful was required by Christ to appoint a man to fill the office as Christ required.

At the heart of Luther's reform of the doctrine of the ministry is his rejection of the Roman notion of the Mass as a sacrifice. First developed in his *Address to the German Nobility* (1520), Luther rejected the notion that it was the priest's primary duty to offer up the sacrifice of the Mass on behalf of the parish community. He repudiated the notion that the priest had the gift, conferred in ordination, to transform the bread and the wine into the body and blood of Christ in the Mass. Luther countered that the real presence of Christ in the Sacrament of the Altar did not depend upon priestly character or authority, but upon the word of God. Thus the ordained Lutheran clergyman's primary responsibility was not to re-sacrifice Christ, but to preach the word and to administer the sacraments: the Lord's Supper, baptism, and absolution. As preacher, teacher, and administrator, the Lutheran clergyman came to be called "pastor," one who shepherds Christ's flock through word and sacrament.

For Luther, there is no essential difference between the layperson and the pastor—there is no special class of order in society known as "the priesthood." Rather, all Christians stand before God under the word with Christ as their only mediator. The difference between pastor and people is not one of standing, but rather that one has received a charge, or call, from God to hold the Office of the Ministry on behalf of the rest of the believing community. Ordination for Luther meant a public recognition of the call that a group of Christians had extended to a particular Christian person.

Thus Luther tried to hold two extremes together without allowing either to dominate the other—the divine institution and necessity of the Office of the Ministry and the "Priesthood of all Believers." Misunderstandings of Luther's doctrine have occurred when one of these is stressed at the expense of the other. Also, we must remember that Luther articulated his doctrine in the midst of controversy, and his thought at any given time reflects those matters that were most pressing on him. For example, early in his reforming career Luther advocated more strongly the priesthood of all believers. In the face of Rome's insistence that ordination conferred a special gift to the priest that empowered him alone to forgive and retain sins, Luther stressed that every Christian by virtue of his or her baptism was given this power. Later, however, some of the more radical Reformers took the doctrine of the priesthood of all believers to an extrabiblical extreme, essentially arguing that no ministry at all was established in the New Testament. Luther reacted strongly against the disorder inherent in the egalitarian stance of this faction and stressed the divine institution and necessity of the Office of the Ministry, as well as its independence from the control of the calling community.

The Reformed Ministry

The Reformed tradition owed much to the thought of Martin Luther and the Lutherans, though its leaders departed from them in significant ways. Like

Luther, the Swiss Reformer Ulrich Zwingli, who was also a Roman Catholic priest, sought to restore a biblical pattern to the ministry of the church. More important for our purposes, however, is the work of John Calvin. Calvin systematized Reformed thought on the doctrine of the ministry. Like Luther, Calvin accepted the authority of Scripture and saw justification by grace through faith as the article on which the church stands and falls. There is no salvation outside the church, because the church is the only place in which the pure word is proclaimed.[3] One can identify the church by its marks. Recalling the language of the Augsburg Confession, Calvin writes: "Wherever we see the word of God sincerely preached and heard, wherever we see the sacraments administered according to the institution of Christ, there we cannot have any doubt that the Church of God has some existence."[4] The ascended Christ, as prophet, priest, and king, continues to rule his church. But because he is at the right hand of God, he has established the office of the ministry as the special medium through which he continues to speak to the church. "He declares his condescension towards us, employing men to perform the function of his ambassadors in the world, to be the interpreters of his secret will; in short, *to represent his own person.*"[5]

In his *Ecclesiastical Ordinances* of 1541, Calvin argued that Scripture teaches (Eph. 4:11; Rom. 2:7; 1 Cor. 12:28) that there are four orders of the Office of the Ministry: pastors, doctors, elders, and deacons. Pastors are to preach and administer the sacraments. Doctors teach the church's doctrine, while the elders' primary task is to administer church discipline, as part of a consistory that includes the pastor. Thus that disciplinary power will not fall into the hands of one person or party. Finally, deacons are to care for the sick and the poor.

Calvin's four orders of ministry found expression in the churches of the Reformed tradition in Scotland and in America. Both the Presbyterians and the Puritans, with their Congregationalist heirs, looked to Calvin as their mentor in these matters. His influence is also evident in the traditions that arose out of English Separatism, for example, the Baptists and the Disciples of Christ, to name only two.

Anglicanism, though dependent on Calvinism for its doctrinal expressions, developed a doctrine of the ministry that differed significantly from its Reformed roots. Henry VIII's *Assertio Septem Sacramentorum* of 1521 censured Luther's sacramental and thus also his ministerial reforms. Henry aimed to establish

---

[3] John Calvin, *Institutes of the Christian Religion*, trans. Henry Beveridge (repr. Peabody, MA: Hendrickson, 2007), 4.1.4.

[4] *Institutes* 4.1.9.

[5] *Institutes* 4.3.1, emphasis added.

the Church of England as a distinct church from Rome without changing its substance or form, and in 1534 the Act of Supremacy declared the monarch "the only supreme head in earth of the Church in England." Henry's daughter Elizabeth I fixed the episcopal ministry as the basic form of the ministry. It has remained so for the worldwide Anglican communion ever since. However, within that tradition there are radically differing opinions as to the nature of the ministry. The high church or Anglo-Catholic group stresses the necessity of apostolic succession and defines the institution of clergy on the basis of transmission of priestly power in the sacrament of ordination. The broad church, or Latitudinarian tradition, holds that ordination is beneficial for the church without saying that holy orders necessarily offer a special gift or power. Finally, the low church or evangelical party holds that the episcopacy, though not absolutely necessary to the church, assures that the church enjoys the fullness of the gifts that Christ has for it when it establishes the ministry in its midst.

Methodism had its roots in the Anglican tradition, and its founder, John Wesley (1703–1791), refused throughout his life to separate himself from the Church of England. Toward the end of his life, Wesley came to the conclusion that New Testament terms for bishops and priests were synonymous and that, therefore, he could rightfully ordain ministers for his "church within the church."

The Ministry in America

It was in America, with its Methodist circuit riders and egalitarian principles, where some of the most important changes to the historic Protestant doctrine of the ministry occurred. We have seen that the Puritans inherited their doctrine of the ministry from the theology of John Calvin and orthodox Calvinism. Their application of that doctrine underscores its fundamental orthodoxy. E. Brooks Holifield has shown that the colonial clergy of the seventeenth century saw their task as the "cure of souls."[6] They were responsible for the spiritual care of the sheep entrusted to their care, and this accountability extended to all fields of their activities as ministers of word and sacraments—for example, preaching, teaching, governing the congregation, and the general nurture of a truly pious life.

However, the eighteenth century's First Great Awakening helped force a shift in ministerial activity. The new minister emphasized the spiritual awakening of the individual. Called "preacher" with greater and greater frequency, the minis-

---

[6] See E. Brooks Holifield, *A History of Pastoral Care in America: From Salvation to Self-Realization* (Nashville: Abingdon Press, 1983).

ter's principal task was to exhort and awaken sinful individuals to move toward a decision for Christ. The style of preaching changed as sermons became more familiar in their address (using the second-person singular and plural "you") and purposeful in their manipulation of the emotions. Those pastors who retained the older model of preaching and cure of souls were frequently rebuked as being "unconverted" and even "dead." The classic expression of this is Gilbert Tennent's *The Danger of an Unconverted Ministry* (1740), in which he castigates the preaching of the orthodox as being so "cold and sapless" as to "freeze between their lips."[7] Paralleling this new stress on vernacular preaching (likely driving it) was a theological shift from Calvinism, as expressed in the likes of the Westminster Confession, to an Arminianism that denied original sin and stressed the freedom of the human will to choose whether it would or would not serve God.

The practical results of this theological change were enormous. No longer would preachers see awakenings as being totally dependent upon the will and grace of God. Nor did they see pastoral care in terms of the care of souls. The new preachers believed their methods could bring about spiritual conversion through the application of the right methods. These budding revivalists strove to drive people to the point of spiritual distress and to place the resolution of the matter in the arena of the hearer's free will. Revivals, whose success did not absolutely depend on God's activity, took the place of the divine service of the Reformation liturgies. "A revival is not a miracle," wrote Charles Finney, "nor dependent on a miracle in any sense. It is a purely philosophical result of the right use of the constituted means."[8] To put it crassly, in American revivalism, emotional manipulation replaced the care of souls.

Not surprisingly, a new doctrine of the ministry developed. The most influential ministers in the new system were not the settled ministers who simply shepherded their flocks. The traveling revivalist, who fanned the revival fires and then moved on, could shape and sway vastly more people to his theology and ideas. The biblical notion of "evangelist" (one who proclaims the good news) took on a new meaning—an itinerant minister whose chief activity was conducting revivals. Thus a new office of ministry was introduced to the church. Stressing the human side of the conversion equation and, ultimately, putting salvation in the hands of his (and, increasingly, her) hearers, the revivalist appealed to the egalitarian democracy that had overcome the republicanism of the early national

---

[7] In *The Great Awakening: Documents on the Revival of Religion, 1740–1745*, ed. Richard L. Bushman (Chapel Hill: University of North Carolina Press, 1969), 90.

[8] Charles G. Finney, *Revival Lectures* (repr., Grand Rapids, MI: Fleming H. Revell, 1993), 5.

period.[9] Not only did it mirror the politics of the Age of Jackson, but it fit hand in glove with the burgeoning market capitalism.

The Evangelical Ministry: *Quo Vadis?*

In 1956, Sydney Mead argued that this conception of the Protestant ministry had become part and parcel of American evangelicalism.[10] What remains for us to look at is the manner in which this ministry has played out in the American religious scene.

It is more than obvious that this Arminian, revivalistic conception of the ministry still holds great sway for evangelicals in the present age. One can see a clear line of evangelical revivalists running from Charles Finney on down to the latest TV evangelist who tops the ratings. Theologically, they are very similar. Though they might differ at points (for example, Finney was a postmillennialist and most current revivalists are dispensational premillennialists), they all share a commitment to Arminianism and a rejection of the theological anthropology embodied in the great confessions of the Reformation (e.g., the Augsburg and Westminster Confessions). The great pressures facing Protestant ministers today are to fall in line with this theological pedigree. As always, the temptation is great, for Finney's new measures (be they the "anxious bench" or Willow Creek), promise—no, guarantee—numerical success and a great harvest of souls. Scripture speaks clearly to this point, and the theological positions of Luther and the other Reformers, biblical as they are, still apply to America today. The question confronting evangelicals is what will drive pastoral care in our churches: a theology that guarantees numerical success, or one that is faithful to the Scriptures? To put it another way, are the models for ministry that we adopt dependent on the orthodox, biblically centered confessions of the Reformation, or do they simply echo theologically the ideas of secular culture?

Perhaps one example will suffice. Willow Creek Church in South Barrington, Illinois, has been all the rage for the last several years. Its "Seeker Services," with their low-profile approach to the gospel and movie theater atmosphere, have gathered great attention. However, one of the principles underlying the life of Willow Creek is its new doctrine of the ministry. In *Preparing Your Church for*

---

[9] See Nathan O. Hatch, *The Democratization of American Christianity* (New Haven: Yale University Press, 1989).

[10] Sydney Mead, "The Rise of the Evangelical Conception of the Ministry in America: 1607–1850," in *The Ministry in Historical Perspectives*, eds. H. Richard Niebuhr and Daniel D. Williams (New York: Harper & Brothers, 1956), 207–49.

the Future, Carl F. George holds up Willow Creek as one of the finest examples of ministry in action. In this book, he outlines a new doctrine of the church and ministry he calls "Meta-Church."[11] George's basic complaint is that "present models for doing ministry are ineffective and inadequate." Why? Because older, traditional churches have limited "pastoral care" to the activity of the ordained clergy. Rather, every individual Christian is responsible for pastoral care. This is one of the primary secrets to Willow Creek's success. For George, everyone is more than a minister; now everyone is a pastor! What then becomes of "the" pastor? He is relegated to status as a CEO—his task is to "manage" his cell group. The effective result of George's plan is that the pastor does less and less "pastoral care," while the lay pastor of the ten or less member cell-group takes center stage. "The pivotal roles in the church will be those of the cell-group leader (X) and the apprentice leader (Xa)."[12]

Not surprisingly, the Meta-Church congregation lacks a firm doctrinal foundation. It is more structurally oriented than belief oriented. In fact, George himself says: "These churches of the future realize that God measures His people more by their obedience than by their knowledge of Bible facts. Therefore, they've shifted their priorities from teaching to caring, from understanding to application."[13] Perhaps I've been too quick to call this a "new" doctrine. Meta-Church doctrine and practice parallels, in striking ways, some of the more shoddy positions of medieval Roman Catholicism. The people were prodded to obedience to the church but were left ignorant of doctrine. Lacking a foundation in biblical theology, they subjected themselves to the doctrinal developments that the Reformation strove so hard to overcome. More seriously, George's subordination of doctrine to experience leaves the very heart of the gospel at risk and threatens to turn Christianity into a religion of the law. After all, if God truly does measure people more by their obedience than by what the Savior has done for them (all of which is revealed in what George dismisses as "Bible facts"), then we have returned to the days of salvation by works, and the grace of God is at the very least obscured, if not utterly destroyed!

One might argue, however, that this critique of George is simply the frustrated howling of a threatened seminary professor. I disagree. George's work is a development of a new doctrine of church and ministry. He himself admits that

---

[11] Carl F. George, *Preparing Your Church for the Future* (Grand Rapids, MI: Fleming H. Revell, 1992).

[12] George, 148. The "X" and "Xa" refer to people in George's cell-grouping scheme. For a pictorial representation of these roles, see p. 149.

[13] George, 154–55.

his work is a "prophetic call" and should elicit from its readers a "compulsion from God" to put it into action. The god of this volume, however, is the god of marketing and management. My response is equally prophetic. Unlike George, though, I am calling the church back to the prophetic voice of Scripture and the confessions of the church catholic.

I believe that George, the Arminian revivalists, and, yes, all orthodox Protestants would do well to recall the words of Martin Luther in the last sermon he preached. Commenting on Matthew 11:25–30, Luther writes:

> For they are always exerting themselves; they want to do things in the Christian church the way they want to themselves. Everything that God does they must improve so that there is no poorer, more insignificant and despised disciple on earth than God; he must be everybody's pupil, everyone wants to be his teacher. . . . They are not satisfied with what God has done and instituted, they cannot let things be as they were ordained to be. They think they have to do something too, in order that they may be a bit better than other people able to boast: This is what I have done. What God has done is too poor and insignificant, even childish and foolish; I must add something to it. . . . These are the real wiseacres, of whom Christ is speaking here, who put the cart before the horse and will not stay on the road which God himself has shown us, but always have to have and do something special in order that people may say: "Ah, our pastor or preacher is nothing; there's the real man! He'll get things done!"[14]

How long this latest church growth fad will last is anyone's guess. My own church has found itself enamored of the approach, but only time will tell whether it's simply another flash-in-the-pan. It is always easy to do theology on the world's terms—sinful human nature will always reward such endeavors. To be faithful to the Scripture's narrow way is more difficult, strewn as it is with the world's enmity and rejection. Be that as it may, that doesn't change the church's task. Nor does it compromise the theme of this article—that biblical doctrine and its historical expression must provide the cues for the church as it moves forward in the twenty-first century. Only as we are firmly grounded in the Scriptures and confessions will we be able faithfully to address the challenges to the church in the new millennium. To lose sight of where we've been doctrinally and to forget our history invites disaster. As Madeline Sadler Waggoner has so aptly put it: "It is well for us to remember. For a faith or a nation that forgets its roots in history loses its vision. And so must perish."[15]

---

[14] The sermon may be found in *Luther's Works*, vol. 51, ed. and trans. John W. Dobberstein (Philadelphia: Fortress Press, 1959), 383–92.

[15] *The Long Haul West: The Great Canal Era, 1817–1850* (New York: G. P. Putnam's Sons, 1958), 301.

CHAPTER 28

Against the Weber Thesis

Diarmaid MacCulloch

Max Weber, a nineteenth-century German sociologist of genius, put forward a theory that still remains influential, particularly among those who are not historians. In a classic work first published in 1904, *The Protestant Ethic and the Spirit of Capitalism*,[1] he suggested that there was a causal link between these two phenomena, more particularly between Calvinist Protestantism and modern capitalism—thus adroitly standing on its head the contention of Karl Marx and Friedrich Engels that Protestant ideology was the superstructure of change in economy and society. Weber's work shaped the English Christian socialist R. H. Tawney's equally influential book, *Religion and the Rise of Capitalism* (1926). Tawney, who had more refined historical instincts than Weber, both widened and restricted the argument. He pointed out that an urge to accumulate capital and monopolize the means of production can be found in many cultures and civilizations, but he also contended that this instinct found a particular partner in "certain aspects of later Puritanism": individual self-discipline, frugality, and self-denial.[2] From vague memories of these two authorities combined comes that still frequently heard cliché, the "Protestant work ethic."

The Weber-Tawney thesis still has defenders, and much in the Reformed Protestant ethos might make it seem plausible. Plenty of Reformed Protestants exemplified the traditional image of disciplined, self-reliant people, with a powerful sense of their elect status, ready to defend their right to make decisions for themselves. Nevertheless, it is missing the larger picture simply to find the Weber-Tawney thesis proved in particular historical situations, like late nineteenth-century southern Germany and Switzerland, the setting for Weber's own observations of contrasting Catholic and Protestant economic and social

---

[1] Max Weber, *The Protestant Ethic and the Spirit of Capitalism*, 2nd ed. (London: Routledge, 2001).

[2] R. H. Tawney, *Religion and the Rise of Capitalism* (London: Harcourt, Brace & Co., 1926), 226–27.

behavior. Tawney was, of course, right in seeing a wider canvas. He would have been further vindicated had he seen the explosion of emphatically non-Christian Indian, Pakistani, and East Asian entrepreneurial energy in the late twentieth century. Above all are major questions of cause and effect. Protestant England and the Protestant Netherlands undoubtedly both became major economic powers in the seventeenth and eighteenth centuries—pioneers in economic production, and virtuosi in commerce and the creation of capital and finance systems—while formerly entrepreneurial Catholic Italy stagnated. Why?

Any simple link between religion and capitalism founders on objections and counter-examples. Rather than taking its roots from religion, this new wealth and power represents a shift from the Mediterranean to the North Sea, which has political roots: particularly the disruption caused by the Italian wars from the 1490s and the long-term rise of the Ottoman Empire, which brought terrible social and economic blight to Mediterranean Christian coastal regions. Striking counter-examples would be the economic backwardness of Reformed Protestant Scotland or Transylvania. That suggests that prosperity in England and the Netherlands arose precisely because they were not well-regulated Calvinist societies, but from the mid-seventeenth century had reluctantly entrenched religious pluralism alongside a privileged church. Just as in the case of Judaism in medieval Europe, tolerated but disadvantaged minorities such as Protestant Dissenters in Stuart England found the best way to the social advancement available to them. Excluded from political power, ecclesiastical office, or the law, they turned to commerce and manufacture. French Huguenots and eighteenth-century English Methodists (who were emphatically not Calvinists) followed their example.

One powerful objection to the notion of a structural or causal link between Reformed Protestantism and capitalism comes from the very dubious further linkage often made between Protestantism generally and individualism. Individualism, the denial or betrayal of community, is after all seen as one of the basic components of the capitalist ethos. It is very frequently suggested that medieval Catholicism was somehow more communitarian and collective-minded than its successor, Protestantism, which was a dissolvent of community and promoted the sort of individualism embodied in that apocryphal cry of Luther, "Here I stand; I can do no other."[3] Yet Calvinism is a Eucharist-centered and there-

---

[3] This assertion is at its most explicit in some of the writings of John Bossy: cf. especially J. Bossy, *Christianity in the West 1400–1700* (Oxford: Oxford University Press, 1985), 140–52, 167–71. It might also be seen as a tendency in classic English "revisionist" work on the Reformation such as J. J. Scarisbrick, *The Reformation and the English People* (Oxford: Oxford University Press, 1983), and E. Duffy, *The Stripping of the Altars: Traditional Religion in England 1400–1580* (New Haven: Yale University Press, 1992).

fore community-minded faith. Its discipline at its most developed was designed to protect the Eucharist from devilish corruption, and the resulting societies formed one of the most powerful and integrated expressions of community ever seen in Europe. Certainly Protestants disrupted some forms of community, the structures created by medieval Catholicism, but they did so precisely because they considered them harmful to the community, just like witches or sacred images. They then rebuilt those communities and did so most successfully where Reformed Protestantism was at its most effective and thoroughgoing: Scotland, Hungary, and New England. Such places were not at the forefront of the birth either of modern individualism or of modern capitalism. In the United States, it is not Congregationalist Salem or Boston that are the best symbols of modern capitalist enterprise, despite their once-flourishing ocean-going trading fleets; it is the determined and foundational pluralism of New York or Pennsylvania's Pittsburgh. The "Spirit of Capitalism" debate shows how sensitive we should be in placing theology in its context before putting together cause and effect. Reformations and counter-reformations always interacted with and were modified by other aspects of the peoples and the societies in which they operated. Equally, we should never forget that theology is an independent variable, capable in the Reformation of generating huge transformations in society, modes of behavior, even the very shape of the ritual year.

CHAPTER 29

Christ in the Heidelberg Catechism

W. Robert Godfrey

The Heidelberg Catechism is arguably the finest catechism produced in the sixteenth century. Its warm piety and clear, biblical theology have made it a favorite summary of Reformed Christianity for many through the centuries. The catechism was completed in 1563 in Heidelberg, the capital city of the Palatinate in Germany. It was intended to aid the movement of the Palatinate from Lutheranism to Calvinism. Its doctrine is expressed largely in positive terms, but does become sharper on the Lord's Supper, where its position is contrasted explicitly with Rome's and implicitly with that of the strict Lutherans.

From the beginning, the catechism was intended for preaching as well as teaching. The Reformers of Heidelberg were convinced that not only children needed catechizing, but that all God's people needed careful, regular instruction in the basics of the faith. The catechism was divided into fifty-two Lord's Days with the purpose of facilitating weekly preaching from the catechism. Especially in the Dutch Reformed tradition, that intention has been preserved to our day. The sermon in one service each Sunday (usually the afternoon or evening service) is based on the catechism for that Sunday.

The personal and Christ-centered character of the catechism is clear right from the beginning. The first question asks, "What is your only comfort in life and death?" The answer is as fine a summary of the gospel as can be found anywhere:

> That I am not my own, but belong—body and soul, in life and in death—to my faithful Savior Jesus Christ. He has fully paid for all my sins with his precious blood, and has set me free from the tyranny of the devil. He also watches over me in such a way that not a hair can fall from my head without the will of my Father in heaven: in fact, all things must work together for my salvation. Because I belong to him, Christ, by his Holy Spirit assures me of eternal life and makes me wholeheartedly willing and ready from now on to live for him.

This first answer is long and stands in marked contrast with the rather short questions that begin other catechisms. The Westminster Shorter Catechism asks,

"What is the chief end of man?" and answers, "To glorify God and enjoy him forever." The Anglican Catechism is even briefer (and easier). Its first question is "What is your name?" But Heidelberg takes the catechumen to the heart of the gospel right at the beginning. Christ stands at the head of the catechism, and the whole catechism is an explication of what it means to belong to him.

The second question of the catechism presents the basic structure of the whole work. It asks, "What must you know to live and die in the comfort?" It answers, "Three things: first, how great my sin and misery are; second, how I am set free from all my sins and misery; and third, how I am to thank God for such deliverance."

The catechism from this point is divided into three sections. Questions 3–11 deal with man's sin and misery. Questions 12–85 cover man's deliverance from sin. Questions 86–129 discuss the life of gratitude to be lived for such a deliverance. These three sections have been called "sin, salvation, and service," or "guilt, grace, and gratitude." This threefold division is often said to parallel the structure of the book of Romans, where Paul moves from his reflections on the sinful human condition to redemption in Christ and then on to the Christian life. This division stands in contrast to the twofold division of the Westminster catechisms into belief and duty.

The first section of the Heidelberg Catechism is quite brief, only nine questions. This brevity may surprise some who might expect Calvinists to dwell on the problem of sin at greater length. But these few questions impress the gravity of the human problem clearly. The law of God—summarized by Jesus in two commandments about loving God and neighbor—reveals sin and shows that "I have a natural tendency to hate God and my neighbor" (Question 5). This nature is inherited from Adam and Eve (Question 7), and unless we are born again (Question 8) will surely lead to judgment: "God is merciful, but he is also just. His justice demands that sin, committed against his supreme majesty, be punished with the supreme penalty—eternal punishment of body and soul" (Question 11).

The theme of judgment is question 11 is the transition to the second section, the one on deliverance. Questions 12–17, very much in the spirit of Anselm's *Cur Deus Homo?*, speak of how justice must be satisfied and redemption accomplished by one who is a perfectly righteous man and yet is also infinite God. Only Jesus meets these qualifications and is the Savior of his people (Question 18). But the saving work of Jesus does not redeem everyone: "Only those are saved who by true faith are grafted into Christ and accept all his blessings" (Question 20).

Question 21 is another of the remarkable points in the catechism. If man is saved only by faith in Christ, then we must ask what faith is, which is just what Question 21 does. Its definition of faith is superb:

What is true faith? True faith is not only a knowledge and conviction that everything God reveals in his Word is true; it is also a deep-rooted assurance, created in me by the Holy Spirit through the gospel, that out of sheer grace earned for us by Christ, not only others, but I too, have had my sins forgiven, and have been made forever right with God, and have been granted salvation.

Faith is not only knowledge that accepts the teaching of the Bible, but it is trust and confidence that Christ is my Savior. A confident assurance that Christ has saved me must be at the heart of my faith. The catechism develops the content of faith in a long section that explains the Apostles' Creed. Medieval catechisms had been basically structured around expositions of the Apostles' Creed, the Ten Commandments, and the Lord's Prayer. The Heidelberg Catechism follows this tradition of catechismal instruction and discusses the Apostles' Creed in Questions 22–58. This use of reiteration is an important dimension of good teaching.

The section on the Apostles' Creed contains many notable statements. Only a taste of it can be presented here. Question 28 is striking:

How does the knowledge of God's creation and providence help us? We can be patient when things go against us, thankful when things go well, and for the future we can have good confidence in our faithful God and Father that nothing will separate us from his love. All creatures are so completely in his hand that without his will they can neither move nor be moved.

Question 31 is also illuminating:

Why is he called "Christ," meaning "anointed"? Because he has been ordained by God the Father and has been anointed with the Holy Spirit to be our chief prophet and teacher who perfectly reveals to us the secret counsel and will of God for our deliverance; our only high priest who has set us free by the one sacrifice of his body, and who continually pleads our cause with the Father; and our eternal king who governs us by his Word and Spirit, and who guards us and keeps us in the freedom he has won for us.

In these two questions there is much to chew on. No Reformation catechism would be complete without a section on justification. Heidelberg has six questions on justification, of which Question 60 is the center:

How are you right with God? Only by true faith in Jesus Christ. Even though my conscience accuses me of having grievously sinned against all God's commandments and of never having kept any of them, nevertheless, without my deserving it at all, out of sheer grace, God grants and credits to me the perfect satisfaction, righteousness, and holiness of Christ, as if I had never sinned nor been a sinner, as if I had been as perfectly obedient as Christ was obedient for me.

The catechism also speaks of the source of faith. Interestingly, the source of faith is not discussed in terms of the electing purpose of God, as a Calvinist might suppose (although election is taught in Question 54). Rather, in a teaching that is perhaps even more controversial today than predestination, Question 65 says of true faith, "The Holy Spirit produces it in our hearts by the preaching of the holy gospel, and confirms it through our use of the holy sacraments." Do we esteem preaching as highly as the catechism does? Perhaps the church would be stronger if solid preaching of the gospel was sought and even demanded by God's people.

A large section of the catechism is devoted to the sacraments (Questions 66–82). Such length is in part attributable to the controversial nature of the sacraments in the sixteenth century. No question was more heatedly debated than the meaning of the Lord's Supper. But such length is a help to us today because the sacraments are so important and so neglected. The catechism follows Calvin in seeing the sacraments as support that God has given us in our weakness as Christians. The theme of strengthening our assurance pervades this section. Consider Question 73:

> Why then does the Holy Spirit call baptism the washing of regeneration and the washing away of sins? God has good reasons for these words. He wants to teach us that the blood and Spirit of Christ wash away our sins just as water washes away dirt from our bodies. But more important, he wants to assure us, by this divine pledge and sign, that the washing away of our sins spiritually is as real as physical washing with water.

The catechism's second major division concludes with a discussion of preaching and church discipline as the keys of the kingdom. Church discipline is necessary so that some who deny Christ in doctrine or life do not delude themselves or others by claiming to be Christians (Question 85). Discipline contributes to deliverance by calling sinners to repentance and purifying the church.

The third major part of the catechism (Questions 86–129) is on the life of gratitude that Christians will lead for the redemption that Christ has brought to them. Christian living is not a voluntary, optional addition to faith, but an inevitable and necessary consequence of true faith:

> We do good because Christ by his Spirit is also renewing us to be like himself, so that in all our living we may show that we are thankful to God for all he has done for us, and so that he may be praised through us. And we do good so that we may be assured that by our godly living our neighbors may be won over to Christ. (Question 86)

The topic of Christian living is divided into two parts in the catechism—repentance and prayer. In the language of Reformed theologians of the sixteenth century, repentance is really a synonym for sanctification. Repentance is the putting to death of the old man and the bringing to life of the new man (Question 88). We are guided in that lifelong process by the Ten Commandments, which are discussed in Questions 94–113. The fine and helpful reflection on the commandments is concluded with this observation: "In this life even the holiest have only a small beginning of this obedience. Nevertheless, with all seriousness of purpose, they do begin to live according to all, not only some, of God's commands" (Question 114).

Prayer, especially the significance of the Lord's Prayer, is the subject of the last questions of the catechism (Questions 116–129). The Christ-centered character of the catechism continues in this section and teaches us the essence of true prayer:

> Why did Christ command us to call God "Our Father"? At the very beginning of our prayer Christ wants to kindle in us what is basic to our prayer: the childlike awe and trust that God (through Christ) has become our Father. Our fathers do not refuse us the things of this life; God our Father will even less refuse to give us what we ask in faith.

The Heidelberg Catechism is an anchor. It anchors us in sound knowledge as it summarizes the basic teachings of Christ's word, the Bible. It anchors us in Christ's work as it clearly and attractively presents to us God's redemption. It anchors us in Christ's church as it explains the content of faith and the support of faith given in Christ's community and Christ's sacraments. It anchors us in living for Christ by Christ's Spirit. It is no wonder that Reformed Christians have treasured, studied, memorized, and preached this catechism for centuries. We will surely be built up in Christ and in faith if we do the same today.

CHAPTER 30

"Servants of Freedom": Luther on the Christian Life

Rick Ritchie

Martin Luther's treatise *The Freedom of the Christian* is a wonderful start-ing point for reading the Reformer's works.[1] It was written in 1520, three years after the posting of the Ninety-Five Theses, and at a time when the differences between Luther's new theology and Roman dogma had clearly become funda-mental. Yet while many of Luther's writings at the time were polemical to refute Roman error, this treatise was unique in being the first real positive exposition of the new evangelical theology. It was also unusual for its irenic tone. In it we can see what Luther was *for* and not merely what he was *against*. The posi-tion about Christian liberty proves to be robust, coherent, and grounded in the Scriptures.

It is helpful to look at this treatise to see the nature of early Protestantism. By comparing it to Roman writings of the period, we can see how the treatise taught a new way of reading Scripture. Both sides in the debates of the day knew how to marshal proof-texts. It might surprise a modern reader to see how many texts the Roman doctrine could produce to support its positions. While these are not the half-verse quotations of today's cultists, cited out of context, they are still the product of a more cursory reading of the texts than that practiced by Luther. The Roman readings would in many cases be quite plausible were it not for the existence of a broader context of Scriptures that put these texts in a different light. Luther's genius was not that he could find texts here or there to support his new theology but that his new theology was the product of a different way of reading Scripture.

---

[1] *Martin Luther's Basic Theological Writings*, ed. Timothy Lull, 3rd ed. (Philadelphia: Fortress Press, 1994).

Some Texts Are More Equal Than Others

One of the chief charges against the Reformation was that the doctrine of private interpretation did not lead to uniform belief. How could the Scriptures be a sufficient rule of faith if people could not agree upon what it taught? I do not intend to offer an exhaustive answer to this question, but I wish to point out how some of Luther's often overlooked insights can be used to explain some of the causes of misunderstanding. It will help to use an example from another area of life. When I was in the fourth grade, I was exposed to some innovative curriculum to teach critical thinking. One of the lessons contained the following directions. The page listed something similar to the following:

Directions: Read all instructions before you begin

1. Draw a box
2. Inside the box, draw a picture of a pig
3. Next to the pig, write "This is me"
4. Ignore the first three directions, and write "Ha ha" on the paper

At the end of this exercise, not everybody's paper looked the same. Some kids had pigs with "This is me" written next to them. Many crossed this out afterward when they saw that they had been tricked. Others had "Ha ha" written on their papers and said the same to their less fortunate classmates. I was usually pretty bad at following directions, but I had looked at the exercise as a puzzle and had solved it correctly. And yes, I gloated.

Now this classroom set of directions is a lot shorter than the Bible, yet even in this exercise we had differences in results. What was the problem? The problem was that some of the "texts" determined the meaning of other "texts." Directions 1–3 were overridden by direction 4; students realized this only if they followed the unnumbered instruction at the top, which said to "Read all instructions before you begin."

I contend that Luther's evangelical breakthrough was the result of discovering something like direction 4 in the book of Romans. There were texts in Romans that ruled the reading of other texts. In a recent work on sanctification, one writer accuses the Reformers of a Pauline imperialism that makes Paul more important than Jesus.[2] Perhaps this sounds plausible on the surface. After all, Jesus is God and Paul is not. Yet this will not do. Paul's writings are Scripture

---

[2] E. Glenn Hinson, in *Christian Spirituality: Five Views of Sanctification*, ed. by Donald L. Alexander (Downers Grove, IL: InterVarsity Press, 1988), 44.

(2 Pet. 3:15–16), and it is the teaching of Scripture that the word of Scripture is the word of God.[3] So if Paul's writings are Scripture, then Paul's writing is the word of God, and since Jesus is God, it is to be assumed that this means that Paul's writing could be said to be the word of Jesus. So we cannot drive a wedge between the words of Jesus and Paul, because they ultimately have the same source. In addition, if some of Paul's writings contain hermeneutical rules, then these texts rule our readings of other texts. It is not that we practice a Pauline imperialism because Paul is "more our type" than Jesus. It is that certain Pauline passages describe Christian doctrine in a way that naturally serves to alter our reading of all kinds of texts. The same thing applies to the Gospels. When the Sermon on the Mount is preached, our understanding of the Old Testament law is altered, for now we have the author's own interpretation. The source of each passage is the same, but some texts will rule our readings of other texts because they were given by God to do so.

As we compare Luther's readings of Scripture against that of his Roman opponents, I would challenge you to look at the clash of readings like the one that occurred in my fourth grade classroom. I do not deny that the Roman side had texts to cite. Yet their citations were similar to what would have happened if one of the children who had messed up the exercise had turned to another and said, "Where's your pig? Direction 2 said to draw a pig, and you disobeyed!" If all we look at is direction 2, then the child is right. Yet a deeper reading shows the clear error. When we are dealing with Scripture, it is easier to see how even educated adults would be open to misreading. Perhaps they never read Romans. If they never saw the rules for reading, then their misreading might be plausible.

While the Reformers insisted on the right of private interpretation, they nevertheless saw the value of tradition. Tradition is something handed down. They believed the Scriptures to be clear but saw multiple layers to them. When they found rules for reading Scripture within Scripture, they saw it as their responsibility to teach these rules to others. The key problem with interpreting the Bible for yourself is the time required. Finding these "rules for reading" takes time. Yet if someone else can point them out to you early on, then you are saved from many misreadings. The church should be the wise tutor who helps you find your way around an unfamiliar book. The advantage tutors have is that they have been reading the book longer. Familiarity, not a secret decoder ring, is what they have to offer us. The church has a responsibility to teach people to read and to show

---

[3] B. B. Warfield argues this point well in the seventh chapter of *The Inspiration and Authority of Scripture* (Philadelphia: Presbyterian and Reformed, 1948). For example, he cites Romans 9:17, "The Scripture saith to Pharaoh," when God spoke to Pharaoh through Moses.

people where to find the heart of the matter, so that they will not make pigs of themselves by starting in the wrong place.

Scripture Is Not the Book of Virtues

Luther's presentation of the nature of Christianity is unusual for his time. I have read the introductory material, or prolegomena, to several works of medieval theology. They softened my view to medieval theologians who were often accused of an "unbiblical scholasticism." The charges I heard gave the impression that you would not find Scripture spoken of, or if it was spoken, it would be twisted to answer obscure questions it had no intention of answering. The works I read, however, were saturated in Scripture. The method was scholastic—that is, schools of thought that developed an approach to explicating theology and explained that approach at the beginning of their work. "Is theology a science?" they would ask and then attempt to resolve the question by lining up the Scriptures on both sides of the question and explaining the apparent tensions. Somewhere down the line, faith would be spoken of and Scriptures concerning faith would be cited.

Luther breaks this tradition and starts at the center. He begins with the subjective center of things—namely, what is faith?—since he had discovered that this is the difference between being condemned and being justified. "Many people have considered Christian faith an easy thing," Luther writes, "and not a few have given it a place among the virtues."[4] With these words, Luther states the problem his new theology constantly faced. The Roman church taught a doctrine of salvation by merit. The individual would judge the acts he was to perform by how much merit was in them. For most, the idea was to spend the least amount of time possible in purgatory. If it meant less time in flames, then who would not judge all actions as to their effect on time in purgatory?

Now this focus on the bottom line was infamous for its small-mindedness. The indulgence salesmen have been rightly seen for their guilt in making people worse off than they were before. Everyday selfishness increases when we are always asking, "What's in it for me?"—which was the question the medievals asked of every good work. Your neighbor thereby becomes an instrument you use to try to get yourself into heaven.

Yet it was not only abuses that fostered this attitude. While the worst applications of this teaching sprung from the minds of crafty indulgence hawkers, sober theologians had done their part in bringing about these misconceptions. The verse "If I have all faith, so as to remove mountains, but do not have love, I am

---

[4]Luther, 343.

nothing" (1 Cor. 13:2) and the verse "Above all these things put on charity, which is the bond of perfectness" (Col. 3:14) were cited to prove that love is a greater virtue than faith.[5] If love were a greater virtue, then how could it be that faith saved? Further, James spoke about how "faith without works is dead" (James 2:20). The Roman theologians thought that these passages dealt the deathblow to Luther's new theology.

But Luther saw that some key distinctions were not being made. First, when the word *faith* is used in the Scriptures, it is not always used in the same sense. A faith that moves mountains is not necessarily one that trusts in Christ alone for salvation. The demons who believe that God is one in James 2:19 do not trust in Christ for salvation. Second, faith does not save as a virtue. These distinctions both need to be made, and when they are not, the passages that speak of saving faith are lost. What is ironic is that the scholastic method is usually good at resolving differences like this. Passages that speak of faith saving without works (e.g., Rom. 4:5) would be placed alongside passages like James 2:24, and the apparent contradictions worked out by showing how terms are being used in different senses. Yet method alone is not enough when a preconceived system is blinding a reader to unexpected meanings in the text.

The problem was that Luther's opponents did not allow Luther's arguments to be understood in its own terms. They taught a meritorious method of salvation and would plug this or that teaching of Luther's theology into their existing doctrine and show how it did not fit. It would be like arguing over two pieces of music, say "The Battle Hymn of the Republic" and Beethoven's Ninth Symphony. Those who preferred "The Battle Hymn" might plug individual notes or measures from Beethoven into their piece to show just how badly they fit. Yet this is not a fair test; you must take the piece of music as a whole and see how it plays.

When you start with the assumption that the gospel is a system of meritorious works whereby we win a place in heaven, then of course Luther's theology will not work. Luther says, following Paul, that we are not saved by works but by faith. Luther's opponents counter that this will not do, since faith is not the most virtuous of works. Yet faith is not being offered as a *virtue* but as an *instrument* that unites the soul to Christ.[6] So its status as a lesser virtue is no point against it. When Luther says that not a few people have granted faith a status among the virtues, he is accusing them of damning it through faint praise.

---

[5] Luther, 343.

[6] "*Confutatio Pontifica*" (Papal Confutation of the Augsburg Confession), in *The Augsburg Confession: A Collection of Sources*, ed. by J. M. Reu (Fort Wayne, IN: Concordia Theological Seminary Press), 352.

Some Dichotomies Cut Deeper Than Others

Luther urges faith against works righteousness first by making a distinction between outer and inner man, or between body and spirit.[7] No outward work will save a man if he is still evil in his heart.[8] Yet Luther does not say this in order to preach salvation through internal change. No, that will not do since we are in spiritual bondage. But the word of God can release a man from that bondage. That word of God divides into commands and promises (what was later termed law and gospel). The commands let us know what we have failed to do so that we might despair of our own efforts and look for rescue. Then the promises declare that Jesus has filled the commands in our place and borne our punishment.

Luther presses the matter in a way that few before him did. Many in the early church would have made the distinction between the outer man and the inner man, yet most would stop there and urge an internal change. If they did go further and bring the word of God in as a remedy, then they typically declared the commands and ignored the promises. Or they might hold out the promises on the condition of fulfilling the commands. But Luther sees this as a misuse of Scripture. He quotes Romans 11:32, where it says, "God has consigned all men to disobedience that he might have mercy on all" to show what God has really intended through the law. He intended to make men disobedient so that salvation would be on account of mercy.[9] If he had wanted to create a meritorious system of salvation, then why consign all men to disobedience? And why this talk of mercy to the disobedient? If faith is an instrument whereby we receive salvation freely, then it makes sense that it doesn't matter how much or how little virtue faith possesses. For God has mercy on the disobedient. He made them disobedient, or shall we say unvirtuous, so that his mercy would be true mercy. If we sneak virtue into faith as a cause of salvation, then we end up saying that God consigned all men to un-virtuousness so that he might make them virtuous again. Why not leave well enough alone if that were his goal?

Faith Produces Virtues

Luther goes on to describe the life of the justified Christian. Salvation is by divine mercy, which saves us through the instrument of faith despite our lack

---

[7] Luther, 351.
[8] Luther, 344.
[9] Luther, 345.

of virtue, or even the lack of virtue in our faith. But there are virtues that spring from that faith. Luther emphasizes the spontaneity of the new life. He even says of the inner man, "He needs neither laws nor good works but, on the contrary, is injured by them if he believes that he is justified by them."[10] This is close to that famous statement by one of Luther's colleagues that "good works are injurious to salvation!" No, they are not injurious in themselves. On the one hand, they spontaneously flow from faith. But on the other hand, they can be the objects of idolatry. If we begin to trust them and not God for salvation, then they really are injurious. They are much like the Scriptures that unstable men twist to their own destruction. The Scriptures are holy and written for the sake of giving life, but destructive use can be made of them. The same is true of good works. Luther says,

> We do not, therefore, reject good works; on the contrary, we cherish and teach them as much as possible. We do not condemn them for their own sake, but on account of this godless addition to them and the perverse idea that righteousness is to be sought through them; for that makes them appear good outwardly, when in truth they are not good.[11]

There is a relational truth here, which is taught in the very chapter of Scripture the opponents use to prove the lesser virtuousness of faith. First Corinthians 13 teaches that many of the most magnificent outward works are worthless apart from love. Well, without faith they are equally worthless (Heb. 11:6). It is not just the work that must be questioned but the heart behind the work. A heart filled with faith will give its money to the poor in trust that God will continue to provide for it. A faithless heart may give its money to the poor, but it will be a statement that God does not care for the poor, so somebody else had better do so. Same action but signifying very different states.

Luther says that proper teaching on these matters cuts through the snares that had been set for people's consciences.[12] The church had added law upon law that the faithful thought they must follow at the risk of damnation. Luther sees this as a bad reason to follow church laws, since it conflicts with the truth that our salvation is provided freely through Christ. But if the laws instruct us in serving our neighbor, then we can freely engage in what they enjoin for the sake of the neighbor, so long as we do not think we thereby are saving ourselves.

Finally, Luther says that men are naturally inclined to be superstitious and to believe that when they follow laws, their obedience saves them. He finds this to

---

[10] Luther, 349.
[11] Luther, 358.
[12] Luther, 363.

be not just a Roman error but an inborn human error. Only God can take it out of the heart. He says it is necessary that we pray for God to make us *theodidaktoi*, or taught by God himself, that we might be delivered from this opinion.

> [If God] himself does not teach our hearts this wisdom hidden in a mystery, nature can only condemn it and judge it to be heretical because nature is offended by it and regards it as foolishness. So we see that it happened in the old days in the case of the apostles and prophets, and so godless and blind popes and their flatterers do to me and those who are like me.[13]

This is the opposite of Rousseau, who says that man is born free and yet everywhere is in chains. Luther sees men as being born bound but free to live when they believe the gospel. Others might wrongly believe that their chains are necessary to life. But the Christian can dispense with them: "God has consigned all men to disobedience that he might have mercy on all."[14] When mercy has come, bondage ceases. Bondage to law and bondage to disobedience are linked. When one ceases, so ought the other.

---

[13] Luther, 370.
[14] Luther, 377.

CHAPTER 31

Being and Remaining: The Apostolicity of the Church in Lutheran Perspective

Mickey L. Mattox

In one of the New Testament's shortest letters, Jude states that, while he had been eager to write to his readers about the salvation he shared with them, he has found it necessary instead to urge them "to contend for the faith that was once for all delivered to the saints" (Jude 3). This plea has always been at the front of Protestant minds when we confess our belief in "one, holy, catholic, and *apostolic* church." It has always played a central role in our answering the question, What is the apostolic church and what is implied in our confessing faith in it? For Lutherans, answering this question raises issues about the nature of the church and its unity and about what it means for the church to abide in the apostolic faith "once for all delivered to the saints."

These issues were crucial in the Reformers' time and they remain crucial today. For example, right now in the more liberal Evangelical Lutheran Church in America a controversy is raging over whether the church can remain faithful to its apostolic tradition if it blesses gay marriages and ordains noncelibate homosexuals. In the more conservative Lutheran Church-Missouri Synod, a battle is being fought over whether that denomination's New York-area district president, David Benke, should have participated in the public, interfaith event that was held in Yankee Stadium following the September 11 terrorist attacks. There Jews, Hindus, Buddhists, Christians, and others met together to pray about the world's perilous state. This raised the issue of whether Christians can stand clearly for the apostolic truth that there is "no other name under heaven that has been given among men by which we must be saved" (Acts 4:12) when they are at the same time seen praying in the company of others who hold to very different faiths. So it should be obvious that a lot rides on our answer to the question, What is this apostolic church in which we confess belief, and what is implied in our confessing belief in it?

The Church and the Apostolic Faith

In spite of past and current controversies, Lutherans have always enjoyed fundamental agreement regarding the doctrine of the church and its apostolicity. Lutheran agreement about these doctrines appears as early as 1530 in the Augsburg Confession that nearly all Lutherans affirm. This confession, consisting of twenty-one articles on doctrine and seven articles on church reform, was penned by Philipp Melanchthon in response to the attempt of Roman Catholic theologian John Eck to identify Lutheranism with all sorts of heresies. In it, and more especially in the *Apology of the Augsburg Confession* (first published in 1531), Melanchthon labored to establish Lutheranism's orthodoxy and catholicity from the Scriptures, as the epigraph that heads the confession's preface portends: "I will also speak of your testimonies before kings and shall not be put to shame" (Ps. 119:46).

The first article of the Augsburg Confession sets the stage for all of its remaining articles by opening with the words, "The churches among us teach with complete unanimity that . . ." Article VII opens by declaring that these Lutheran churches teach "that at all times there must be and remain one holy, Christian church," which is "the assembly of all believers among whom the gospel is purely preached and the holy Sacraments are administered according to the gospel." This is what the first Lutherans confessed as their faith—and all who claim confessional fidelity to the evangelical Lutheran church continue to believe, teach, and confess it today.

Lutherans hold that the church is not, as one might otherwise imagine, an invisible spiritual community known and apparent only by faith. Instead, the "one, holy Christian church" is radically empirical. It is a decidedly this-worldly "assembly" (that is, *ekklesia*) of believers, a living communion of the faithful created and established by the all-powerful Word of the Triune God. Indeed, the church is, in the Latin shorthand of the sixteenth century, a *creatura verbi divini*, a "creature of the Word." In this divinely created assembly, believers hear and receive the spoken word of the gospel as the very power of God unto salvation (see Rom. 1:16–17; 1 Thess. 1:4–5; 1 Pet. 1:25). In the washing with water of holy baptism, they are raised by God the Father to new life (see Col. 2:12–13), united to Christ the Son (see Rom. 6:3–11), sealed by the Holy Spirit (see Eph. 4:30), and "marked with the cross of Christ forever." In the holy absolution spoken by their priest or pastor, they are continuously reconciled to God and to one another through confession and the forgiveness of sins. And at the Lord's Table they are offered by the hand of the minister and receive with their bodily mouths (!) Christ's true body and blood in, with, and under the bread and wine.

If the Augsburg Confession's affirmation of the church, which "must be and remain," can be taken as the classic Lutheran *definition* of the church, then it is hard not to notice that this definition presupposes that the apostolic church is a community of people at work. Believers assemble and busy themselves with all the tasks we associate with Sunday morning services: preaching and hearing, baptizing and confirming, absolving and communing, and so forth. They rise and sit, kneel to confess, close and open their eyes, bow their heads, speak and sing, pray inwardly and process forward in faith to receive the sacrament at the altar—and much more. This "liturgy" (in the Greek, *leitourgia*)—or "work of the people"—the confession takes for granted; indeed, it assumes it as the empirical context where the church happens. Wherever the faithful are gathered around the gospel and the sacraments, they join in the orthodox praise of God. And there the church is and remains. There, by means of the visible marks that were identified above, we find the true church of Jesus Christ, the church that is not only "one, holy, [and] catholic" but also *apostolic*.

Apostolicity and Continuity

But when we affirm that the "one, holy Christian church" found in this assembly of believers is *apostolic*, exactly what do we mean? Among other things, we mean that the faith of the apostles is *constitutive* for the church—that is, this faith, and no other, constitutes the church as church. The church identified in the Lutheran confessions thus stands in historic and confessional continuity with the church of apostolic times. Their faith is our faith, for "Jesus Christ is the same yesterday and today and forever" (Heb. 13:8). We devote ourselves unreservedly "to the apostles' teaching and fellowship, to the breaking of bread and the prayers" (Acts 2:42). The faith believed and practiced in the church is the one faith, given in "the pattern of the sound words" (2 Tim. 1:13) by which the apostles witnessed to Christ the Savior. The Word proclaimed and administered by the apostles unites us and makes us their successors.

Our devotion to the truth of the apostolic faith does not stand alone, however, but is complemented by a commitment to reject false doctrine (see Acts 20:27–31; 1 Tim. 6:20; 2 Tim. 1:14; 1 John 4:1). Lutherans from the beginning adopted critical principles according to which flawed Christian faith or practice should be reformed in a manner consistent with the apostolic witness as we have it in Holy Scripture. As Reformers such as Luther and Melanchthon saw the matter—and as is generally conceded today, by both Lutheran and Roman Catholic scholars—the church's faith and practice in the later Middle Ages were flawed and needed reformation. In response, Lutherans called for a return to the sources of the faith. In order that the apostolic faith should be rightly taught and handed on to coming generations, they strove to bring Christian proclamation and practice into conformity with Scripture. At the very least, they argued, what we believe and do must not contradict the apostolic witness. Once again, what is crucial is that the apostolic faith—the *evangel*—should be clearly preached and the sacraments faithfully administered. The apostolicity of the church today consists in our holding to the teaching and practice of the apostles, Christ's first and faithful witnesses, as they are preserved for us in God's Holy Scriptures.

In itself, the claim that the church should be reformed based on the apostolic witness in Holy Scripture was neither new nor particularly threatening, even in Luther's day. Church-dividing differences arose only when the Lutherans—whose representatives were mostly secular princes, pastors, and university professors— came into conflict with the church's established leaders: the Roman Catholic bishops. Yet even this conflict was by no means necessary. Early Lutherans were willing to concede a lot to the structure and authority of the church's ordered ministry as it had existed since at least the times of the early church fathers.

The church's ministry of service to the whole people of God had long been structured and apportioned according to a threefold order: *deacons* were responsible for the church's caring ministry to the poor and needy (see Acts 6:1–4); *priests* administered the sacraments and tended the local congregations (see 1 Cor. 11:23–26; Eph. 4:11; 1 Tim. 4:11–16; 2 Tim. 4:1–5); and *bishops* held the "ministry of oversight" (*episkop*: see Acts 20:28; 1 Tim. 3:1; Titus 1:7 ESV margin), attending to the unity of the local congregations in the apostolic faith. At Augsburg, Lutherans recognized and affirmed the bishops' leading role in the church, and they freely admitted that Christ had entrusted to them the "power and command of God to preach the gospel, to forgive or retain sin, and to administer and distribute the sacraments" (Augsburg Confession, Article XXVIII). Christ had established, in other words, the church's ordered ministry and charged it with the duty and responsibility of publicly ministering to the faithful through preaching and the administration of the sacraments. As loyal sons of the church, the Lutherans vigorously asserted their willingness to be obedient to their bishops, provided only that the bishops would allow the preaching of that faith. When the bishops refused to do so, what had been a protest became a revolt, a rejection of ecclesiastical tyranny in defense of the apostolic faith.

Still, the Lutherans were not opposed to the church per se. In fact, the vital connection they saw between salvation and the church is made clear in the progression from the fourth to the fifth articles of the Augsburg Confession. According to Article IV, justification is a gift given by grace alone for Christ's sake alone through faith alone. But if faith is the medium of salvation, then there should be means through which it is given and effected in the Christian. The Holy Spirit works faith in us through the "external Word" present in the gospel and the sacraments. Therefore, the church must have a ministry. So, "to obtain such faith, God instituted the office of preaching, giving the gospel and the Sacraments" (Augsburg Confession, Article V). The office of the ministry is necessary for faith, that is, as the instrument through which the means of grace—gospel and sacraments—are administered and applied. Thus in the "true, holy Christian church," it is clearly possible to speak of a *successio apostolica*, a succession of the apostolic faith down through the generations. Likewise, we can also affirm a succession in the church and its ministry, for if there is a historical continuity in saving faith, then there must also be continuity in the ministry of the gospel and sacraments through which saving faith is given and imparted.

Consequently, the Lutheran doctrine of the church cannot be understood as in any way anti-institutional, as if saving faith could somehow "liberate" us from dependence on the church and its ministry. To the contrary, Lutherans teach that God has instituted the office of the holy ministry and that this ministry is essential to the matter of salvation by grace through faith alone. Lutherans never even imagine Christians without a church. Nor do they expect a church where there are not rightly called and ordained servants of the Word carrying out the divinely appointed tasks of preaching the gospel and administering the sacraments. The church is a tangible institutional reality and it will always remain so, for the "gates of Hades will not prevail against it" (Matt. 16:18).

Lutherans have long been wary, however, of any move that would seem to make the gospel the servant of the church, rather than the church the servant of the gospel. Classically, this wariness is perhaps most powerfully expressed in Lutheran opposition to the notion that what is called "apostolic succession" can be reduced to the merely tactile—that is, as consisting in a continuous series of episcopal ordinations stretching back to the apostolic age. Lutherans, along with many others, have often spoken derisively of this understanding of apostolic succession. In its crassest form, this "pipeline theory" would make the implausible claim that a bishop's tactile relation to the apostles by means of the continuous historical application of the rite of the laying on of hands in episcopal consecration guarantees the apostolicity of the church's faith. Against this theory Lutherans have argued that a bishop's actual fidelity (or infidelity) to the apostolically delivered faith trumps any claim based solely on historic episcopal succession. In the sixteenth century, there were any number of rightly ordered bishops standing in historic succession who the Lutherans thought were unfaithful to the apostolic gospel and who, therefore, could not be understood as the apostles' successors. For Lutherans, when there is a conflict between the gospel and established authorities in the church, the gospel wins every time. The necessity of the church as an institution can never be pitted against the Word that the church was instituted to serve.

Apostolicity and Historical Episcopal Succession

As nervous as Lutherans tend to get when the talk turns to apostolic succession understood in strictly episcopal terms, we nevertheless believe firmly in a tangible church and ministry that are historically continuous over time. There have always been faithful pastors preaching the gospel and administering the sacraments to faithful people. In fact, in classical Lutheran thought continuity in the apostolic faith extends back not only to the time of the apostles, but through the days of the prophets and patriarchs right back to the household of Adam and Eve. The promise made to the first fallen human beings in Genesis 3:15 (the so-called *protoevangelium*) is the very promise fulfilled in Christ. The Old Testament faithful looked ahead to his coming, while we, with the apostles, look back on it as an accomplished fact. Yet the faith of us all is the same (see Rom. 4:11, 16–25; Gal. 3:7–9). Thus we privilege the apostles' witness to the gospel, but we do not separate their faith from our own. The communion in Christ given in the word and the sacraments brings us into fellowship with the apostles and all the saints in the "true holy, Christian church" (see 1 John 1:3).

Therefore, in Christ we stand united both with the living who share the apostolic faith and with the dead who kept and still keep it (see Rev. 6:9–10). To be sure, this fellowship is spiritual. But because it is realized preeminently in the assembly of the faithful around word and sacraments, this fellowship leaves tangible external signs. For example, it leaves church buildings that witness powerfully to the continuity of the apostolic faith over time even when those buildings have long since fallen into disuse. Who could fail to be impressed by the faith of the Christian people who built the churches and monasteries in the Holy Land? Granted, the archaeological remains of church buildings are insufficient to demonstrate that their builders or users kept the apostolic faith. But we know that the apostolic faith has been kept, at least by a few, and that people of faith build churches. The ruins—and in many places the continuing vitality—of ancient Christian churches speak powerfully, if not necessarily, of the faith of generations gone by.

Enduring Christian institutions can also be tangible signs of apostolic faith; and as long as we do not look to them to supply us with what can only be found in the means of grace themselves, Lutherans are free to affirm and accept them. The Evangelical Lutheran Church in America has done this in its recent adoption of the historic episcopacy. The fact that there have been Christian bishops exercising a ministry of oversight in particular places for centuries or millennia testifies powerfully to the church's continuity over time. Archbishops have exercised their ministry as "Primate of All England," for example, since St. Augustine of Canterbury in the late sixth century. Of course, this does not demonstrate the apostolicity of the faith believed and confessed by Augustine's current successor. But the fact that Augustine's successors have included great Christians such as St. Anselm should suffice to impress even the more skeptical that an impressive tradition of faith is embodied in the institution itself. Examples like this could be multiplied. It was, after all, the episcopally ordered church that bequeathed us the canon of Scripture and the great ecumenical creeds; and many bishops have given heroic testimony to "the faith that was once for all delivered," including Augustine of Hippo, Athanasius, Cyril of Alexandria, and Gregory the Great.

We Lutherans make the history of the church our own and claim its apostolic heritage not only, of course, by means of this particular element of historical continuity. Our form of public worship, hymnody, and catechetical traditions likewise celebrate the faith of our patristic, medieval, and Reformation ancestors. We honor them on saints' days, and in the recognition of blessed Mary as the true mother of God. Our faith that the church of the apostles must "be and remain" means that it has not been invisible, so we eagerly take our own history captive in service to the church and its abiding apostolicity.

CHAPTER 32

"Comfort Ye My People": A Reformation Perspective on Absolution (Lutheran View)

Rick Ritchie

Some years back, I viewed *Amadeus* in the student lounge of the Assemblies of God college my friend was attending. In this film about Mozart, a Roman Catholic priest visits a lunatic asylum where Salieri, a court musician of mediocre talent, is pining away his last days. The priest seems sincere and has a good pastoral manner. Nobody reacted negatively to this character until he announced the purpose of his visit. He spoke the words "I come to offer you the forgiveness of God," and the room exploded in mockery. Several students immediately pointed to their chests and said, "*I* come to offer you the forgiveness of *God*." Their emphasis on the words *I* and *God* was meant to demonstrate the ludicrous arrogance of any man claiming to offer God's forgiveness to another. This is considered by many to be the worst form of Roman Catholic arrogance. This opinion is by no means confined to the radical fringe of Protestantism. I remember the evangelical pastor of a church I used to attend saying that if any pastor of his denomination claimed to be able to forgive sins, he or she ought to be defrocked.

These opinions were familiar to me growing up. In fact, I shared them. It wasn't that I had heard careful proof-texting for the evangelical position. The Roman position simply seemed absurd on the face of it. Human analogies sprang quickly to mind. "If Tom totals your car, I am in no position to forgive him for what he did to you. He must approach you himself." Besides this, the Roman Church was well known for giving priests powers that didn't belong to them. Not long ago, they were the only ones allowed to read the Scriptures. At one time they were immune from paying the civil penalty for crime. Why should it surprise us, then, that they would presume the divine power of forgiveness?

When I was later exposed to confessional Lutheranism, some surprises awaited me. Holy Absolution was yet another place where the Lutheran mode of reformation differed from that of most of American Protestantism. The reformation with which I was familiar could be summarized as "out with the old and in with the new." In this view, the Reformation began with the discovery that the church was grossly corrupt and unbiblical in its practice. Reformation consisted in starting from scratch and learning what the Bible taught afresh, without looking for direction from the Catholic past. Soon, I discovered that while this characterized the Anabaptists, it differed from the more conservative Lutheran stance.

While the Lutheran Reformers were convinced that the medieval Catholic Church was guilty of gross corruption, their method was to carefully evaluate old practices. Where they were helpful to the gospel, they were retained. Where they were unbiblical and dangerous to the gospel, they were jettisoned. Where they were biblical practices corrupted by unbiblical additions, they were cleaned up. I had always assumed that absolution was an abuse in and of itself. The Lutheran Reformers saw it differently. They viewed it as a biblically grounded practice that had been abused. Their intention was to retain the practice purged of abuses. This mirrored their—and the other Reformers'—method of dealing with baptism and the Lord's Supper. All considered these biblical practices that the medieval church had overlaid with superstition. The biblical practice was retained, but the abuses were eliminated.

The mere knowledge that there is more than one way to reform a church does not in itself answer the question of whether absolution is a sound practice. Nor does our knowledge that some Reformers taught the doctrine establish it. Still, it is helpful to remember the old proverb that abuse does not prohibit legitimate use. There have been obvious misuses of the practice of absolution (indulgence sales, for example). Yet this does not by itself prove there is no good use of the practice.

The Biblical Grounds

I was surprised to find out how biblical the grounds were for absolution. Yet some of the passages upon which it rested were familiar to me. In some cases I had ignored their implications, using the argument: Whatever this means, it can't mean *that* (by *that*, I meant the obvious meaning of the text); *that* is just what the Catholics say, and they can't be right. In other cases, I had been directed to the wrong portion of the text for my understanding of the doctrine.

One of the clearest passages on absolution is also the most often misread. It is not that the language is unclear, but that attention is paid to the wrong portion of the passage. Consider the healing of the paralytic, found in Matthew 9:2–8:

> And behold, they brought to him a paralytic, lying on his bed; and when Jesus saw their faith he said to the paralytic, "Take heart, my son; your sins are forgiven." And behold, some of the scribes said to themselves, "This man is blaspheming." But Jesus, knowing their thoughts, said, "Why do you think evil in your hearts? For which is easier to say, 'Your sins are forgiven,' or to say, 'Rise and walk'? But that you may know that the Son of man has authority on earth to forgive sins"—he then said to the paralytic—"Rise, take up your bed and go home." And he rose and went home. When the crowds saw it, they were afraid, and glorified God, who had given such authority to men.

I am sure this passage is familiar to most readers. A good teacher ordinarily points out that Jesus establishes his authority to forgive through his miracle. We aren't expected to believe that anyone who makes claims to forgive can do so. They must have divine authority. Jesus proves his divine authority by means of a healing. So far so good.

What is overlooked, however, is that when people glorify God, they glorify him for giving such authority "to men." As Christians who know the identity of Jesus, it is easy to think that Jesus is proving here that he is divine and that his divinity is the reason he can forgive sins. This is understandable, yet it leads to problems. It would take a unique display of power to demonstrate the deity of Jesus. The resurrection is such a demonstration (see John 20:28; Rom. 1:4). A healing is not. Jesus' disciples could heal. Did this prove them to be divine? Of course not.

The right principle to draw from this passage is that the ability to heal was a manifestation of divine authority. If an individual heals someone, he or she exercises an authority given from heaven. That healing is a manifestation of divine authority is supported by another passage in Matthew: "And he called to him his twelve disciples and gave them authority over unclean spirits, to cast them out, and to heal every disease and infirmity" (Matt. 10:1). If it is true that the ability to heal requires divine authority, and that the divine authority to heal can be used as evidence for the ability to forgive sin, then isn't it clear that the divine authority to forgive might be transferable to other men? The people who witnessed the healing of the paralytic seemed to reason this way. What is ironic is that sometimes by direct statement and sometimes by implication, evangelical teachers suggest that the unbelieving Pharisees were better theologians than the believing crowds. The response muttered by the unbelieving Pharisees "Who can forgive sins but God alone?" is considered an example of good reasoning. That the crowds "glorified God, who had given such authority to men," however, is considered an example of bad reasoning. Isn't this a strange use of a passage? Where else are the Pharisees right and the believers wrong? Yet this is exactly the way the case is argued by so many.

Frequently, Mark 2:7 is quoted: "Who can forgive sins but God alone?" This passage, though, is a quotation of the unbelieving Pharisees. The full quotation is: "Why does this fellow talk like that? He's blaspheming. Who can forgive sins but God alone?" If everything the Pharisees say is so true that their quotations in Scripture can be identified as the teachings of Scripture itself, then we have to say that the Scriptures teach that Jesus is a blasphemer too! Of course, this is unacceptable. The point is that the argument against absolution seems so self-evident to some that they are careless about whom they quote in their favor.

Of course, God is the only one who naturally holds the authority to forgive sins. The important questions are, "Could God authorize the use of that authority by others if he so chose?" and "Has he in fact done so?" I could understand a reader answering these two questions differently. It is possible to say that God could choose to authorize others to forgive sins in his name but has not in fact chosen to do so. But are we prepared to say that God could not give this authorization to others even if he so chose?

Protestants' case for absolution must rest on passages and not on rational speculation. The following passage is an even clearer statement of the doctrine of absolution. (Although it is the clearest, I chose to present the above-quoted passages first, so that I could establish the grounds for the following passage to be taken according to its natural sense.) The passage is found in John, where Jesus appears to his disciples after the resurrection: "And when he had said this, he breathed on them, and said to them, 'Receive the Holy Spirit. If you forgive the sins of any, they are forgiven; if you retain the sins of any, they are retained'" (John 20:22–23). The first time I read this passage, I concluded that Jesus gave his disciples the authority to forgive sins. I showed the passage to another evangelical who explained it away by saying, "But it can't mean that. That's what the Catholics teach." There was no real attempt to explain what the passage did mean. I was just told that the natural sense was ludicrous.

The fact that the Catholics teach a doctrine is no proof that it is false. Most would agree. We have to look to Scripture to determine whether a doctrine is true or false. But what happens when the Catholic reading is the natural reading of the text and the evangelical reading is not (or when there is no evangelical reading of the text!)? "That's what the Catholics say" is considered a sufficient refutation. This form of reasoning has got to stop.

According to the natural sense of Scripture, God has given the authority to forgive sins to men. If we do not bring preconceived ideas to the text, then I believe this is what we must conclude. Of course, we will have questions and concerns. If God has granted this authority, then who possesses it? How are they obliged to use it? What if they misuse it? I worry about two classes of readers. First I am concerned about the reader who is so bound to preconceived ideas that he or she cannot see that God has granted to men the power to forgive sins. Second, I worry about those who accept any implications drawn from it too easily. The preferred reader is the one who accepts that God has granted men the power to forgive sins since Scripture so clearly teaches it, but remains a skeptic until convinced that a certain theory about how that forgiveness is to be applied is a scriptural theory. The early Lutherans held to this middle course. They had grown up in the medieval church, so they had better reasons than we to fear priestcraft. Yet they considered Scripture authoritative, requiring them to bow to its teaching even if it seemed in some way to uphold a practice that the Roman church had abused.

Speaking in Christ's Stead

That Jesus had the authority to heal and forgive sins, and could give that authority to others, is an established fact. The question remains: "How does this concern us?" So far, readers might be a little disturbed that the ability to forgive and retain sins is transferable but feel that the matter is still distant. Jesus told his hearers to do this, but can anyone else? If not, we are left with a curiosity, like Peter's handkerchief in Acts. It was a strange thing to discover, and must have been useful at the time, but has little pertinence to us. Jesus' hearers did many things we wouldn't expect our own pastors to do.

Establishing the link between Jesus' granting of authority in Scripture and authority in our day appears difficult to us even when we believe he did grant it. Part of the reason lies within us. Once we accept that this authority existed, it is easier to believe that the disciples once had it than it is to believe that someone might have it today. After all, eleven out of twelve disciples turned out well, and this authority may only have been given out after the bad one died. (I think it plausible that the disciples were able to forgive when they were first commissioned, though this is not required by the text.) The eleven were no doubt careful in their use of authority. But what if this authority was given to priests and a priest to whom I was assigned had it in for me? Could he really damn me? Who would dare do business with such an individual? It is easy to imagine some grouchy priest going through a day saying, "I retain his sins, and his sins, and her sins, and their sins . . ." What would this say of God if he managed things like this? It is bad enough to know that religious authorities, like other authorities, may become corrupt and arbitrary in their use of power. Who wants to believe that when this happens, God has placed his stamp of approval on the situation?

Again, however, we must understand what God has revealed before deciding what he can or cannot have said. I do not doubt that people's fears of possible misuse are well grounded. But the same can be said of baptism and the Lord's Supper. Their misuse is even documented in Scripture itself! Yet we do not abolish them for that reason.

It is important to reiterate that the Lutheran practice of absolution is primarily based upon Scripture. Consequently, Lutherans use a stronger form in pronouncing absolution than many Christians do. They sometimes say, "By the authority and in the stead of Jesus Christ, I forgive you your sins, in the name of the Father, the Son, and the Holy Spirit." This is acting in Christ's place, with the understanding that he has explicitly authorized it. When the teaching of absolution is derived from somewhere other than Scripture, there will be a tendency to favor weaker expressions, often because the early church supposedly did. It may sound more Protestant to some to say "God forgives you your sins" than ". . . and in the stead of Christ, I forgive you your sins," because it seems to leave the matter to God. In fact, it does not. If we didn't have explicit authorization to do this in Scripture, even the weaker forms of speech would be presumptuous. But if we have explicit authorization (the words being "If you forgive the sins of any they are forgiven"), well then, why not use it? We are not to reason out for ourselves how strongly we ought to speak. We must have a clear word from God. If he authorizes strong speaking, let us speak strongly.

The Keys of the Kingdom

It is ironic that Protestants speak of the priesthood of all believers but deny what this entails. They teach that all believers are ministers, but nobody is a priest. In another article I have argued that teaching that all believers are ministers is like teaching that every sheep is a shepherd.[1] But I do not deny to believers their royal priesthood. The power to forgive and retain sins is a priestly power. Here the Roman church is right. What the Lutherans did was to recognize that

---

[1] "Every Sheep a Shepherd?" *Modern Reformation* 6, no. 2 (March/April 1997): 28–33. (I must credit pastors Kenneth Korby and William Cwirla for much of the material contained in this article. They are not, however, responsible for any of its shortcomings.)

priestly powers belong to all Christians. Some Protestants abolished priestly powers, or at least the most notable ones.

Regarding absolution, Lutherans did not just argue from the doctrine of the royal priesthood that all believers were given the authority to forgive. There are reasons to believe so from the text. As Luther argued, the John passage says that when he gave out the authority to forgive sins, he breathed out the Holy Ghost on his hearers. Now it is not just ordained priests and ministers who have the Holy Spirit, but all Christians. If he did not limit the Spirit to the one group, neither did he limit the authority to forgive to them.

> *Does this mean that you and I can go around forgiving sins?*
> Yes, absolutely. In fact, it is our responsibility to do so.
> *But won't that give people the wrong idea?*
> Only if we haven't been empowered to do so. If we are empowered to forgive, then if people who are forgiven by us "get the wrong idea," they didn't get it from us.

Perhaps a comparison with the evangelical use of another passage might be helpful. In 1 John we are told, "If we confess our sins, God who is faithful and just will forgive us our sins, and cleanse us from all unrighteousness." This is private confession directly to God. It is biblical, and Lutherans hold to it as well as evangelicals. Lutherans state that when people do this, they in effect pronounce absolution on themselves. Why? Because in order to benefit from the confession, I must believe God's promise. I confess, I look to the promise, and then conclude, "I am forgiven." This is a declarative form of absolution. If I do not conclude this, then I charge God with falsehood. Have I given myself the wrong impression? No.

The only wrong impression I might come to is that my sins are easy to forgive because they are insignificant. But this ignores the cross. God's promise to forgive the penitent assumes that I am trusting that the forgiveness I receive is based upon Christ's perfect payment on the cross. Apart from faith, I do not receive the benefit of the forgiveness, even if the forgiveness itself was valid.

The same is true of absolution however it is received, whether pronounced by myself, another Christian layperson, or a pastor.

> *So why go to another Christian if I can pronounce absolution on myself?*
> Because I might think I am being easy on myself just to feel better. If I hear the words from another, they may benefit me more and do more to strengthen my faith.

Then why go to a pastor if a layperson has so much to offer? For at least two reasons. First, the pastor is under the seal of the confessional. (Make sure your pastor understands and agrees with this before you charge ahead and tell him something that could be dangerous.) What is said to him is to be repeated to no one. If it is, he should be defrocked. This ensures greater safety to your reputation. If you have committed a serious crime, then he might strongly urge you to turn yourself in to the authorities, but he is under obligation to leave doing that to you. A layperson is in no such position. Second, when the pastor forgives, he does it not only as a representative of God but as a representative of the congregation. If the pastor says you are now innocent, then fellow members of the congregation are not to treat you as a guilty individual.

In the Lutheran church, only ministers absolve publicly, but this is for the sake of order in the church. As Luther says, if everyone tried to do publicly in the church everything they had the power to do, we would have chaos. If everyone in the congregation wanted to baptize a child just because they had the power to do so, and a thousand people rushed to the font to exercise their authority, the child would be drowned! Things work best when the laity are free to exercise their priestly authority in the world, since pastors cannot be everywhere absolution needs to be spoken. And when pastors alone absolve publicly, it is clear to the congregation who has been absolved.

The Historical Case

The historical case for absolution can argue in favor of the practice, but not so effectively against it. If the Scriptures back the practice, then an absence of the practice in the early years would cause us to wonder, but not to give up our doctrine. If, however, the early church always practiced absolution as we read about it in Scripture, then the burden of proof shifts. Not only do we have Scripture on our side, but the early church read the pertinent Scriptures the way we do.

The actual historical practice seems to have developed as follows. In the early church, the Scriptures I have mentioned in favor of confession and absolution were used to establish the practice of public confession before the congregation, followed by a public pardon. The *Westminster Dictionary of Church History* tells us, "Confession of sin as the first step was already traditional in the first century; the Didache speaks of 'confession in church,' presumably a public declaration (*exomologesis*) of wrongdoing."[2] This was practiced for a few centuries but then discontinued because of the problems it caused. The practice was discontinued in the Eastern Church in the AD 390 and condemned by Pope Leo

---

[2] *Westminster Dictionary of Church History*, ed. Jerald C. Brauer (Philadelphia: Westminster Press, 1971), 645.

in AD 459. The problems that led to the abolition of public confession included scandal, gossip, and destroyed reputations. Perhaps it was also noticed that Matthew 18 set a precedent for sins being made public to as few people as possible. Whatever abuses auricular confession may have been subject to later, the reasons for establishing it were valid.

According to a Lutheran reading of church history, it is not the practice of auricular confession itself that is abusive, but specific additions to it. One of the worst additions is the teaching that confession is necessary to salvation. Pope Innocent III decreed that all who failed to go to confession at least once a year were guilty of mortal sin. In addition, the Council of Trent decreed that every mortal sin had to be confessed to be forgiven. These two elements of the Roman teaching, the necessity of confession and the necessity to enumerate sins, were rejected by the Lutherans even as they retained the practice.

Fear of Priestcraft

The chief fear that the doctrine of confession and absolution occasions is the fear of priestcraft. Just what will men do when they are invested with the power to remit and retain sins? This is an awesome power that in the wrong hands could do untold damage. The Roman church has historically had a tendency to ignore these dangers, and Roman writers scoff at accounts of priests abusing the confessional as Protestant propaganda.

In early Protestantism, attacking the confessional was an easy way to attack the Roman church. In his book, *The Reformation in the Cities*, Harvard historian Steven Ozment documents how this was done in early Protestant tracts. Some of the accounts are humorous, making use of sexual innuendo and double entendre. (The priests were portrayed as dirty old men who made sport of seducing innocent girls, and asking them if they had committed indecent acts that they would never have imagined had they not gone to confession.)

The Lutherans retained the confessional but made it less onerous by making it optional. Confession was not mandatory nor were penitents required to enumerate sins. This changed the practice's whole character. Sinners whose consciences were sore because of particular sins, and who had a hard time believing that God had forgiven them, could go and have a minister forgive them in God's stead. While this forgiveness was no more genuine than the one they received after confessing privately to God, it might sink in more easily.

Yet even after seeing that the Bible teaches confession and absolution, some might still worry. How will it be for me if I start going to confession?

Personally, I have found the practice helpful if I have particular past sins that weigh on my mind. If after confessing directly to God, I find that these sins still come to mind, I have found that taking them to private confession keeps them from coming back to torment me. On the other hand, I have not found the practice of going weekly to be helpful, at least as far as I am conscious of this. Weekly confession made me feel as if the forgiveness was wearing off over the course of the week. I felt forgiven on Wednesday nights after confession, but felt as if I had to be careful on the freeway on the weekends. This was not what I was taught, but when I saw how the practice was affecting me, I eliminated weekly confession.

Two groups will fault me for this account. First, the more evangelical party will suggest that the fear of mortal sin I experienced was part-and-parcel of the practice of confession. "This is how Catholics think," they will say. "Why should you be surprised if acting like a Catholic makes you think like a Catholic?" On the other hand, the Catholic party will suggest that my decision to leave off the practice when it did not leave me "feeling more forgiven" was too subjective. If valid forgiveness is offered, that is all that matters. So why do I take a middle course?

I believe that absolution exists for the sake of my conscience. God does not need my confession to forgive me. But hearing the gospel addressed individually to me and my particular sins is helpful to my faith. The practice of confession and absolution is not to be taken as yet another thing we need to do to be saved. It is another way of delivering the gospel we have already heard and received.

This being so, it is my own "Roman" conscience that concocts a fear of absolution wearing out during the week. Yet I have found that the confessional can actually be a place where consciences are de-Romanized, as pastors challenge their parishioners to stop thinking of their sins the way Roman Catholics do (at least at their worst). But, likewise, if absolution exists for my benefit, if I see the opposite of the intended result coming from it and leave feeling less forgiven, then it makes sense to discontinue the practice. It grants a valid forgiveness to be sure. But if it exists to strengthen faith, and my faith is not, in fact, strengthened, then it is not working for me, however valid it might be.

I view going to confession similarly to going to the doctor. It beats operating on myself, especially when I need major surgery. But if I find that the lesser treatments do more harm than good, I as the patient am in the best position to know what is best. This really is a middle course between a Catholic "trust everything the doctor tells you even if you feel like it's killing you" philosophy and an evangelical "I'm my own surgeon" credo.

I have gone to confession.[3] Have I lost all fear of priestcraft? No. I still do not know the limits of pastoral power as it is practiced in my church, and I am uncomfortable about the idea of its misuse. I do not laugh at evangelicals who have this fear. I do not consider them ignorant for their fear of the unknown. But I am convinced that confession and absolution is a biblical sacrament. I have seen its value. I don't doubt it can be misused. I still have a lot to learn about how these powers are to be regulated in a congregation. To anyone who thinks these powers in the hands of men could be dangerous, I say amen. But I am still convinced that God has given these powers to men, and that they can be used for the good of the church. Further, I believe that all would benefit from a deeper investigation of the nature and history of the practice. We can make more intelligent decisions about our own involvement with it if we know facts and not propaganda.

I hope readers will be convinced by the Scriptures to recognize that God has been generous in the ways he has chosen to convey the forgiveness of sins. What I have argued for does not make it harder to be forgiven, since the practice is not mandatory. Rightly understood, it can only make it easier. The Reformation did have a case to make concerning Catholic abuses of this practice. However, we lose something dear if in our anti-Roman crusades we throw out the keys of the kingdom along with the chains of bondage. There is an evangelical practice of confession and absolution we need to recover. God's voice of freedom should be echoing out of as many mouths as possible.

---

[3] I write of my experience, not to suggest that everyone will find the same to be true for themselves. I don't know how lifelong Lutherans experience this sacrament. But it may be helpful for evangelicals who have not experienced this but are convinced that it is scriptural to read the experience of someone else.

CHAPTER 33

"Comfort Ye My People": A Reformation Perspective on Absolution (Reformed View)

Michael S. Horton

Growing up in evangelicalism, I have found that there is a healthy suspicion of unbiblical ceremonies. At least in theory. In practice, we often substituted our own "sacraments." Where Rome offered forgiveness if the penitent met the conditions and claimed the inherent powers of the priesthood, we evangelicals were nevertheless often led to ourselves, to wander in the caverns of our own subjectivity. As I began to read the Reformers and their criticism of a church that led people into terrible insecurities—wondering if they had been sufficiently sorry for their sins, if they had confessed every one—I saw striking parallels with my own experience.

Reformation theology provides profound biblical insights into the meaning of guilt and its cure. It also offers us a concrete model of churches that actually dealt with the practical consequences of guilt. Even many Reformed people today would be surprised to discover some of these rich resources. For instance, preaching was viewed as a miraculous event where Christ met the sinner and brought him or her into saving union with himself. It was not chiefly information or exhortation, but a saving encounter with the Living God by the power of the Holy Spirit working through the preached word. Added to the proclamation of the gospel was the regular administration of the Lord's Supper. Why did Calvin believe it should be celebrated every time the word is preached, or at least weekly? Knowing he could not prescribe something that was not explicitly required by Scripture, Calvin nevertheless emphasized the importance of frequent Communion solely because he was an evangelical (that is, "gospel-centered") in the best sense. As he argues the case, we are weak and feeble. If God does

not constantly convince us of our misery and of his forgiveness and reconciliation, then we will invariably return to self-confidence or despair. The same sort
of pastoral intuition led the Genevan Reformer to argue for the recovery of an
evangelical practice of public and private confession and absolution.

Like the other Reformers, Calvin was eager to see all of ecclesiastical action as ministerial rather than magisterial. In other words, officers are given
the "ministry of reconciliation" (2 Cor. 5:21), not the power of lords and masters.
Rome exercised tyranny by attributing powers to priests that belong to God alone.
However, this did not mean that ministers had not been authorized to bring forgiveness to the lost. In Calvin's section on confession and absolution in the *Institutes* (3.4.1–14), the evangelical concerns are primary. While Rome prescribed
private confession as part of its sacrament of penance—contrition (feeling sorry
for the sin), confession, and satisfaction (making amends to God and the offended
party)—Calvin insisted that this was a terrible parody of the biblical doctrine of
repentance. In recovering the apostolic and ancient church's understanding of
"the keys" (John 20:23; Matt. 18:18; 2 Cor. 5:20), Calvin urged a wise and guarded,
evangelically shaped practice of private and public confession and absolution. For
Calvin, private confession and absolution were simply a one-on-one version of the
public proclamation of the gospel, much as private administration of Communion
to shut-ins is an extension of the public administration earlier that day or week. It
is not a different gift, nor is it a different degree of forgiveness, than one receives
by taking advantage of confession and absolution. Rather, it is a greater sight of
that forgiveness that all Christians receive from God's gracious hand. Calvin offers rich insights as a pastor who understood guilt and its remedies.

First, he contrasts the New Testament doctrine of repentance and the medieval doctrine of penance. Although he is sarcastic in pointing out the speculative
labyrinth erected out of the medieval imagination, he insists that this is serious
business:

> But I would have my readers note that this is no contention over the shadow of an ass,
> but that the most serious matter of all is under discussion: namely, forgiveness of sins.
> . . . Unless this knowledge remains clear and sure, the conscience will have no rest at
> all, no peace with God, no assurance or security; but it continuously trembles, wavers,
> tosses, is tormented and vexed, shakes, hates, and flees the sight of God. (*Inst.* 3.4.2)

To be sure, we must exercise godly sorrow for our sins, confess them to God,
and make necessary changes. "But if forgiveness of sins depends upon these
conditions which they attach to it, nothing is more miserable or deplorable for
us." At its root, Rome's mistaken view of repentance is that it somehow pacifies
God when we sin. Calvin replies,

Repentance is not the cause of forgiveness of sins. Moreover, we have done away with those torments of souls which they would have us perform as a duty. We have taught that the sinner does not dwell upon his own compunction or tears, but fixes both eyes upon the Lord's mercy alone. We have merely reminded him that Christ called those who "labor and are heavy-laden" [Matt. 11:28], when he was sent to publish good news to the poor, to heal the broken-hearted, to proclaim release to the captives, to free the prisoners, to comfort the mourners [Isa. 61:1; Luke 4:18]. (*Inst.* 3.4.3)

In the ancient church, confession to the minister was not a condition of forgiveness, but an aid for those who needed to be convinced that they were forgiven. It was Pope Innocent III in the thirteenth century, Calvin says, who introduced this tyranny of the priesthood.

The General Confession

But Calvin certainly did not completely abandon confession and absolution. They still have their place in the context of the church. First, they occur in the public worship:

For this reason, the Lord ordained of old among the people of Israel that, after the priest recited the words, the people should confess their iniquities publicly in the temple [cf. Lev. 16:21]. For he foresaw that this help was necessary for them in order that each one might better be led to a just estimation of himself. And it is fitting that, by the confession of our own wretchedness, we show forth the goodness and mercy of our God, among ourselves and before the whole world. (*Inst.* 3.4.10)

Hardly an add-on for those weeks in which we feel particularly liturgical, "this sort of confession ought to be ordinary in the church." Calvin adds:

Besides the fact that ordinary confession has been commended by the Lord's mouth, no one of sound mind, who weighs its usefulness, can dare disapprove it. For since in every sacred assembly we stand before the sight of God and the angels, what other beginning of our action will there be than the recognition of our own unworthiness? But that, you say, is done through every prayer; for whenever we pray for pardon, we confess our sin. Granted. But if you consider how great is our complacency, our drowsiness, or our sluggishness, you will agree with me that it would be a salutary regulation if the Christian people were to practice humbling themselves through some public rite of confession. (*Inst.* 3.4.11)

This is why the practice of public confession and absolution was retained in Reformed and Presbyterian churches. Calvin adds:

And indeed, we see this custom observed with good result in well-regulated churches; that every Lord's Day the minister frames the formula of confession in his own and the people's name, and by it he accuses all of wickedness and implores pardon from the Lord. In short, with this key a gate to prayer is opened both to individuals in private and to all in public.

Private Confession

Next, Calvin turns to private confession, pointing out that Scripture "approves two forms of private confession: one made for our own sake, to which the statement of James refers [James 5:16]" and the other "for our neighbor's sake, to appease him and to reconcile him to us" (*Inst.* 3.4.12). It is the first that concerns us here. To be sure, James 5:16 has every believer in mind. The "priesthood of all believers" means that any Christian is authorized to hear confessions and pronounce God's pardon.

Yet we must also preferably choose pastors inasmuch as they should be judged especially qualified above the rest. Now I say that they are better fitted than the others because the Lord has appointed them by the very calling of the ministry to instruct us by word of mouth to overcome and correct our sins, and also to give us consolation through assurance of pardon [Matt. 16:19; 18:18; John 20:23]. For, while the duty of mutual admonition and rebuke is entrusted to all Christians, it is especially enjoined upon ministers. *Thus, although all of us ought to console one another and confirm one another in assurance of divine mercy, we see that the ministers themselves have been ordained witnesses and sponsors of it to assure our consciences of forgiveness of sins, to the extent that they are said to forgive sins and to loose souls.* When you hear that this is attributed to them, recognize that it is for your benefit.

Therefore, let every believer remember that, if he be privately troubled and afflicted with a sense of his sins, so that without outside help he is unable to free himself from them, it is a part of his duty not to neglect what the Lord has offered to him by way of remedy. Namely, that, for his relief, he should use private confession to his own pastor; and for his solace, he should beg the private help of him whose duty it is, both publicly and privately, to comfort the people of God by the gospel teaching. (*Inst.* 3.4.12; italics added)

Summarizing the argument, then, private confession and absolution ought to be retained in an evangelical form, with the following conditions:

1. It is for the good of someone who needs it, not a requirement for all.

2. It is made to a pastor (or elder) because the pastor is the minister of the word and this is a part of that ministry, "to the extent that they are said to forgive sins and to loose souls."

3. It is for comfort in the gospel teaching, not a condition for forgiveness to be superstitiously invoked. Later (3.4.18), Calvin shows the impossibility of the medieval conditions. For instance, how could we possibly recall all of our sins?

> But he should always observe this rule: that where God prescribes nothing definite, consciences be not bound with a definite yoke. Hence, it follows that confession of this sort ought to be free so as not to be required of all, but to be commended only to those who know that they have need of it. Then, that those who use it according to their need neither be forced by any rule nor be induced by any trick to recount all their sins. But let them do this so far as they consider it expedient, that they may receive the perfect fruit of consolation. Faithful pastors ought not only to leave this freedom to the churches, but also to protect it and stoutly defend it if they want to avoid tyranny in their ministry and superstition in the people. (*Inst.* 3.4.12)

However, our public or private confession cannot speak comfort to our guilty conscience alone. Therefore, absolution also belongs to the ministry as part of "the power of the keys" (John 20:23; Matt. 18:18). After all,

> it is no common or light solace to have present there [at the front of the church] the ambassador of Christ, armed with the mandate of reconciliation, by whom [the church] hears proclaimed its absolution [cf. 2 Cor. 5:20]. Here the usefulness of the keys is deservedly commended, when this embassy is carried out justly, in due order, and in reverence. Similarly, when one who in some degree has estranged himself from the church receives pardon and is restored into brotherly unity, how great a benefit it is that he recognizes himself forgiven by those to whom Christ said, "To whomsoever you shall remit sins on earth, they shall be remitted in heaven." And private absolution is of no less efficacy or benefit, when it is sought by those who need to remove their weakness by a singular remedy. (*Inst.* 3.4.14)

Here Calvin strikes that familiar note of his: the weakness of our faith and the need to be strengthened. We also see God's fatherly condescension to meet us in our weakness. Instead of scolding us for not being sufficiently strengthened by the publicly preached word, God stoops to convince us by the privately preached word that is individualized:

> For it often happens that one who hears general promises that are intended for the whole congregation of believers remains nonetheless in some doubt, and as if he had not

yet attained forgiveness, still has a troubled mind. Likewise, if he lays open his heart's secret to his pastor, and from his pastor hears that message of the gospel specially directed to himself, "Your sins are forgiven, take heart" [Matt. 9:2], he will be reassured in mind and be set free from the anxiety that formerly tormented him. (*Inst.* 3.4.14)

But whatever we choose to do in this matter, we must not make out of this practice a means of grace separate from (or even distinct from) the preached gospel. Here is where the Reformed diverge from our Lutheran brothers and sisters in their claim that confession and absolution constitute a third sacrament in addition to baptism and the Eucharist. We Reformed folks have no stock in the number "two," but we can find no scriptural evidence for our Savior's institution of this practice as a sacrament. In both baptism and the Supper, we see clear institutions established, but not so with respect to confession and absolution. If the Lutheran cites texts such as "Whoever's sins you forgive are forgiven," then we share their exegesis. Ministers forgive sins: that is what the biblical text says, and our confessions do not shrink from that conclusion. However, how is this a distinct sacrament rather than the exercise of the office of the keys—more specifically, the ministry of the word privately applied?

But the Reformed join Lutherans in affirming this practice, in contrast to both evangelical individualism and Roman Catholic sacerdotalism (i.e., "priestcraft"). Rome never tired of discussing "the power of the keys," but for her this meant that she could dispose of the eternal destinies of her subjects. Control, power, and subservience were uppermost in such discussions. Calvin was prepared, for biblical and evangelical reasons, to retain the practice of public and private confession/absolution. Yet it must be viewed as a ministry of the gospel in weakness leading to life and not a ministry of judgment in power leading to death. "For when it is a question of the keys, we must always beware lest we dream up some power separate from the preaching of the gospel." Writing about excommunication, Calvin insists on letting the gospel have the last word. In fact, he sees this most extreme form of discipline as a law—work that will lead the person to see his or her need for Christ. Knowing how prone we all are to tyranny and "lording it over people as the gentiles do," Calvin is anxious to keep this from becoming an independent power that the minister has over his congregation.

Calvin's view is by no means eccentric but characterizes the confessional and dogmatic heritage of the Reformed and Presbyterian communions. While denying any "priestcraft," theologian Francis Turretin (1623–87) nevertheless argued that Christ had given the "power of the keys" to his ministers.

But they loose and remit sins ministerially, both to the penitent and believers in common. . . . The absolution committed to the ministers of the gospel is not judicial, such as belongs to a judge or lord; but ministerial, such as is partly by the preaching of the gospel (which consists in remission of this kind) or by his heralding or ministry of it, and in the exercise of ecclesiastical discipline, as it is subordinated to that preaching of the gospel.[1]

The sixteenth-century Second Helvetic Confession warns against the tyranny of auricular confession as practiced by Rome.

> If, however, anyone is overwhelmed by the burden of his sins and by perplexing temptations, and will seek counsel, instruction and comfort privately, either from a minister of the Church, or from any other brother who is instructed in God's Word, we do not disapprove; just as we also fully approve of that general and public confession of sins which is usually said in Church and in meetings for worship. . . . Thus, ministers remit sins. . . . Ministers, therefore, rightly and effectually absolve when they preach the Gospel of Christ and thereby the remission of sins, which is promised to each one who believes, just as each one is baptized, and when they testify that it pertains to each one peculiarly. Neither do we think that this absolution becomes more effectual by being murmured in the ear of someone or by being murmured singly over someone's head. We are nevertheless of the opinion that the remission of sins in the blood of Christ is to be diligently proclaimed, and that each one is to be admonished that the forgiveness of sins pertains to him. (Ch. 14)

Similarly, the Westminster Confession (1647) declares, "To these officers the keys of the Kingdom of Heaven are committed, by virtue whereof they have power respectively to retain and remit sins" (Ch. 32). This is no arbitrary power: it does not reside within the minister himself, but belongs to all elders and ministers as they are Christ's ambassadors.

The power of the keys in general and confession and absolution in particular are, in the Reformed tradition, often linked to both the public word and sacrament ministry as well as to private discipline. For instance, a repentant person who is struggling with a particular sin may not only need to hear that he or she is absolved, but might also need practical help and ongoing accountability. In our own church, private confession is just that—private. Nevertheless, in most cases the individual is actually surprised and relieved to interact with the elders. As Matthew 18 teaches, private sins are dealt with privately, while public sins are handled publicly. When someone is unrepentant and completely resistant to correction, the law is needed. They need to have their presumption shaken so that they will flee to Christ and the gospel.

---

[1] Francis Turretin, *Institutes of Elenctic Theology*, ed. James T. Dennison, trans. George Musgrave Giger (Phillipsburg, NJ: P&R Publishing, 1997), 3:554–5.

Consequently, according to the Reformed tradition, confession and absolution are entrusted particularly to the officers of the church in three ways: (1) public worship, with the general confession in the liturgy; (2) privately, to assure the conscience that the forgiveness is not merely offered generally but applies specifically to this struggling person; and (3) privately or publicly in the practice of ecclesiastical discipline.

In this regard, new Calvinists tend to overreact to their backgrounds. Former Roman Catholics flatly reject penance and its practice of private confession and absolution. And those of us who were formerly Arminians simply jettison the altar call and regular evangelistic preaching as human-centered manipulation. (Of course, there is something in that, and such illegitimate practices as the altar call should not have any place in rightly ordered churches.) Nevertheless, what happens in the course of the Christian life is this: a person is converted by the preaching (hopefully!) of the death, burial, and resurrection of Christ for sinners, and then finds in years to come that he or she is still struggling. Sin and temptation undermine the person's confidence: Was I really converted? Maybe I didn't really mean it? Surely if I were really a Christian I wouldn't have this much trouble with sinful desires and habits. "Means of grace," such as Roman Catholic penance and Arminian altar calls, were invented just for the crisis that occurs when grace is considered conditional.

Instead of merely reacting, we need to go back and examine how theology leads to particular practices and then carefully examine the Scriptures to see how we can more faithfully apply our theology. For instance, many sermons repeatedly try to persuade people to "make a decision." This emphasis is not consistent with the apostolic preaching of the cross. But it is clear from the Scriptures that the church, as well as unbelievers who might be in attendance, needs to be evangelized weekly. Furthermore, if we shun the altar call, why not have regular Communion and an invitation for those who wish to talk to the pastors and elders after the service? Perhaps an extended time of private ministry of the word could follow the public ministry each Lord's Day. Clearly, such ministry should be available not only for new converts but also for the oldest Christian.

We are given ministers not to trouble our conscience as masters, but to lift the burden in Christ's own name. Servants rather than lords, they apply the salve that alone can heal our soul's sores. It is because this is a ministry of life that we can rejoice that Christ has given his servants these keys. "Therefore," Calvin writes, "when you hear that this is attributed to them, recognize that it is for your benefit."

CHAPTER 34

The Reformation and Spiritual Formation

Michael S. Horton

Luther and Calvin have a lot to teach us about heady doctrines such as justification and election. We have to look elsewhere, though, when it comes to the brass tacks of Christian living. Any real engagement with the Reformers' work, however, dispels this widespread misunderstanding.

They knew nothing of the modern dichotomy between doctrine and life; like the ancient fathers, Luther and Calvin used the word *piety* to encompass both. The problem I suspect is that many evangelicals today have in mind a rather narrow definition of piety and a list of spiritual disciplines that are almost exclusively private and method oriented. It's the whole framework, not just the details, that distinguishes Reformation piety from other approaches. Here are several such hallmarks of Reformation piety:

1. Reformation piety is not about moving higher than the gospel but growing deeper into it.

2. It is more communal and covenantal. It's the external ministry through which the Spirit unites us to Christ and therefore to his visible church, and this public ministry defines our private piety, rather than vice versa.

3. Reformation piety treats good works not as something we do for God, or even for ourselves, but for others: fellow saints, our family, and our neighbors through our various callings in the world. Hence, Reformation piety is extrospective more than introspective—looking up in faith to God and out to our neighbors in love.

When *we* think we're talking about piety, many of our brothers and sisters think we're talking about something else. They are often focused on means of commitment that lead to grace, where we're thinking of means of grace that produce commitment; private disciplines that we sometimes can do together, where we have in mind a public ministry that shapes our private disciplines; withdrawing from the world in solitude, when we're imagining a piety that drives us out into the world.

In many ways, contemporary evangelical approaches share more affinities with medieval than reformational piety. In fact, popular evangelical writers such as Dallas Willard and Richard Foster make this connection explicit by encouraging a revival of the practices that marked monastic spirituality. This more intensely personal relationship to God is promised by practicing the spiritual disciplines—especially private prayer, fasting, silence, contemplation, and solitude. Even in evangelical Calvinist circles, as well as Lutheran pietism, the Christian life is often individualistic and introspective. Even when informed by evangelical doctrine, the picture evoked is of the lonely pilgrim making his way to the Celestial City more than the "cloud of witnesses" cheering from the heavenly stands and the communion of saints on earth. While it is certainly better to preach the gospel than other things to ourselves, isn't it more important to hear the gospel proclaimed objectively and publicly to us and ratified in sacraments? Often, the Christian life is identified primarily with things we do by ourselves, to ourselves, and for ourselves.

The Medieval Sources of Evangelical Spirituality

Reacting against individualism, some people put transforming the world above transforming themselves. From the Reformation perspective, this is an in-house debate within medieval spirituality. Should primacy be given to the contemplative life or the active life? Different monastic orders were founded in answer to that question. From the Reformers' perspective, however, the whole paradigm needed rethinking.

The connection with medieval piety should not be surprising, since in many ways the Anabaptist movement grew in that soil. This is true especially of the Brethren of the Common Life, a remarkably effective lay movement that anticipated the parachurch network of evangelical pietism. The basic approach was captured by the title of a best-seller by Brethren alumnus Thomas à Kempis, *The Imitation of Christ*.

Like the Brethren movement generally, Anabaptists showed little interest in debates over justification and in some cases outright rejected it. In fact, many went beyond the more moderate mysticism of monastic spirituality, drawing especially on radical mystics such as Meister Eckhart and Johann Tauler. A sharp antithesis was maintained between spirit and matter, inner and outer, and direct experience within and the external ministry of preaching and sacrament.

The main difference between medieval and Anabaptist-Pietist spirituality was that the latter expected not only an elite group of monks and nuns, but all truly regenerate disciples to commit themselves to the separated life of rigorous introspection and holy solitude. By separating from the world—and a worldly church—their souls could ascend away from everything material and achieve union with God in all of his majesty. This trajectory is evident in Lutheran pietism and among some Puritans, such as Richard Baxter, who were more inclined toward Arminian views. It continued with William Law, in John Wesley's "Holy Club," the Keswick "higher life" movement, and myriad evangelical leaders and movements that have been shaped by this trajectory. Whatever their differences on various points, Luther and Calvin were at one on the chief emphases of biblical piety.

Union, Not Just Imitation

At the very outset, Calvin, like Luther, put the brakes on the monastic ascent toward the God of majesty:

> The situation would surely have been hopeless had the very majesty of God not descended to us, since it was not in our power to ascend to him. Hence, it was necessary for the Son of God to become for us "Immanuel, that is, God with us," and in such a way that his divinity and our human nature might by mutual connection grow together. Otherwise the nearness would not have been near enough, nor the affinity sufficiently firm, for us to hope that God might dwell with us. . . . Therefore, relying on this pledge, we trust that we are sons of God, for God's natural Son fashioned for himself a body from our body, flesh from our flesh, bones from our bones, that he might be one with us. (*Inst.* 2.12.1–2)

The object of faith is not merely "God," Calvin argues, but the *Triune* God, revealed in *Christ*, "as he is clothed in his *gospel*" (*Inst.* 3.2.32). To attempt direct union with God apart from Christ is to "seek God outside the way." It is to be trapped in a labyrinth, as one finds in Roman Catholic piety.

While the monk ascends to the God of majesty through contemplation, speculation, and merit, in the gospel God descends to us in humility, in our flesh, to rescue us. All of our salvation is found in Christ, not in ourselves. Indeed, "if you contemplate yourself," Calvin warns, "that is sure damnation."[1]

---

[1] John Calvin, *Commentary on the Gospel According to John*, 107.

The Spirit who united the Son to us in the incarnation also unites us to Christ by his gospel. "As long as Christ remains outside of us, and we are separated from him," says Calvin, "all that he has suffered and done for the salvation of the human race remains useless and of no value for us. Therefore, to share with us what he has received from the Father, he had to become ours and dwell within us. For this reason, he is called 'our Head' [Eph. 4:15], and 'the first-born among many brethren' [Rom. 8:29]" (*Inst.* 3.1.1). From this saving union we discover our election, redemption, effectual calling, justification, adoption, sanctification, and glorification. All of these benefits belong to every believer in Christ alone through faith alone.

In union with Christ we receive justification and sanctification as gifts. There isn't one gift (justification) and then some other supposedly higher gift (sanctification) reserved for those who experience a "second blessing." Calvin explains that faith embraces *Christ* himself and therefore *all* of his gifts together. Justification speaks to the legal aspect of this union, while Scripture draws on organic imagery for sanctification, such as vine and branches, head and members. The piety in which he was reared emphasized imitating Christ by following his example ("What would Jesus do?"). Calvin pointed to something deeper:

> Let us know that the Apostle [in Romans 6] does not simply exhort us to imitate Christ, as though he had said that his death is a pattern which all Christians are to follow; for no doubt he ascends higher, as he announces a doctrine with which he connects an exhortation; and his doctrine is this: that the death of Christ is efficacious to destroy and demolish the depravity of our flesh, and his resurrection, to effect the renovation of a better nature, and that by baptism we are admitted into a participation of this grace. This foundation being laid, Christians may very suitably be exhorted to strive to respond to their calling.[2]

This is true of everyone who is united to Christ, he adds, not just to a superior class. Thus this "ingrafting is not only a conformity of example, but a secret union."[3]

Christ is not only our hero, model, or pattern, but our vine and we are branches. He is the head of his body of which we are members, the firstfruit of the whole harvest to which we belong. Calvin says that we are "in Christ (*in Christo*) because we are out of ourselves (*extra nos*)," finding our sanctification as well as our justification not by looking within but by clinging to Christ.[4] The

---

[2] Calvin on Romans 6:4 in *Calvin's Commentaries Vol. 19*, trans. John Owen (Grand Rapids: Baker, 1996), 221.

[3] Calvin on Romans 6:5 in *Calvin's Commentaries Vol. 19*, 222.

[4] Quoted in Mark A. Garcia, *Life in Christ: Union with Christ and Twofold Grace in Calvin's Theology*, Studies in Christian History and Thought (Milton Keynes: Paternoster, 2008), 116.

Christian life is not only a matter of getting used to our justification, but also of getting used to being in Christ, from whom we receive both justification and sanctification through the same gospel. Therefore, in justification and in sanctification, faith receives every good from Christ alone as the source.

There is no place for "first-class" saints who move on from the gospel to a higher state of "victorious living" through monastic practices. "Certain Anabaptists of our day conjure some sort of frenzied excess instead of spiritual regeneration," Calvin relates, "thinking that they can attain perfection in this life" (*Inst.* 3.3.14).

> Removing, then, mention of law, and laying aside all consideration of works, we should, when justification is being discussed, embrace God's mercy alone, turn our attention from ourselves, and look only to Christ. . . . If consciences wish to attain any certainty in this matter, they ought to give no place to the law. (*Inst.* 3.19.2)

Those who are preoccupied with raising their standing in God's estimation offend God, deepen their guilt, and do nothing for their neighbors. The monk was the ideal portrait of this confused spirituality.

The Direction: Outside to Inside, Public to Private

In various ways, Roman Catholic teaching collapsed personal faith into the believing act of the church and its sacramental operations. At the other extreme, radical Protestants tend to separate the personal from the public, the external from the internal, and the formal from the spontaneous. It is what the individual does with the word that saves, rather than what the word does with the individual. Baptism is the believer's decision and pledge, not God's. The Supper merely offers an opportunity for individual believers to reflect on Christ's death and recommit their lives, but it is not itself the gift of Christ with all of his benefits. Even in public prayers, the emphasis falls on spontaneous expression— either of the individual pastor or of the people offering their own private prayers independently.

This approach is especially true of the pietistic and revivalist traditions that have had such a wide impact. The apostles teach that we are born again by the preaching of the gospel (1 Pet. 1:23–25; Rom. 10:6–17; and so on). "So then faith comes by hearing and hearing by the word of Christ" (Rom. 10:17). The gospel is "the power of God for salvation" (Rom. 1:16). In Acts, conversion is identified with the public hearing of the gospel, baptism, and being added to the church. "And they gathered regularly for the apostles' teaching and fellowship, the breaking of the bread, and the prayers" (Acts 2:42). In radical Protestantism, however, we are born again by inviting Jesus into our hearts. It is a personal relationship with Jesus that "none other has ever known." "This is just between you and the Lord," we are told. "Getting saved" is not only distinguished from but often contrasted with "joining a church." One has a relationship with Christ that may be expressed publicly, but authentic faith is deeply individual, personal, and private. It begins privately, within, and expresses itself publicly.

In the Reformers' view, biblical faith is created by the Spirit through the external and public word, creating faith within each of us. What results from this divine action are not only individual deciders but a communion of forgiven sinners. There can be no doubt that the Reformers impressed hearers with their need for personal faith. They opposed with might and mane the idea of implicit faith, the corporate church acting as a surrogate for individuals. Nevertheless, personal faith is shaped by the public means of grace, as described in the following four points.

1. There Is the Public Preaching of the Word. Ministers are trained to interpret the Scriptures in the original languages, aware of the history of church teaching, and grounded in the creeds and confessions, as well as how to bring this word effectively to the people of God. Their calling by Christ through his church is to full-time study and prayer, and to share the burden of spiritual care of the flock along with the elders. According to the Apostle Paul, pastors and teachers are "the gifts [Christ] gave" for the building up of his church as one body, rooted in his word (Eph. 4:1–16). When I read Scripture with my family or even alone, I am reading with the church. My reading is guided by what I have heard—together with my brothers and sisters—in the public assembly of Christ's covenant people, through his appointed ambassadors.

2. There Is Public Baptism. The Reformers saw the whole Christian life as a daily living out and returning to our baptism, dying and rising with Christ. Again, in family life, friendships, and callings in the world, we are shaped by what God did to us and gave to us in baptism. Our personal relationship with Christ in daily life is formed by our sharing in "one Lord, one faith, one baptism" (Eph. 4:5).

3. There Is the Regular Administration of the Lord's Supper. The Supper confirms and deepens our union with Christ, as the Spirit delivers Christ's body and blood to us through his word and the bread and wine. As we

grow more and more in our union with Christ, we grow more and more in the communion of saints. While Luther and Calvin disagreed over some important details, they were at one in opposing both the Roman tendency to collapse personal faith into the public ministry of the church and the Anabaptist tendency to separate them. "We are assailed by two sects," Calvin told Cardinal Sadoleto, "the pope and the Anabaptists." Both tend to separate the Spirit's work from the external word. According to Calvin, Rome binds God to earthly means, while the Anabaptists disallow that God can freely bind himself to them (*Inst.* 4.1.5).

4. Even the Public Prayers in Church Shape Our Family and Private Prayers. Indeed, writes Calvin, "whoever refuses to pray in the holy assembly of the godly knows not what it is to pray individually, or in a secret spot, or at home" (*Inst.* 3.20.29). Even in our private prayers we are not alone but joined with the Father, the Son, and the Holy Spirit. And, united to Christ, we are joined to our brothers and sisters beside us—indeed the whole church everywhere. Just as our private Bible reading is informed and enriched by the communal faith proclaimed and confessed in the church, our private prayers are as well.

Elsie Anne McKee explains, "Although Calvin provided guidelines for private prayers, he was primarily interested in defining public prayers, the liturgy, because he understood all personal or individual devotional acts as an extension of the corporate worship of the body of Christ."[5] We have to resist the false choice between public and private, formal and informal, planned and spontaneous.[6] A

---

[5] Elsie Anne McKee, "Context, Contours, Contents: Towards a Description of Calvin's Understanding of Worship" in *Calvin Studies Society Papers, 1995, 1997: Calvin and Spirituality; Calvin and His Contemporaries*, ed. David Foxgrover (Grand Rapids: CRC Product Services, 1998), 78.

[6] McKee, 79–80: McKee puts it well: "Calvin, like most clerical reformers, gives more attention to liturgy than to devotional acts. It is significant that the two marks by which he identifies the true church, the pure preaching and hearing of the Word and the right administration of the sacraments, are both central to the liturgy. On the other hand, many lay reformers seem to give particular stress to the devotional life....Although it has long been popular to assume that Reformed Christians were fiercely opposed to written liturgies, this common notion is in fact false for the sixteenth century and even for many later Reformed communities. (A primary reason for the misinterpretation is owed to the effect of revivalism on parts of the Reformed tradition.)" One should add that even the Puritan's antipathy toward the Book of Common Prayer lay principally in its being imposed by the monarch as necessary for worship.

rich life of prayer in the family and in private will flourish in the fertile soil that has been tilled and tended by "the apostles' teaching and fellowship, the breaking of the bread, and the prayers" (Acts 2:42). Anyone reared in synagogue worship would have known that "the prayers" meant communication with God—prayers the whole church said and sung as one body. When the disciples asked Jesus to teach them to pray, he gave them—and us—the Lord's Prayer. Like a trellis, common prayer trains our hearts to conform our communication with God to his word. A trellis can't make plants grow, but it helps them grow in the right direction.

The public prayers we pray together do not stifle our more informal and spontaneous prayers in daily life. On the contrary, the public prayers train us to bring our thanksgiving, confessions of sin and faith, and laments and petitions to the Father with the whole church spread throughout the world. Because of this public ministry, there is a place for more informal, individual, and spontaneous ways of interacting with God and his word. Only now—even in our private praise, laments, confessions, and petitions—we are never alone. Our meditation on Scripture is now part of the creedal and confessional interpretation that we share in common with the whole church as we snack throughout the week on the rich morsels from the weekly feast. We live out our baptism in the concrete circumstances of daily life, and the body and blood of Christ we received sustains us in our fellowship with the saints and our witness to the world.

The Gift-Giving Ethic: Where Good Works Go

Theologies of glory ascend to heaven with humanly devised methods for bringing Christ down or for descending into the depths to make his living real to us; but a theology of the cross receives him in the humble and weak form of those creaturely means he has ordained.[7] "And the ministry of the Church, and it alone, is undoubtedly the means by which we are born again to a heavenly life."[8]

The Reformers were attracted to Augustine's description of the essence of sin as being "curved in on ourselves." Yet this was precisely what monastic piety encouraged: an inward-looking and upward-striving piety that ignored both God's gifts and neighbors' needs. Nobody benefited from the monastic life. Far from being pleased, God was offended with works he had not commanded being

---

[7] Herman Selderhuis, *Calvin's Theology of the Psalms*, 203, on Ps. 42:2 and 24:7.

[8] Calvin on Psalm 87:5 in *Calvin's Commentaries Vol. 5*, trans. James Anderson (Grand Rapids: Baker, 1996), 402.

offered to him as meritorious claim. The monk himself was not saved by such service, and the neighbor was not served. In short, the monastic life reversed the flow of God's gifts.

Taking a different approach, the Reformers understood Scripture to teach that we come to church first of all to be served rather than to serve. The result of the gospel ministry is faith and this faith bears the fruit of love and good works—not for us, but for others. The fountain is the public ministry of word and sacrament, and its gifts flow in ever-expanding concentric circles from the communion of saints to callings in the world. The flow of gifts is from God to us and, through us, out to others we encounter every day. God is pleased, we are delighted in God's glory and our neighbors' good, and our neighbors have a little more of what they need for that day. Although we may be surprised to learn that such an ordinary piety transformed millions of people, historians document how it happened—even if they don't understand the reasons. May God send us a revival of this genuinely evangelical piety.

CHAPTER 35

"By These Means Necessary": Scriptural and Sacramental Spirituality for All Nations

John Nuñes

If Lutheran theologian Paul Raabe in *A Confessing Theology for Postmodern Times* (Crossway, 2000) is right, then an examination of any cultural group's practice of Christianity must be rooted in the religion and God of Israel: "The only hope for Hispanics or Chinese or Germans or Americans is to come to Zion and worship the God of Israel, not to build their own Gentile religion or Gentile temple." God's people live their earthly lives as a pilgrimage of faith based in a particular Christian spirituality. By faith, eyes, hearts, and hopes are fixed on the final city of God. But in the meantime, like Jesus in Jerusalem, God's people are to be passionately consumed with the things of the Father's house—"for my house will be called a house of prayer for all nations" (Isa. 56:7).

A popular proverb says that "faith is lived most abundantly by looking forward, but faith is understood most completely by looking backward." Christian faith offers a fullness of life in Christ, leaning forward toward this soon-coming King of kings while looking backward to the presence of God in his visible Word who won the victory of salvation by acting in history. It remembers deliverance's strong hand—"We've Come This Far by Faith"—even as it anticipates God's return in Christ—"Soon and Very Soon."

Faith's journey begins sacramentally with three splashes of water—Father, Son, and Holy Spirit. Baptism is performed once, applying the eternal, once-and-for-all, life-giving benefits of Jesus' death and resurrection to his people. The ensuing pilgrimage's struggles do not make us more acceptable before God. No *hajj*, prayer-vigil, or cultural practice such as Kwanzaa can make us righteous before the Father. It is from their faith in Christ's righteousness that disciples embark on the perilous, cross-laden path that follows the rest-giving One who calls out to them, "Come unto me."

On this journey, Christians may slip into sin or slide into doubt. But God's word of promise spoken at baptism is not thereby broken. When we fall from our faith, Scripture does not tell us to get rebaptized. It tells us to reaffirm the faith of our baptism—a faith that rests in God's promise (Mark 16:16; Acts 2:38–39).

Today, many people are tragically going off track, derailed by false doctrine. The church has fallen for Satan's deceptive traps of humanly manufactured, plastic teaching—literally, *plastoi logoi* (2 Pet. 2:3)—and this has thrown her into crisis. But doctrinal corruption is seldom innovative, and so looking backward to Martin Luther's battle for the means of grace can be useful in our pluralistic times.

No Magic in These Means

Luther railed against Roman Catholicism's "magical" conception of the means of grace, charging it with devaluing both the potency and efficacy of God's word. The devaluation of God's word through a denial of the inspiration and inerrancy of Scripture is central to our modern church crisis. Luther viewed God's word as the power for the justification of everyone who believes (Rom. 1:16), as well as the church's only doctrinal norm.

In Luther's time, renewed appreciation for God's word was prompted primarily by God's Spirit moving his people to read, mark, learn, and inwardly digest the Bible—especially in the original languages of Greek and Hebrew. At the same time, late medieval humanism benefited the Reformation by its commitment to return to original sources, as expressed in the motto, *Ad fontes!* ("To the sources!"). This resulted in the Reformers' investigating the teachings of the early church. In this way, much of their work was catalyzed by the recovery of many stifled or forgotten voices.

Thus Ambrose, the St. Augustine-mentoring bishop of Milan, influenced Luther's view of the word and the Lord's Supper by linking the consecration of the bread and the cup of Communion with the speaking of God's word—specifically, with the repetition of Jesus' words as Paul reports them in 1 Corinthians 11. In contrast, by the time of the Reformation the so-called transubstantiation of the elements into Christ's body and blood had been linked to a human uttering, a human prayer. Ambrose helped Luther see that this view had not always been the case by observing that in all that is said prior to the moment of consecration, "the priest offers praise to God and renders intercession for the people, for the kings, and for others. But at the point where the Holy Sacrament is effected, the priest no longer employs his own speech but the speech of Christ." Thus with the Lord's

Supper as with baptism, it is God's word that effects the sacrament. And so there is no magic in these means of grace.

Luther's affirmation of Scripture as the church's only doctrinal norm extended to what Scripture says makes a sacrament. He consequently came to see that sacraments were not made through incantations, smells (incense), or bells (which were rung at key points during Mass). Over against such sacramental mechanism in Roman Catholicism, the Reformers restored God's word to a central place.

Lutherans use the word *sacrament* to refer to ceremonies instituted in Christ's preaching. They identify three: baptism, the Lord's Supper, and absolution. Each of these external rites are signs of the entire gospel, testimonies of the remission of sins or of reconciliation, that convey God's grace to his pilgrim people, given for Christ's sake and proclaimed in his word.

A Battle from Both Sides

Some church historians, especially among the Roman Catholics and Eastern Orthodox, accuse the Reformers of dismantling essential church systems. Luther, Philipp Melanchthon, John Calvin, and other Protestants are repeatedly accused of sowing the seeds for the innumerable denominations that have sprouted, especially in American soil, with the decline of pastoral authority and the rise of Pentecostalism. For example, Swiss Catholic theologian Hans Küng claims that there "is no doubt that in fact enthusiasm very largely triumphed over Luther."

Enthusiasm, commonly understood, involves positive, passionate energy. Without this kind of enthusiasm, nothing great is ever accomplished. But this is not the way that reformational Christians understand it. For us, the word *enthusiasm* possesses a technical and negative sense. It refers to those fanatical, heretical "ravers" (*Schwaermer* in German) who boast that "God dwells in them" (*en-theou*). These enthusiasts maintain that God deals directly and immediately with human beings—apart from the external, objective word and the sacraments. Modern-day church ravers manipulate their hearers emotionally, especially in evangelism.

Frankly, I find God's promise to work through word, water, bread, and wine to be a greater source of strength and divine engagement than any unbiblical claim that God will work in us directly and immediately. Yes, God's Spirit like the wind blows where he wills, and one must never quench the Spirit, but "faith comes from hearing the message, and the message is heard through the Word of Christ" (Rom. 10:17). A means-of-grace-based theology such as Luther's can generate exuberant faith. In fact, as Melanchthon said, it is enthusiasm, technically understood, that can lead to "dissolute," "indolent, and sluggish" spirituality.

Often, when I emphasize in Bible classes that the Spirit usually works through the designated means of grace, it prompts questions such as, "Well, can't God just touch us directly?" or "Are you telling me that God can't come to me in a dream?" Double-edged questions like these are pastorally and philosophically tricky. Pastorally, we know that Christ's love compels us to give every answer with "gentleness and respect" (1 Pet. 3:15)—without doing more damage than wretched presuppositions like these are already doing to our questioners. Philosophically, whenever someone asks a question that starts with "Can God . . . ?" the answer is almost always yes. So after conceding God's ability, I raise a question frequently found on the lips of our Pentecostal friends: "God is bound to his word, isn't he?" In Scripture, God reveals how he has bound himself regarding his dispensation of forgiveness and grace. Word, water, bread, and wine are his self-designated means. Here Jesus' words through father Abraham to the rich man whose greed gained him hell can help: "If they do not listen to Moses and the Prophets, they will not be convinced if someone rises from the dead" (Luke 16:31).

Luther's battle for the priority of Scripture and sacraments as the means of grace was fought, then, not only with Roman Catholics. To the Scylla of Rome was added the Charybdis of the enthusiasts. "Suddenly," Luther said, "there arise fanatical spirits [who] . . . in a short time . . . subvert everything that we had been building for such a long time and with so much sweat." In his customary caustic way, Luther ascribes the rise of these sectarian opinions to the devil. Modern confessional evangelicals find themselves between a similar rock and a hard place. In addition, however, we have an encroaching pluralism that strikes at concepts such as objective truth.

The Reformation Continues

Luther proclaimed that the church always needed to be reformed—*ecclesia semper reformanda*. Biblically faithful women and men must fight relentlessly to reclaim the reformational *solae: sola scriptura* ("scripture alone!"), *sola gratia* ("grace alone!"), *sola fide* ("faith alone!"), *solus Christus* ("Christ alone!"), and *soli Deo gloria* ("Glory to God alone!"). We must continue reforming the church at the rocks and hard places we now find ourselves between.

During the Reformation, debates raged over both the number and definitions of the sacraments. Today, we must confront theological pluralism and religious syncretism if we are to maintain that women and men can be saved in only one way—by grace alone, through faith alone, in Christ alone.

In his day, Luther felt compelled to denounce those who were coopting the term "evangelical." Today, to hear the preaching and see the piety of many so-called evangelicals is, likewise, to encounter a plethora of ideas about God and faith. Where word and sacrament do not link the holy God and human faith, we find sentimentalism and subjectivism. People seek to experience God's power directly and immediately. And, consequently, at the level of much popular piety, knowledge about God is confined to the domain of feelings, emotions, and "heartfelt" religion.

When we think about our hearts, we often start with a skewed definition. In Jewish-Christian thought, the heart is much more than emotions and feelings. It is the seat of our personalities (Gen. 6:5; Ps. 84:2), the source of our vitality (Josh. 5:1; Ezek. 21:6–7), the wellspring of courage (2 Sam. 22:46; Ps. 27:3), the root of our rationality (1 Kings 3:12; Prov. 2:2), and the center of our moral character (Deut. 8:2; Matt. 5:8). Scripture seldom uses the word *heart* to refer simply to feelings and emotions. And no wonder, since basing our assurance of eternal salvation on feelings and emotions sets us up for a wild roller coaster ride of religious highs and lows.

Today, especially, we should remember that salvation comes from outside us—*extra nos*—by means of our hearing God's external, objective word. As pilgrims, our hearts must be firmly grounded in the strength of this word. Psalm 84:5 alludes to this: "Blessed are those whose strength is in you, who have set their hearts on pilgrimage." This psalm's last phrase literally translates as "in whose heart are the highways to Zion" (ESV). These are the roads trustingly taken in life, the discipleship decisions made, the concrete confidence a believer has that God's word as it is found in the Scriptures can be a "lamp to my feet and a light for my path" (Ps. 119:105).

The truth and efficacy of God's word is under attack in our pluralistic society. In conscious contrast, we must preach and teach it with zeal, zest, and accuracy. In the end, we confront our pluralistic and syncretistic time with words, just words—but they are the powerful, efficacious words of the gospel. The church is meant to be the "mouth house" of God. We know that it is God's word that presents Christ; it is this word, spoken by us, that is the means through which God speaks. Where God's word is present, the Holy Spirit is working; and where the Holy Spirit is working, things are happening: disciples are being made, sin is being jettisoned, lives are being transformed, and communities are improving. In the end, "the grass withers and the flowers fall, but the Word of our God stands forever" (Isa. 40:8).

The Means Are Meant for Every Tribe and Every Nation

Sunday morning service is still the most segregated hour of the week in America. We have been successful to a fault in reversing the diversity of Pentecost. This is due in part to our church growth mania that often succumbs covertly to the sacrilegious principle of homogeneous units. Most American churches are monocultural islands in a sea of multiethnic opportunity. "I do not agree with those who cling to one language and despise all others," Martin Luther declared.

> The Holy Spirit did not act like that in the beginning. He did not wait till all the world came to Jerusalem and studied Hebrew, but gave manifold tongues for the office of the ministry, so that the apostles could preach wherever they might go. I prefer to follow this example. It is also reasonable that the young should be trained in many languages; for who knows how God may use them in times to come?

Luther's words loom large in our rapidly increasing multilingual reality. We who are committed to the truth and efficacy of God's external, objective word ought to scrutinize the curricula we employ and the languages we use, perhaps especially in those regions where there is a rapid rise of Spanish language and cultures. Demographers suggest there are seventeen emerging Hispanic subcultures in the United States, and in some areas of the nation the Hispanic presence is growing 400 percent faster than any other ethnic group.

In a pluralistic and syncretistic time like ours, the watchword of many is "tolerance." The way to celebrate and embrace diversity is to be tolerant. This invocation of tolerance can approach the level of religion. For some, this thinking is a kind of faith in the secular, civic realm. These secular religionists dismiss the preaching of God's word as unhelpful even as they view secular tolerance as salvific. For others, tolerance has become an essential part of their religion. Their churches possess their own rare, in-house language, their own predictable patterns of ritualized behavior, and their own approved liturgies of social orthodoxy. But the difference between this and true religion is simple: true religion rests on biblical truth, and its practice requires the recognition of transcendence—of God's coming to us from outside our cultures by means of his external, objective word and his other self-designated means of grace—and of the need for relational depth. The creeds of tolerance are artificial, earthbound, and surprisingly superficial in an age allegedly yearning for authenticity. Tolerance's proponents dismiss the "otherworldly" and distrust absolutes with an ironic, dogmatic ardor often tinged with self-righteousness.

Attempts to create righteous and socially correct communities apart from the gospel are always contrived. They may scratch at sin's superficial symptoms, but they cannot cure its deadly plague. Their treatments may seem salutary, but they are, in fact, deeply unhealthy since they are only skin deep.

In contrast, God's designated means of reconciling human beings with himself have multiple dimensions. In the preaching and teaching of his word, in baptism and the Lord's Supper, God creates a connection to himself by faith. The promise of life in God is conveyed to the baptized through water and the word. Inherited sin is thereby exchanged for Christ's righteousness and full and free forgiveness is extended. A new orientation and destination is adopted and a new pilgrimage begins.

On this journey, our fellow-travelers change forever. We must seek inclusive fellowships that confess Trinitarian truth. Authentic multiethnic communities should come out of baptismal and Eucharistic living, as John's vision of robed palm-branch wavers from every nation, tribe, people, and language attests (Rev. 7:9–12). These communities cannot be manufactured, manipulated, or replicated merely by raising ethnic consciousness.

We must lay claim bravely to that which has already claimed all of us who believe and are baptized and thus become a community of one Lord, one faith, one baptism (Eph. 4:5). This water is "thicker" than any blood except the blood of Christ by which our sin has been washed away. God's self-designated means of grace bind us together more effectively than any sociological principle. What he has joined together in baptism, and what he keeps together at the table of Holy Communion, no racism, no sexism, or no ethnocentrism can ever put asunder.

So it is this kind of sacramental spirituality that defines who we are when we say "we." Who are we? Well, we are those who have put our faith in the gospel, who have been baptized, and who together celebrate Communion.

The church has a long way to go, but it has a helpful legacy and a glorious future. Along its pilgrims' way, it has a God who feeds his weary people with his gifts of forgiveness and reconciliation as conveyed by the sacraments that Christ instituted in his preaching. God's word, water, bread, and wine really are bread from heaven that make us, his weary pilgrim people, fresh and clean. The prolific Welsh hymn writer William Williams (1717–1791) expressed this poetically:

Guide me, O Thou great Jehovah,   *Bread of heaven, Bread of heaven,*
Pilgrim through this barren land;   *Feed me till I want no more;*
I am weak, but Thou art mighty,   *Feed me till I want no more.*
Hold me with Thy pow'rful hand.

CHAPTER 36

A Brief History of the Westminster Assembly

Michael S. Horton

It is impossible to read the history of modern Britain or the United States without realizing at once that it is simultaneously the history of Puritanism. After the "first Reformation," which is how the Puritans referred to the sixteenth century led by Luther and Calvin, it became increasingly clear that many in Britain were simply moving from nominal Roman Catholicism to nominal Protestantism. Baptized in the Church of England, every native son or daughter was generally regarded as a citizen of heaven, in spite of so many learned and godly bishops and archbishops who insisted on further reformation of the church.

The Puritans were simply Protestants who thought that the English Reformation had not gone far enough. Unlike the Anabaptists, they did not think this meant a rejection of infant baptism or involvement in society. In fact, the Puritan-dominated House of Commons prior to the English Civil War in the mid-seventeenth century was on the vanguard of democratic thinking. The problem was that the Reformed Church of England had inherited a monarch for its head. When Henry VIII made the Church of England independent of the Rome in 1534 and himself head of the church under the Act of Supremacy, it was not for all the right reasons, as we recall from high school history lessons. In fact, Henry had earlier earned for himself the title "defender of the faith" from the pope for writing a tract against Luther; but as his leading scholars, bishops, and his own archbishop of Canterbury were turning to the Reformed faith, the ruthless monarch knew he would have to make certain concessions in order to win and keep his church. "This King wants to be God," Luther charged. "He founds articles of faith, which even the Pope never did."

Henry's son, Edward, succeeded and encouraged Reformed faith throughout the realm, for he was himself an avid reader of the Reformers as well as the Greek New Testament. The young king's favor for some of the greatest names in the Reformation (Martin Bucer, Calvin's mentor, and Peter Martyr Vermigli) brought them to England's universities as jewels in the nation's crown. As these continental Reformed theologians taught and inspired an entire generation of bright young scholars, Edward's untimely death at the age of fifteen placed "Bloody Mary," his half-sister, on the throne. Between the years 1555–1558, Mary had nearly three hundred Protestants, including bishops and the archbishop of Canterbury, burned at the stake. Furthermore, in spite of the national and religious sentiment against Spain, Mary married King Phillip II. In 1558, the queen was laid to rest, and the nation joyously acclaimed Elizabeth I the "Virgin Queen." The scores of young Reformed scholars who had fled England during Mary's persecutions returned, with a firsthand knowledge of the Reformed Churches of Europe.

The Protestants who sought a more complete reformation of the Church of England—patterned on the models of Geneva, Strasbourg, and Zurich—saw in Elizabeth a sign of hope for their spirits after such bitter disappointments. The new queen seemed to support their hopes by appointing the newly returned Reformed exiles to be her archbishops, bishops, and chaplains. Nevertheless, Elizabeth declared herself, like her father before her, to be governor of the church and set out to steer a middle course between Rome and Geneva with what came to be called the "Elizabethan Settlement."

For many Englishmen, however, it did not settle anything. Just when Protestantism was restored in England, the further reformation for which so many Protestants had longed seemed stillborn. These were the beginnings of frustration. With so many who had tasted the best theological fare in the Reformed centers of Europe now in ecclesiastical power, and so many more trained by these returned exiles, the key question became: Do we put up with an unreformed church, so long as the gospel is purely preached? Even Bullinger and Calvin answered yes and generally sided with the Elizabethan bishops, counseling the "Puritans" (i.e., those who wanted to model the church's government and liturgy on Geneva or Zurich) to pursue a moderate course of reformation.

At first, the Puritans heeded, but when Presbyterian Thomas Cartwright was deprived of his living and his post at Cambridge, things definitely began to make a turn for the worse. Across Europe, wars over religion were breaking out and the Roman Catholic princes formed a league to drive Protestantism off the continent. In 1572, over three thousand French Calvinists were slaughtered in Paris alone and many thousands more in the countryside, which Pope Gregory XIII celebrated with a *Te Deum*. But the massacre, led by the queen, gave Protestants in Europe and England the impression that Roman Catholicism equaled despotism in government and tyranny on the throne. Elizabeth was succeeded by her nephew, James of Scotland, who had been trained by Presbyterians. When the Puritans of England met up with the new monarch on his way down to be crowned, their hopes again were raised, only to be dashed after successive attempts to reform the liturgy and church government and to allow for liberty in matters of Christian conscience.

But the trouble really began in earnest when James was succeeded in 1625 by his son, Charles I. Marrying a Roman Catholic princess, Charles began to favor those who had been won over to the arguments of the Dutch heretic Arminius. In the eyes of the Puritans (indeed, many Protestants), this was tantamount to giving England back over to the religion of Rome. When Charles declared war on Scotland, the Puritan-controlled Parliament would not fund the war against its Presbyterian brethren and the king responded by dissolving Parliament. Meanwhile, William Laud, Charles's archbishop of Canterbury, was depriving Calvinists of their posts and livings and ejecting ministers from the land. A trickle to the New World became a stream, as New England became the center for ejected Puritans. Of course, the affairs in England presented a constitutional as well as religious crisis.

Finally, in 1642, the English Civil War broke out. In 1643, in the heat of military battle, Parliament called for an assembly of "learned, godly, and judicious divines" to meet at Westminster for the purpose of forming a confession, catechism, and directory of worship for the uniform worship of God in the three kingdoms of Scotland, Ireland, and England. It is against this dramatic backdrop that the assembly of thirty laymen, a few Scottish observers, and one hundred twenty-five ministers (mainly Presbyterian, but also Episcopalian and Congregational) gathered to bind the divided kingdoms into one united kingdom. The basis of unity was the one church that was patterned on "the example of the best reformed churches and according to the word of God." The Civil War concluded with the trial and execution of Charles and Laud by Parliament as traitors and tyrants, along with the abolition of the House of Lords as "useless and dangerous." Oliver Cromwell took the helm until the monarchy was restored in 1660.

The very name "Puritan" has become a form of derision for those whom we consider prudish or indefatigably opposed to pleasure or joy. Despite much scholarship pouring off the press that dispels these myths, even from secular historians who have little sympathy for their views, the popular misconceptions persist. Unless we are opposed to Christ-centered, biblical preaching, godly living, constitutional democracy, the beauty of the arts and sciences, and the excellence of education, we have nothing to lose as heirs of the Puritans and everything to gain. Perhaps the portrait provided by C. S. Lewis will encourage us to take the Puritans more seriously at a time when we seem to be at a loss for the depth of biblical wisdom, richness of language, and clarity of insight that these sturdy souls provided for their time and place:

Nearly every association which now clings to the word *puritan* has to be eliminated when we are thinking of the early Protestants. Whatever they were, they were not sour, gloomy, or severe; nor did their enemies bring any such charge against them. . . . For [Thomas] More, a Protestant was one "dronke of the new must of lewd lightnes of minde and vayne gladnesse of harte. . . ." We must picture these Puritans as the very opposite of those who bear that name today: as young, fierce, progressive intellectuals, very fashionable and up-to-date. They were not teetotalers; bishops, not beer, were their special aversion. . . . They wanted English drama to observe the (supposedly) Aristotelian "unities," and some of them wanted English poets to abandon rhyme—a nasty, "barbarous" or "Gothic" affair—and use classical metres in English. There was no necessary enmity between Puritans and humanists. They were often the same people, and nearly always the same sort of people.

May God visit us with another Reformation and the warmhearted, zealous, and deeply thoughtful Christianity we find represented in this confession and these catechisms.

CHAPTER 37

A Defense of Reformed Liturgy

Michael S. Horton

If anyone had told me that I would one day write an article defending any kind of liturgy, much less something called "Reformed liturgy," I would have politely changed the subject. But here I am, writing that very article and almost giddy with enthusiasm for the project. If the reader will permit a bit of brief autobiography, it may help make the point.

Raised in mainstream conservative evangelicalism, wrestling with God and his people became somewhat commonplace for me. In my early teens, I began questioning things and turned to the book of Romans, at my brother's suggestion, for answers. What I found there contradicted much of what I was being taught in an Arminian private school and church, but there was no church in town that seemed to serve up a diet of "sovereign grace," so off I went to the "big city" next door, to Bidwell Presbyterian Church, a distinguished United Presbyterian congregation in Chico, California, whose well-preserved Victorian architecture and vaulted ceilings inspired a mixture of enchantment, awe, unfamiliarity, and no small degree of fear. "Isn't this awfully 'Catholic?'" I recall having asked myself. The service itself contributed little to ease my worries in that regard, as the congregation in unison recited a creed, a confession of sin, and heard a declaration of pardon from the minister up front. It was all very strange. The songs were not the Bill Gaither choruses I had come to know and loathe. (I have always had trouble understanding the charge of contemporary worship that traditional worship music is boring, given the repetitious and unimaginative style of many of the praise choruses.) Instead, the almost demonic bass end of the organ's pipes nearly unhinged my jaws, as the processional made its way down the aisle with "For All the Saints." The pastor got me reading serious theological work, and I finally found compadres, soul mates, in this passion for the theology of the book of Romans.

In later years, I would reflect on the harmony between that service and Romans. Each Sunday at Bidwell, the focus of the liturgy and singing was on God and his saving work in Christ for his whole church; while at my home church, the focus was on me and my personal "willing and running," as Paul put it (Rom. 9:12). Since then, I have studied liturgy in some depth and have come to believe that it is impossible to be Reformed in theology and have one's worship shaped by music companies in Nashville owned and operated by Pentecostals. I do not hate Pentecostals; but having experienced the deeply Arminian (even Pelagian) theology that fuels their experience-oriented style, I have come to believe that style and substance are indivisible. God-centered theology requires God-centered worship and piety, while human-centered theology will always lead to entertainment, emotional exuberance, subjective fanaticism, and the never-ending roller-coaster of repeating the same "high" next week. There is no reason why a Reformed church needs to adopt the resources of charismatic and Pentecostal groups, since the Reformed tradition has, by God's grace, produced some of the greatest hymns and choral music in church history. Its heritage of psalm singing, including the full range of psalms set to appropriate tunes, is rich. There is a reason why that organ with its imposing and ominous-sounding pipes is given priority over the guitar. The ministry of word and sacrament is one of proclamation, not chiefly of informal storytelling. The whole service centers not on an experience but on an announcement! How do we best convey this sense to the people?

According to *The Encyclopedia of the Reformed Faith*, "Reformed worship glorifies God, the holy God, whose gracious salvation is a free, undeserved gift. Therefore, Reformed worship can be described as 'objective'; with awe it glorifies the sovereign God, yet it is essentially thankful." It is important for those of us who call ourselves "Reformed" to realize that Reformed theology is not simply a new way of thinking or believing, but a new way of worship and service.

First, Reformed worship is dialogical. That is, God speaks to us (guilt, followed by grace), and we respond (gratitude). This, by the way, is the division of the Heidelberg Catechism (1563): Guilt, Grace, and Gratitude. As David G. Buttrick points out, "If medieval worship had become an 'office,' a propitiatory work offered to God securing mercy, Reformation worship was responsive—like the biblical leper who, healed, turned back to praise God." In the Reformed tradition, he notes, "worship is neither a transactional sacrifice nor an awareness of religious experience. God acts empty-handed and we respond to God's goodness in a 'sacrifice of praise and thanksgiving.'" But, as Buttrick also observes, the Reformers were not innovators. On the contrary, they thought the medieval church had added too many new services and ceremonies that obscured the law and the gospel and the centrality of Christ.

Origins of Reformed Liturgy

While the differences pale in comparison to today's free for all, Reformed patterns varied slightly even during the Reformation. Zurich, for instance, led by Ulrich Zwingli, was largely out of fellowship with the rest of the Reformed movement until after Zwingli's death, especially for its extreme views on the Lord's Supper (i.e., a memorialist view, chided as "the Real Absence" doctrine). One might expect Zwingli to have been a liturgical radical, as he had silenced the organs and whitewashed the walls. Yet his service actually retained the sung "Ave Maria" and a commemoration of the dead; only under strong pressure from the people did he abandon Latin, ceremonies, and vestments.

More principled reflection on biblical worship took place in Strasbourg, a German city during the Reformation, led by the Reformed theologian Martin Bucer, Calvin's mentor. In 1524, the Reformed service was the German Mass purged of its errant theology. The goal was to find the most ancient threads of the Mass (which were in some way centered on a progress of guilt, grace, and gratitude) and expunging the more recent accretions that tended toward works-righteousness and the re-sacrifice of Christ. It was here that John Calvin developed his liturgical views and took them back to Geneva, where he had already attempted unsuccessfully to reform the liturgy away from Zwinglian lines that William Farel had established. In Strasbourg, Calvin pastored the French refugees and adapted Bucer's service. "Thus," writes Buttrick, "Calvin's new liturgy incorporated the basic shape of the Mass, Word, and sacrament, rather than the stark 'preachiness' of Farel's" service. "No meeting of the church," Calvin wrote, "should take place without the Word, prayers, partaking of the Supper, and almsgiving" (*Inst.*4.17.44).

Although the Reformed departed from the Lutheran understanding of the Lord's Supper in certain essential respects, both agreed that Christ was actually present and was not only exhibited but given through the preached word and received sacrament. Both rejected any Zwinglian interpretation of the sacraments as "bare and naked signs" (see the Belgic, Second Helvetic, and Westminster Confessions on the point), and emphasized the connection between word, sacrament, and Spirit. While the Spirit is active in every aspect of our lives as Christians, he only dispenses his saving blessings in Christ through word and sacrament. Thus the service must be a "word and sacrament" service, not cluttered with special music, excessive singing, and lavish ceremonies.

The outline of a Lutheran and Reformed service was basically identical. As Bryan Chapell points out, the Liturgy of the Word for both groups began with the call to worship (hymn and blessing), recitation of a prayer of general confession, absolution or declaration of pardon, pastoral prayer (including specific requests on behalf of the congregation), Scripture readings, the Apostles' Creed, and sermon. Hymns and psalms, of course, were interspersed throughout. The Liturgy of the Upper Room (i.e., the Communion service, for both Lutheran and Reformed churches began with the offering, intercessions, the Lord's Prayer, followed by the Exhortation (i.e., warning against unlawful eating and drinking), the Creed (sung in the Reformed churches), Words of Institution, Prayer of Consecration, and the Fraction (breaking of the bread or wafer). Communicants then came forward to receive the common cup and the bread from a common loaf. As in the Liturgy of the Word, here hymns and psalms were interspersed as appropriate and the Aaronic Blessing was pronounced as a benediction.

What is the point in all of this? First, it is biblical. All of the described elements are evident in Scripture and are present in these services. Paul's warnings about properly exhorting the congregation and fencing the Table are taken seriously here. As the early church simply adapted the synagogue worship (in which Jesus himself was reared and, when he taught his disciples to pray according to the form of the Lord's Prayer, seems to have endorsed) to Christian use. Jesus was raised with a service book, full of prayers and the psalms, as were many of the first Christians. The basic elements of the services thus described are actually patterned on the earliest forms of Christian worship available.

Second, Reformed worship is God-centered. It focuses on the objective, what God has done in Christ for the salvation of sinners, applied by the Holy Spirit. Calvin himself insisted, against opposition on the city council, that there be an assurance of pardon and weekly Communion. Believers must constantly be reminded that they are sinners who require divine forgiveness even for the sinfulness that clings to their best works. They must never be allowed to fall back on themselves for assurance nor live again for themselves, so the service must concentrate on guilt and grace, with gratitude as the only appropriate creaturely response. Medieval worship had degenerated into a show, Calvin lamented in a number of places. Since people could not read or follow the Latin sermon and liturgy, their only point of contact with the service was emotional. In fact, morality plays—dramas—often overshadowed or even replaced sermons. Similarly today, images prevail and sermons and worship styles are increasingly reduced to the lowest common denominator. What results, of course, is another tyranny of images over words, "orthofeely" over orthodoxy, experience and entertainment over proclamation and announcement.

CHAPTER 38

Calvin and Anglicanism

C. FitzSimons Allison

Although Archbishop Thomas Cranmer was in significant and amicable correspondence with John Calvin during Edward VI's reign, the enormous influence of Calvinism on the English Church occurred after the death of Queen Mary (1558) with the return of the "Marian exiles" who had lived among Calvin scholars on the continent. Archbishop Edmund Grindall (d. 1583) was one of the exiles who lived in Frankfurt until Elizabeth succeeded Mary. He had tried to mediate among the exiles and was regarded as a "moderate" Calvinist. However, he so favored attention to Scripture on the part of Puritan conventicles called "prophesyings" that he refused Queen Elizabeth's demand to shut them down and was forced to relinquish much of his authority. The high water mark of Calvinism in England is considered to be under Grindall's successor, John Whitgift (1583–1604). Although Grindall was a vigorous opponent of the Puritan Thomas Cartwright in debates at Cambridge, he showed himself to be a staunch defender of episcopacy against Presbyterian claims. Yet he was a decided Calvinist in theology if not in polity. At that time, Cambridge University was beset by a most acrimonious division over questions of indefectibility of grace, whether it applied to all who were regenerate and justified or only to the elect. The latter was deemed "Augustinian" and the former "Calvinist."

Whitgift helped formulate the Lambeth Articles of 1596, which leaned toward the Calvinist side of the debate. In spite of careful qualifications as to the authority of the articles, they brought down a heavy barrage of criticism from the queen, Lord Burleigh, and leading scholars across England. After 1596, Calvinism was never again the leading theological party in England.

The most remarkable evidence of the trend away from Calvinism (and from the Reformation) was the conference led by Bishop William Laud (1573–1645) and "Fisher" the Jesuit. It had been called by the king to settle the claims of Roman Catholicism against those of the Church of England. Laud, then bishop of St. David's, was the English Church's spokesman and later archbishop. In defending his church against Roman Catholic claims, he never mentions either the Thirty-Nine Articles or the doctrine of justification.

The very term "Calvinism" is an awkward one, especially in light of the on-going debate as to how much and on what issues later Calvinists differed from Calvin himself. In the matter of the Eucharistic presence, there is a consensus that Cranmer's gradual change of mind led him from Luther's position to something closer to that of Calvin.[1]

The Synod of Dort (1618–19) gave to Calvinism a precise definition: (1) Total depravity (fallen humans cannot choose to serve God); (2) Unconditional election (God's choice of the elect is not conditional on any action by them); (3) Limited atonement (Christ died for the elect only); (4) Irresistible grace (divine grace cannot be rejected by the elect); and (5) Perseverance of the saints (once elect, always elect). These issues had divided "Calvinists" from "Remonstrants," but the political and military divisions made open dialogue impossible. The Remonstrants were barred from or refused to attend the synod and were condemned on the basis of their writings. Some followers of Calvin were aware that Calvin himself in his *Institutes* put the question of election and predestination in the section on soteriology (how we are saved) and not in the doctrine of God (how God manages things). These followers remained unwilling to press the logic of doctrines where Scripture is silent.

King James I was himself a Calvinist and sent five delegates to the synod. They issued the following statement attempting to qualify the one-sided victory at Dort:

> We suggest, moreover, that of those things which are established on the sure foundation of the Word of God, there are some, which ought not to be promiscuously inculcated upon all, but touched in the proper time and place with tenderness and judgment. One of them is the sublime mystery of predestination, sweet indeed and most full of comfort, but to them who are rooted in the faith, and exercised in holy living; for to such only will it prove an unfailing bulwark in the midst of the grievous struggles of the conscience.[2]

"Arminianism" became the term used to describe much of the reaction against Dort in the subsequent history of the Church of England. The term itself derives from James Arminius who had died in 1609. In spite of what he himself

---

[1] Diarmaid MacCulloch, *Thomas Cranmer* (New Haven: Yale University Press, 1996), and Ashley Null, *Thomas Cranmer's Doctrine of Repentance* (Oxford: Oxford University Press, 2000).

[2] C. Hardwick, *A History of the Articles of Religion* (Philadelphia: G. Bell, 1852), 186.

taught, his name has been given to the belief that humans are naturally free before grace, free when accepting or rejecting grace, thereby giving credence to the presumption that we are free when we sin. Overlooked was Jesus' warning that "he who sins is a slave to sin. . . . When the Son makes you free you are free indeed" (John 8:34, 36). Arminius never taught that we are free when we sin, but that we are in bondage and slavery. We are "free" to reject God in the sense that our wills are uninhibited and unconstrained in the choice to reject him, but the will is itself in bondage until the Son makes it free. Our wills are not free simply because they are unrestrained.

This human and fallen pretension that we are born free began to work its way through seventeenth-century England in R. Montague's *Appello Caesarem* (1626), the works of Jeremy Taylor (1613–67) and Henry Hammond (1605–60), the anonymous *The Whole Duty of Man*, and into the eighteenth century through the Cambridge Platonists and the Latitudinarians.[3] Samuel Taylor Coleridge (1772–1834) looked back to Jeremy Taylor as a symbol of the doctrinal drift of two centuries: "Socinianism is as inevitable a deduction from Taylor's scheme as Deism or Atheism is from Socinianism."[4] In the eighteenth century, there was a revival of Calvinism in the works of Anglican evangelicals: Augustus Toplady (1740–78), author of the hymn "Rock of Ages," and more moderate Calvinists such as John Newton (1726–1807), author of "Amazing Grace," Selina, countess of Huntingdon (1707–91), and George Whitefield (1714–70).

Fear of antinomianism was an important factor in discrediting Calvinism with its claim to free grace without requiring works for justification. Whereas Calvin had counseled acceptance, obedience, or exile under tyranny, his successor Theodore Beza (1519–1605) affirmed the option of rebellion. In 1628, the assassination of the duke of Buckingham gave rise to fear that rebellion and lawlessness would be products of Calvinism. The English Civil War increased this fear and encouraged Pelagianism as a counter to social disruption. The eighteenth century also fed the fear of antinomianism and the belief in the role of religion to quell sin in society. This very fear led John Wesley to embrace the term "Arminian," which provoked a serious split among evangelicals. Wesley even dropped the article on predestination in the Thirty-Nine Articles from the Methodist articles.

Since the eighteenth century, that aspect of Arminianism, which assumed freedom in the initial situation, has been a common element in most of Angli-

---

[3] C. F. Allison, *The Rise of Moralism* (Vancouver: Regent College, 2003).
[4] Samuel Taylor Coleridge, *The Complete Works of S. T. Coleridge*, vol. V (New York: Harper, 1876), 172.

canism, with the exception of Archbishop William Temple (1881–1944). The pastoral cruelty of assuming sinners are free instead of in bondage to sin was caught by Coleridge's dictum that Calvinism "is as a lamb in the wolf's skin to the [Arminian's] wolf in the lamb's skin."[5]

---

[5] Coleridge, 200.

CHAPTER 39

Calvin and the Continuing Protestant Story

Serene Jones

One doesn't have to look very far or very hard to realize that we are living in uncertain times—not just uncertain, downright cataclysmic. As the world waits anxiously for news of the market's every fluctuation, new poverty for some means an exponential increase in suffering for those who have always been on the underside of global prosperity. As patterns of immigration and migration shift and people find themselves living, by choice and necessity, in closer proximity than ever, a new generation of North America begins to navigate waters swelling with the waves of greater human diversity. The web of these events, and the sense of crisis it engenders, covers all aspects of our common life, including the stories we tell about who we are. For North American Protestants formed in the Calvinist heritage, our theological story about humanity and the meaning of life hold special treasures for us as we grapple with these pressures and possibilities.

Having moved to New York, I am more aware of these global changes than ever. In addition to the lasting monuments to Calvinism in the grand churches on our boulevards—First Presbyterian, Fifth Avenue Presbyterian, St. John the Divine, The Riverside Church—every day new strands of Calvinism are pouring into the city from places such as South Africa, St. Petersburg, and Sao Paolo. Unlike anything our New York forbearers would have imagined, these forms of Calvinism express an emerging global Christianity that is both exciting and perplexing. In these new communities, one finds old-fashioned, resonant strands such as the story of grace and sin and God's absolute sovereignty. Right next to them, however, are strong claims of God's immediate presence and Pentecostal experience of the Spirit's ecstasies. Just to complicate the picture even more, living right next door to these two jostling versions of Calvinism are practitioners of other faiths—Roman Catholics, Eastern Orthodox, Jews, Hindus, Muslims, Buddhists—and that strange new demographic that is growing faster than them all: the so-called unaffiliated. These are folks who know themselves to be religious, who engage in a variety of religious and spiritual practices, but who do not affiliate with any one tradition. Unlike the Seekers of the Sixties, these folks are not looking for a definite spiritual home. Their "home" is the pastiche of practices that hold their lives in crisscrossing lines of belief and belonging. They are yoga practitioners who also chant the Lord's Prayer; praise music junkies who identify as agnostic; Sikh women who pray at Islamic shrines; Rastafarians who also practice Vodun and pray the rosary.

Standing in this new landscape can be disorienting, like wandering into a Van Gogh painting—vibrant colors, unclear lines, and blurred horizons draw us into a world that is both beautiful and overwhelming. For a mainstream Calvinist like myself, raised in the Christian Church, Disciples of Christ, and the United Church of Christ, it's often hard to get my head around it. But this is where returning to Calvin himself can be so helpful. Despite historical distance, Calvin might recognize the world we live in today, because he too lived in a time of cataclysmic changes. Calvin's Geneva was comprised of an immigrant population significantly larger than the size of its citizenship. And Calvin himself was one— an immigrant who, like the others, wasn't able to vote on civic issues because he was not a native citizen, until near the end of his life. Refugees and immigrants, displaced businesspeople and peasants, royalty and clergy, all of them came to Calvin's Geneva in search of new life and new possibility. Like us, what they discovered was that new life had to be newly "made-up" in a great experiment: there was no template, no easy answer. And out of this experiment came the foundations for democracy, the rule of law, and more variations of Christianity and politics than can be easily counted in any history class.

As a pastor and writer in these tumultuous times, Calvin's theology offers me hope. He knew that in times of rapid change, people are likely to grasp for things that promise to anchor them. It is hard to live in such flux. But wisely, Calvin knew that our very human need for stability could lead us to make idols of objects that are not holy. A person, a religious or political system, a clear line drawn between "us" and "them," or even a set of cherished beliefs—all can become idols we promote to the place of God. To counter this most pernicious—and most natural!—impulse, Calvin's theology insists on only one steadfast principle: we must be reformed and always reforming. We move forward practically, forging pragmatic solutions to real social problems, anchoring ourselves in communities and laws and practices. And then we open our eyes again, under the ever-loving gaze of an all-present God, unclasp our clutching hands, and face the possibility that our good work—even our deepest religious beliefs—might have turned into idols in our eagerness to do the work of God.

And having humbled us by lifting up our capacity for idol-worship, Calvin would have eagerly reminded us that even in a world-undone, grace abounds and stabilizes us, through the simple of wonder of unstoppable hope and the insistent presence of the Divine with you. To the Glory of God.

CHAPTER 40

Ten Ways Modern Culture Is Different Because of John Calvin

David W. Hall

1. Education: The Academy

Calvin broke with medieval pedagogy that limited education primarily to an aristocratic elite. His Academy, founded in 1559, was a pilot in broad-based education for Geneva. Although Genevans had sought for two centuries to establish a university, only after Calvin's settlement did a college finally succeed.[1] By the time of Calvin's arrival, city officials yearned for a premier educational institution, but in 1536 most Genevans thought this was a target too ambitious. Regardless of the unsuccessful starts in education that had occurred between Geneva's adoption of the Reformation in 1536 and Calvin's return from his Strasbourg exile in 1541, it is clear that success in establishing a lasting university did not occur until Calvin set his hand to the educational plow after Geneva became settled in its Protestant identity in the 1550s.

Calvin's Academy, which was adjacent to St. Pierre Cathedral, featured two levels of curricula: one for the public education of Geneva's youth (the college or *schola privata*) and the other a seminary to train ministers (*schola publica*).[2] One should hardly discount the impact that came from the public education of

---

[1] The most recent history of the university recounts several abortive efforts, including one in 1420 under Roman Catholic authority and another in 1429 by Francois de Versonnex. See Marco Marcacci, *Historie de l'Universite de Geneve 1558–1986* (Geneva: University of Geneva, 1987), 17. For a prehistory of the Genevan Academy, see also William G. Naphy, "The Reformation and the Evolution of Geneva's Schools," in Beat Kumin, ed., *Reformations Old and New* (London: Scholar Press, 1996), 190–93. Until recently, Charles Borgeaud's *Historie de l'Universite de Geneve* (Geneva, 1900) was the standard history.

[2] E. William Monter, *Calvin's Geneva* (New York: John Wiley & Sons, 1967), 112. The *schola privata* began classes in fall 1558 and the *schola publica* commenced in November 1558. Marcacci, 17.

young people, especially in a day when education was normally reserved only for aristocratic scions or for members of Catholic societies. Begun in 1558,[3] with Calvin and Theodore Beza chairing the theological faculty, the Academy building was dedicated on June 5, 1559, with 600 people in attendance in St. Pierre Cathedral. Calvin collected money for the school, and many expatriates donated to help its formation. The public school, which had seven grades, enrolled 280 students during its inaugural year, and the Academy's seminary expanded to 162 students in just three years. By Calvin's death in 1564, there were 1,200 students in the college and 300 in the seminary. Both schools, as historians have observed, were tuition-free and "forerunners of modern public education."[4] Few European institutions ever saw such rapid growth.

To accommodate the flood of students, the Academy planned to add in what would become characteristic of the Calvinistic view of Christian influence in all areas of life—departments of law and medicine. Beza requested prayer for the new medical department as early as 1567, by which time the law school was established. Following the St. Bartholomew's Day massacre (1572), Francis Hotman—and several other leading constitutional scholars—taught at the Genevan law school. The presence of two legal giants, Hotman (from 1573–78) and Denis Godefroy, gave Calvin's Academy one of the earliest Swiss legal faculties. The medical school, attempted shortly after Calvin's death, was not successfully established until the 1700s.[5] Calvin's Academy became the standard bearer for education in all major fields.

Historically, education, as much as any other single factor, has fostered cultural and political advancement. One of Calvin's most enduring contributions to society—a contribution that also secured the longevity of many of the Calvinistic reforms—was the establishment of the Academy in Geneva. Through his Academy, Calvin also succeeded where others had failed. Worth noting, none of the other major Protestant Reformers are credited with founding a university that would last for centuries, even becoming a sought-after property by some surprising suitors such as Thomas Jefferson.[6]

---

[3] Public records for January 17, 1558, refer to the establishment of the college with three chairs (theology, philosophy, and Greek). Notice was also given commending the college as a worthy recipient of inheritance proceeds. See Henry Martyn Baird, *Theodore Beza* (1899; repr., Charleston, SC: BiblioLife, 2010), 104.

[4] See Donald R. Kelley, *Francois Hotman: A Revolutionary's Ordeal* (Princeton: Princeton University Press, 1973), 270.

[5] Baird, 106, 113.

[6] See my summation in *The Genevan Reformation and the American Founding* (Lanham, MD: Lexington Books, 2003), 2–4. I am indebted to Dr. James H. Hutson for this

2. Care for the Poor: The Bourse Française

Most people don't associate Calvin with sympathy for the poor or indigent. However, a cursory review of his care for orphans, the indigent, and displaced refugees in a period of crisis not only shows otherwise but also provides enduring principles for societal aid for the truly needy.

Calvin thought that the church's compassion could best be expressed through its ordained deacons, the epitome of private charity. The challenge for Calvin was to derive practical protocols that would care for the poor, using the diaconal mechanisms that God had already provided through the church's ministry of mercy.

Jeannine Olson's able historical volume *Calvin and Social Welfare: Deacons and the Bourse Française* is an eye-opening study of Calvin's impact on Reformation culture, focusing particularly on the enduring effect of his thought on social welfare through the church's diaconate. In her treatise, she noted that, contrary to some modern caricatures, the Reformers worked diligently to shelter refugees and to minister to the poor. The Bourse Française became a pillar of societal welfare in Geneva;[7] in fact, this mercy ministry may have had nearly as much influence in Calvin's Europe as his theology did in other areas.

The activities of the Bourse were numerous. Its diaconal agents were involved in housing orphans, the elderly, or those who were incapacitated. They sheltered the sick and dealt with those involved in immoralities. This ecclesiastical institution was a precursor to voluntary societies in the nineteenth and twentieth centuries in the West. Calvin was so interested in seeing the diaconate flourish that he left part of his family inheritance in his will for the Boys School and poor strangers.[8]

Its initial design was to appease the suffering of French residents who, while fleeing sectarian persecution in France, settled in Geneva. It has been estimated that in a single decade alone (1550–1560) some 60,000 refugees passed through Geneva, a number capable of producing significant social stress.

The deacons cared for a large range of needs, not wholly dissimilar to the strata of welfare needs in our own society. They provided interim subsidy and job

---

fascinating anecdote, which he presents in his *The Sister Republics: Switzerland and the United States from 1776 to the Present*, 2nd. ed. (Washington, DC: Library of Congress, 1992), 68–76.

[7] Jeannine Olson, *Calvin and Social Welfare: Deacons and the Bourse Française* (Cranbury, NJ: Susquehanna University Press), 11–12.

[8] Cited by Geoffrey Bromiley, "The English Reformers and Diaconate," in *Service in Christ* (London: Epworth Press, 1966), 113.

training as needed; on occasion, they even provided the necessary tools or supplies so that an able-bodied person could engage in an honest vocation. Within a generation of this welfare work, Calvin's diaconate discovered the need to communicate to recipients the goal that they were to return to work as soon as possible. They also cared for cases of abandonment, supported the terminally ill who, in turn, left their children to be supported, and also included a ministry to widows who often had dependent children and a variety of needs.

Naturally there were theological peculiarities, and these theological distinctives led to certain practical commitments. Modern leaders might be better off to see what they can learn from the past; in summary, the following list illustrates principles of Calvin's influential welfare reform:

1. It was only for the truly disadvantaged

2. Moral prerequisites accompanied assistance

3. Private or religious charity, not state largesse, was the vehicle for aid

4. Ordained officers managed and brought accountability

5. Theological underpinnings were normal

6. Productive work ethic was sought

7. Assistance was temporary

8. History is valuable

One of Calvin's fellow Reformers, Martin Bucer, went so far as to say of the diaconate that "without it there can be no true communion of saints."[9] In a sermon on 1 Timothy 3:8–10, Calvin himself associated the early church's compassion as the measure of our Christianity: "If we want to be considered Christians and want it to be believed that there is some church among us, this organization must be demonstrated and maintained." On one occasion, Calvin rhetorically asserted, "Do we want to show that there is reformation among us? We must begin at this point, that is, there must be pastors who bear purely the doctrine of salvation, and then deacons who have the care of the poor."

---

[9] Basil Hall, "Diaconia in Martin Butzer," *Service in Christ* (London: Epworth Press, 1966), 94.

3. Ethics and Interpretation of the Moral Law: The Decalogue

Calvin's interpretation of the Ten Commandments as ethical pillars was widely influential for generations of character development. In his discussion, he argued that this moral law was necessary; for even though man was created in God's image, natural law alone could only assist in pointing toward the right direction. Although acknowledging conscience as a "monitor," Calvin knew that depravity affected such conscience and people were "immured in the darkness of error." Thus humanity was not left to natural law alone, lest it be given over to arrogance, ambition, and a blind self-love. The law, then, was as gracious as it was necessary. Such a fundamentally positive view of God's law would become a distinctive ethical contribution of Calvinism.

The law also shows people how unworthy they are and leads them to distrust human ability. Calvin frequently used phrases such as "utter powerlessness" and "utter inability" to make the point that people are dependent on God's revelation if they are to do well. The law is a "perfect rule of righteousness," even though our natural minds are not inclined toward obedience.

Calvin noted that the law is full of ramification, and that it should not be limited to narrow applications. There is always, he wrote, "more in the requirements and prohibitions of the law than is expressed [literally] in words." Each commandment also required its opposite. If one was not to steal, then he also should protect his and others' property. If one was not to lie, then he was to tell the truth, and if one was not to commit adultery, then he should support marital fidelity. Calvin believed that we must reason from the positive command to its opposite in this way: "If this pleases God, its opposite displeases; if that displeases, its opposite pleases; if God commands this, he forbids the opposite; if he forbids that, he commands the opposite." This wide application of the moral law created the basis of an ethical theory that spread in time throughout the West, and it also exhibited a sophistication that was not always present in some theologies.

Calvin believed that the law had many practical functions: it convinced like a mirror; it restrained like a bridle; and it illumined or aroused us to obedience. Another chief design of God's law, however, was to guide and remind believers of God's norms.

Calvin's commentary on sexuality (when discussing the seventh commandment) spans less than a thousand words in the *Institutes* but is ever so profound. His discussion of "thou shalt not steal" was rich with texture, calling for a person not only to avoid theft but also to "exert himself honestly to preserve his own" estate (*Inst.* 2.8.45). These and other commentaries formed the Protestant work

ethic. Similarly, when he spoke of the internal scope of the commandment pro-
hibiting false testimony, he noted that it was "absurd to suppose that God hates
the disease of evil-speaking in the tongue, and yet disapproves not of its malig-
nity in the mind" (*Inst.* 2.8.48). While those expositions may be brief, they are
excellent and so worthy of consulting that most Protestant confessions thereafter
did just that. Some of the codifications in various Puritan contexts would follow
Calvin's train on the need and proper use for the law.

Calvinists, then, were not legalists but admirers of the perfections and wisdom of God's law, which they trusted more than themselves. Calvin's followers
regarded their own native abilities with such low esteem and God's revealed law
in such high esteem that they became the creators and supporters of constitutionalism and law as positive institutions. Moreover, charity was the aim of law,
and purity of conscience would be the result.

4. Freedom of the Church: The Company of Pastors

Calvin labored extensively to permit the church to be the church—and culture
was impacted by a robust, vibrant church. Less than two years after Calvin's arrival
in Geneva,[10] he was exiled. The struggle was an important one, involving whether
the church and her ministers could follow their own conscience and authority, or
whether the church would be hindered by state or other hierarchical interference.

In 1538, Calvin and William Farel (who pastored the Genevan churches of St.
Pierre and St. Gervais, respectively) declined to offer Communion to the feuding
citizenry, lest they heap judgment on themselves.[11] In return, on April 18 of that
year, the city council exiled them for insubordination. In 1541, however, Calvin
was implored to return to Geneva.

When he returned, rather than seeking more control for himself over church
or civic matters, he sought to regularize a republican form of church government.
One of Calvin's demands before returning to Geneva in September 1541 was that
a collegial governing body be established of pastors and church elders from the
area.[12] When it came time to replace ineffective centralized structures, rather

---

[10] Henri Heyer, *Guillaume Farel: An Introduction to His Theology*, trans. Blair Reyn-
olds (Lewiston, NY: The Edwin Mellen Press, 1990), 60.

[11] Arthur David Ainsworth, *The Relations between Church and State in the City and
Canton of Geneva* (Atlanta: The Stein Printing Company, 1965), 15, reports that the un-
rest began with a minister denouncing the political government from the pulpit, which
led to his arrest.

[12] Theodore Beza, *Life of John Calvin* (Darlington, UK: Evangelical Press, 1997), lxxvi.

than opting for an institution that strengthened his own hand, this visionary Reformer lobbied for decentralized authority, lodging it with many officers. He also insisted that the church be free from political interference—separation of jurisdictions, not a yearning for theocratic oppressiveness, helped also to solidify the integrity of the church—and his 1541 *Ecclesiastical Ordinances* specifically required such a separation.

The first priority of Calvin and Farel upon their reengagement in Geneva was the establishment of the protocols in Calvin's *Ecclesiastical Ordinances*, a procedural manual that prescribed how the city churches would supervise the morals and teaching of their own pastors without hindrance from any other authorities. The priority that Calvin assigned to this work shows how important it was for him that the church be free to carry out its own affairs, unimpeded by the state. The sovereignty of the ministerial council (Consistory)[13] to monitor the faith and practice of the church was codified in these 1541 *Ordinances*. They were later revised in 1561, just prior to Calvin's death, and provided enduring procedures for a free church. Obviously, this arrangement marked a departure from the traditional yoking of political and ecclesiastical influence under Roman Catholic auspices. The Genevan innovation also differed slightly from the current practices in Bern and Lausanne, both of which were also Protestant.

In nations or regions where the civil government has ever or often sought to influence the church to change its views, this Calvinistic signature is greatly appreciated. A church free from external, hierarchical, or civil control was a radical and lasting contribution that Calvin made to the modern world. When the church is effective at promoting her God-given virtues, that free church is a powerful influence for society's good.

5. Collegial Governing: The Senate

Calvin argued long and hard that government should not and could not do everything; it had to be limited in its task and scope. If it was not, it would run aground as in the time of the Hebrew prophet Samuel.

---

[13] The first Consistory in 1542 was comprised of twelve elders elected annually by the magistrates and nine ministers. By 1564, the number of ministers grew to nineteen. The Consistory met each Thursday to discuss matters of common interest and church discipline. Alister McGrath, *A Life of John Calvin* (Oxford: Wiley-Blackwell, 1993), 111. Since Calvin insisted so strongly on this institution after his Strasbourg period, some believe that he imitated the practice of Bucer (McGrath, 13).

Calvin's sermon on 1 Samuel 8[14] addresses one of the most widely expounded passages about political thought in Scripture. His 1561 exposition
discusses the dangers of monarchy, the need for proper limitation of government, and the place of divine sovereignty over human governments. It is an
example of Calvinism at its best, carefully balancing individual liberty and
proper government.

Calvin began his sermon on 1 Samuel 8 by asserting that the people of Israel
were—even at the last minute prior to electing a king—still free to change their
minds; such freedom rendered the kingship optional. Then Samuel warned them
"that the king who will reign over them will take their sons for his own purposes
and will cause much plundering and robbery." Calvin preached that "there are
limits prescribed by God to their power, within which they ought to be satisfied:
namely, to work for the common good and to govern and direct the people in
truest fairness and justice; not to be puffed up with their own importance, but
to remember that they also are subjects of God."

Calvin's calls to submit to the governor were not without limit. God established magistrates properly "for the use of the people and the benefit of the
republic." Accordingly, kings also had charters to satisfy: "They are not to undertake war rashly, nor ambitiously to increase their wealth; nor are they to govern
their subjects on the basis of personal opinion or lust for whatever they want."
Kings had authority only insofar as they met the conditions of God's covenant.
Accordingly, he proclaimed from the pulpit of St. Pierre, "Subjects are under the
authority of kings; but at the same time, kings must care about the public welfare
so they can discharge the duties prescribed to them by God with good counsel
and mature deliberation."

The republican-type plan suggested by Jethro (Exod.18) appears as an innovation that did not originate in the mind of man, thought Calvin. Other commen-
tators, ranging from Aquinas and Machiavelli to Althusius and Ponet, viewed
Jethro's advice as a pristine example of federalism or republicanism. Commenting on a similar passage in Deuteronomy 1:14–16, Calvin stated:

> Hence it more plainly appears that those who were to preside in judgment were not
> appointed only by the will of Moses, but elected by the votes of the people. And this
> is the most desirable kind of liberty, that we should not be compelled to obey every
> person who may be tyrannically put over our heads; but which allows of election, so
> that no one should rule except he be approved by us. And this is further confirmed

---

[14] Quotations in this section are from Douglas Kelly's translation of Calvin's "Sermon
on 1 Samuel 8," in *Calvin Studies Colloquium*, eds. Charles Raynal and John Leith (Davidson, NC: Davidson College Presbyterian Church, 1982).

in the next verse, wherein Moses recounts that he awaited the consent of the people, and that nothing was attempted which did not please them all.

Thus Calvin viewed Exodus 18 as a representative republican form.[15] Geneva's smallest Council of Twenty-Five was also known as the Senate.

This Genevan beacon, whose sermonic ideas later reached the shores of America, enumerated from the Samuel narrative the ways kings abuse their power, and he distinguished a tyrant from a legitimate prince in these words: "A tyrant rules only by his own will and lust, whereas legitimate magistrates rule by counsel and by reason so as to determine how to bring about the greatest public welfare and benefit." Calvin decried the oppressive custom of magistrates "taking part in the plundering to enrich themselves off the poor."

The character of Calvinism is exhibited in this (and other) sermons that advocated limited government. Calvin was correct that individual responsibility was a good speed bump to a government taking over more than it should. He altered the trajectory of governance, no less.

6. Decentralized Politics: The Republic

One of the procedural safeguards of the 1543 civic reform—a hallmark of Calvinistic governing ethos—was that the various branches of local government (councils) could no longer act unilaterally; henceforth, at least two councils were required to approve measures before ratification.[16] This early mechanism, which prevented consolidation of all governmental power into a single council, predated Montesquieu's separation of powers doctrine by two centuries, a Calvinistic contribution that is not always recognized. The driving rationale for this dispersed authority was a simple but scriptural idea: even the best of leaders could think blindly and selfishly, so they needed a format for mutual correction and accountability. This kind of thinking, already incorporated into Geneva's ecclesiastical sphere (imbedded in the 1541 *Ecclesiastical Ordinances*) and essentially derived from biblical sources, anticipated many later instances

---

[15] For more support of this thesis, see my "Government by Moses and One Greater Than Moses," in *Election Day Sermons* (Oak Ridge, TN: Kuyper Institute, 1996).

[16] E. William Monter, *Calvin's Geneva* (Huntington, NY: Krieger, 1975), 72. In 1542, the General Council adopted this proviso: "Nothing should be put before the Council of Two Hundred that has not been dealt with in the Narrow Council, nor before the General Council before having been dealt with in the Narrow Council as well as the Two Hundred" (trans. Kim McMahan).

of political federalism. The structure of Genevan presbyterianism began to influence Genevan civil politics; in turn, that also furthered the separation of powers and provided protection from oligarchy. The result was a far more open and stable society than previously, and Calvin's orientation toward the practical is obvious in these areas.

The process of Genevan elections itself was a mirror of Calvin's view of human nature and the role of the state. In one of the earliest organized democratic traditions, Calvin's fellow citizens elected four new syndics (commissioners) from a slate of eight for an annual term. Various levels of councils were then elected by the citizens.

This Calvin-shaped polity, which appeared to be either liberal or daringly democratic for its day, provided checks and balances, separation of powers, election by the residents, and other elements of the federal structure that would later be copied as one of Geneva's finest exports. Additional features of federalism, including an early appellate system, were developed by the late 1540s. Not only was Calvin's Geneva religious,[17] she also sought the assent of the governed to a degree not previously seen, leading the world to new and stable forms of republicanism. At the very least, one should acknowledge "the rather striking correlation, both in time and in place, between the spread of Calvinist Protestantism and the rise of democracy."[18]

In keeping with the teachings of Calvin,[19] elected governors perceived themselves as having a duty to God, one that compelled them to serve the public good and avoid pursuing personal benefit. This notion of selfless political duty owed much of its staying power to Calvin, and it soon became an integral feature of Genevan public culture. Municipal officials were not full-time salaried employees in the time of Calvin, and the combination of checks and balances between the various councils required government to be streamlined and simple. Political offices in Geneva, in contrast with medieval and some modern customs, were not profitable for office holders. Service in such offices was even avoided by some, requiring the threat of a fine if a citizen refused to serve after election.[20]

---

[17] In early Massachusetts, church attendance was sanctioned. Absenting oneself from church in Reformed Geneva drew a fine. E. William Monter, *Studies in Genevan Government, 1536–1605* (Geneva: Droz, 1964), 79.

[18] Robert M. Kingdon, *Calvin and Calvinism: Sources of Democracy* (Lexington, MA: D. C. Heath and Company, 1970), vii.

[19] Monter observes that Calvin did not so much purpose to instruct the existing magistrates "as to show others what magistrates are and for what end God has appointed them." Monter, *Studies in Genevan Government, 1536–1605*, 58.

[20] Monter, *Studies in Genevan Government, 1536–1605*, 57.

Geneva became the chief laboratory for the implementation of many of Calvin's republican ideas. As such, her local political model yields hints about the character of Calvinism, complete with its tendency to limit government. Features such as limited terms, balance of powers, citizen nullification, interpositional magistracies, and accountability were at the heart of New World governments—which further amplified Calvinism to other generations and locales.

Many ideas that began with Calvin's reformation in Geneva and later became part of the fabric of America were cultivated and crossbred in the seventeenth century. Customs now taken for granted—such as freedom of speech, assembly, and dissent—were extended as Calvin's Dutch, British, and Scottish disciples refined these ideas.

7. Parity Among All Professions: The Doctrine of Vocation

Another culture-shaping aspect of Calvin's thought was his emphasis on the sacredness of ordinary vocations. Before Calvin and the Protestant Reformation, the doctrine of vocation or calling was thought to be exclusively for the clergy. However, his view of work as inherently dignified by our Creator elevated all disciplines and lawful vocations to the status of holy calling. One could, after Calvin, be as called to medicine, law, or education as a clergyman was called to serve the church.

Calvin's call for hard work did not necessarily equate success or prosperity with divine blessing. His views, though, did have a persistent tendency of ennobling various areas of human calling and labor. Business, commerce, and industry were all elevated by Calvin's principles, and those who adhered to these became leaders of modern enterprise. Max Weber and others are correct to identify that Calvinism dignified work and callings of many kinds.

Prior to his time, many workers felt little sense of calling unless entering the priesthood. Due primarily to the priestly emphasis of the Roman Catholic Church, prior to the Reformation "calling" or vocation was largely restricted to ecclesiastical callings. Calvin taught that any area of work—farming, teaching, governing, business—could be a valid calling from God, every bit as sacred as serving as a minister. This was a radical change in worldview, which would ultimately alter many economies, cultures, and human lives.

The formation of the Genevan Academy under Calvin called for general education (not only in religious studies), and it provided for studies in law, medicine, history, and education. Calvin and other Reformers helped retire the sacred/secular distinction. He realized that a person could serve God in any area of labor and glorify him. Calvin counseled with many leaders, entrepreneurs, printers, and merchants in his time, and he did not revile any lawful calling. The character of Calvinism ennobles all good work. Despite its faith in the afterlife, Calvinism called its adherents to be leaders in all fields.

His commentary on the fourth commandment in Exodus 20 also underscores the dignity of work. Just as God commanded people to rest on the seventh day, so the Lord expected them to work six days. Work was vital for all people made in God's image; thus for Calvin, all callings were important.

Whether we eat or drink, as Calvin agreed with Paul in the New Testament, we do all to the glory of God. That is why the great post-Reformation composer Johann Sebastian Bach signed each of his original scores with the initials "SDG." Those letters stood for the Latin phrase *sola Dei gloria* ("to God alone be the glory"). Bach knew the character of Calvinism and applied it to his craft. Some of the finest Christians in history have also applied the Lordship of Christ to their own vocations and served as leaders in fields for the glory of God.

8. Economics and Profit: The Invisible Hand

Of interest to historians, both sympathetic and unsympathetic to Calvin, is that whatever Calvin was doing during this time transformed Geneva into a visible and bustling forum for economic development. With a growing intellectual ferment, evidenced by the founding of Calvin's Academy and the presence of modern financial institutions (e.g., a Medici bank), Geneva became an ideal center for perfecting and exporting reform.[21]

Wherever Calvinism spread, so did a love for free markets and capitalism. If one valid measurement of leadership is its impact on its immediate environment,

---

[21] Several studies detail Calvin's Geneva. Among the best are: E. William Monter, *Calvin's Geneva* (New York: John Wiley & Sons, 1967); *Calvinism in Europe, 1540–1610: A Collection of Documents*, eds. Alistair Duke, Gillian Lewis, and Andrew Pettegree (Manchester, UK: Manchester University Press, 1988); J. T. McNeill, "John Calvin on Civil Government," *Calvinism and the Political Order*, ed. George L. Hunt (Philadelphia: Westminster Press, 1965), 22–45; William A. Dunning, *A History of Political Theories: From Luther to Montesquieu* (New York: Macmillan, 1919), 26–33; W. Fred Graham, *The Constructive Revolutionary: John Calvin, His Socio-Economic Impact* (Richmond, VA: John Knox Press, 1975); and William G. Naphy, *Calvin and the Consolidation of the Genevan Reformation* (Manchester, UK: Manchester University Press, 1994). Two other biographies also add to our understanding: William Bouwsma, *John Calvin: A Sixteenth-Century Portrait* (New York: Oxford University Press, 1988); and Alister McGrath, *A Life of John Calvin* (Oxford: Basil Blackwell, 1990).

one might well compare Geneva before and after Calvin. The socioeconomic difference between *before* and *after* Calvin may be noted by comparing three key occupational segments. In 1536, prior to Calvin's immigration, Geneva had fifty merchants, three printers, and few, if any, nobles. By the late 1550s, Geneva was home to 180 merchants, 113 printers and publishers, and at least 70 aristocratic refugees who claimed nobility.[22]

It is certainly erroneous to think, however, like Max Weber in his *The Protestant Ethic and the Spirit of Capitalism* (1905), that Calvinists equated material success with a sign of being the elect. To rebut that idea, one may simply consult Calvin's teaching on the eighth commandment. On this commandment that forbade stealing, Calvin interpreted that the holding and protecting of personal property was by implication perfectly normal. In fact, that commandment, properly understood, called for avoidance of greed for what others have, and it required every person to "exert himself honestly in preserving his own [property]." He warned believers not to squander what God providentially gave and also to care for their neighbor's well-being. He saw this commandment as calling for contentment with

> our own lot, we study to acquire nothing but honest and lawful gain; if we long not to grow rich by injustice, nor to plunder our neighbor of his goods . . . if we hasten not to heap up wealth cruelly wrung from the blood of others; if we do not . . . with excessive eagerness scrape together whatever may glut our avarice or meet our prodigality. On the other hand, let it be our constant aim faithfully to lend our counsel and aid to all so as to assist them in retaining their property.

A prayer by Calvin makes Weber's oft-repeated confusion fall to the ground more rapidly. The commonly mistaken caricature of Calvin as a crass capitalist should be contrasted with the prayer he suggested before beginning work, which is included in the 1562 Genevan Catechism. In that prayer, he led the people in asking God to bless their labor, noting that if God failed to bless it, "Nothing goes well or can prosper." He prayed for the Holy Spirit to aid workers in this calling "without any fraud or deception, and so that we shall have regard more to follow their ordinances than to satisfy our appetite to make ourselves rich." Along with this, Calvin prayed that workers would also care for the indigent and that

---

[22] Monter's numbers, of course, may be challenged. It is possible that records were kept better after 1536, which could explain some of the rise of the merchant class (*Calvin's Geneva*, 5.). Even if that should be established, however, the astronomic rise of printers and nobility is certain. Nobles, mainly from France, fled to Geneva since adhering to Protestantism at home could have meant their death.

the prosperous would not become conceited. He prayed that God would diminish prosperity if he knew the people needed a dose of poverty to return them to their senses. Far from callousness toward the less fortunate, Calvin prayed that workers would "not fall into mistrust," would "wait patiently" on God to provide, and would "rest with entire assurance in thy pure goodness."[23]

He also asserted that any endeavor that ceased to have charity as its aim was diseased at its very root. Elsewhere, Calvin warned that luxury could incite great problems and produce "great carelessness as to virtue." Moreover, he warned against "eagerly contend[ing] for riches and honors, trusting in our own dexterity and assiduity, or leaning on the favor of men, or confiding in any empty imagination of fortune; but [that we] should always have respect to the Lord." Lest Calvin be misunderstood, he also called for a "curb to be laid on us" to restrain "a too eager desire of becoming rich, or an ambitious striving after honor." Although Calvin advocated reliance on God and not wealth, the prosperity ethic that followed his time in Geneva is one of the wide-ranging effects of his thought and practice.

9. Music in the Vernacular: The Psalter

One of Calvin's early initiatives was to translate music designed for use in public worship into the language of the day. Realizing that what people sing in a holy context has enduring impact on how they act, Calvin wanted worship—in all its aspects—to be intelligible. Shortly after his settling in Geneva, he urged a talented musician, Clement Marot, to translate the Psalms into mid-sixteenth-century French. Calvin wanted participants in worship, not only the clergy, to be able to understand and reiterate the truths of Scripture—this time in poetic structure. His democratizing of holy song and other elements of worship made parishioners participants in Divine Liturgy; simultaneously, it also boosted the endeavor of artists.

Hymns and songs powerfully lodged distinct ideas in the popular mind, especially when aided by reading the Bible in the common language and sermons that were understood by the masses. The singing of the Psalms afforded these Protestants the occasion to confess their beliefs, and some anti-Protestants even went so far as to view the singing of the Psalms as an inherently subversive act![24]

---

[23] *Calvinism in Europe, 1540–1610: A Collection of Documents*, 34.

[24] W. Stanford Reid, "The Battle Hymns of the Lord: Calvinist Psalmody of the Sixteenth Century," *Sixteenth Century Journal* 2, no. 1 (1971): 43, 45. Reid comments:

Marot never completed his translation and arrangement of the Psalms, but Calvin's disciple Theodore Beza was as committed—if not more so—to this project, which would both alter the nature of Protestant worship as well as further engrain scriptural teachings into the Puritan mind. Beza even sponsored a hymn-writing contest shortly after Calvin's death in his attempt to match the poetry of the Psalter with sing-able tunes.

Perhaps the largest single printing venture of the sixteenth century, Beza's French translation of the Psalms in metrical form went to press in Geneva's old town.[25] This Psalter, which became the international songbook of expansionistic Calvinism,[26] went through numerous editions (27,400 copies were printed in 1562 alone). Stanford Reid notes that to a greater degree than "all the fine theological reasoning, both the catechism and the Psalter entered into the very warp and weft of the humblest members' lives. For this the credit must largely go to the first pastor of Geneva."

Other importers of Calvinism to the West, besides the various Psalters, were the Geneva Bible and Beza's *New Testament Annotations*, which inspired readers ranging from Shakespeare (in his plays composed during the 1590s, Shakespeare quoted from the Geneva Bible)[27] to American colonists with "scores of marginal notes on covenant, vocation . . . deposition of kings, the supremacy of God's Word [over human tradition], and the duty of orderly resistance to tyranny."[28] Beza and Marot's hymnbook of metrical Psalms, which became surprisingly popular, paved the way for acceptance of other ideas championed by

---

"Whether one thinks of the fourteen martyrs of Meaux who sang the 79th Psalm, the five scholars of Lausanne in Lyon who sang Psalm 9, or others who turned to other parts of the Psalter as they went to their deaths, one can see how in the last great struggle of faith, the Psalms indeed were true battle hymns" (46). These Psalms, once engrained, fit "every occasion and form of resistance."

[25] E. William Monter, *Calvin's Geneva* (New York: John Wiley & Sons, 1967), 181.

[26] Reid, 36–54, speaks of the Psalms as the battle hymns of "one of the earliest modern resistance movements." Reid also describes Calvin's view of church music as a via media between Luther's liberal embrace of contemporary music and Zwingli's elimination of music at the Grossmunster.

[27] See David L. Edwards, *Christian England: From the Reformation to the Eighteenth Century* (Grand Rapids: Eerdmans, 1983), 146. In "A Translation Fit for a King," *Christianity Today* (22 October 2001), David Neff argues how biblical translation powerfully aided the flow of liberty: "Logically, it is a fairly short step from the biblical language of liberty to the secular politics of liberty." For more, see: http://www.christianitytoday.com/ct/2001/013/6.36.html.

[28] Robert M. Kingdon, *Calvin and Calvinism: Sources of Democracy* (Lexington, MA: D. C. Heath and Company, 1970), 40.

the enormously influential Beza.[29] Accordingly, art was elevated and became useful for cultural progress.

When Puritan settlers colonized North America, one of the consistent best-sellers of the day was the Bay Psalter, a thinly disguised revision of Calvin's Psalter. Calvin's disciples knew that the faith that sings powerful truths will also pass those truths on to future generations, and worship music set in the vernacular was a strong step in that direction.

10. The Power of Publishing Ideas: The Genevan Presses

If Martin Luther seized on the potential of the printing press, Calvin and his followers elevated the use of the press to an art form. With the rise of the Gutenberg press, the Reformers seized the new media with a vengeance to multiply their thought and action plans. Perhaps no first-generation Reformer seized the moment like John Calvin. Expressing his thoughts with clarity and regularity was part of his life.

The ability to defend the views of Calvin rapidly in print magnified the lasting impact of his thought.[30] The number of books published in Geneva rose from three volumes in 1536 to 28 in 1554 and to 48 by 1561. The number of volumes printed in Geneva the five years prior to his death was a stunning average of 38 volumes per year (a tenfold increase in 25 years). The average dropped to 20 per year after his death.[31] By 1563, there were at least 34 presses, many manned by immigrants.[32] Shortly after Calvin's death, one contemporary wrote: "The printed works flooding into the country could not be stopped by legal prohibition. The more edicts issued by the courts, the more the booklets and papers increased."[33]

---

[29] Herbert D. Foster, *Collected Papers of Herbert D. Foster* (privately printed, 1929), 93.

[30] Alister McGrath contrasts Calvin's success with that of Zurich reformer Vadian and identifies Calvin's "extensive publishing programme" as one of the differences. Alister McGrath, *A Life of John Calvin: A Study in the Shaping of Western Culture* (Oxford: Wiley-Blackwell, 1993), 124–26.

[31] Monter, 79.

[32] Robert Kingdon explains that the number was likely more since some were coopted by others. In 1562, neighbors complained that paper mills were running round the clock. Robert M. Kingdon, *Geneva and the Coming Wars of Religion in France, 1555–1563* (Geneva: Librairie Droz, 1956), 94. Jean Crespin even contracted to purchase bales of paper from outside Geneva (95).

[33] *Documents on the Continental Reformation*, ed. William G. Naphy (New York: St. Martin's Press, 1996), 87.

Geneva also developed an extensive and efficient literary distribution system. A childhood friend of Calvin, Laurent de Normandie (who later became mayor of Noyon), developed a network of distributors who took Genevan Calvinist publications into France and other parts of Europe. Many of the books were designed to be small for quick hiding, if need be, within clothing.[34] Thousands of contraband books were spread throughout Europe during Calvin's time, and several distributors of literature became Protestant martyrs.[35]

So successful was Calvin's city at spreading the message that all books printed in Geneva were banned in France beginning in 1551. Calvin's *Institutes* (along with at least nine of his other writings) had been officially banned in France since 1542, but that could not halt the circulation of his books. As a result, Geneva was identified as a subversive center because of its publishing; and the 1551 Edict of Chateaubriand forbade, among other things, importing or circulating Genevan books.[36] Distributing such works for sale could incur secular punishment. However, many books still filtered across porous European borders. Some shrewd printers, unwilling to be thwarted by state censorship, cleverly responded by employing typeset fonts that were commonly used by French printers and published under fictitious addresses.[37] This new medium and its energized distribution pipeline allowed Calvin's message to transcend Geneva's geographical limitations.

Calvin's thought spread throughout Europe and sailed over the Atlantic with various colonists, cropping up frequently in sermons and pamphlets in different colonies. If English sermons in the seventeenth century were still referencing Calvin's *Institutes* as a robust source for opposing governmental abuse, American colonial sermons conveyed his sentiments even more. "Probably no other theological work," writes Dartmouth historian Herbert Foster, "was so widely read and so influential from the Reformation to the American Revolution. . . . In England [it] was considered 'the best and perfectest system of divinity' by

---

[34] Monter, 82. Robert Kingdon notes that the books were so well circulated that as early as 1560 the cardinal of Lorraine had successfully collected twenty-two pamphlets that had criticized him. Kingdon, 103. Another historian in 1561 reported the spread to Paris of Beza's Psalter, catechisms, and popular Christian books, "all well bound in red and black calf skin, some well gilded" (103).

[35] Monter, 82.

[36] *Calvinism in Europe, 1540–1610: A Collection of Documents*, trans. and ed. by Alistair Duke, Gillian Lewis, and Andrew Pettegree (Manchester: Manchester University Press, 1992), 57.

[37] McGrath, 12. See also E. Droz, "Fausses adresses typographiques," *Bulletin of Historical Research* 23 (1961): 380–86, 572–74.

both Anglican and Puritan until [Archbishop William] Laud's supremacy in the 1630s. Oxford undergraduates were required to read Calvin's *Institutes* and his Catechism in 1578."[38] "Most colonial libraries seem to contain some work by Calvin," and "scarcely a colonial list of books from New Hampshire to South Carolina appears to lack books written by Calvinists."[39]

Even the Scottish philosopher David Hume, a fan of neither Knox nor Calvin, admitted: "The republican ideas of the origin of power from the people were at that time [about 1607] esteemed as Puritan novelties."[40] Calvin's ideas, then, took on a life of their own and became the actions emulated by many others, due in no small measure to the printing press and Calvin's wise employment of the latest technology. A strong case can be made that the most determinative religion at the time was Calvinism or one of its offshoots. Long after his death in 1564, Calvin would live on and continue to mentor many through his writings, which are still widely available today.

Epilogue

The Calvinist view of liberty, wherever it spread, gave citizens confidence and protections. Within a century, the American colonies would exhibit these Calvinistic distinctives. Not incidentally, one of the first colonial law codes was named "The Massachusetts Body of Liberties." So close were law and liberty that Calvin's disciples customarily associated law codes with tables of liberties. The reason was that a proper understanding of liberty is essential for any successful venture, whether it is business, civic, or religious. Calvin had seen an oppression of liberties—both in Paris as Protestants were persecuted, and in the eyes of the

---

[38] Kingdon, *Calvin and Calvinism*, 37. The sermon referred to by Foster is a 1663 sermon by British minister Robert South, who referred to Calvin as "the great mufti of Geneva." *Collected Papers of Herbert D. Foster* (privately printed, 1929), 116.

[39] Kingdon, *Calvin and Calvinism*, 37. Other historians argue that the Puritanism of New England was "patterned after the Westminster Catechism and embodied the type of Calvinistic thought current in all of New England at that time." See Peter De Jong, *The Covenant Idea in New England Theology, 1620–1847* (Grand Rapids: Eerdmans, 1945), 85. Foster, 79, lists the numerous Americans who owned copies of Calvin's *Institutes*. Patricia Bonomi has also firmly established that the majority of seventeenth-century Americans followed "some form of Puritan Calvinism, which itself was divided into a number of factions." See Patricia U. Bonomi, *Under the Cope of Heaven: Religion, Society, and Politics in Colonial America* (New York: Oxford University Press, 2003), 14.

[40] Cited in Charles Arrowood posted at: http://www.visi.com/~ contra_m/ab/jure /jure-chapter3.html.

many Roman Catholic refugees who arrived regularly at Geneva's walls—and he formed his view of liberties based on God's word and also in a fashion that avoided misuses of it.

Few thinkers with a lineage as ancient as Calvin have as much future promise. Calvin set forth both the positive necessity for well-ordered government as well as the limitations of its scope. His Reformed theology compelled government to be limited to the role of servant of the people; his political insights helped restrain the Leviathan. Today, when individuals frequently act as if centralized government agencies can provide lasting solutions to a wide range of social and individual problems, Calvinistic realism is one of the few substantial intellectual traditions that cogently warns against the twin dangers of utopianism and the threat of expansive governmental power.

Of all the theologies, Calvinism has made the most significant contribution to democracy. One summary of political Calvinism reduced Calvin's ideas to five points that may be of continuing validity. Herbert Foster noted the following as hallmarks of Calvin's political legacy,[41] and these permeate the cultural contributions noted above:

1. The absolute sovereignty of God entailed that universal human rights (or Beza's "fundamental law") should be protected and must not be surrendered to the whim of tyranny.

2. These fundamental laws, which were always compatible with God's law, are the basis of whatever public liberties we enjoy.

3. Mutual covenants—as taught by Beza, Hotman, and the *Vindiciae*—between rulers and God, and between rulers and subjects, were binding and necessary.

4. As Ponet, Knox, and Goodman taught, the sovereignty of the people flows logically from the mutual obligations of the covenants above.

---

[41] Herbert D. Foster, *Collected Papers of Herbert D. Foster* (privately printed, 1929), 163–74. I have summarized the five points of political Calvinism slightly differently, referring to: depravity as a perennial human variable to be accommodated; accountability for leaders provided via a *collegium*; republicanism as the preferred form of government; constitutionalism needed to restrain both the rulers and the ruled; and limited government, beginning with the family as foundational. The resulting mnemonic device, DARCL, though not as convenient as TULIP, seems a more apt summary if placed in the context of the political writings of Calvin's disciples.

5. The representatives of the people, not the people themselves, are the first line of defense against tyranny.[42]

At least an elementary grasp of Calvin is essential to any well-informed self-understanding of Western democracy—indeed, for modernity itself. Unfortunately, many remain unaware of the signal contribution that the leadership of Calvin has made to open societies. We may even credit Calvin's Reformation with aiding the spread of participatory democracy. Even if this heritage no longer holds a place of honor in our textbooks or in our public tradition, we owe our Calvinistic forefathers a large debt of gratitude for their efforts to establish limited government and personal liberty grounded in virtue. A single man with heart aflame changed the world.

American Supreme Court Justice Antonin Scalia once estimated the paramount political accomplishment of the millennium as law established by elected representatives instead of by the king or his experts. His candidate for the *fin-de-millénaire* award in late 1999 was

> the principle that laws should be made not by a ruler, or his ministers, or his appointed judges, but by representatives of the people. This principle of democratic self-government was virtually unheard of in the feudal world that existed at the beginning of the millennium. . . . So thoroughly has this principle swept the board that even many countries that in fact do not observe it pretend to do so, going through the motions of sham, unopposed elections. . . . We Americans . . . have become so used to democracy that it seems to us the natural order of things. Of course it is not. During almost all of recorded human history, the overwhelming majority of mankind has been governed by rulers determined by heredity, or selected by a powerful aristocracy, or imposed through sheer force of arms. Kings and emperors have been always with us; presidents (or their equivalent) have been very rare.[43]

It should be noted, however, from the highlights above that Justice Scalia is describing the kind of republicanism pioneered by Calvin and his disciples—a republic grounded in the eternal truth of morally ordered liberty.

Even during the twentieth century, intellectuals certainly remained aware of Calvin. In fact, in the words of contemporary theologian Douglas Kelly, Calvin's legacy continues and is "perhaps the stronger and deeper for the very fact that its roots are largely unperceived." Large segments of political thought have often embraced such forward-looking Calvinistic concepts as respecting fixed limits on governing

---

[42] Foster, 174. Besides Calvin, this idea is reiterated in Buchanan, Beza, Peter Martyr, Althusius, Hotman, Daneau, *Vindiciae*, Ponet, William the Silent, and others.

[43] Antonin Scalia, "The Millennium That Was: How Democracy Swept the World," *The Wall Street Journal* (7 September 1999), A24.

power and permitting people the rights to resist oppression, with little awareness of their genesis.[44] Calvin's original formulation of these ideas was eventually "amplified, systematized, and widely diffused in Western civilization. . . . Thus modified, it would prevail across half of the world for nearly half a millennium."[45]

Calvin should certainly be acknowledged for his overall contribution to the legacy of freedom and openness in democratic societies. It is undeniable that he had a large influence on the American founding fathers, who had absorbed much more Calvinism—particularly in their views of the nature of man and the need for limited government—than some realize.

John Calvin was much more than a theologian, and his influence extended far beyond churches.[46] Calvin and his disciples, when measured by this new millennium, will probably make more lasting contributions than Karl Marx, Napoleon Bonaparte, Albert Einstein, Bill Gates, or Henry Ford. Calvin inspired the cultural changes that gave rise to the political philosophy of the American founders, a truly extraordinary event in world history. Founding fathers—such as George Washington, James Madison, Samuel and John Adams, Patrick Henry, and Thomas Jefferson[47]—stood on the shoulders of some of history's greatest philosophers, not the least of whom was a pastor from Geneva hundreds of years ago.

That he is still commemorated five hundred years after his birth as a culture-shaping leader indicates the robust character of his thought and a sturdy legacy for generations to come.

---

[44] Douglas Kelly, *The Emergence of Liberty in the Modern World* (Phillipsburg, NJ: Presbyterian and Reformed Publishing, 1992), 4, 27.

[45] Kelly, 32.

[46] Some of the foregoing work was also contained in my dissertation, "The Calvinistic Political Tradition, 1530–1790: The Rise, Development, and Dissemination of Genevan Political Culture to the Founders of America through Theological Exemplars" (Whitefield Theological Seminary, 2002).

[47] A recent article further corroborates Jefferson's ease with religion. See "What Would Jefferson Do?" in *The Wall Street Journal* (9 March 2001), D26. That editorial contains a finding by Kevin Hasson, to wit: "The Framers did not share the suspicion that religion is some sort of allergen in the body politic. Quite the contrary, they welcomed public expression of faith as a normal part of cultural life." It is also noted that in Jefferson's day, the Treasury Building was used for a Presbyterian communion, Episcopal services were held in the War Office and, as the Library of Congress exhibition states, "the Gospel was also preached in the Supreme Court chambers." That America today doesn't know its own history here is a reflection of the larger revisionism that today portrays the churches, synagogues, and mosques that crisscross the country not as bulwarks of freedom but as incipient threats to the American way of life. The editorial concludes by suggesting that if future Supreme Court justices are hostile to the free expression of religion, "they'll have to do it without Jefferson."

CHAPTER 41

Was Geneva a Theocracy?

Michael S. Horton

From the firsthand accounts, Gillian Lewis notes: "The city of Geneva possessed a significance which was symbolic and mythical. Her friends saw her as the mirror and model of piety, a haven of refuge, a roosting-place for fledglings, a stronghold to train and dispatch abroad soldiers of the Gospel and ministers of the Word." And yet, there were enemies as well, enemies who saw Geneva as "Satan's sanctuary, a source of heresy, atheism, and libertinage and a centre for the active dissemination of sedition."[1]

As soon as Geneva embraced the Reformation officially and severed its loyalties to the bishop and duke of Savoy, the city was flooded with refugees from all over Europe. Overnight Geneva became—after Wittenberg, Zurich, and Strasbourg—a capital of the Protestant faith. Foreign visitors expressed amazement as they observed both the theological and practical attractions of the city.

Nevertheless, the impressions we received from our high school teachers more than likely had little in common with those reported by firsthand witnesses, friend or foe. Images abound of a tyrant in a black academic gown, organizing a sixteenth-century equivalent of the secret police to ensure that no one, at any time or any place, was enjoying himself. The amazing thing about this is not the image itself but the fact that it has survived in the public imagination, even though it has been refuted by the consensus of the world's leading Renaissance and Reformation historians for over half a century. The foundation for this public myth is the assertion that Geneva was a theocracy and Calvin was its pope.

The Reluctant Reformer

Alister McGrath writes, "Before the Reformation Geneva was an episcopal city in decline."[2] In 1535, the city council abolished the Mass, and the bishop

---

[1] Gillian Lewis, "Calvin and Geneva," in *International Calvinism 1541–1715*, ed. Menna Prestwich (Oxford: Oxford University Press, 1985), 39.

[2] Alister McGrath, *A Life of John Calvin* (Cambridge: Basil Blackwell, 1991), 86.

responded by excommunicating the Genevan population. Months later they minted their first coins, which read, "After darkness, light!" Protestant Berne came to Geneva's defense militarily, and Geneva gained its independence from the duke of Savoy. Nevertheless, the city was in severe debt and administratively confused, much as we are used to seeing with new independent republics around the world today. While the bishop threatened the use of force, the people voted for the Reformation on May 25, 1536. But that is only the beginning. Without qualified leadership, Geneva was on the verge of collapse. What the new republic desperately needed was a young visionary.

John Calvin was trained in theology and law, the latter being his chosen course, and he studied under some of the most sensitive intellects of the Renaissance. He finished his first published work, a commentary on Seneca's *De Clementia*. Combining his interests in language and civil law, this work explored the Roman philosopher's concern (and, no doubt, Calvin's as well) for leniency and compassion in the execution of civil justice. Seneca and Calvin both lived during difficult times, when power was used for personal advantage to such a point that church and society both had become demoralized.

At this time, Calvin was becoming a "Lutheran" and read every evangelical tract he could find. Fleeing the authorities in Paris, Calvin set off on July 15, 1536, for the Reformed city of Strasbourg, where Martin Bucer was centered. However, the French king and the emperor were engaged in a war that blocked the road to Strasbourg from France. Frustrated, but undaunted, Calvin took a detour to Geneva for the night. That's right, for the night. Little did Calvin know what awaited him in God's providence. The chief Reformed pastor, Guillaume Farel, a stern older gentleman, greeted the young Reformer. Calvin was anonymous and wanted it to stay that way. Here is his own account:

> Nobody there knew I was the author [of *The Institutes*] . . . until finally Guillaume Farel kept me at Geneva, not so much by advice and argument, as by a dreadful curse, as if God had laid his hand upon me from heaven to stop me. . . . Then someone . . . discovered me and made it known to others. Upon this Farel . . . went out of his way to detain me. And after having heard that I had several private studies for which I wished to keep myself free . . . he gave vent to imprecation, that it might please God to curse my leisure and the peace for my study that I was looking for, if I went away and refused to give them support and help in a situation of such great need. These words so shocked and moved me that I gave up the journey I had intended to make. However, conscious of my shame and timidity, I did not want myself to be obliged to carry out any particular duties.[3]

---

[3] McGrath, 95.

McGrath observes, "Withdrawn in personality and intellectual in inclination, he gave little indication of being of potential value in the cut-and-thrust world of Genevan politics of the 1530s."[4] At this time, Calvin was no more than a lecturer in the Bible and theology.

The big moment apparently came when Berne, attempting to convert the city of Lausanne via a public debate, invited Farel to represent the Reformed position and Farel brought Calvin along. Caught in a bit of a pinch over how to handle the Catholic representative's claim that the Reformed ignore the church fathers, Calvin rose to answer. "Reeling off a remarkable chain of references to their writings, including their location—apparently totally from memory—Calvin virtually destroyed the credibility of his opponent."[5] After winning Lausanne to the Reformation, Calvin was asked to write the Confession of Faith for the city. Thereupon he was appointed pastor of St. Peter's, the cathedral church of Geneva.

After years of clerical domination, the city council was not about to give the church its proper spiritual authority much less civil power. "Unlike their catholic predecessors," writes McGrath, "they were devoid of power and wealth within the city; indeed, they were not even citizens of Geneva, with access to decision-making bodies."[6] Tension began to build between Calvin and the city council. Calvin wanted Communion to be administered frequently (preferably, every time the word was preached); he insisted on the authority for excommunication resting with the church, not with the state—the latter often using it as a threat against political enemies. In other words, Calvin wanted more of a separation between the religious and civil spheres. However, the city council, for political reasons, denied Calvin and Farel their reforms. When they refused to tolerate the interference of the city council in spiritual affairs, they were exiled to Strasbourg.

The Reluctant Returner

In Strasbourg (1538–41), Calvin felt as though he were in heaven. Martin Bucer became his mentor, and Calvin assumed the pastorate of the French Reformed church there. During this time, Calvin published some of his most noted works and settled down enough to marry Idelette de Bure, the widow of an Anabaptist friend. With every success, Calvin became more satisfied in Strasbourg, but once again Geneva was calling.

---

[4] McGrath, 96.
[5] McGrath, 97.
[6] McGrath, 97.

First, the city council asked Calvin to write a response to Cardinal Sadoleto's appeal for the Genevans to return to the Roman fold. This Calvin did, and a convincing defense it is, and the Reformer thought the project was harmless enough, since he could write it in the leisure of Strasbourg's more supportive environment. Geneva issued its apology and a plea for Farel and Calvin to return, but neither appeared particularly moved by the invitation. Finally, in February 1541, Farel persuaded Calvin to return, though he himself did not, and Calvin arrived September 13.

McGrath points out "how deeply the myth of 'the great dictator of Geneva' is embedded in popular religious and historical writings," and points to the work of Balzac and Huxley as examples of writers who made assertions without any historical facts supporting them, but who nevertheless seem to have had more influence in the shaping of the modern view of Calvin than the facts of history.[7] The Genevan Reformer was "denied access to the city's decision-making machinery. He could not vote; he could not stand for office."[8] In fact, he still had little power over his own church affairs!

Did Calvin Have Servetus Burned at the Stake?

There is one event that stands out in our minds concerning Calvin's leadership in the Genevan church, however, which deserves closer consideration. On October 25, 1553, the city council issued the decree that Michael Servetus be burned at the stake for heresy.

Did Calvin have Servetus burned at the stake, as is the popular impression? The answer, clearly, is no! First, Calvin had corresponded with Servetus, and there is some evidence to suggest that he had even tried to clandestinely meet with the anti-Trinitarian in order to try to convince him of his error. After escaping certain execution from Roman Catholic authorities in France and Vienna, Servetus arrived in Geneva and made himself known to Calvin in public. Servetus was arrested and—although Calvin was both a theologian and trained lawyer who had been employed by the city council to draft legislation concerning social welfare, city planning, sanitation, and the like—he was not the prosecuting attorney. Remember, he did not even have the rights of a common citizen!

Second, Calvin was at the height of his battles with the city council at this time. Had he, in fact, urged the execution of Servetus, this might have been just the thing to have saved the victim's life! When Servetus was given the option

---

[7] McGrath, 105ff.
[8] McGrath, 109.

of facing trial in Vienna or Geneva, Servetus chose Geneva. For some reason, he must have thought his chances of survival were better in Geneva. However, the council, led by the anti-Calvin faction at this time, was determined to demonstrate that Geneva could be trusted as a Reformed city committed to upholding the creeds and Servetus was sentenced to death by burning. Calvin pleaded with the council to execute Servetus in a more humane manner than the traditional ritual burning for heretics. But, of course, the city council refused Calvin's plea. Farel visited Calvin during the execution and was, reportedly, so disturbed that he left without even saying farewell.

During this same period, by the way, thirty-nine heretics were burned in Paris, and the Inquisition was being enforced in Spain, Italy, and other parts of Europe. In spite of the fact that many sought refuge in Geneva who were less than orthodox and who were fleeing Catholic authorities, Servetus was the only heretic burned there during Calvin's distinguished career.

In fact, it must be noted that Jews were invited by the Reformed cities to find safety from the Inquisition. The Puritan Cromwell was later to make England a safe haven for dissenters, even for those with whom he dissented, and especially for Jews. The same is true of the Netherlands and Strasbourg. It is no small wonder that when we think of human rights and international relations, these Reformed (or once-Reformed) capitals—Geneva, Strasbourg (home of the International l Institute of Human Rights, the European Parliament, and other relief and human rights agencies), Amsterdam, and London—find their way to the top of the list.

Will the Real Calvin Please Stand?

The fact is that Calvin was a caring pastor who visited patients dying of the contagious and deadly plague in the newly organized hospital he had established, even though he was warned of the dangers of contact. He "not only risked his life," according to Dutch historian L. Penning, "but accomplished more for the patients by adopting sophisticated hygienic measures."[9] He was the genius behind the establishment of the network of deacons who, according to Gillian Lewis, "took charge of the day-to-day care of the sick and impotent poor," giving the position "the dignity of being a part of the four-fold ministry of the church."[10]

---

[9] L. Penning, *Life and Times of Calvin*, trans. B. S. Berrington (London: Kegan, Trench, Trubner, 1912), 287.

[10] Lewis, op. cit., 44.

It was he who urged the council to secure low-interest loans in banking for the poor but entrepreneurial exiles, who had been trained in a craft through the training and employment agency that was the functioning diaconate.

It was Calvin who urged universal, free education to all inhabitants of the city, as Luther and the other Reformers had done, and "from 1541 he always rose and went to bed with this thought uppermost in his mind: 'How can we give Geneva a University?'"[11] It was his students who spread the gospel, as well as proto-democratic ideals throughout the Western world.

For the Reformers in general and for Calvin in particular, *soli Deo gloria* (to God only be glory) was the design of life and good works were caring for one's neighbor, working for justice and right dealings, building churches, pubs, hospitals, and universities for the honor of the Great King.

So here is our "tyrant of Geneva," whose ministry was first opposed and then summoned with repeated pleas, then frustrated and finally held in high honor by the people he is supposed to have abused. Penning writes that, toward the end of his life, when Calvin was seen in the streets, citizens and "famous strangers" would say, "Look, there goes our Master Calvin!" On March 10, 1564, the council decreed a day of prayer for Calvin's health, and the Reformer recovered for a time. On Easter, April 2, Calvin was carried to St. Peter's in his chair and, after he received communion from Beza, his successor, the congregation began weeping.

The council, which had years earlier determined the length of sermons in Geneva and opposed so much of his pastoral ministry, voted to give Calvin a substantial financial gift, but he refused to accept any money since he could no longer fulfill the functions. On Saturday, May 27, Calvin died, aged fifty-five years. "When late at night the news of Calvin's death spread, there was much weeping in the town, as a nation weeps when it loses its benefactor," writes Penning. "Cannon Street was crowded with people; it became a pilgrimage to the Reformer's death-bed, and the Government had to take measures to prevent too great a pressure."[12] The city, with its thousands of exiles, citizens, and foreign dignitaries, followed the procession. Calvin had insisted that he be placed in a simple pine box, buried in an unmarked grave. This surely was not the funeral of a despot.

Even the greatest heroes of the past have blemishes and have made decisions or statements that cause us, centuries later especially, to flinch and Calvin is no exception. But at a time when preachers, much less politicians and celebrities, appear to offer some less than heroic role models, the shy and reluctant man

---

[11] Penning, op. cit., 288.
[12] Penning, 391.

of Geneva seems to have weathered the disdain of those today, like those of his own day, who cannot understand what it is like to be possessed by a passion for God. Tom Wolfe, author of *Bonfire of the Vanities*, told *TIME* Magazine, "Ours is not an age likely to produce great heroes." May today's Bible-believing heirs of the Reformation prove him wrong.[13]

---

[13] For further reading on this subject, see Ralph Hancock, *Calvin and the Foundations of Modern Politics* (repr. South Bend, IN: St. Augustine's Press, 2011); J. T. McNeill, *The History & Character of Calvinism* (Oxford: Oxford University Press, 1967); Ronald Wallace, *Calvin, Geneva, and the Reformation* (repr. Eugene, OR: Wipf & Stock, 1998); Alister McGrath, *A Life of John Calvin: A Study in the Shaping of Western Culture* (Oxford: Wiley-Blackwell, 1993).

CHAPTER 42

Is Calvin Still Relevant After 500 Years? It All Depends

Michael S. Horton

According to many Protestants—including some evangelical leaders—the Reformation may be over. In an age of rampant secularism, the threat of militant Islam, and moral relativism, surely the issues that unite us are greater than our differences. It seems that a lot of today's heirs of the Reformation are weary of fighting age-old battles and most people in the pews cannot even identify the flash points. Something about the pope, and Mary and the saints, or something.

For that matter, surveys reveal that most evangelicals hold views about salvation that are, if anything, worse than the official position of the Roman Catholic Church. While it's undeniable that Calvin had a major impact on Western history, it is not clear at all whether his driving concerns are still regarded widely as relevant in contemporary Christianity.

I have to admit that I've been a little uneasy with this whole "Calvin 500" celebration. And I'm not sure that a rigorously God-centered minister such as Calvin—who demanded to be buried in an unmarked grave, within a plain pine casket—would appreciate all the attention. I am even a little more confident that he would not approve of all the attempts to turn him into an important person for all the wrong reasons. This is where Calvin is brought out by some as the tyrant of Geneva and by others as the pioneer of modern liberties and all sorts of other concerns that were, at best, tangential to the Reformer's interests.

What was central to Calvin's interest also happens to make him more relevant than whatever he may have incidentally and inadvertently done to improve Western culture. Calvin's obsession, the nearest I can tell, was the tender mercy of the Father shown toward sinners in the Son and through the Spirit. I agree with B. B. Warfield's assessment that Calvin was even more interested in God's fatherhood than his sovereignty. Calvin's robust doctrine of the Holy Spirit leaves its mark on every theological topic. And as for the "in Christ" part of it all, this is the nearest thing to a "central dogma" I can think of for Calvin.

Is the Reformation Over?

Not out of any relish for the five-century split, but out of concern for the only source of the church's existence, unity, and mission, a couple of fairly recent news items are worth bearing in mind when we ask whether John Calvin is still relevant after five centuries.

U.S. newspapers have recently been running stories on the Vatican's "Year of St. Paul." The focus of most articles is the pope's decision to offer indulgences to celebrate the 2000th anniversary of the apostle's birth. Best known for his rich proclamation of free grace and severe condemnation of any church that would preach a different gospel, Paul's birth being celebrated with indulgences is ironic in the extreme. The special year is to last until June 2009. According to the Vatican website:

> The gift of Indulgences which the Roman Pontiff offers to the universal Church, truly smoothes the way to attaining a supreme degree of inner purification which, while honouring the Blessed Apostle Paul, exalts the supernatural life in the hearts of the faithful and gently encourages them to do good deeds. . . . [Supplicants who do this] will be granted the Plenary [full] Indulgence from temporal punishment for his/her sins, once sacramental forgiveness and pardon for any shortcomings has been obtained. . . . The Christian faithful may benefit from the Plenary Indulgence both for themselves and for the deceased, as many times as they fulfil the required conditions but without prejudice to the norm stipulating that the Plenary Indulgence may be obtained only once a day.

The conditions of the indulgence are also clearly stipulated. Absolution will be granted to the soul that does penance, receives Communion, makes a pilgrimage to the Papal Basilica of St. Paul in Rome, "devoutly recites the Our Father and the Creed, adding pious invocations in honour of the Blessed Virgin Mary and St. Paul . . . and who prays for the Supreme Pontiff's intentions." If they do this "in a spirit of total detachment from any inclination to sin," and also "take part devoutly in a sacred function or in a pious public exercise in honour of the Apostle to the Gentiles" during this "Pauline Year," they may receive time off in purgatory up to full (plenary) exoneration.

For anyone who might not recall, the sale of indulgences built St. Peter's Basilica in Rome and provoked Luther's Ninety-Five Theses. Since the mid-nineteenth century, direct payment of money is forbidden, but charitable contributions are part of the penance that contributes to the indulgence. Like Luther, Calvin criticized indulgences not merely for overcharging for salvation, but because of the grotesque distortion of the gospel that could make such a travesty possible.

After years of discussion between representatives from the Vatican and the Lutheran World Federation, the Joint Declaration on Justification was signed on Reformation Day 1998. The declaration concluded that differences over this issue were no longer church-dividing because the condemnations of each body no longer apply to their conversation partner. Only because the Lutheran partner no longer holds the views condemned at the Roman Catholic Council of Trent in the mid-sixteenth century could the Vatican recognize this conclusion as valid. It should be noted that the Lutheran World Federation, like the World Alliance of Reformed Churches, represents the more liberal wing of Lutheranism. Their confessional rivals (including the Lutheran Church Missouri Synod) rejected the Joint Declaration, however, because they still hold the views condemned by the Council of Trent and all subsequent reaffirmations by the magisterium.

Yet, in mid-celebration, the Vatican's Pontifical Council for the Promotion of Christian Unity issued a caution. The statement began by praising the consensus announced in the Joint Declaration but then added, "The Catholic Church is, however, of the opinion that we cannot yet speak of a consensus such as would eliminate every difference between Catholics and Lutherans in the understanding of justification" (*L'Osservatore Romano*, weekly edition in English, 8 July 1998). Citing the Council of Trent, the Pontifical Council reminded Roman Catholics that they must hold as dogma that "eternal life is, at one and the same time, grace and the reward given by God for good works and merits."

Christ Alone

John Calvin considered himself a Catholic Christian who simply wanted to reform the church, bringing it back to the faith and practice of the apostles. He never left the Church of Rome but was excommunicated along with all others who followed the "evangelical way." Calvin also considered himself a pupil of Martin Luther, although he exhibited a rare exegetical ability in his own right that brought deeper insight and refinement to the Reformation cause.

Like Luther and the other Reformers, Calvin emphasized that human beings are born into the world under God's wrath. Everyone wants to ascend to God through their own works, devotion, speculations, and pious experience, but Calvin warned that no good can come of any approach to the Father apart from the incarnate Son. A thread of quotations from the *Institutes* provides a flavor of Calvin's concentrated emphasis:

> The situation would surely have been hopeless had the very majesty of God not descended to us, since it was not in our power to ascend to him. Hence, it was necessary

for the Son of God to become for us "Immanuel, that is, God with us," and in such a way that his divinity and our human nature might by mutual connection grow together. Otherwise the nearness would not have been near enough, nor the affinity sufficiently firm, for us to hope that God might dwell with us [2.12.1]. . . . Therefore, relying on this pledge, we trust that we are sons of God, for God's natural Son fashioned for himself a body from our body, flesh from our flesh, bones from our bones, that he might be one with us. Ungrudgingly, he took our nature upon himself to impart to us what was his, and to become both Son of God and Son of man in common with us [2.12.2]. . . . Therefore, in order that faith may find a firm basis for salvation in Christ, and thus rest in him, this principle must be laid down: the office enjoined upon Christ by the Father consists of three parts. For he was given to be prophet, king, and priest [2.15.1]. . . . In short, from the time when he took on the form of a servant, he began to pay the price of liberation in order to redeem us. [2.16.5]

It is in Christ, not in the church, that the treasury of merit is to be found, and he dispenses it freely to all who throw themselves upon him in faith. Although there is no salvation outside of the church, there is no salvation from the church. Although the church is "the mother of the faithful," she is not the source or object of faith.

Calvin challenged both Rome and the Anabaptists for encouraging people to look to Christ for only some gifts. Everything that we have in our heavenly inheritance is granted to every believer, *extra nos* (outside of us), in Christ alone. In a moving passage, he testifies,

We see that our whole salvation and all its parts are comprehended in Christ. We should therefore take care not to derive the least portion of it from anywhere else. If we seek salvation, we are taught by the very name of Jesus that it is "of him." If we seek any other gifts of the Spirit, they will be found in his anointing. If we seek strength, it lies in his dominion; if purity, in his conception; if gentleness, it appears in his birth. For by his birth he was made like us in all respects that he might learn to feel our pain. If we seek redemption, it lies in his passion; if acquittal, in his condemnation; if remission of the curse, in his cross; if satisfaction, in his sacrifice; if purification, in his blood; if reconciliation, in his descent into hell; if mortification of the flesh, in his tomb; if newness of life, in his resurrection; if immortality, in the same; if inheritance of all blessings, in his Kingdom; if untroubled expectation of judgment, in the power given to him to judge. In short, since rich store of every kind of good abounds in him, let us drink our fill from this fountain, and from no other. (*Inst.* 2.16.19)

For Calvin, Christ is not a means to an end. He is not merely a great example to imitate, an important bridge to cross from wrath to grace so that we may go on to other mountains to climb for spiritual blessings. He is the source, the means, and the destination. "The apostle does not say that [Christ] was sent to help us attain righteousness but himself to be our righteousness" (*Inst.* 3.15.5).

In his preface to the *Institutes*, addressed to King Francis I, the vicious persecutor of the church in France, the Reformer pleads,

> For what is more consonant with faith than to recognize that we are naked of all virtue, in order to be clothed by God? That we are empty of all good, to be filled by him? That we are slaves of sin, to be freed by him? Blind, to be illuminated by him? Lame, to be made straight by him? Weak, to be sustained by him? To take away from us all occasion for glorying, that he alone may stand forth gloriously and we glory in him? When we say these and like things our adversaries interrupt and complain that in this way we shall subvert some blind light of nature, imaginary preparations, free will, and works that merit eternal salvation. . . . For they cannot bear that the whole praise and glory of all goodness, virtue, righteousness, and wisdom should rest with God. But we do not read of anyone being blamed for drinking too deeply of the fountain of living water. (Prefatory Address to King Francis I, *Inst.* 13)

The Reformers were not innovators; it was the medieval church that had corrupted the worship and doctrine of Christ's assembly with a perpetual string of novelties. "But he who knows that this preaching of Paul is ancient, that 'Jesus Christ died for our sins and rose again for our justification,' will find nothing new among us" (*Inst.* 16).

Calvin believed that all of Scripture pointed to Christ—and, specifically, to Christ's death and resurrection for sinners: "Whenever we take the sacred books [of Scripture] into our hands, the blood of Christ ought to occur to our minds, as if the whole of its sacred instruction were written therewith" (*Four Last Books of Moses* III:320). In his *Commentary on Corinthians*, he wrote, "All the wisdom of believers is comprehended in the cross of Christ" (I:74). Further interpreting Paul, he adds, "There is no tribunal so magnificent, no throne so stately, no show of triumph so distinguished, no chariot so elevated, as is the gibbet on which Christ has subdued death and the devil" (*Commentary on Philippians-Colossians*, 191).

Justification: "The Hinge on Which All True Religion Turns"

At least since Albert Schweitzer there has been a trend in Protestant studies of Paul to treat justification as a "subsidiary crater" in the apostle's theology. Following this trend, some heirs of Luther and Calvin have sought to downplay the centrality of justification in the Reformers' teaching.

However, this trend is as bound to fail in consideration of the Reformers as in its treatment of Paul. According to Calvin, "Justification . . . is the principal hinge by which religion is supported" (*Inst.* 3.11.1) and "the sum of all piety" (*Inst.* 3.16.7). "Whenever the knowledge of it is taken away, the glory of Christ is extinguished, religion abolished, the Church destroyed, and the hope of salvation utterly overthrown" (Calvin's Reply to Cardinal Sadoleto, in *Tracts* I:41). "There is nothing intermediate between being justified by faith and justified by works" (*Commentary on the Psalms* V:251). Furthermore, "Whatever mixture men study to add from the power of free will to the grace of God is only a corruption of it; just as if one should dilute good wine with dirty water" (*Inst.* 2.5.15). "Therefore, we explain justification simply as the acceptance with which God receives us into his favor as righteous. And we say that it consists in the remission of sins and the imputation of Christ's righteousness" (*Inst.* 3.11.2).

Calvin believed that the whole Epistle to the Romans can be summarized as saying "that man's only righteousness is through the mercy of God in Christ, which being offered by the Gospel is apprehended by faith."[1] Calvin knew that faith will never rest unless it is firmly secured by God's promise of plenary indulgence (free favor) in Christ alone, through faith alone. On Romans 4, he comments,

> All things around us are in opposition to the promises of God: He promises immortality; we are surrounded with mortality and corruption: He declares that he counts us as just; we are covered with our sins: He testifies that he is propitious and kind to us; outward judgments threaten his wrath. What then is to be done? We must with closed eyes pass by ourselves and all things connected with us, that nothing may hinder or prevent us from believing that God is true. . . . For if justification means renovation, then that he died for our sins must be taken in the same sense, as signifying that he acquired for us grace to mortify the flesh, which no one admits. . . . He therefore still speaks of imputative justification.[2]

Faith

Just as "God" and "Christ" have lost much of their specificity in contemporary life, "faith" has become a generic term for religious commitment. For many, it is nothing more than a positive outlook on life. However, Calvin understood

---

[1] *Commentaries on the Epistle of Paul the Apostle to the Romans*, trans. and ed. John Owen (repr., Grand Rapids: Baker, 1996), xxix-xxx.

[2] *Commentaries on the Epistle of Paul the Apostle to the Romans*, 180, 186.

faith as "a sure and steadfast knowledge of the fatherly goodwill of God toward us, as he declares in the gospel that for the sake of Christ he will be our Father and Savior" (Geneva Catechism, 1536, in *Tracts* II:132).

> [Faith] is a steady and certain knowledge of the Divine benevolence towards us, which, being founded on the truth of the gratuitous promise in Christ, is both revealed to our minds and confirmed to our hearts by the Holy Spirit" (*Inst.* 3.2.7).

That is not to say that we are justified by faith, as if faith itself were the ground of our favor with God. There is no inherent virtue in faith. "With respect to justification, faith is a thing merely passive, bringing nothing of our own to conciliate the favor of God, but receiving what we need from Christ" (*Inst.* 3.13.5). Apart from any virtues or actions that might improve our inherent moral condition, "faith adorns us with the righteousness of another, which it seeks as a gift from God" (*Commentary on Romans*, 159). In fact, it is never perfect in this life. "Some portion of unbelief is always mixed with faith in every Christian" (*Inst.* 3.2.4). "Our faith is never perfect; . . . we are partly unbelievers" (*Commentary on the Synoptic Gospels* II:325).

> Faith then is not a naked knowledge either of God or of his truth; nor is it a simple persuasion that God is, that his word is the truth; but a sure knowledge of God's mercy, which is received from the gospel, and brings peace of conscience with regard to God, and rest to the mind. The sum of the matter then is this,—that if salvation depends on the keeping of the law, the soul can entertain no confidence respecting it, yea, that all the promises offered to us by God will become void: we must thus become wretched and lost, if we are sent back to works to find out the cause or the certainty of salvation . . . for as the law generates nothing but vengeance, it cannot bring grace. (*Commentary on the Synoptic Gospels* II:171)

United to Christ by faith, by the powerful working of the Spirit through the gospel, faith discovers sanctification as well as justification. Christ is the source not only of relief from the fear of judgment and the assurance of peace with God, but of the defeat of sin's bondage.

> Although we may distinguish them [justification and sanctification], Christ contains both of them inseparably in himself. Do you wish, then, to attain righteousness in Christ? You must first possess Christ; but you cannot possess him without being made partaker in his sanctification, because he cannot be divided into pieces [1 Cor. 1:13]. Since, therefore, it is solely by expending himself that the Lord gives us these benefits to enjoy, he bestows both of them at the same time, the one never without the other. Thus it is clear how true it is that we are justified not without works yet

not through works, since in our sharing in Christ, which justifies us, sanctification is just as much included as righteousness. (*Inst.* 3.16.1)

Therefore, the Roman Catholic charge that the Reformation's doctrine of justification is a "legal fiction" that cuts off all hope of sanctification is completely groundless.

> Christ was given to us by God's generosity, to be grasped and possessed by us in faith. By partaking of him, we principally receive a double grace: namely, that being reconciled to God through Christ's blamelessness, we may have in heaven instead of a Judge a gracious Father; and secondly, that sanctified by Christ's spirit we may cultivate blamelessness and purity of life. (*Inst.* 3.11.1)

> This alone is of importance: having admitted that faith and good works must cleave together, we still lodge justification in faith, not in works. We have a ready explanation for doing this, provided we turn to Christ to whom our faith is directed and from whom it receives its full strength. (*Inst.* 3.16.1)

> The believer does not keep one eye on Christ for justification and the other eye on his or her own works with the other, but looks to Christ for both. For in Christ he offers all happiness in place of our misery, all wealth in place of our neediness; in him he opens to us the heavenly treasures that our whole faith may contemplate his beloved Son, our whole expectation depend upon him, and our whole hope cleave to and rest in him. This, indeed, is that secret and hidden philosophy which cannot be wrested from syllogisms. But they whose eyes God has opened surely learn it by heart, that in his light they may see light [Ps. 36:9]. (*Inst.* 3.20.1)

Furthermore, this union brings not only the immediate possession of justification and the beginning of sanctification, but the hope of glorification: "The spiritual connection which we have with Christ belongs not merely to the soul, but also to the body" (*Commentary on Corinthians* I:217). In short, clinging to Christ for all saving benefits, we are assured that we will be raised on the last day: without passing through purgatory.

So, as Rome celebrates the "Year of St. Paul" with indulgences, many so-called Reformed and Presbyterian bodies around the world are remembering Calvin and his legacy, while burying, obscuring, or denying the central message that consumed his energies. Only if the gospel they preached is true are these figures still relevant today. And if it is true, then the Reformation is not over. Indeed, a new one must begin. The best way we can honor both the apostle and one of his best interpreters in history is to revive and unleash the revolutionary message of which they were heralds.

Is the Reformation Over?

Michael S. Horton

Several years ago, Mark Noll and Carolyn Nystrom wrote a thoughtful and engaging book, *Is the Reformation Over?*[1] It was particularly interesting because Mark Noll is one of the deans of the evangelical world, a thoughtful historian from a Reformed background. The argument was that, yes, the Reformation is probably over.

For many Christians today, even on the Protestant side, the Reformation now seems like an episode in the deep-dark past whose relevance is unclear. For others, including Protestants, it was a wasteful enterprise that left countless divisions in its wake. But are the teachings that the Reformation recovered, first of all true and do they matter even for us today? Do they resonate with believers struggling with a hostile culture or with the daily challenges of life? Interestingly, some of the New Testament's richest articulations of justification in Christ alone through faith alone are found in passages intending to bring practical comfort in daily struggles.

There are a couple of places in Paul's letters to Timothy where he seems to need to steel his young disciple against all sorts of conflict, including questioning his call as a minister.

> Therefore do not be ashamed of the testimony about our Lord, nor of me his prisoner, but share in suffering for the gospel by the power of God, who saved us and called us to a holy calling, not because of our works but because of his own purpose and grace, which he gave us in Christ Jesus before the ages began, and which now has been manifested through the appearing of our Savior Christ Jesus, who abolished death and brought life and immortality to light through the gospel, for which I was appointed a preacher and apostle and teacher to the Gentiles, which is why I suffer as I do. But I am not ashamed, for I know whom I have believed, and I am convinced that he is able to guard until that Day what has been entrusted to me. Follow the pattern of the sound words that you have heard from me, in the faith and love that

---

[1] Mark A. Noll and Carolyn Nystrom, *Is the Reformation Over? An Evangelical Assessment of Contemporary Roman Catholicism* (Grand Rapids: Baker Academic, 2008).

are in Christ Jesus. By the Holy Spirit who dwells within us, guard the good deposit entrusted to you. (2 Tim. 1:8–14)

In the Middle Ages, the Roman Catholic Church didn't deny that salvation was by grace, nor did they deny that salvation was by Christ or that salvation was through faith. The Reformation conflagration was over whether we are saved by grace *alone* because of Christ *alone* through faith *alone*. John Calvin said,

> True, in our day he [Christ] is called a redeemer, but he's a redeemer in a manner which implies that men do also, by their own free will, redeem themselves from the bondage of sin and death. True, he is called righteousness and salvation, but so that man still pursues salvation by his own obedience. Nay, Jesus was not sent to help us to attain righteousness, says the Apostle, but to be our Righteousness.[2]

It was *that* understanding of the gospel the Reformers were willing to bet all of their chips on; *that* understanding that the Roman Catholic Council of Trent in clear terms condemned in the sixteenth century:

> If anyone says that the sinner is justified by faith alone, let him be anathema.
>
> If anyone says that men are justified either by the sole imputation of the righteousness of Christ, or by the sole remission of their sins, let him be anathema.
>
> If anyone says that justifying faith is nothing other than confidence in divine mercy, which remits sins for Christ's sake alone, or that it is this confidence alone that justifies us, let him be anathema.
>
> If anyone says that the justice or righteousness received is not preserved and also not increased before God through the merit of our good works, but that those works are merely the fruits and signs of justification obtained, but not the cause of the increase of their merits, let them be anathema.[3]

The above quote from Trent is pretty clear. A lot of people say, "They just didn't understand each other. If they just spent more time talking, more time at conferences, well, everything would have been sorted out." They were burning

---

[2] John Calvin, "The Necessity of Reforming the Church," *Selected Works of John Calvin: Tracts and Letters*, ed. Henry Beveridge and Jules Bonnet, 7 vols. (Grand Rapids: Baker, 1983), 1:192.

[3] Twelfth Session, Canons 9, 11–12, and 24, in *Canons and Decrees of the Council of Trent: Original Text with English Translation*, trans. H. J. Schroeder, OP (St. Louis: B. Herder Book Co., 1960), 43, 45–46.

the midnight oil at conferences! This condemnation is finally what came down from the Vatican. "Well, things are a lot different today." That's often what you hear, especially since 1999, when the Lutheran World Federation said, "This is not an issue for us anymore." Why? Because the partners in this discussion are no longer holding to what was condemned in the sixteenth century.

Now, Rome did not take that view. Rome never said they would step away from the condemnations above. They said, "We can't—the church can't step away from condemnations of a Council." But of course Protestants can. They can step away from anything, and they did. They walked away from it by saying that justification of sinners is forgiveness *and* being made righteous: justification *is* sanctification, which is the very reason for the Reformation. The whole dispute with Rome was regarding that point, and now everybody says that people are in agreement. Maybe it's true that the Reformation is over in much of Protestantism. It all depends on what we mean when we ask, "Is the Reformation over?" Maybe Protestantism is over. Mainline Protestants have been euthanizing themselves for a couple of generations now.

The greater danger is what's happening in evangelicalism. "Evangelical" comes from the Greek word *evangel*, which means "gospel"—evangelicals are those who follow and teach the gospel. The term "evangelical" was first used by Martin Luther, who said we shouldn't call ourselves Lutherans but evangelicals: we're recovering the gospel; we're all about the gospel. Fifteen years ago, while I and my colleagues participated in the Evangelicals and Catholics Together debate, I was greatly dismayed to see even one of my mentors go from saying that justification is the great Atlas that holds the Christian faith on its shoulder, to saying that justification is the "fine print." Another member of the committee on the evangelical side said that the Reformation was "a tempest in a teapot." One of my favorite statements from an evangelical leader is that "Martin Luther was right in the sixteenth century, but now it's not really of great concern." I scratch my head at that one. One could say that Martin Luther was wrong, or that he misunderstood Scripture—that makes sense. But it's absolutely ridiculous to say that he was right about justification by grace alone through faith alone in Chris alone, but that that's wrong today. That's like saying that Nicaea got the Trinity right in the fourth century, but today, not so much—God is no longer a trinity because we live in the modern world.

It's greatly dismaying when you see that for a long time, in America especially, Protestants have misunderstood the heart of the gospel. Here's what Charles Finney, regularly cited as the greatest evangelist in American history before Billy Graham, said concerning the doctrine of justification:

This error has slain more souls, I fear, than all the false teachings that ever cursed the world. [Rome has never said anything that horrible.] As has already been said, there can be no justification in any legal or forensic sense at all, but upon the ground of the believer's universal, perfect and uninterrupted obedience to the law. Christ's righteousness can never be imputed to us. It was naturally impossible, then, for him to obey in our behalf. Representing the atonement as the ground of the sinner's justification has been a sad occasion of stumbling to many people.[4]

There have been wonderful alternatives to Charles Finney, a great witness to the great truth of justification. Most of the great missionaries sent out from this country to the rest of the world were joyfully bringing the gospel of God's free justification of sinners. But there has always been this confusion of justification and sanctification (particularly in American Protestantism), so much so that when Dietrich Bonhoeffer was asked, "How would you characterize American Protestantism?" he answered, "I would call it Protestantism without the Reformation."

Is the Reformation over? The real question is: Is the gospel that the Reformers taught in the sixteenth century biblical? If it is biblical, then the Reformation represented the greatest missionary advance and the greatest evangelization of an enormous number of people on the planet that we've seen since the Apostle Paul. If not, then it was the greatest act of schism and one of the most serious heresies ever to have bedeviled the church, and we ought to repent of it. Whatever it is, it is not a tempest in a teapot—that's the one thing we can't say about it.

That's why my White Horse Inn co-hosts and I talk about this message. Not because we think it's the only thing the Bible teaches, but because if we're not clear about this, then nothing else we teach matters. Even in churches that officially hold to this, or maybe refer to it in confirmation or profession of faith, don't necessarily incorporate it into their regular diet in preaching, teaching, or Sunday school materials. Graeme Goldsworthy, an Anglican in Australia, calls attention to this when he says that "the pivotal point of turning in evangelical thinking which demands close attention after my many years of teaching is the change that has taken place from the Reformation emphasis on the objective facts of the gospel in history to the medieval emphasis on the inner life." The evangelical who sees the inward transforming work of the spirit as the central element of Christianity will soon lose even that, and will surely lose contact with the historic faith in the historic gospel.

We have to get the message right, and we have to get the message out. There is no luxury in getting the message right if you don't care about getting it out. What's the purpose of having all the i's dotted and t's crossed, but not taking

---

[4] Charles G. Finney, *Systematic Theology* (repr., Minneapolis: Bethany, 1976), 57.

it out there to people? But also, what is the benefit of going around the world, evangelizing, bringing missions and Christian activity to the rest of humanity without the gospel itself? We have to get the gospel right, and that's the first part the apostle focuses on when he's talking to Timothy. Every time he writes to Timothy, Paul reminds him: "Be rooted and grounded in the gospel. Do not be ashamed."

To the Ephesians, Paul says, "Even though I am in chains, the gospel is not." Now Timothy too is called to suffering. "Therefore do not be ashamed of the testimony about our Lord nor of me his prisoner but share in suffering for the gospel by the power of God" (2 Tim. 1:8). As in Romans 10, Paul knows that the gospel is a stumbling block. It is a rock of offense to those convinced that their own righteousness can in any way commend them to God. He's very clear about that. In Romans 10 he says that there are two ways: the righteousness that is by works (i.e., how can I ascend into heaven to pull Christ down?), and the righteousness that comes through faith, that sits down and hears the gospel as it is preached and receives Christ there.

"I am not ashamed of the gospel," Paul tells the Romans, "because it is the power of God unto salvation for everyone who believes" (Rom. 1:16). The gospel's content is clear. First of all, it's the testimony about our Lord. There's no reason for us to get all hot and bothered about what the Roman Catholic Church teaches today or in any day, or when you hear evangelicals talking about "being" the gospel, "living" the gospel, "doing" the gospel, or saying things such as "Our lives will preach better than anything that we ever say." No, it won't—the testimony is not about me. When I was growing up, giving your testimony meant talking about you. There's nothing wrong with talking about your experience with the Lord; there's certainly a place for talking about how Jesus changed and continues to change our life. But if you've talked about who Jesus is for you and how he's changed your life and how you have become a better person since you invited Jesus into your heart, and you haven't talked about who Jesus is and what Jesus accomplished, then you haven't shared the gospel. Paul says, "Don't be ashamed of the testimony concerning our Lord"—not the testimony concerning me, but the testimony about Jesus. We're not the center. Like John the Baptist, we're pointing away from ourselves to the Lamb of God who takes away the sin of the world.

The gospel isn't only a testimony to historical facts. It's also a testimony to saving deliverance to those who believe it, for those who embrace it: it's not only drama but doctrine. Not only was he crucified and raised, but he was crucified for our sins and raised for our justification. It's the strangest thing in the world that God justifies the wicked. Nobody wants to believe it. Everybody wants it to be on easier terms, but they still want it to be the law. Oprah wants it to be the law. God justifies the wicked? Well, of course he doesn't justify the wicked. He's lenient. First of all, none of us are wicked. Let's start there.

Pope Francis recently proclaimed the "Jubilee Year of Mercy: Mercy Triumphs over Justice," which included the granting of plenary indulgences (which means time off in purgatory). The Vatican announced that people are also going to be able to be absolved of sins such as abortion. One wonders why people couldn't be absolved of grave sins before this. It's still works, but it's buying heaven cheaply. As we see also in Protestant, even evangelical, circles a similar concept of love triumphing over justice, which of course vitiates any notion of mercy. There are obvious similarities at the level at least of assumptions between Rob Bell's *Love Wins* and Pope Francis's *The Name of God Is Mercy*.

In contrast, Scripture teaches that it cost God the Son condemnation in the flesh for you and me. It cost us nothing, but it cost him everything. It is not cheap. It's not a little bit of works along with grace. Paul says that God has saved us and called us not according to our works at all, but according to his own purpose and grace given to us before time began, which is now revealed by the appearing of our Savior Jesus Christ who has abolished death and has brought life and immortality to light (2 Tim. 1:9–10).

It's not just some works that he opposes to grace; it is anything we do, anything we purpose. We're not saved according to decisions we make or purposes we have or are driven by, but by his own purpose and grace given to us—not because we chose Christ, but because God gave grace to us in his eternal plan before time began by choosing us in Jesus Christ. Talk about taking it out of our hands! I don't know where you were before the foundation of the world, but I wasn't responding to "Just As I Am." Now that does not mean we don't choose Christ; it doesn't mean we don't love God. It doesn't mean we don't serve him. It doesn't mean we don't perform good works. What it means is that contrary to what the Council of Trent says, those choices, that service, and those works are the fruit of God's justifying, saving work. Because he has chosen me, I choose him. Because he surrendered all for me, he calls me to lay down my life and say I am not my own, but belong both body and soul in life and in death to my faithful Savior Jesus Christ. It's this gospel, Paul says, that has appeared in Jesus Christ. He is the incarnate gospel, and in his appearing, we come to know that death and hell are abolished, and life and immortality are ours. This is not a tempest in a teapot. Believe it or don't believe it; it is not insignificant. Paul says it is this gospel, not what we have done but what God has done, that brings life and immortality to light. Extinguish that part of the message, and the light of the gospel itself goes out.

The character of it is good news, which is why Timothy, like Paul, was enjoined to be a herald, an ambassador. The gospel is something you preach. Our lives don't preach—they testify to what we preach. Our lives can drive people away from the gospel, or draw people toward the gospel—that's absolutely true. But the gospel itself is an announcement about someone else's life—an accomplishment, an achievement, brought about by someone else in history for us. And that's why it has to be news shared. It is not our life but the gospel that has to be the content of our preaching and teaching.

J. Gresham Machen, in the face of Protestant liberalism in the 1920s, said what could sadly be said today in much more conservative churches: "What I need first of all is not an exhortation, but a gospel. Not directions for saving myself with God's help, but knowledge of how God has saved me." Have you any good news? That's the only question I ask of you. I know your exhortations will not help me, but if anything has been done to save me—why don't you just give me the facts? No, the Reformation isn't over if this is the gospel. Now, if the sections on justification from the confessions we have don't accord with what we've just read from Paul in Romans and 2 Timothy and elsewhere, then the Reformation should have been over in the sixteenth century. But if it does accord, if that is in fact the gospel, then the Reformation won't be over until the second coming of Jesus. The church will always derive its life and existence from this gospel or it will perish. But Jesus promised that until he returns, the church will not perish, not even the gates of hell will prevail against it.

Not only do we have to get it right, we have to get it out. Christianity seems divided sometimes between those who want to get it right and those who want to get it out. In some of my own circles, I wonder sometimes if we can sit around debating what we would say to a non-Christian if we ever met one. I think of the line of D. L. Moody, the famous evangelist, to some critics nipping at his heels: "I like my way of doing it better than your way of not doing it." It stings a little bit, and it hasn't always been that way. The Reformation was the greatest missionary movement since the days of the Apostle Paul. The modern missionary movement was fueled by people who were as convinced as the Reformers that this message is the gospel. Paul says at the beginning of 2 Timothy that he was appointed a preacher, apostle, and teacher to the Gentiles (2 Tim. 1:11). This was not a ministry he made or chose; it was chosen for him and given to him. The gospel not only is a message; it has means that go along with it. It is a message that has to be proclaimed.

Paul reminds Timothy that God uses means, and that Timothy is one of those means. He reminds him of the means that God used to bring Timothy to an understanding of the gospel when he writes, "I am reminded of your sincere faith, a faith that dwelt first in your grandmother Lois and your mother Eunice and now, I am sure, dwells in you as well" (2 Tim. 1:5). Many of you here are Loises and Eunices. Where would the church have been without Timothy? And where would Timothy have been without Lois and Eunice, catechized at their knee? God uses means.

Another means God uses is, as Paul says, ordination: "Fan into flame the gift of God, which is in you through the laying on of my hands" (2 Tim. 1:6). He also writes in the 1 Timothy 4:14, "Do not neglect the gift you have, which was given you by prophecy when the council of elders laid their hands on you." Timothy hadn't sent himself out any more than he had saved himself. He was saved, sent, and gifted by God. Now he was to fan that gift into a flame. "For God gave us a spirit not of fear but of power and love and self-control" (2 Tim. 1:7). Paul says in verse 15, "You are aware that all who are in Asia turned away from me, among whom are Phygelus and Hermogenes." Paul says that although everybody in Asia had turned against him, Timothy shouldn't be afraid. It's God's church and gospel, but he uses means. We have to get the gospel right, but we also have to get the gospel out.

Paul finally tells Timothy, "Don't think you're it." He says that the same gospel Timothy had been given should be entrusted to others:

> You then, my child, be strengthened by the grace that is in Christ Jesus, and what you have heard from me in the presence of many witnesses entrust to faithful men who will be able to teach others also. Share in suffering as a good soldier of Christ Jesus. (2 Tim. 2:1–3)

And that's what has happened from the time of Jesus and the apostles, when that good news was entrusted to a new generation of faithful people. The gospel has gone forward—even under great hardship, even when not everybody believed it—because that word, as we have heard, above all earthly powers, will continue to break down Satan's kingdom.

Paul wasn't trusting in his own testimony about his accomplishments or achievements as an apostle: "But I am not ashamed, for I know whom I have believed, and I am convinced that he is able to guard until that Day what has been entrusted to me" (2 Tim. 1:12). He is convinced about Christ; about what he has accomplished, that it is sufficient, that it is enough for him. He can keep plugging away without fear or compromise, because he knows who's holding onto him.

Finally, Paul says, "Follow the pattern of the sound words that you have heard from me, in the faith and love that are in Christ Jesus" (1 Tim. 1:13). That's an interesting phrase. "The pattern of sound words" is a confession or a creed. In other words, there is a right way of delivering a message. It is that discernment we desperately need today. Tragically, today you could say the gospel in an orthodox way to an audience in the church to resounding applause and affirmation, and the next minute say it in a completely heterodox or heretical way, and those same people will cheer.

Discernment is often what's lacking. Creeds and confessions are there for the mission; the mission isn't there for the creeds and the confessions. We have a "pattern of sound words" so we can get this message out to the world. Far from exhibiting sectarianism, the form of "sound words" Paul here enjoins on Timothy provides the magnet for unity and the motive for mission. That's what pushes him out there. Why? "Because the Lord has many people in this city." Salvation isn't ultimately in their hands, but it's because of the purpose and grace given to them in Christ Jesus before time began.

The Reformation is not over because the gospel is not over. May God use our meager efforts to help each other plumb the depths of this glorious gospel, to seek out its wonderful connections to the whole mystery of salvation and series of doctrines we prize in the Christian faith, and help us to look beyond ourselves to a world full of misery, but to a God full of grace.

Who Were the Reformers?

Martin Luther (1483–1546)

Luther is credited as the founder of the German Reformation. Luther's study of the writings of the Apostle Paul and Augustine of Hippo led him to the belief that men and women could be justified only by the grace of God, through faith rather than through good works or religious observances. Luther's writings include *On Christian Liberty* (1519), *To the Christian Nobility* (1520), *The Babylonian Captivity of the Church* (1520), and On the Bondage of the Will (1525). In his *Small Catechism* (1529), Luther commented briefly in question-and-answer form on the Ten Commandments, the Apostles' Creed, the Lord's Prayer, baptism, and the Lord's Supper. The *Small Catechism* explains the theology of the Lutheran Reformation in simple yet colorful language.

Philip Melanchthon (1497–1560), Lutheran

Melanchthon shared a lifelong friendship with Luther. Having arrived at Wittenberg with a strong humanist background, he was won over to the Reformation by Luther and became the Reformer's leading associate. It was Melanchthon who urged Luther to translate the Bible into the German of his day for the common people. In Wittenberg, Luther had little time to systematize the various doctrines of evangelical theology, so in 1521 Melanchthon took on this task, writing the first systematic summary, titled *Loci Communes*. Based on several already completed writings and on the negotiations of Augsburg, Melanchthon also wrote the first great confession of the Reformation, the Augsburg Confession (1530). Lutheran pastors to this day are ordained with this confession.

John Calvin (1509–1564), Reformed

Calvin was the French Reformer best known for his work in Geneva and his seminal work, *The Institutes of the Christian Religion* (1536). Calvin's teachings shaped the beliefs of most Reformed churches. He had a great commitment to the absolute sovereignty and holiness of God. Because of this, he is often associated with the doctrines of predestination and election, but it should be noted that he differed very little with the other magisterial reformers regarding these difficult doctrines. Although the "Five Points" of Calvinism are a reflection of the thinking of the great Reformer, they are actually a product of the Synod of Dort, which issued its judgments in response to five specific objections that arose after Calvin's time. In 1541, Calvin began to reform the institutional church in Geneva. He established four categories of offices: (1) doctors held an office of theological scholarship and teaching for the edification of the people and the training of other ministers; (2) pastors were to preach, to administer the sacraments, and to exercise pastoral discipline, teaching and admonishing the people; (3) deacons oversaw institutional charity, including hospitals and physical welfare; and (4) elders were twelve laymen whose task was to oversee the spiritual well-being of the church.

Heinrich Bullinger (1504–1575), Reformed

After the death of Ulrich Zwingli in 1531, Bullinger became pastor of the principal church in Zurich and a leader of the Reformed party in Switzerland. He played an important part in compiling the First Helvetic Confession (1536), a creed based largely on Zwingli's theological views as distinct from Lutheran doctrine. In 1549, the Consensus Tigurinus, drawn up by Bullinger and Calvin, marked the departure of Swiss theology from Zwinglian toward a more Calvinist theory. His later views were embodied in the Second Helvetic Confession (1566), which was accepted in Switzerland, France, Scotland, and Hungary, becoming one of the most generally accepted confessions of the Reformed churches.

Thomas Cranmer (1489–1556), Anglican

In 1533, Cranmer was chosen to be archbishop of Canterbury. With Thomas Cromwell, he supported the translation of the Bible into English. In 1545, he wrote a litany that is still used in the church. Under the reign of King Edward VI, Cranmer was allowed to make the doctrinal changes he thought necessary to the church. He is credited with writing and compiling the first two Books of Common Prayer (1549, 1552), assisted by the Strasbourg Reformed leader Martin Bucer, and the Thirty-Nine Articles, which established the basic structure of Anglican liturgy for centuries.

Hugh Latimer (c. 1485–1555), Anglican

Hugh Latimer was bishop of Worcester in the time of King Henry VIIII but resigned in protest against the king's refusal to allow the Protestant reforms that Latimer desired. When Mary came to the throne, Latimer was arrested, tried for heresy, and in October 1555 burned at the stake with his friend Nicholas Ridley. His last words at the stake are well known: "Be of good cheer, Master Ridley, and play the man, for we shall this day light such a candle in England as I trust by God's grace shall never be put out." The deaths of Hugh Latimer, Nicolas Ridley, and later Thomas Cranmer are now known as the Oxford Martyrs.

John Knox (c. 1513–1572), Reformed

John Knox was a Scottish teacher who embraced the principles of the continental Reformation. As chaplain to King Edward VI, he was involved in the revision of the Anglican Book of Common Prayer. After a period in exile following the ascension of Queen Mary, he returned to Scotland, where he pioneered changes along Reformation principles. He was primarily responsible for the First Book of Discipline and the Book of Common Order, which were adopted by the newly formed Church of Scotland.

A Reformation History Lesson

Throughout the Middle Ages, the Western church was discussing and debating the nature of justification. The Reformers really believed that the popular (and, by the mid-sixteenth century, official) Roman Catholic position was self-salvation. By "Roman Catholic," we don't mean what's going on at your local Catholic Church today. Rather, it is to the medieval position that we refer: the Roman Catholic theology that was represented in the Council of Trent from 1545 to 1563. What, then, were the medieval positions on this doctrine?

Thomas Aquinas, the great Catholic theologian of the mid-thirteenth century, had a doctrine of justification, but for him it was just one doctrine among many (Aquinas makes this point in his *Summa Theologiae* 1–2, q. 113). Somewhere tucked behind, around, and under such subjects as regeneration, predestination, and sanctification was his position on justification. It was a doctrine of justification that involved God loving the sinner insofar as he or she was not a sinner. He did not love the sinner as sinner. How could a holy and just God love a sinner? But he loved sinners insofar as they had the potential not to be sinners.

Another Catholic theologian, John Duns Scotus (who lived in the early fourteenth century), spoke of the necessity of an absolutely selfless act of contrition (sorrow) and love for God by natural means if a person was to be saved. Think about that for a moment. At least once during your life, you would have to perform an utterly selfless act that had no vested interest for you whatsoever, or you would not be saved. Luther believed that this way of justification prevented God from befriending publicans and sinners, and that if it were true, then God was not truly free.

Of course, there were many other views, but the medieval consensus that won out has come to be known by the technical name semi-Pelagianism (from the late fourth- to fifth-century debate between Augustine, defender of grace, and Pelagius, a monk who denied original sin and therefore the need for supernatural grace). While the Synod of Orange (AD 529) condemned both Pelagianism and semi-Pelagianism, the heresy of works-righteousness, erected on the foundation of free will, grew increasingly popular among the masses and even among theologians.

What the Reformers said of the position was that it was by necessity a theology of doubt, of fear, and finally of despair of ever being saved. One had to be sanctified enough first in order to merit justifying grace, and the essence of justification was a real change within the human heart. Justification, in mainstream Roman Catholic theology, is primarily a real, empirical change in the human heart. Aquinas argued that justification involves a gradual change from unjust to just, thus justified. Grace amounts to an infused power to lead a God-pleasing life, to cooperate with the Spirit, to gradually move oneself from the category of "ungodly" to that of "righteous." And this would be evident in fewer and fewer sins by the believer. Luther, however, did not agree that the word *grace* in the Bible means an *infused power to live a God-pleasing life*, as though grace were a substance. He said rather that grace is the opposite of merit—unmerited favor. We are saved by God's graciousness to us. God has decided to be gracious to sinners; we are saved by his graciousness.

Grace is not even a principle. It is an attribute, a disposition, of the living God. He is gracious. To be saved by God's graciousness is to give up on merit, or to use Luther's phrase, to "let God be God." Luther believed that to let God be God is to recognize that it is he who does the saving, and part of what is requisite in that is for us to quit trying to do the saving. The Roman Catholic position was that God and the believer working together can save, whereas the Reformation position insisted that God can save sinners only if they stop trying to save themselves. The cause of God's graciousness to sinners is not our faith, the Reformers insisted; the cause of God's graciousness to sinners is his graciousness. In other words, we do not leverage the love of God out of heaven. We do not have an Archimedean point for a lever to pry it down toward us. Our openness, our yearning for him, our longing to be part of his gracious plan—none of this justifies; none of these dispositions or desires on our part can pry open the gate of heaven.

If the Reformers were correct in interpreting what Paul was getting at in his Epistle to the Romans, 100 percent of our salvation is due to God's graciousness, and 0 percent is due to anything in us. The Reformation's answer to the question "Do I contribute anything to my salvation?" is "Yes, your sin!" The value, then, of saving faith is only a value in virtue of the object grasped. Faith itself has no virtue; it connects us to the One who is virtuous.

Key Concepts in Reformed Spirituality

Union with Christ. Every doctrine related to salvation and the Christian life must be oriented around this touchstone of faith. No theory of Christian growth or development can obscure or ignore this central fact. In Reformation spirituality, the objective and subjective, external and internal, are linked inseparably by this reality. "In Christ" we are justified and are being sanctified.

Justification by Faith Alone. "To declare righteous," this courtroom term is the core of the good news. If we seek to attain divine favor by our own willing and running, then we will quickly end up in either self-righteousness or despair. Progress in obedience comes only as we acknowledge Christ to be our righteousness, holiness, and redemption.

Sanctification. Here is another essential biblical word. Once declared righteous by the imputation of Christ's righteousness, we now grow in personal righteousness in union with Christ and his righteousness. In our salvation we contribute absolutely nothing except sin. But once regenerated by God's grace (apart from our cooperation), we are free to cooperate with the Holy Spirit for the first time. Sanctification therefore—unlike regeneration, justification, and so on—requires our energies and participation. We grow in the grace and knowledge of Christ, actively animated by the gospel. Both justification and sanctification are the gift of God by virtue of our union with Christ.

Calling/Vocation. Also related to the "priesthood of all believers," this Reformation doctrine emphasized the fact that everything we do honors God if done in faith. A ditch-digger is no less spiritual than a missionary. God has created each of us with certain gifts, and we are meant to find meaning and fulfillment not only in church-related things, but in our work and leisure as well. This doctrine, more than any other, was responsible for what has come to be identified as "the Protestant work ethic."

Sacraments. Baptism and Holy Communion, in Reformation spirituality, figure prominently as "means of grace." Baptism is the beginning of our life in Christ, and in Communion we feed on Christ—the Bread of Life—throughout our wilderness journey.

Contributors

Michael Allen is associate professor of systematic and historical theology at Reformed Theological Seminary-Orlando in Florida.

C. FitzSimons Allison is the retired bishop of South Carolina, who now serves as a pastoral bishop for churches in the Anglican Communion Network, a network of orthodox churches in the Episcopal Church in the United States of America.

Peter D. Anders is a systematic and historical theologian. He has taught at Talbot School of Theology, Gordon-Conwell Theological Seminary, and most recently at Gordon College in Wenham, Massachusetts.

David R. Andersen is author of *Martin Luther: The Problem with Faith and Reason: A Reexamination in Light of Epistemological and Christological Issues* (Wipf & Stock, 2012).

R. Scott Clark is professor of church history and historical theology at Westminster Seminary California in Escondido.

Alexandre Ganoczy is a Hungarian catholic theologian and writer. He taught dogmatic theology at the Catholic Institute of Paris and at the universities of Münster and Würzburg in Germany.

Ryan Glomsrud is associate professor of historical theology at Westminster Seminary California in Escondido, and book review editor for *Modern Reformation* magazine.

W. Robert Godfrey is president and professor of church history at Westminster Seminary California in Escondido.

David W. Hall is senior pastor of Midway Presbyterian Church in Powder Springs, Georgia. In 2009, he served as executive director of Calvin500.

Paul Helm is a British philosopher and theologian. He is a teaching fellow at Regent College. He also served as professor of theology at Highland Theological College in Scotland.

Michael S. Horton is the J. Gresham Machen Professor of Systematic Theology and Apologetics at Westminster Seminary California in Escondido and editor-in-chief of *Modern Reformation* magazine.

Frank A. James III is president of Biblical Theological Seminary in Hatfield, Pennsylvania. He formerly served as provost and professor of historical theology at Gordon-Conwell Theological Seminary in South Hamilton, Massachusetts.

Serene Jones is president of the faculty and the Johnston Family Professor for Religion and Democracy at Union Theological Seminary in the City of New York.

Scott L. Keith is the director of operations and scholarship for *1517. The Legacy Project* and adjunct professor of theology at Concordia University, Irvine, California.

Eric Landry is executive editor of *Modern Reformation* and pastor of Redeemer Presbyterian Church in Austin, Texas.

Diarmaid MacCulloch is university lecturer at St. Cross College, University of Oxford.

Keith A. Mathison is professor of systematic theology at Reformation Bible College in Sanford, Florida.

Mickey L. Mattox is professor of historical theology at Marquette University in Milwaukee, Wisconsin.

Alister McGrath is the Andreas Idreos Professor of Science and Religion at the University of Oxford, director of the Ian Ramsey Centre for Science and Religion, and fellow of Harris Manchester College, Oxford.

John Nuñes is president of Concordia College-New York. He previously served as the Emil and Elfriede Jochum Chair at Valparaiso University in Indiana.

Lawrence R. Rast Jr. is president of Concordia Theological Seminary-Fort Wayne, Indiana.

Rick Ritchie is a long-time contributor to *Modern Reformation*.

Rod Rosenbladt is currently involved in *1517. The Legacy Project*, a nonprofit initiative he helped launch. Previously, he served as professor of theology at Concordia University, Irvine, California, and cohost of the *White Horse Inn* syndicated radio program.

Benjamin Sasse is the United States Senator for Nebraska and a former editor/writer for *Modern Reformation* magazine.

Dennis Tamburello is professor of religious studies at Siena College in Loudonville, New York.

David VanDrunen is the Robert B. Strimple Professor of Systematic Theology and Christian Ethics at Westminster Seminary California in Escondido.

Gene E. Veith is provost emeritus and professor of literature emeritus at Patrick Henry College in Purcellville, Virginia.